Motherhood and Mental Illness 2

Causes and consequences

Edited by
R Kumar and I F Brockington

Wright
London   Boston   Singapore   Sydney   Toronto   Wellington

Wright
is an imprint of Butterworth Scientific

First published, 1988

©Butterworth & Co. (Publishers) Ltd, 1988

British Library Cataloguing in Publication Data
Motherhood and mental illness 2.
   1. Women. Mental disorders. Role of childbirth
   I. Kumar, R. (Ramesh), *1938–*
   II. Brockington, I.F.
   616.89′0088042

   ISBN 0–7236–0766–4

Library of Congress Cataloging in Publication Data
Motherhood and mental illness 2, causes and consequences / edited by
   R. Kumar and I. F. Brockington.
      p. cm.
   Includes bibliographies and index.
   ISBN 0–7236–0766–4 :
   1. Postpartum psychiatric disorders. 2. Mother and child.
3. Infants–Death–Psychological aspects. I. Kumar, R. Ramesh, 1938–
II. Brockington, I. F.
   [DNLM: 1. Attitude to Death. 2. Death – in infancy & childhood.
3. Mental Disorders – in pregnancy. 4. Mother–Child Relations.
5. Puerperal Disorders – etiology. 6. Puerperal Disorders – psychology.
WQ 500 M9185]
RG850.M67   1988
616.7′6—dc19
DNLM/DLC
for Library of Congress   88–20540
                                            CIP

Typeset by TecSet Ltd., Wallington, Surrey
Printed in Great Britain at the University Press, Cambridge

Preface

The publication in 1982 of our first collection of review articles under the title of *Motherhood and Mental Illness* coincided with the formation of the Marcé Society—an international society dedicated to improving the understanding, prevention and treatment of psychiatric disorders related to childbearing. The scientific and clinical reviews which we commissioned for our first book were intended to promote the aims of the Marcé Society by summarizing the state of knowledge on puerperal psychosis, neurotic disorders during pregnancy and after childbirth, the maternity blues, normal attachment and disorders of the mother-infant relationship, inpatient psychiatric mother and baby units and drug prescription and abuse in pregnancy.

It has been very gratifying to discover that *Motherhood and Mental Illness* has become established in many countries as a useful and important reference book for clinical practice, for research and for teaching. We also hope that it may have contributed to the growth of interest in the past few years in the psychology and psychopathology of childbearing. At the point of producing a follow-up volume, it seems appropriate to ask what has changed over the past six years.

In 1982, it seemed that the whole subject of postnatal mental illness had somehow only just been kept alive during the post-war years by the work of a scattered and often solitary band of investigators and clinicians. Now there are clear signs that this subject is beginning to be recognized as an important health problem, which affects not only the mothers but also their families and especially the developing child. The most obvious signs are to be found in the increasing numbers of relevant publications in books and journals, in the many scientific meetings that have taken place during the past few years in Britain, Western Europe, North America, Australia, India and in Japan. At these meetings the interest and enthusiasm of the expert participants has been mirrored by an equally important and parallel development among the consumers—women have been setting up self-help organizations to provide information and support for mothers with psychiatric problems related to childbearing. The dialogue between the researcher and the clinician will be of little value if it does not incorporate the consumer in a true exchange of information about problems, symptoms, resources, available therapies and their possible usefulness. We still know very little about the causes of postnatal illnesses and about their consequences; understanding the mechanisms behind causes and effects will lead to focused interventions both for treatment and for prevention. At present the allocation of resources for mentally ill mothers and their families by health planners and politicians can be placed firmly between two points ranging from 'none' to 'pathetic'. Nevertheless, despite the lack of 'official' awareness there is much that can be done.

Our original aim was regularly to update knowledge in the field and, therefore, we have solicited a series of reviews which will supplement our 1982 publication. In this collection we include sections on the impact of maternal mental illness on the infant, and on the loss of a baby through stillbirth or neonatal death. The theme of postpartum psychosis is continued with a further article on its nosology and differentiation from other puerperal mental disorders and the role of biochemical and neuroendocrine dysfunction in postnatal illness is critically examined. There is a comprehensive review of postnatal depression from a methodological and conceptual standpoint as well as a consideration of transcultural explanations for it. Finally, a pioneering community-based service for puerperal mental illness is described, with home treatment of puerperal psychotic disorders, including manic syndromes.

This book serves as a progress report on the activities of the Marcé Society *inter alia*. We hope that it will be the second of a series of volumes marking an accelerating progress in the understanding and control of mental illness related to childbirth. In order to maintain the identity of the proposed series we have thought it best to retain the general title of *Motherhood and Mental Illness* and to mark each volume by a subtitle, in this instance 'Causes and consequences'.

Contributors

Kerry Bluglass MB, ChB, DPM, FRCPsych
Consultant Psychiatrist and Deputy Medical Director, Woodbourne Clinic, Birmingham; Senior Clinical Lecturer in Psychiatry, University of Birmingham, UK.

IF Brockington MD, FRCP, FRCPsych
Professor of Psychiatry, University of Birmingham, UK.

JL Cox DM, FRCPsych, DPM, FRCP(Ed)
Professor of Psychiatry, Department of Postgraduate Medicine, University of Keele, Staffordshire; Consultant Psychiatrist, City General Hospital, Stoke on Trent, UK.

Anne Cox-Roper BSc, RMN
Research Worker, Department of Psychiatry, University of Birmingham, UK.

JFW Deakin PhD, MRCPsych
Senior Lecturer in Psychiatry; Honorary Consultant Psychiatrist, University Hospital of South Manchester, UK.

A Dyregrov PhD
Senior Research Scientist, Center for Occupational Health and Safety, University of Bergen, Norway.

Carol Gambles MA, BSc
Clinical Child Psychologist, Leeds Eastern Health Authority; Formerly, Research Psychologist, Institute of Psychiatry, London, UK.

A George BSc, PhD, MIBiol
Senior Lecturer in Pharmacology, School of Pharmacy, Liverpool Polytechnic; Honorary Research Fellow, Department of Psychiatry, Liverpool University, UK.

R Kumar MD, PhD, FRCPsych
Reader in Psychosomatic Medicine, Institute of Psychiatry; Honorary Consultant Psychiatrist, Bethlem Royal and Maudsley Hospitals, London, UK.

EC Melhuish BSc, PhD
Senior Research Officer, Thomas Coram Unit, Institute of Education, University of London, UK.

Lynne Murray MA, PhD
Winnicott Fellow and Senior Research Associate, Child Care and Development Group, Department of Paediatrics, University of Cambridge, UK.

Margaret Oates MB, ChB, DPM, MRCPsych
Senior Lecturer in Psychiatry, University of Nottingham; Honorary Consultant Psychiatrist, University Hospital, Nottingham, UK.

MW O'Hara PhD
Associate Professor, Department of Psychology, University of Iowa, USA.

M Sandler MD, FRCP, FRCPath, FRCPsych
Professor of Chemical Pathology, Royal Postgraduate Medical School, University of London, UK.

Wendy Savage BA, MB, BChir, FRCOG
Senior Lecturer in Obstetrics and Gynaecology, London Hospital Medical College, London, UK.

Ellen Zekoski MA
Graduate Student, Department of Psychology, University of Iowa, USA.

Contents

Chapter 1

The nosology of puerperal mental illness

Ian Brockington and Anne Cox-Roper

Introduction

When one considers the reasons why our knowledge of the psychiatric complications of childbirth has made so little progress since the days of Marcé (1858), one must bear in mind difficulties which are not peculiar to psychiatry. Clinical science suffers from the difficulty of controlling the supply of subjects; it is at the mercy of opportunist 'samples' of patients. It has to rely on natural experiments, and can with difficulty isolate and control the conditions. Psychiatric research has additional problems—the notorious difficulty of objectifying and measuring disorders of emotion, behaviour and relationship; the difficulty of isolating and unravelling interactive psychological processes; and the complexity and inaccessibility of intracerebral biology. These difficulties are all shared with other psychiatric disorders.

Within psychiatry, the postpartum disorders have fallen foul of nosological fashions. In the nineteenth century, puerperal insanity seemed a clear-cut entity—easily defined, homogeneous and promising a unitary cause—and was clearly identified before ideas which are now more influential (e.g. schizophrenia) were conceived. Unfortunately the appeal of the 'two entities principle', which provided a simple structure covering the whole range of psychotic illness, proved too strong, and the idea of puerperal psychosis was eclipsed for three generations. The reason for the resurrection of this pre-kraepelinian concept is probably also related to the waning fortunes of kraepelinian classification, since it has now been realized that schizophrenia and manic depressive (affective) psychoses are difficult to define and heterogeneous, and investigators are searching for more discrete and definable disorders (Kendell and Brockington, 1979; Brockington, 1986). It has in any case been realized that classifications are arbitrary and provisional and there is no reason why scientists should not use their own concepts alongside 'official' nosologies, provided that the criteria for diagnosis are made explicit.

Although puerperal psychosis is linked to a precisely timed event, there are still problems in its temporal definition and differential diagnosis. To the present writers it seems often to have been defined too broadly. Some studies have included patients whose illness began three, six or even 12 months after delivery. Some investigators group together all psychiatric

1

disorders loosely related to childbirth, without subclassification. This is an anachronism because psychiatrists are now aware of a variety of psychological complications of motherhood, some of which are quite different from puerperal psychosis as originally described. It has become important to find boundaries between these conditions lest this area of psychiatry be subject to the same lack of diagnostic clarity which plagues psychiatric research as a whole. This chapter is written with this purpose in mind. It discusses in some detail the nosology of puerperal psychosis and then briefly reviews other postnatal disorders which should be distinguished from it.

Puerperal psychosis

The idea of 'puerperal insanity' 'puerperal mania' or 'puerperal psychosis' stems from the sudden onset of extreme mental derangement in 'hitherto peaceable and well-conducted' women. Since the defining characteristic is a temporal association (presumably resulting from a causal link), the first task in reaching a definition is to define the time period within which puerperal psychosis develops.

Temporal definition

Paffenbarger's research showed that hospital admissions were concentrated within the first postpartum month. In his first paper (Paffenbarger, 1961) he found that 18 patients from Cincinnati were admitted during pregnancy (two per month), 96 during the first month after childbirth, 13 in the second month and 16 in the next four months (average of four per month). When he extended his study to the whole of Hamilton county, Ohio (Paffenbarger, 1964), the figures were eight per month during pregnancy, 164 in the first month postpartum, 27 during the second month, 21 in the third, 17 in the fourth and 10 in the fifth. These figures show that something leads to a huge increase in hospitalization during the first month. There is also an increase in months 2–4 when compared with pregnancy. This has been confirmed by a more recent study from Edinburgh (Kendell, Chalmers and Platz, 1987), based on record linkage between obstetric and psychiatric registers, which showed that 181 patients with functional psychoses were admitted during the two years after childbirth, compared with only 49 during the two years before delivery; 89 of these were admitted in the first trimester, of which 51 were in the first month, 25 in the second and 13 in the third. The number admitted in the second month is still high compared with the mean for the prepartum period, and the rate remains somewhat elevated throughout the first two years after childbirth, compared with the two years before.

    Clearly there is a need to progress the argument to a discussion of onset of illness rather than hospital admission. The determination of onset involves error of two kinds—rating error and data error. Rating error can be reduced by using two or more raters. Data error can be reduced by interviewing patients and relatives. Brockington and Cernik (Brockington,

Winokur and Dean, 1982) carried out a study of the onset of the illness in 241 patients admitted to the Manchester Mother and Baby Unit between 1971 and 1979; two raters were used, but in most patients the only data available were the case records, since only 103 patients were included in a prospective study which began in July 1976. In the patients studied prospectively, it was shown that the reliability of the judgement that an illness had begun during the first two weeks postpartum was 0.61 (Cohen's kappa). This is a high reliability and would be still higher if the consensus judgement of two raters was compared with the consensus judgement of another two raters. The results of this study were reported (with minor errors) in Brockington, Winokur and Dean (1982). The corrected results are given in *Table 1.1*.

Table 1.1 Onset of illness in patients admitted to Manchester Mother and Baby Unit 1971–9

Group	No. of patients
Exclusions:	
Onset during pregnancy	41
Onset more than one year after delivery	2
Addiction	2
Insufficient information	6
	51
Onset in 1st week after delivery	81
Onset in 2nd week	46
Onset in 3rd week	13
Onset in 4th week	8
Onset in 2nd month	21
Onset in months 3–6	15
Onset in months 7–12	6
	190
Total	241

The steep fall in the number of patients beginning their illness with the passage of time after delivery suggests that the time interval for any mental illness statistically associated with parturition is a short one, and (on the basis of these figures) two weeks was suggested. These results can be compared with the Edinburgh series reported by Dean and Kendell (1981). Of their series of 41 patients whose illness began during the postpartum period, 21 began in the first week, four in the second, five in the third and 11 during the remaining 10 weeks of the first trimester. Meltzer and Kumar (1985) in a case record study of 142 mothers admitted to various hospitals in the South-East Thames Region found that 65 had onset during the first week, 22 in the second, only one in the third, and five in the fourth week. Kendell's register study, quoted above, also gives data on the timing of onset. Of 111 with onset in the postpartum period, 54 began in the first week, 12 in the second and 21 in the third and fourth weeks. These figures all confirm the very early onset of most patients admitted during the first month postpartum.

The onset of schizophreniform and manic illness

To make any further progress, it is necessary to consider clinical features and diagnosis as well as onset. Definition in terms of a time interval can never be fully satisfactory. Childbirth is a complex event; the puerperium is packed with somatic and emotional incident, and is a period of rapid biological, social and psychological transition. It would be surprising if only one form of mental illness was aetiologically related to parturition and the arrival of the newborn. What seems obvious to the clinician is that much depressive illness in the perinatal period is related to stress, such as illness or malformation in the baby, emotional rejection of the infant and other social and psychological difficulties. For this reason it seems wise to examine the data for onset after excluding depressive illness of all kinds.

When the Manchester data are analysed in this way, the timing of onset of the illness is shown in *Table 1.2*. In this analysis only patients studied prospectively (between July 1976 and May 1981) have been included. These data show that when puerperal psychosis is defined in terms of manic and schizophreniform psychoses (excluding depression), and data from prospective interviews are used, 57 of 64 episodes had onset in the first two weeks. There was only one patient whose onset was considered to be in the third or fourth week, and six patients with onset much later in the first postpartum year.

Table 1.2 Onset of illness in 86 psychotic[a] patients admitted to Manchester Mother and Baby Unit, 1976–81

Exclusions	
Onset during pregnancy	18
Not yet diagnosed and timed	4
	22
Onset within two weeks	
RDC[b] diagnosis:	
Schizophrenia or probable schizophrenia	13
Schizoaffective mania	16
Mania or hypomania	18
Mixed manic and depressive states	7
Undiagnosed functional psychosis	3
Total	57
Onset during third and fourth weeks	
RDC diagnosis: schizophrenia	1
Onset more than one month after delivery	
RDC diagnosis:	
Schizophrenia	4
Mania	1
Undiagnosed functional psychosis	1
Total	6
Grand total	86

[a]Here the term 'psychotic' excludes delusional and schizoaffective depression.
[b]RDC = Research Diagnostic Criteria (Spitzer, Endicott and Robins, 1978)

Comparing these results with others in the literature is not easy, because few studies have presented data on onset and diagnosis. Karnosh and Hope (1937) found that almost all postpartum illnesses which had a component of delirium began within two weeks. Dean and Kendell (1981) reported that all their manic patients became ill during the first 19 days. Meltzer and Kumar (1985) reported that only one manic patient had onset in the fourth week postpartum. Both these studies were based on case record data. We conclude that cases of manic and schizophreniform illness beginning outside the two-week period are so uncommon that they could well be sporadic (i.e. of an aetiology different from the early onset cases). The data from the most severe and easily timed illnesses emphasize the very early onset of 'puerperal psychosis'.

Homogeneity of puerperal psychosis

We must next consider whether it is legitimate to include in one category a group of patients with diverse clinical pictures. Those listed in *Table 1.2* include substantial numbers of patients from both sides of the 'two entities' dichotomy. It was the appreciation that the Kraepelin/Bleuler diagnostic principle split the puerperal patients into two fragments which caused the concept of puerperal psychosis to fall into disrepute, and it cannot be reinstated without addressing this question.

Considering the patients listed in *Table 1.2*, all clinicians would regard hypomania and mixed manic and depressed patients as variants of manic depressive disease; they account for 25 of 57 patients. Research carried out in the last 15 years has also strongly suggested that schizoaffective mania should also be regarded as a variant of mania (Brockington and Meltzer, 1983; Taylor and Abrams, 1983). It remains to consider the four patients with undiagnosed functional psychosis and the 13 patients with 'schizophrenia'. This is an example of the former group:

> A 20-year-old unmarried mother, living with her supportive family, was delivered of a male infant. She discharged herself from the maternity hospital after one week. At home she was overactive and slept little, tidying her drawers in the middle of the night. She laughed and cried inappropriately, ate little and neglected her baby. On admission to hospital, she was rather careless with the baby whom she carried around like a doll. She answered questions coherently and relevantly, and complained that her thoughts were in a jumble. She was irritable and resented supervision. She said that the staff had put poison in her tea. She rapidly returned to normal.

In this patient there is at least some overlap with hypomania, even though she failed to meet Research Diagnostic Criteria (RDC), and the same is true of the other patients with this diagnosis.

As for the 13 patients with 'schizophrenia', it must be remembered that RDC were used (Spitzer, Endicott and Robins, 1978), and that they allow a diagnosis of schizophrenia to be made in an illness lasting only two weeks; all these patients would have been diagnosed as 'schizophreniform' psychoses by the DSM-III (Diagnostic and Statistical Manual, 3rd Edition, (American Psychiatric Association, 1980). Nevertheless, the proposition that DSM-III schizophreniform psychosis (acute schizophrenia) is related to mania, although suggested by Ollerenshaw (1972), would be controversial: most psychiatrists would consider it to be a violation of the two entities principle. There has been little time since the introduction of DSM-III to evaluate 'schizophreniform psychosis'. A small study comparing 19 DSM-III schizophrenic patients with seven schizophreniform psychoses showed that the latter had an excellent outcome and significantly more manic symptoms than the former (Helzer, Brockington and Kendell, 1981). Another small study by Fogelson, Cohen and Pope (1982) of only six patients showed that three of them had a history of typical manic episodes, one a history of cyclothymia and major depression, one a history of depression and family history of bipolar disorder and the sixth patient had a personal and family history of depression only. Another large study of 93 patients from the 'Iowa 500 series' by Coryell and Tsuang (1982) did *not* suggest that schizophreniform psychosis belonged to the affective disorders but, as Fogelson and colleagues point out, selection was heavily in favour of schizophrenic patients; moreover the outcome study did not examine the presence of manic episodes.

The literature on 'cycloid psychosis' is relevant, especially in view of the fact that Perris has claimed that puerperal psychosis is a manifestation of cycloid psychosis. The clinical picture of 'cycloid psychosis' differs completely from that of mania. In a series of 30 patients diagnosed by Perris, 18 were considered to be suffering from schizophrenia by their British psychiatrists. However, patients with cycloid psychosis share many characteristics with manic depression, including high heritability, endogenicity, a benign relapsing course, and response to lithium and electroconvulsive therapy (Brockington *et al.*, 1982).

The best evidence that postpartum schizophreniform clinical pictures are alternative manifestations of puerperal mania is the observation that patients given this diagnosis after one pregnancy have suffered a recurrence after the next with a picture of schizoaffective mania or even hypomania. This is an example of such a patient:

A 28-year-old woman was admitted to hospital in 1978 one week following the birth of a male infant. The illness began four days after the birth. The content of the illness was centred on delusions of parasitosis, ideas of reference, repetitive washing, severe insomnia, slow monotonous speech with gaps when she would stare and pick at her hands, dreamy distant rapport and walking around in a trance. She became briefly overactive with rapid incoherent speech and smashed several items on the ward. She was completely disorientated and misidentified several members of staff as her own family. Some of her ideas were grandiose, e.g. her father was the Pope. She described thought insertion and withdrawal and believed she was controlled by God.

Her next baby was born two years later. She had already developed symptoms before her discharge from the maternity unit. This time she had marked insomnia and disinhibition and her husband described typical hypomanic behaviour. She started undressing other people's babies and she thought she was Queen Victoria.

In this example the first episode was given a diagnosis of schizophrenia because, in the absence of elation, RDC for schizoaffective mania were not met, but there were some manifestations of mania even though only briefly present. While accepting that further evidence is required to establish the point, patients like this argue that puerperal schizophreniform states are a variant of mania and should be included within the category of 'puerperal psychosis'. We propose, therefore, to include within a single category all those acute non-depressive psychoses which begin within two weeks of delivery, standing in sharp contrast to the normal mental functioning present at that time. This category should be defined as follows:

Puerperal psychosis
Patients meeting RDC for mania, schizoaffective mania, schizophrenia or undiagnosed functional psychosis beginning within two weeks of childbirth, irrespective of social circumstances. Exclude patients who manifested similar symptoms during the ninth month of pregnancy, but include patients who suffer from depression or neurotic symptoms before delivery.

Is puerperal psychosis a bipolar disorder?

The next question is whether puerperal psychosis is a bipolar illness. Since psychiatrists are conditioned to expect manic patients to suffer from depressed phases, there is a prejudice in favour of this proposition. However, it is not necessarily true. Puerperal psychosis could be a unipolar disorder, and all postpartum and postnatal depression might be unrelated to it aetiologically.

The evidence in favour of the existence of a depressed pole of a bipolar puerperal psychosis includes:

(1) Puerperal mania does not wholly account for the flood of admissions during the first month postpartum noted by Paffenbarger: when manic patients are omitted, there is still an excess of patients with very early onset; in the Manchester study there were 44 depressions starting within the first two weeks, 16 in the third and fourth weeks and only 21 beginning during the remaining 11 months of the first year.

(2) Some patients are seen with a mixed or alternating picture of depression and mania. Seven such patients were studied at Manchester between 1976 and 1981.

(3) Among the depressed patients with early puerperal onset there are some with unusual clinical features. In particular, there are those who have marked confusion similar to that seen in the puerperal manic patients. Indeed, occasional patients have been seen with such severe cognitive change in the absence of affective symptoms that they fitted Marcé's description of 'transitory intellectual enfeeblement'. Examples of such patients were given by Brockington, Winokur and Dean (1982).

(4) The strongest evidence comes, again, from occasional patients who have presented with a depressive clinical picture following one pregnancy and a manic following the next, or a switch of polarity between the primary episode and a relapse.

Collectively these points offer a strong case for regarding puerperal psychosis as a bipolar condition.

The recognition of the depressed form of puerperal psychosis, however, is not easy. As with manic depression it is hard to determine the clinical picture of the depressive pole. Pending the clarification of the clinical features of puerperal psychosis in its depressed form, we propose the following definition for a puerperal depressive psychosis:

Puerperal depressive psychosis

1. Depression meeting RDC, or other widely used criteria, for major depression.
2. Onset in first two weeks after childbirth. If the depression started a longer time after delivery, the word 'probable' should be added to the diagnosis.
3. Presence of delusions, hallucinations or confusion.

Relation of these definitions to other nosological systems

These recommended definitions are not offered in competition to other systems. In the climate of uncertainty which prevails about psychiatric classification, research workers should use several diagnostic approaches to their patients. This 'polydiagnostic technique' was first used by Hawk, Carpenter and Strauss (1975) and by Kendell and Brockington (1978) in relation to schizophrenia, and has subsequently been advocated by Berner and Katschnig (1982) in Vienna, and seems generally applicable to psychiatric research. We recommend that these definitions of puerperal psychosis are used in parallel with those recommended by the World Health Organization and American Psychiatric Association.

It is, nevertheless, regrettable that the WHO and American official classificatory systems have paid so little attention to puerperal mental disorders. This has had a negative effect on the clinical and epidemiological study of this important group. Furthermore there has been a deterioration in the last 25 years—Paffenbarger's research, which did so much to revive interest, would not be possible now. The eighth revision of the International Classification of Diseases included 294.4, 'unspecified psychoses that have occurred within six weeks (42 days) following delivery', but this was dropped from the ninth revision, while in the 494-page DSM-III, postpartum psychoses are specified in the section on 'atypical psychosis' where they should be classified if they do not meet criteria for an organic mental disorder, schizophreniform disorder, paranoid disorder or affective disorder. Members of the Marcé Society have had discussions with Drs Spitzer and Sartorius about remedies for this unfavourable situation. We agreed that one solution was to apply a biaxial classification of clinical syndrome and aetiological association, as suggested originally by Essen-Möller (1961). We were concerned, however, that psychiatrists would not pay sufficient attention to the proper coding of the aetiological axis. When under time pressure they were likely to diagnose the clinical syndrome in all cases, and aetiological association only in some. We therefore requested the insertion of a paragraph in the introduction outlining the reasons why puerperal psychoses should always be identified by the biaxial coding, with reminders in the appropriate sections (especially that dealing with affective or bipolar disorders).

At the beginning of this chapter, reference was made to the apparent conflict between the ancient concept of puerperal insanity and the two entities principle, one seeming to exclude the other. In the authors' view this is a mistake. The recognition of puerperal psychosis is no threat to the two entities principle. It merely argues for a redrawing of the boundaries between the affective psychoses and schizophrenia. All the evidence supports the classification of puerperal psychosis with other bipolar disorders such as manic depression and cycloid psychosis. The boundaries between the 'two entities' have shifted far during the last 10 years, with the term 'schizophrenia' now being employed (especially in the USA) for a small group of chronic psychoses. Research into puerperal psychosis has been part of a large body of clinical research leading to a restriction of the term 'schizophrenia' to disabling and pernicious disorders. The findings from the study of patients with the puerperal illness continue to challenge the specificity of schizophrenic symptoms because all the most characteristic symptoms are found in a disorder which has been considered the most benign of all psychoses (Herman, 1896). Furthermore some of the puerperal patients seem to have characteristic symptoms in the absence of a full manic or depressive syndrome. The study of puerperal psychosis, therefore, throws light on the symptomatology and definition of schizophrenia and manic depressive illness, even though it does not challenge the idea (which some find clarifying, some obfuscating) of the 'two entities' principle.

Other disorders occurring in the postnatal period

Table 1.3 lists a number of psychiatric disorders and psychological phenomena which may cause concern in the aftermath of childbirth. These will be

Table 1.3 Classification of puerperal mental disorders

	Frequency[a]
1. Puerperal psychosis	
(a) Manic or schizophreniform states	1:1000
(b) Depression	1:1000
2. Disorders of the mother-infant relationship	
(a) Delayed attachment	1:10
(b) Obsessions of hostility to the infant	1:100
(c) Rejection of infant	1:100
(d) Child abuse	1:1000
(e) Infanticide (neonaticide and filicide)	1:50 000
3. Depressive disorders	
(a) Maternity blues	1:2
(b) Grief due to stillbirth, neonatal death or deformity	1:100
(c) 'Postnatal depression'	1:10

[a]These figures are only approximations; where research data are absent (e.g. for obsessions of hostility, rejection), clinical impressions are used (and may be inaccurate). The denominator is the number of deliveries.

considered briefly, not in order to give a comprehensive description but to clarify their relationship to puerperal psychosis.

Reactive (psychogenic) psychoses

In the authors' opinion not all psychoses occurring in the puerperium should be called 'puerperal psychosis'. There is another small group of psychoses which are also related to childbirth but with completely different characteristics. These are the 'reactive' or 'psychogenic' psychoses according to a Danish/Norwegian tradition (Faergeman, 1963).

> A reactive psychosis is . . . defined as a psychosis in which the development . . . seems understandable in terms of the . . . person's constitutional background and personality development within a life situation which facilitated a mental disturbance in that . . . person and at that particular time . . . . The psychosis will bear relation to acute mental trauma; the content of the psychotic symptoms reflects the traumatic experience, and the course of the psychosis is usually benign and termination of the psychosis is expected upon liquidation of the traumatic experience (Retterstöl, 1983).

Here is an example of such a patient:

> A 25-year-old woman living in poverty and social isolation failed to 'bond' with her first child, and was suspected of battering him. She became depressed during her second pregnancy, and was given ECT. She was delivered of a premature infant weighing 1.5 lb. The baby was treated in an intensive care ward for several weeks. The patient seldom visited him and, some weeks after delivery, developed the delusion that a transfer of babies had taken place during pregnancy, so that her own baby had been born to a neighbour up the street. She 'remembered' a tearing sensation in her womb while travelling with this woman in a car, and the sensation of emptiness in her womb. She could hear this baby calling for her and asking to be taken home. She pursued the other woman, calling on her house and demanding 'her' baby. ECT and neuroleptic treatment failed to cure her, but her husband insisted, on pain of divorce, that she go to the premature baby unit, collect her own baby and care for it. This she did, whereupon she rapidly formed a strong normal attachment, lost her delusions and recovered from her depression.

To such a group belong also the onset of morbid jealousy during the puerperium, and querulous reactions to obstetric procedures, as in the following patient:

> A 42-year-old single woman was delivered of a baby with the help of forceps under epidural anaesthesia, occasioned by occipitoposterior presentation and fetal distress. Six months later she began telephoning the Maternity Hospital (sometimes in the middle of the night) to abuse the nursing and medical staff and express her bitterness about her 'high technology delivery'. Two years later she was still pursuing the hospital and its staff, expressing venomous hatred against them and from time to time venting her rage in visits to the unit and tirades against anyone she could find.

The distinction between puerperal psychosis and psychogenic psychoses will no doubt be the subject of debate. Parturition is itself a major event, and some may be tempted to consider all puerperal psychoses as reactive, though empirical research shows that for most such patients childbirth does not occur in a stressful setting (Brockington *et al.*, unpublished data). At the moment the distinction depends on clinical intuition, which sees an obvious contrast between the incomprehensible, unexpected quality of puerperal psychosis and this smaller group of psychotic disorders whose timing and content is related to psychological stress.

Disorders of the mother-infant relationship

There has been some misunderstanding about the status of mother-infant relationship disorders as a 'separate entity'. The authors believe that this relationship is a psychological phenomenon quite independent of the mental health or illness of the mother, and that it may be disturbed in the absence of major mental illness. Thus disorders of mother-infant attachment may or may not coexist with psychiatric illness such as depression. Those working in a specialist psychiatric service will, no doubt, commonly find them to be associated with depression, but this is not always so, and we quote an example of such a patient on p.12. The association with depression may be less frequent in the general community. The nub of this controversy is the view held by some that such disorders are always secondary to depression, and never primary. Against this view we can quote patients in whom the successful treatment of a profound disturbance of the mother-infant relationship has been followed by prompt recovery from prolonged and treatment-resistant depression (Brockington and Brierley, 1984).

Table 1.3 lists some disturbances of the mother-infant relationship. We have omitted from the list minor disorders such as abnormal irritability occurring in mothers deprived of sleep, and incompetent mothering associated, for example, with mental handicap or social defect states.

Delayed attachment

It is common for mothers to experience some delay in the full development of affectionate feelings for their infants (Robson and Moss, 1970). This may be distressing, and may be associated with depression. Whether this is cause or effect is difficult to determine, and to the clinician appears sometimes the one and sometimes the other. It is outside the scope of this chapter to discuss the manifestations, determinants and treatment of delayed attachment. This subject has been addressed by Margison (1982) and Robson and Powell (1982).

Obsessional thoughts of hostility to the infant

Mothers with an anankastic personality may experience intrusive and distressing thoughts about their babies, including impulses to inflict bodily harm. Button, Reivich and Kan (1972) described 42 patients with 'obsessions of infanticide' in a review of 605 consecutive admissions and 712 outpatient referrals to Kansas Medical Centre (3.4% of psychiatric referrals). These thoughts coexist with a normal mother-infant relationship, though they may cause distress, and may lead to some avoidance of contact with the infant. The following is an example of the phenomenon:

A 34-year-old woman with meticulous traits and a previous history of ereuthophobia (fear of blushing) and alcohol abuse, developed severe depression during pregnancy. This continued into the puerperium, and was successfully treated with electroconvulsive therapy. During the period of outpatient follow-up, she stated that she was very fond of the baby, but kept getting 'these thoughts—evil thoughts blaming him for things which have happened, swearing at him, e.g. "bloody baby" '. She was considerably distressed by the thoughts, but otherwise well. The nature of these thoughts as obsessional phenomena was explained to her, and she was advised to label them as 'stupid irrational ideas', not to feel ashamed of them, but rather to react with amusement at the tricks her mind was playing on her. This helped her a good deal. The thoughts worried her less and became less frequent.

Rejection of the infant

It is clinically useful to distinguish delayed attachment and obsessional thoughts from rejection of the infant, in which there is not only a lack of feeling, but also persistent hostility and a determined effort to avoid the maternal role. Such disorders are intractable and lead to intense friction within the nuclear and extended families. To illustrate this phenomenon two examples are given and a third has already been given on p.10.

A 25-year-old woman was raised in a quarrelsome family. Her father was aggressive and criminal. She was expelled from school for 'insubordination' and developed as a strongly independent and rather masculine person, with trans-sexual urges. She married, but sought sterilization at 23. This was resisted and she was delivered of a son at 25. Five weeks later she deliberately immersed him in water, believing him dead. He was resuscitated by remarkably prompt action on the part of the general practitioner. She later became rather depressed and was admitted to the Mother and Baby Unit with her baby. The depression was mild and lifted completely but it was obvious she had no feeling whatever for the baby, who was offered for adoption.

A woman with a 7-year-old child greatly desired another and became pregnant. She visited a fortune teller who told her the child would be handicapped. She sought an abortion, which was prevented by her husband. The infant was born with a congenital abnormality. She developed an intense hatred for the baby, whom she called 'the bitch'. In turn, she was rejected by her husband, his family and her son. She became deeply depressed, with delusions of zoophilic metamorphosis. ECT relieved the depression, but the rejection remained unresolved, and family discord continued for years.

Child abuse and neglect

The subject of child abuse has not been addressed in the two volumes of *Motherhood and Mental Illness*, in spite of the fact (indeed, because of the fact) that its literature is perhaps equal to that of all the remaining postnatal mental disorders. The present volume is largely written by those practising within the adult mental illness service, while child abuse is a major preoccupation of the paediatric and social services. In this place, therefore, we can only emphasize the importance of this subject, refer the readers elsewhere (e.g. Taylor and Newberger, 1979) and point out how most child abuse differs from the disorders described here. When a baby is starved or neglected, it may be an extreme manifestation of rejection. When it is injured by blows, shaking, scalding or burning, it may be a complication of psychosis or severe depression. However, the majority of instances of child abuse probably occur outside the context of severe mental illness. Frequently they occur in a setting of impulsive violence on the part of an inadequate often unsupported parent who is at the end of his or her tether, i.e. they are manifestations of personality disorder or neurosis (sometimes aggravated by a degree of mental impairment). Child abuse occurs in families of low social standing, often with a history of familial violence. There is often severe marital disharmony or lack of kinship support and isolation. The mothers themselves have often been ill-used, and feel worthless, rejected and criticized. They have had very poor models of motherhood and lack understanding and maternal skills. This brief and grossly oversimplified statement is included here to emphasize that child abuse is a different phenomenon from the other forms of disturbed mother-infant relationship.

Infanticide

The subject of child murder has been greatly clarified by the work of Resnick (1969, 1970). He reviewed the world literature from 1751 until 1968 and drew the important distinction between 'neonaticide' and 'filicide'.

Neonaticide is the murder of the newborn within 24 h of its birth. In Resnick's review of 37 cases in the literature, the mothers were usually under 25 and unmarried without evidence of psychosis or depression. Suicide attempts were never seen. In almost all cases the reason for the killing was simply that the child was unwanted. Many of these women were passive individuals who failed to square up to an unwanted pregnancy, did not seek an abortion, were greatly afraid of revealing the pregnancy to their mothers, made no advance preparations and responded to the reality of a crying baby by suffocating him or drowning him in the toilet.

In contrast, *filicide* is defined as murder of a child by his parent more than 24 h after the birth. It is usually associated with mental illness. Among the 131 cases Resnick collected, only 18 killed their babies or children because they were unwanted. The largest group of 50 killed them during a suicidal attempt, to relieve the expected suffering of children about to be abandoned. The next largest group of 28 occurred (often without clear motive) during an acute psychotic episode. Sixteen were killed accidentally, most of them during a violent outburst, without any intention to kill (i.e. they were complications of child abuse). Fourteen were deliberately killed (almost all by their mothers) in order to relieve real or imagined suffering. Finally, five were killed in revenge against the husband ('Medea complex').

Depressive disorders

Maternity blues
Many or most mothers experience mild weepiness and emotionality about 4–5 days after delivery, lasting a matter of hours. It is important to distinguish this from depression. The subject has been reviewed by Stein (1982).

Postnatal depression
This concept came to prominence as a result of surveys which showed that unusually large numbers of women became depressed during the first postpartum year; it has received further support from follow-through studies which have shown a high frequency of new episodes during this time. Although the notion of 'postnatal depression' has aroused much interest, there are many difficulties about it. It has not been demonstrated by controlled studies that new episodes of depression are more common after childbirth than at other times; thus the first stage in the search for a specific aetiological link—the demonstration of a temporal association—has not been reached. From the point of view of the psychiatric services (which deal largely with severe psychoses and depressions of early puerperal onset), postnatal depression fails to reach the threshold of referral, so that it has become a mystery disease hidden in the homes or the hearts of the sufferers. From the scientific point of view, the weakness of most research so far has been the limitation of the diagnostic approach to depressive symptoms, without taking into account duration, impairment of role and other indices of severity. The doubts expressed here about 'postnatal depression' as a medical concept or psychological phenomenon do not detract from the authors' conviction that depression in the mothers of young children (whatever its nature and cause) is a serious and indeed neglected public health problem with far-reaching consequences. This matter is discussed in some detail in Chapter 2.

A special cause of distress after childbirth is the grief experienced by a mother after stillbirth or neonatal death, or following the birth of a handicapped child. These are discussed in Chapters 9 and 10.

Further clinical studies

We have some way to go in the clinical study and definition of the puerperal mental disorders. As far as puerperal psychosis is concerned, it is unsatisfactory that the definitions given above are stated mainly in terms of background factors (personality and stress, history and timing), and that clinical features hardly enter into the classification, except to distinguish between depressed and psychotic patients. Clinicians need all the help they can get when reaching the diagnostic decisions which are the prelude to intervention, and we hope that future generations of psychiatrists will know far more about the features which are typical of specific puerperal disorders and those which are not. Further clinical studies are required to determine:

(1) whether patients with puerperal schizophreniform psychosis have manic features;

(2) whether puerperal mania differs in important respects from non-puerperal mania;

(3) whether the depressed pole of a bipolar puerperal psychosis can be recognized from its clinical features.

One should not, however, underestimate the difficulty of studies of symptomatology. Even in the 1980s studies have emerged which are based on case records. It is essential to study patients prospectively. Structured psychiatric interviews and operationally defined diagnoses have, for 10–20 years, been the basis of good clinical research and are the minimum requirement. While these are necessary, they are not sufficient to tackle such difficult clinical problems. The latest attempt to discover the features of puerperal depression (Brockington *et al.*, 1988) employed a synoptic assessment using multiple information sources (psychiatric and relatives' interviews, nursing observations and case records) together with self-rating and the measurement of non-verbal behaviour from videotapes in a total series of over 100 patients. Rating error was reduced by the use of multiple raters and consensus judgements. Even this battery of measures was not very successful in discovering specific features.

Improvements to classification and diagnosis are an important but preliminary objective. The goal is to understand the cause of these disorders. Advances may result from the alertness and curiosity of clinicians capable of recognizing the unusual instance. In the field of the puerperal mental disorders the progress of the last 20 years has resulted from a measure of specialization. There are now a few practitioners who are prepared to devote at least a few sessions per week to this important area of psychiatry, and when regular practice in a clinical specialism is allied to scientific discipline and powers of observation, progress is inevitable.

References

AMERICAN PSYCHIATRIC ASSOCIATION (1980). *Diagnostic and Statistical Manual of Mental Disorders*, 3rd Edition. Washington: American Psychiatric Association

BERNER, P., KATSCHNIG, H. and LENZ, G.(1982). Poly-diagnostic approach: a method to clarify incongruences among the classification of the functional psychoses. *Psychiatric Journal of the University of Ottawa*, 7, 244–248

BROCKINGTON, I. F. (1986). Schizophrenia: fact and fiction. Inaugural lecture, University of Birmingham

BROCKINGTON, I. F. and BRIERLEY, E. (1984). Rejection of a child by his mother successfully treated after three years. *British Journal of Psychiatry*, 145, 316–318

BROCKINGTON, I. F. and MELTZER, H. Y. (1983). The nosology of schizoaffective psychosis. *Psychiatric Developments*, 1(4), 317–338

BROCKINGTON, I. F., WINOKUR, G. and DEAN, C. (1982). Puerperal psychosis. In: *Motherhood and Mental Illness*, (I. F. Brockington and R. Kumar, eds), pp. 37–69. London: Academic Press

BROCKINGTON, I. F., PERRIS, C., KENDELL, R. E., HILLIER, V. E. and WAINWRIGHT, S. (1982). The course and outcome of cycloid psychosis. *Psychological Medicine*, 12, 97–105

BROCKINGTON, I. F., MARGISON, F. R., SCHOFIELD, E. and KNIGHT, R. J. E. (1988). The clinical picture of the depressed form of puerperal psychosis. *Journal of Affective Disorders* (in press)

BUTTON, J. H., REIVICH, R. S. and KAN, L. (1972). Obsessions of infanticide. *Archives of General Psychiatry*, **27**, 235–240

CORYELL, W. and TSUANG, M. T. (1982). DSM-III schizophreniform disorder. *Archives of General Psychiatry*, **39**, 66–69

DEAN, C. and KENDELL, R. E. (1981). The symptomatology of puerperal illnesses. *British Journal of Psychiatry*, **139**, 128–133

ESSEN-MÖLLER, E. (1961). On classification of mental disorders. *Acta Psychiatrica Scandinavica*, **37**, 119–126

FAERGEMAN, P. M. (1963). *Psychogenic Psychoses*. London: Butterworths

FOGELSON, D. L., COHEN, B. M. and POPE, H. G. (1982). A study of DSM-III schizophreniform disorder. *American Journal of Psychiatry*, **139**, 1281–1285

HAWK, A. B., CARPENTER, W. T. Jr. and STRAUSS, J. S. (1975). Diagnostic criteria and five year outcome in schizophrenia. *Archives of General Psychiatry*, **32**, 343–347

HELZER, J. E., BROCKINGTON, I. F. and KENDELL, R. E. (1981). Predictive validity of DSM-III and Feighner definitions of schizophrenia. *Archives of General Psychiatry*, **38**, 791–797

HERMAN (1986). See Critchton Browne, J. (1896). Prevention and treatment of insanity of pregnancy and the puerperal period. *Lancet*, **i**, 164–165

KARNOSH, L. J. and HOPE, J. M. (1937). Puerperal psychoses and their sequelae. *American Journal of Psychiatry*, **94**, 537–550

KENDELL, R. E. and BROCKINGTON, I. F. (1978). Definitions of schizophrenia: concordance and prediction of outcome. *Psychological Medicine*, **8**, 387–398

KENDELL, R. E. and BROCKINGTON, I. F. (1979). The distinction between the affective psychoses and schizophrenia. *British Journal of Psychiatry*, **135**, 135–243

KENDELL, R. E., CHALMERS, J. C. and PLATZ, C. (1987). Epidemiology of puerperal psychosis. *British Journal of Psychiatry*, **150**, 662–673

MARCÉ, L. V. (1858). *Traité de la Folie des Femmes Enceintes, des Nouvelles Accouchées et des Nourrices*. Paris: Baillière

MARGISON, F. (1982). The pathology of the mother-child relationship. In: *Motherhood and Mental Illness*, (I. F. Brockington and R. Kumar, eds), pp. 191–232. London: Academic Press

MELTZER, E. S. and KUMAR, R. (1985). Puerperal mental illness, clinical features and classification: a study of 142 mother-and-baby admissions. *British Journal of Psychiatry*, **147**, 647–654

OLLERENSHAW, D. P. (1972). The classification of the functional psychoses. *British Journal of Psychiatry*, **122**, 517–530

PAFFENBARGER, R. S. Jr. (1961). The picture puzzle of the postpartum psychoses. *Journal of Chronic Disorders*, **13**, 161–173

PAFFENBARGER, R. S. Jr. (1964). Epidemiological aspects of postpartum mental illness. *British Journal of Preventative and Social Medicine*, **18**, 189–195

RESNICK, P. J. (1969). Child murder by parents: a psychiatric review of filicide. *American Journal of Psychiatry*, **126**, 325–334

RESNICK, P. J. (1970). Murder of the newborn: a psychiatric review of neonaticide. *American Journal of Psychiatry*, **126**, 1414–1420

RETTERSTÖL, N. (1983). Course of paranoid psychoses in relation to diagnostic grouping. *Psychiatria Clinica*, **16**, 198–206

ROBSON, K. M. and MOSS, H. A. (1970). Patterns and determinants of maternal attachment. *Journal of Pediatrics*, **77**, 976–985

ROBSON, K. M. and POWELL, E. (1982). Early maternal attachment. In: *Motherhood and Mental Illness*, (I. F. Brockington and R. Kumar, eds), pp. 155–190. London: Academic Press

SPITZER, R. L., ENDICOTT, J. and ROBINS, E. (1978). *Research Diagnostic Criteria for a Selected Group of Functional Disorders*, 3rd Edition. New York State Psychiatric Institute

STEIN, G. (1982). The maternity blues. In: *Motherhood and Mental Illness*, (I. F. Brockington and R. Kumar, eds), pp.119–154. London: Academic Press

TAYLOR, L. and NEWBERGER, E. H. (1979). Child abuse in the international year of the child. *New England Journal of Medicine*, **301**, 1205–1212

TAYLOR, M. A. and ABRAMS, R. (1983). Schizo-affective disorder, manic type. A clinical laboratory and genetic study. *Psychiatria Clinica*, **16**, 234–244

Chapter 2

Postpartum depression: a comprehensive review

Michael W. O'Hara and Ellen M. Zekoski

Introduction

The study of puerperal mood disorders has intensified in recent years. Psychotic disorders associated with childbearing have long been studied (Marcé, 1858; Turnbull, 1969). However, there were few systematic studies of less severe psychiatric disorders of the puerperium prior to the pioneering work of the Gordons (Gordon and Gordon, 1959, 1960) in the late 1950s. Within a few years, larger scale studies by Ryle (1961), Tod (1964), and Pitt (1968) had begun to provide the first data regarding prevalence and correlates of what is commonly called postpartum depression. Since this time, a number of well designed studies have been carried out primarily by researchers in the United Kingdom, the United States, and Scandinavia.

The spectrum of 'affective disorders' following childbirth has frequently been divided into three classes in ascending order of severity:

(a) postpartum blues;
(b) postpartum depression; and
(c) postpartum psychosis.

The postpartum blues are generally regarded as a fleeting phenomenon characterized by sad or labile mood and tearfulness lasting from a few hours to a few days (Pitt, 1973; Yalom *et al.*, 1968). Postpartum psychosis is an incapacitating disorder that usually requires hospitalization (Brockington *et al.*, 1981; Brockington, Winokur and Dean, 1982). Postpartum depression constitutes those affective disorders whose severity falls in between the blues and psychosis. With respect to the validity of the distinctions among these three 'disorders', it is as yet unclear whether they are distinguishable on grounds other than severity and length of impairment. This problem will be examined later.

The purpose of this chapter is to address several methodological and substantive questions in the postpartum depression literature. The first section will examine methodological issues. Next, there will be a brief review of normal postpartum adjustment that will provide a context for the examination of disordered adjustment. In the third section incidence and prevalence will be discussed to determine whether the incidence of depression following childbirth is actually elevated relative to other times.

Fourthly, we will consider factors related to the aetiology of postpartum depression, i.e. what are the risk factors? Fifthly, the relations among the postpartum affective disorders will be explored and sixthly, we will review the small literature related to treatment and prevention of postpartum depression. In the seventh section recommendations for future research will be made and finally, we will briefly comment on public policy and postpartum depression.

Methodological issues

In this section we will discuss sample size, retrospective versus prospective design, outcome measures, timing of assessments, control for chance findings, and reliability of psychiatric diagnosis. Possible methodological shortcomings of individual studies are noted in *Tables 2.1, 2.2* and *2.3*.

Sample size

The size of a sample being studied determines the confidence that one has in estimating the prevalence of depression. In small samples, small changes in the number of recorded cases of postpartum depression will have relatively greater impact on prevalence estimates than in studies with large numbers of subjects. Also, it should be noted that in studies where there are questions regarding the precision with which variables of interest can be measured, such as family history of psychopathology, number of past episodes of depression, larger sample sizes are necessary to ensure a fair test of the research hypotheses. This is necessary because the greater the potential error in measurement, the larger the sample size necessary to detect true associations between variables. This problem has been especially acute in studies of hormonal correlates of postpartum mood disturbance (*see Table 2.3*).

Retrospective versus prospective design

Most recent studies of postpartum depression have used prospective designs (Kumar and Robson, 1984; O'Hara, Neunaber and Zekoski, 1984) in which women are recruited during pregnancy or shortly after delivery and followed through the postpartum period. There are several advantages of prospective designs. Subjects are more likely to report accurately on their current feelings and current events than on feelings or events that have occurred in the past. If putative predictor variables are measured prior to the measurement of the outcome variables, e.g. postpartum depression, there is less chance that bias on the part of the subject or investigator will colour the measurement of the predictor variables. In retrospective studies such bias would work in favour of confirming both the subjects' and the investigators' hypotheses regarding the causes of postpartum depression. An example of this bias would be the depressed woman who reports selectively on the negative aspects of her prepartum marital relationship during a postpartum interview.

Most studies, even those that are designed to be prospective, have some variables that are measured at the same time that postpartum depression is assessed. For example, it is usually the case that stressful life events since delivery or even since the beginning of pregnancy are assessed at the time of the follow-up postnatal assessment. Depressed subjects may be biased toward reporting more negative events in the retrospective assessment of life events relative to non-depressed subjects. In other cases variables that are measured prior (i.e. have a prospective relevance) to one outcome are measured at the same time (i.e. have a retrospective relevance) as another outcome. For example, family history of psychopathology assessed during pregnancy would have a retrospective relation to depression during pregnancy, i.e. family history is assessed *after or during* a prenatal episode, but a prospective relation to postpartum depression, i.e. family history is assessed *prior* to the postpartum episode.

Outcome measures

Several types of outcome measures of depression have been used in studies of postpartum depression. Often in early work a simple judgement was made by the obstetrician or researcher regarding the presence of depression (e.g. Tod, 1964). More recent work has included the use of standard depression symptom scales such as the Beck Depression Inventory (BDI) (Beck *et al.*, 1961) and the General Health Questionnaire (GHQ) (Goldberg, 1972). In addition, semi-structured interviews are often conducted in order to allow for diagnostic judgements to be made regarding the presence or absence of a postpartum depression. With respect to judgements by clinicians regarding depression, the use of a standardized assessment can significantly reduce the risk of bias in determining 'caseness'. Otherwise, it is not possible to know whether or not the clinician's personal criteria for depression are similar to conventionally accepted criteria, e.g. ICD-9, RDC (Spitzer, Endicott and Robins, 1978), DSM-III (American Psychiatric Association, 1980).

Self-report
Standard symptom scales have the advantage of objectivity, but are usually designed to provide diagnostic information. The practice of using a 'cutoff' on a rating scale such as the BDI or the GHQ to identify women experiencing postpartum depression may lead to misclassification. High scores on these measures may reflect factors other than depression, including physical ill health. For example, the BDI has many items that would be expected to give elevated scores even in the course of a normal pregnancy or puerperium, e.g. fatigue, body image, sleep disturbance, loss of interest in sex. Anxiety-based problems such as generalized anxiety or agoraphobia may also lead to elevated scores on self-report measures. In making a diagnosis of depression, the length of time that the symptoms have been present and the extent to which the dysphoric mood and symptoms interfere with a woman's daily life are also germane. These considerations are rarely addressed in self-report measures.

When self-report measures are used to pick out subjects for more detailed investigation, some depressed women achieve low scores on a screening measure (*see* Pitt, 1968; O'Hara, Neunaber and Zekoski, 1984) and are thus not followed up with an interview. Finally, there are few self-report measures of depressive symptomatology that have been validated for use with pregnant and postpartum women, although this situation is changing (Cox, Holden and Sagovsky, 1987).

Diagnostic interview
Most of the issues that pertain to interview assessments of postpartum depression relate to the reliability of the diagnostic assessment (*see* p. 22). Many recent studies have used standard diagnostic criteria for postpartum depression. The current assumption is that postpartum depression is no different in kind from depression occurring at other times. A major issue, however, is the social significance of what researchers are diagnosing as postpartum depression when standard criteria such as the RDC or the ICD-9 are used. Most cases of postpartum depression diagnosed by researchers are never treated. This situation is not uncommon in community studies of psychopathology (Weissman and Myers, 1978; Myers *et al.*, 1984). In some cases the reason for not seeking treatment may have to do with the unavailability of treatment resources, and in other cases it may have to do with the woman or her family not recognizing the need for treatment.

Because most conceptions of depression as a disorder include a component of impaired functioning due to the presumed disorder, it is fair to ask whether these untreated 'depressions' really should be diagnosed as depression. The RDC (Spitzer, Endicott and Robins, 1978) have addressed this issue rather directly. One of the criteria for major or minor depression is evidence of help-seeking or functional impairment. A woman seeking or being referred for treatment would automatically meet this criterion. In the absence of treatment seeking, women must provide some evidence that they are impaired in their work (at home or on the job), or in their intimate relationships (e.g. with husband, children, parents), or in their casual interpersonal relationships (e.g. friends, store clerks).

Timing of assessments

Both the time at which a postpartum depression assessment is made and the period covered by the assessment vary considerably from three days (Manly *et al.*, 1982) to one year (Feggetter and Gath, 1981). There has been considerable debate as to what constitutes the limit of the postpartum period. For postpartum psychosis, Brockington *et al.* (1981) have argued that onset within two weeks is necessary (also *see* Meltzer and Kumar, 1985). There is, by contrast, almost no agreement regarding the limits for the onset of postpartum depression. A major problem in determining a time limit for the onset of postpartum psychosis or depression is our continuing ignorance of the specific aetiological or risk factors for postpartum depression that are associated with childbirth. For example, if there was clear evidence that fatigue due to lack of sleep was an important aetiological factor in postpartum depression, the limits for the onset of postpartum depression might be defined in terms of when normal sleep patterns return for most women. Or, if a hormonal disturbance was thought to be a prime aetiological factor, then the return to normal hormone levels might be seen as the limit for the beginning of what is called a postpartum depression. This argument assumes that the effects of sleep deprivation or hormonal disturbances would have rather immediate effects or known delayed effects.

A second method for determining a reasonable time limit for the beginning of a postpartum depression episode is to examine the natural history of depressions occurring during the puerperium. Unfortunately, while there are rather convincing data regarding an increased risk for psychosis in the first trimester after birth (Kendell *et al.*, 1976), there are less adequate data regarding postpartum depression. For example, although Kumar and Robson (1984) and Watson *et al.* (1984) found that the greatest risk for depression was in the first trimester after delivery, Nott (1982) did not replicate these results with treated depressives. Given that no birth-specific aetiological factor can be identified and the period of increased risk is unclear, the time limit for the beginning of a postpartum depressive episode (though probably within 3–6 months after delivery) will be to some degree arbitrary.

As implied from what has been described above, a researcher's decision about when to assess for postpartum depression depends on what period of time the researcher believes is the high risk period for depression in the puerperium. The general strategy of most researchers is to assess for postpartum depression at the earliest time that they believe most women will become depressed. There are two reasons for this strategy. First, fewer resources are required to follow subjects for shorter rather than longer periods and fewer subjects will be lost to follow-up for reasons such as moving away. Second, subjects will be better able to provide reliable descriptions of any episode of postpartum depression that had developed and then remitted prior to the assessment the closer in time the assessment is to the episode. The principal risk is that depressions that begin relatively late will be missed. Some of these depressions might even have begun prior to the assessment but were not sufficiently severe or of sufficient duration to be diagnosed as cases of depression.

Control for chance findings

One of the most serious problems with the current postpartum depression literature is the evident misunderstanding of multiple tests of statistical significance on the part of many researchers. The problem with multiple tests of statistical significance is that the actual alpha level, i.e. the probability of the finding occurring by chance, is often greater than that which is indicated, i.e. the nominal alpha level. For example, if the nominal alpha level is set at 0.05 for four statistical tests, the actual alpha level for those four tests is 0.19. Often researchers who set their nominal alphas at 0.05 for multiple tests argue that they have found more significant associations (each at the 0.05 level) than would be expected by chance, implying that this outcome somehow mitigates the effects of very high actual error rates. It does not. Care must be taken in interpreting outcomes of studies when multiple tests have been conducted without appropriate adjustment of significance levels. The extent to which findings replicate earlier work and are sensible within a theoretical framework is also critical in interpreting studies with large numbers of variables.

Reliability

The reliability of psychiatric diagnoses was unacceptably low for many years (Beck *et al.*, 1962). This problem was attacked in two ways. First, operationally defined diagnostic criteria were developed in order to reduce the ambiguity of what constituted a specific symptom for a disorder (Spitzer, Endicott and Robins, 1978). Second, semistructured interviews were developed to provide a guide for diagnosticians so that subjects would be exposed to relatively similar questions about their difficulties (Wing, Cooper and Sartorius, 1974; Endicott and Spitzer, 1978). These advances have made it more likely that a clinical interviewer will make reliable judgements regarding the presence or absence of a disorder. Moreover, a number of studies have shown that many psychiatric disorders can be reliably diagnosed in the context of operational diagnostic criteria and a semistructured interview (e.g. Spitzer, Endicott and Robins, 1978). Nevertheless, it cannot be assumed that a clinical interviewer/diagnostician is making reliable diagnoses in the absence of a reliability study. At a minimum, what is required is that two interviewers overlap in their judgements about some subset of subjects being studied. This overlap may result from one interviewer observing (live, video, or audio) the other and making similar ratings or actually having a subset of subjects interviewed twice. Many studies of postpartum depression in which diagnostic judgements are made are lacking evidence regarding the reliability of those judgements.

Summary

Inspection of *Tables 2.1 2.2* and *2.3* makes it clear that many researchers have not used methodologically sound methods of diagnosis and assessment. Some have not fully considered issues of sample size and design. Others have not attended to factors such as subject and experimenter bias, the use of symptom as opposed to syndrome measures, and statistical control for chance findings.

Perspectives on postpartum adjustment

In order to understand abnormal postpartum adjustment, one must know what is meant by normal adjustment. Defining normality is a difficult task, subject to an individual's personal and professional experiences, values and expectations. Offer and Sabshin (1984) have attempted to avoid biases and subjectivity by defining four perspectives of normality found in the research literature on mental health. The first perspective is that of normality as health. This perspective incorporates the traditional medical-psychiatric approach which focuses on defining pathology. Thus, normality is the absence of pathology. In the context of much of the literature on postpartum depression, the normal response to the puerperal period simply is the lack of a postpartum depression or other disorder. Thus, many investigators who have studied the incidence and prevalence of the syndrome of postpartum depression (Cox, Connor and Kendell, 1982; O'Hara, Neunaber and Zekoski, 1984) have found that the majority of women are 'normal' after delivery. In contrast, those researchers who focused on depressive symptomatology rather than syndromal depression (Nilsson, 1970) have found fewer 'normal' women than investigators who used RDC or DSM-III criteria.

The second perspective is that of normality as utopia, i.e. the ideal. This perspective is propounded by psychoanalytical and humanistic theorists who define normality as ideal functioning or 'self-actualization'. Offer and Sabshin (1966) noted that this perspective implies that the normal individual is 'one who is seldom, if ever, seen in flesh and blood' (p. 104). Investigations of such individuals often appear in the form of case studies. Needless to say, no systematic research on postpartum women has been conducted from this perspective.

The third perspective is that of normality as average. This perspective which is often employed by sociologists is based on the normal distribution, with the middle range viewed as normal and both extremes as deviant. According to this definition, normal postpartum women are not necessarily asymptomatic. As long as symptomatic women fall in the main portion of the normal bell-shaped curve, their adjustment is viewed as normal.

The fourth perspective is that of normality as transactional systems. This perspective stresses that normal behaviour is the end result of interacting systems that change over time. What is viewed as normal behaviour changes as a function of development, e.g. infancy to childhood to adulthood, and as a function of the type of environment to which the individual is exposed, e.g. supportive family versus harsh punitive family. In the case of postpartum depression, an investigator using this approach would be interested in the ongoing psychological development of the pregnant and postpartum woman and any factors which contribute to her development, plus how any changes in the mother affect the environment around her. Because this approach is the most complex of the four perspectives on normality, theories and hypotheses derived from it are the most difficult to test empirically.

Both psychoanalytical researchers and sociologists have investigated postpartum adjustment from the viewpoint of normality as transactional systems. Psychoanalytical researchers such as Shereshefsky and Yarrow (1973) and Leifer (1977) describe the transition to parenthood as a time of crisis, in which the mother enters a stage of disequilibrium. In order to adapt successfully to motherhood, the women must make significant changes intrapsychically and in her relationships with others or she will become emotionally distressed. Sociologists such as Breen (1975) and Rossi (1968) perceive the transition to motherhood as a stage in development which does not necessarily involve the risk of a decline in psychological functioning.

The bulk of postpartum depression research has been conducted by researchers who view normality as health, as evidenced by their emphasis on psychopathology. In the rest of this chapter we will primarily discuss postpartum depression from the perspective of normality as health, although research from other perspectives will also be examined.

Incidence and prevalence

The incidence of a disorder refers to the number of new cases arising over a specified period of time. The prevalence of a disorder refers to the number of cases present during a specified period of time. This distinction takes on special significance when considering disorders that persist over long periods of time, e.g. schizophrenia. For researchers who study postpartum depression the distinction is important because of the need to distinguish between depressive episodes that arise before delivery and persist into the puerperium and those episodes that arise during the puerperium. From a public health or clinical perspective, it may not matter whether a depressive episode arose during pregnancy or after delivery; treatment resources still must be brought to bear. However, to understand the factors that cause postpartum depression, it may be important in research to separate those episodes that begin during pregnancy and continue from those episodes that begin after delivery.

Studies of incidence and prevalence

The criteria for postpartum depression have varied widely across studies. Moreover, many studies do not specifically investigate depression but rather consider any emotional symptom that is detected. In this section, however, we will review primarily the studies that have focused on depression and that have assessed it as a syndrome. That is, we will consider studies that have used diagnostic criteria (e.g. RDC) or a recognized diagnostic scheme (e.g. ICD-9, DSM-III, Pitt criteria) or studies that consider functional impairment and length of episode in their criteria for depression. Nevertheless, early studies that did not use standard diagnostic criteria will be commented on briefly.

Estimates not based on psychiatric diagnosis (see Table 2.1)
There have been several studies that have either relied on global judgements regarding the presence or severity of depression, or that have focused on emotional distress in general rather than depression. These studies are less informative regarding the prevalence of postpartum depression than studies using well-defined diagnostic criteria. For example, Gordon and Gordon (1959) studied 98 American women at four months postpartum. The patients' obstetrician made a three-point rating regarding the amount of emotional upset each woman experienced (none, slight and much). In a later study by these workers (Gordon, Kapostins and Gordon, 1965), 306 American women were followed up at six weeks and six months after delivery. Patients were rated on a five-point scale (normal postpartum reaction, mild, moderate, or severe emotional upsets, and required psychiatric attention) by their obstetrician and public health nurses who visited them at home. Other studies have also relied on ratings from general practitioners, obstetricians or nurses regarding the presence of emotional distress or depression (Tod, 1964; Braverman and Roux, 1978). Another common criterion used in these studies was the seeking of

treatment from a general practitioner or a psychiatrist (Ryle, 1961; Dalton, 1971; Brown and Shereshefsky, 1973). Of course, in these studies all of the serious depressions that were not treated would have been missed using a treatment criterion.

The Scandinavian studies (e.g. Nilsson, 1970; Uddenberg, 1974), though generally well done, did not specify what percentage of their subjects were experiencing depression as opposed to other disorders. Nevertheless, based on the work of several British investigators (e.g. Wolkind, Zajicek and Ghodsian, 1980; Kumar and Robson, 1984; Watson et al., 1984), who found that the great majority of postpartum disorders are affective in nature, it is reasonable to assume that the rates of depression for the Scandinavian samples are close to those rates ascribed to 'pronounced psychiatric symptoms' (Nilsson, 1970) or 'severe mental handicap' (Uddenberg, 1974).

Estimates based on psychiatric diagnosis (see Table 2.2)
One of the earliest studies of postpartum depression which used relatively conventional diagnostic criteria was conducted by Pitt (1968). Pitt developed a screening questionnaire that was given to women during their 28th week of pregnancy and again about 6–8 weeks postpartum. Those women whose postpartum score was six points higher than their prenatal score were interviewed to determine if a postpartum depression had occurred. Also, a random sample of women whose scores had not increased appreciably were interviewed. Interestingly, in the first table of Pitt's paper, there is an indication that six women whose questionnaire score had *not* increased by six or more points were diagnosed as depressed based on the clinical interview. A re-analysis of Pitt's data suggested that a better estimate of the incidence of postpartum depression in this sample was 19.7% (Neugebauer, 1983). The Pitt study illustrates the problem of using a screening questionnaire that is less than perfectly sensitive (i.e. one that misses some true cases of depression) in studies of the prevalence or incidence of postpartum depression.

In a unique study, Nott (1982) matched maternity records from a two-year period in Southampton, UK with a case register of inpatient and outpatient psychiatric visits for the preceding and subsequent two years for each woman. Although this strategy has been used in studies of postpartum psychosis (Kendell et al., 1976, 1981), Nott's study is the only one in which rates of non-psychotic depression were reported. The overall prevalence of depressive neurosis in treatment in the nine months following delivery was 0.27% compared with 0.21% during pregnancy.

Watson et al. (1984) studied 128 British women from the first trimester of pregnancy until one year postpartum. All subjects participated in at least two diagnostic interviews (16th week of pregnancy and six weeks postpartum) with a research psychiatrist. Subjects were also evaluated six more times during pregnancy and five more times in the first year after delivery by a psychologist who arranged for additional psychiatric interviews when warranted. In this way the researchers were able to date rather precisely the onset and offset of episodes of depression occurring during pregnancy and the first postpartum year. A major contribution of this report is the graphical picture that the authors provide of the timing of

Table 2.1 Prevalence of prenatal and postnatal depression: estimates not based on psychiatric diagnosis

Study	Sample size and country of investigation	Prenatal prevalence (time of assessment)	Postnatal prevalence (time of assessment)	Criteria	Comments
Gordon and Gordon (1959)	98 USA	—	16% slight emotional upset 13% much emotional upset (4 months)	Obstetrician rating regarding amount of postpartum emotional upset (3-point scale)	1,2
Ryle (1961)	137 (313 full-term pregnancies) UK	2.6% (entire pregnancy)	4.8% (within one year)	Disorder necessitated at least three consultations with the investigator (GP); neurotic and endogenous depression	1
Tod (1964)	700 UK	—	2.9% (possibly up to a year)	Serious depression (no other criteria)	1
Gordon et al. (1965)	306 USA	—	30% (6 weeks) 11% (6 months)	Obstetrician rating on a 5-point scale; at least mild level of emotional upset	1,2,6
Nilsson (1970)	152 Sweden	27.6% moderate symptoms 17.1% pronounced symptoms (entire pregnancy)	26.3% moderate symptoms 19.1% pronounced symptoms (6 months)	Moderate symptoms affecting subject's wellbeing; pronounced psychiatric symptoms indicating clear mental disturbance	1,2,5
Dalton (1971)	189 UK	—	7.4% depression 25.4% mild depression (6 months)	Depression requiring treatment; mild depression (no criteria)	1,3

Study	Sample	Incidence	Prevalence	Definition	Comments
Brown and Shereshefsky (1973)[a]	62 USA	—	4.8% (6 months)[a]	Psychiatric disorder requiring treatment	1,2,4
Uddenberg (1974)	95 Sweden	21.8% moderate mental handicap 16.8% severe mental handicap (17 weeks)	27.4% moderate mental handicap 20.0% severe mental handicap (4 months)	Moderate mental handicap were symptoms resulting in mild deterioration in social and interpersonal relationships; severe mental handicap reflected by symptoms resulting in significant deterioration in social and interpersonal fucntioning	1,2
Braverman and Roux (1978)	120 Canada	—	2.5% mild to moderate 0.0% moderate to severe 0.8% very severe (6 weeks)	Mild to moderate emotional reaction: more complaints than average; moderate to severe emotional reaction: overt signs of persistent depression such as sad expression; frequent crying; very severe emotional reaction: severe depression requiring psychiatric consultation	1
Oakley (1980)	55 UK	—	24% (5 months)	Presence of two or more symptoms lasting two or more weeks	1,4
Paykel et al. (1980)	120 UK	—	20% (5–8 weeks)	Score greater than 6 on Raskin Three Area Depression Scale (Raskin et al., 1970)	1,5

For many women more than one pregnancy was represented in the sample.

[a]Incidence.

Comments:

1 Study characterized by use of criteria that do not relate to any established diagnostic system.
2 Prevalence estimates include other disorders in addition to depression.
3 Excessive dropouts.
4 Small sample size.
5 Structured diagnostic interview.
6 Assessment of reliability of diagnoses.

Table 2.2 Incidence and prevalence of prenatal and postnatal depression: studies using conventionally defined diagnostic criteria

Study	Sample size and country of investigation	Prenatal incidence/prevalence (time of assessment)[a]	Postnatal incidence/prevalence (time of assessment)	Criteria	Comments
Pitt (1968) Neugebauer (1983)	305 UK	—	—/10.8% —/19.7% (6–8 weeks)	Depressive symptoms that developed since delivery lasting longer than two weeks, unusual in experience and to some degree disabling	1,2
Martin (1977)	401 Ireland	—/23% (time frame unspecified)	14.0%/23% (5–6 weeks)	Pitt (1968) criteria	2
Wolkind et al. (1980)	117 UK	—/16% (7th month)[b]	—/10% (4 months)[b] —/18% (14 months)[b]	Definite psychiatric disorder (mostly depression assessed in context of modified Present State Examination) (Rutter, 1976)	3,6
Cox et al. (1982)	105 Scotland	—/4% (20 weeks)[c]	—/13% (4 months)	Pitt (1968) criteria assessed in context Goldberg interview (Goldberg et al., 1970)	2,6
Nott (1982)	5200 UK	—/0.21% (entire pregnancy)	—/0.27% (9 months)	Depressive neurosis assessed in context of inpatient or outpatient psychiatric care	4,5
Cox (1983)	183 Uganda	—	—/10% (3 months)	Depressive illness based on ICD-8 assessed in context of Goldberg interviews	6
Cutrona (1983)	85 USA	—/3.5% (3rd trimester)[c]	4.7%/4.7% (2 weeks)[c] 3.5%/3.5% (8 weeks)[c] 8.2%/8.2% (combined)	DSM-III (American Psychiatric Association, 1980); major depression	6,7

Study	N	Country	Pregnancy	Postpartum	Diagnostic criteria	Comments
Kumar and Robson (1984)	119	UK	12.0%/13.4% (1st trimester) 2.5%/7.6% (2nd trimester) 2.7%/6.3% (3rd trimester)	14.0%/14.9% (3 months)(c) 4.5%/11.2% (6 months)(c) 4.6%/6.5% (12 months)(c)	Research Diagnostic Criteria (RDC) (Spitzer et al., 1978) major and minor depression in context of Goldberg interview	6
O'Hara et al. (1984)	99	USA	—/9.0% (2nd trimester)(b)	10%/12.0% (9 weeks)	RDC major and minor depression assessed in context of modified Schedule for Affective Disorders and Schizophrenia (Endicott and Spitzer, 1978)	6,7
Watson et al. (1984)	128	UK	—/9.4% (entire pregnancy)	7.8%/12.0% (6 weeks) —/22.0% (entire postnatal year)	Neurotic depression as defined by ICD-9 assessed in context of Goldberg interview	6

(a)Period of coverage of assessment is entire pregnancy up to time of assessment or entire postpartum period up to time of assessment unless otherwise noted.
(b)Period of coverage is the previous 30 days.
(c)Period of coverage is the previous 7 days.
Comments:
1 The estimate of 19.7% represents a revision by Neugebauer of Pitt's original estimate.
2 Validity of diagnostic criteria not established.
3 Anxiety disorders were included in addition to depression.
4 No control over method of diagnosis.
5 Case register study.
6 Structured interview.
7 Assessment of reliability of depression diagnoses.

onset and durations of the episodes of depression. It can be seen in *Figure 2.1* that women who have an episode of depression during pregnancy are highly likely to have another episode in the first postpartum year. Also, it can be seen that about 29% of the 28 postpartum depressed subjects had episodes lasting three months or more and another 29% of the 28 postpartum depressed subjects had episodes lasting six months or more.

Other studies that have followed subjects for up to a year postpartum have confirmed the findings of Watson *et al.* (1984) that many postpartum depressions are not short-lived. Pitt (1968) found that 43% of the 28 postpartum depressed subjects who responded to a follow-up questionnaire had made little recovery by one year postpartum. They complained of symptoms such as loss of sexual and other interests, irritability and fatigue. Wolkind, Zajicek and Ghodsian (1980) reported that, based on

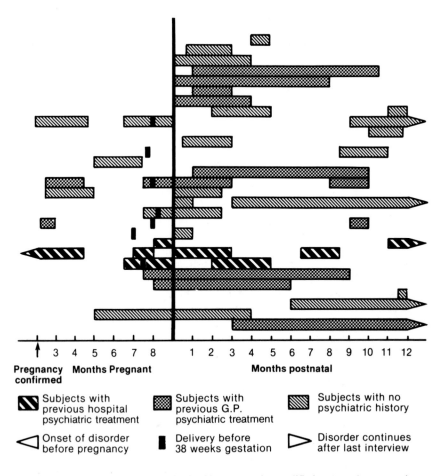

Figure 2.1 Episodes of depression in the 29 women who qualified as 'cases' at some time during pregnancy or in the first postpartum year. For clarity, birth and episodes of disorder ending at birth are shown at nine months gestation. Deliveries before 38 weeks are indicated to convey more precisely the duration of the prenatal episode. (Adapted from Watson *et al.*, 1984, reproduced with permission.)

diagnostic interviews, five of the eight (63%) subjects for whom postpartum depression was their first psychiatric disorder were significantly impaired at 14 months after delivery compared to eight of 82 (10%) subjects who had not experienced a psychiatric disorder either before or after delivery. All women diagnosed with a psychiatric disorder (predominantly depression and anxiety) had to evince significant impairment in their daily functioning and relationships. Cox, Connor and Kendell (1982) and Cox *et al.* (1984) reported that postpartum depressed women frequently had episodes lasting between three and six months, with many women reporting in retrospect that their episode had lasted a year or more. The authors indicated that these depressions, assessed in the context of diagnostic interviews, impaired the ability of subjects to carry out their household tasks and caused much family distress. Moreover, most of these women were distressed by their difficulty in coping with their baby and were excessively concerned with its health. Finally, based on diagnostic interviews at six months postpartum, Kumar and Robson (1984) reported that 50% of their subjects who met diagnostic criteria for postpartum depression (at 12 weeks postpartum) were still depressed. Among the 16 women experiencing postpartum depression, 10 sought help from a professional and at least six of these women received help intermittently for the next four years.

Analysis of incidence and prevalence studies
The common element regarding each of the studies reviewed in this section is that some diagnostic judgement was made regarding the presence of psychiatric disorder (usually depression) during the puerperium. Nevertheless, there was considerable variability across studies with respect to how these judgements were made and the extent to which depression was the focus. Ten of the studies used rather conventional criteria and reported diagnostic data on depression (*see Table 2.2*). In these studies the prevalence of postpartum depression ranged from 8.2% (DSM-III—major depressive episode; Cutrona, 1983) to 23% (Pitt criteria; Martin, 1977). Three studies have used Pitt's criteria and the incidence of postpartum depression ranges from 14% (Martin, 1977) to 19.7% (Pitt, 1968; Neugebauer, 1983). Studies that have used standard diagnoses (i.e. ICD-9, RDC, DSM-III) have found that postpartum depression prevalence ranges from 8.2% (Cutrona, 1983) to 14.9% (Kumar and Robson, 1984). The incidence estimates have ranged from 7.1% (Cutrona, 1983) to 14% (Kumar and Robson, 1984).

Many studies found a higher risk for depression after delivery relative to comparable periods of time during pregnancy. For example, Kumar and Robson (1984) found an increased risk ranging from 1.3 (relative to first trimester) to 5.3 (relative to second and third trimesters). These findings are consistent with other studies (e.g. Cutrona, 1983; Watson *et al.*, 1984). Cox, Connor and Kendell (1982) reported a tripling of risk; however, the period under study during pregnancy was about one week (around the 20th week of gestation) and the period under study after delivery was about four months. Moreover, O'Hara, Neunaber and Zekoski (1984) found a risk ratio of only 1.3 even though the period under study was longer after delivery than during the second trimester. Also, with respect to treated cases, Nott (1982) found very little difference between prevalence of neurotic depression during pregnancy (0.21%) and neurotic depression in the nine months after delivery (0.27%).

The methods of reporting the incidence and prevalence of depression during pregnancy and after delivery have been inconsistent, making comparison across studies difficult. The Kumar and Robson study (1984) might serve as a model for reporting incidence and prevalence of pre- and postpartum depression. They reported the incidence and prevalence separately for each trimester of pregnancy and the first two trimesters after delivery. The period of time under consideration (one month) in each assessment was the same, making comparisons between the probability of affective disorder arising during pregnancy and after delivery much more comparable than in other studies.

The study by Watson et al. (1984) also makes clear the degree to which timing of assessment affects reported prevalence rates for postpartum depression (see Figure 2.1). If additional follow-up interviews had not been done later in the postpartum period, a number of cases would have been missed. For example, four cases all lasting three months or more had their onset between the second and third postpartum month. These data suggest that multiple postpartum assessments are warranted accurately to estimate the prevance and timing of depression after delivery (Kumar and Robson, 1984; Watson et al., 1984).

Prevalence of depression in non-puerperal women

Are pregnancy and the puerperium high-risk periods for the development of depression in the lives of women? Certainly, the significance of rates of depression during pregnancy and the puerperium can only be understood in the light of the knowledge of rates of depression among women who are not pregnant or recently delivered. Three strategies have been used to answer these questions. One strategy has been to conduct a retrospective assessment of depression prior to pregnancy. A second strategy is to compare rates of depression during pregnancy and after delivery with published accounts of other epidemiological studies. The third strategy is to follow a control group and assess them at the same time as the pregnant group.

Prevalence of depression prior to pregnancy
Kumar and Robson (1984) found a prevalence of depression of 4.2% in their sample in the three months prior to pregnancy and an incidence of depression of 1% during that period. Nilsson (1970) found a prevalence of pronounced psychiatric symptoms (not necessarily depression) of 14.5%, and of moderate psychiatric symptoms of 17.8% prior to pregnancy (time period unspecified). Finally, Uddenberg (1974) found a prevalence of severe mental handicap of 13.9% and of moderate mental handicap of 28.7% in the year prior to pregnancy.

Prevalence of depression in other populations
Comparing rates of depression observed in studies of postpartum depression with rates obtained in other epidemiological studies can be proble-

matic. Very often, different criteria will be used across studies and the period under study may be quite different (e.g. period prevalence estimates versus point prevalence estimates). Also, the characteristics of the populations may be quite different. Nevertheless, Watson *et al.* (1984) noted a one-month period prevalence of depression in women of 14.9% in a nearby community (Bebbington *et al.*, 1971), a figure very similar to their own estimate of 12%. They also noted that Brown and Harris (1978) obtained a one-year period prevalence rate of psychiatric disorder of 17% (depression = 14.8%) compared to their own postpartum rate of psychiatric disorder of 26% (depression = 22%) in neighbouring Camberwell. O'Hara, Neunaber and Zekoski (1984) noted that Myers *et al.* (1984) obtained a six-month period prevalence of depression in women between 18 and 24 of 6.1% in several urban communities, a rate about half of what O'Hara, Neunaber and Zekoski (1984) reported for the first nine weeks postpartum. However, Myers *et al.* (1984) employed more stringent criteria (DSM-III) than did O'Hara, Neunaber and Zekoski (1984) (RDC).

One of the most interpretable sets of data was reported in an early study by Ryle (1961). He found that the one-year period prevalence of depression among women in his general practice was 10% (9.5% reactive and 0.5% endogenous). The rate of depression within a year following childbirth that he reported was 4.8% (1.9% reactive, 2.6% endogenous depression and 0.3% uncertain). Ryle argued that postpartum women were at increased risk for endogenous but not reactive depression; nevertheless, Ryle did not specify in detail his criteria for depression.

Control groups

There have been discussions of the need for control groups (Nilsson, 1970) and a few studies have actually employed comparison groups. None of the studies that have employed control groups have followed them prospectively and assessed depression on more than one occasion. Cox (1976) compared 89 pregnant women and 89 matched controls and found that the pregnant women had a rate of certain psychiatric morbidity twice that of the non-pregnant controls (25.9% versus 12.4%). Rees and Lutkins (1971), using the Beck Depression Inventory score of 10 or greater as an indication of at least mild depression, found a prevalence of 12.5% in a control group of 24 women compared to a prevalence of 34% for 47 women during pregnancy and 30% for 67 women sometime between three and 12 months postpartum. Breen (1975), though she followed a control group prospectively, did not assess depression in the control group.

Our own research team is currently following a large group of pregnant/postpartum women and an equal sized group of their non-pregnant acquaintances (O'Hara, 1986a). Each control subject undergoes the same assessments at the same times as her pregnant/postpartum acquaintance. Preliminary results are based on 97 pregnant/postpartum and 95 control subjects. The depression prevalence rate in the second trimester of pregnancy was 5.2% for pregnant subject and 5.3% for control subjects. The depression prevalence rate for the first nine weeks postpartum was 10.6% for the postpartum subjects and 10.0% for the control subjects.

Although these results are preliminary and based on half of our eventual sample, there is no evidence that the pregnant/postpartum subjects were at any greater risk for depression than the control subjects.

Course of mood change over pregnancy and the puerperium

The findings regarding the course of mood across pregnancy and the puerperium are consistent. Both self-report and interview-based measures of symptoms show a decrease in dysphoric mood from pregnancy to the puerperium (Cox *et al.*, 1983; Elliott *et al.*, 1983; O'Hara, Neunaber and Zekoski, 1984). The studies that have found an increase in symptom reports after delivery usually have conducted the first postnatal assessment early in the puerperium (Manly *et al.*, 1982; Cox *et al.*, 1983; Cutrona, 1983). These changes are often trivial in their extent and probably reflect symptoms of the blues.

One of the most thorough investigations of the course of mood changes across pregnancy and the puerperium was conducted by Elliott *et al.* (1983). They obtained self-ratings of mood (e.g. depression, tension, irritability, boredom, tiredness) on seven occasions during pregnancy beginning about week 13 and on 11 occasions during the first year postpartum beginning at week 3. They included several self-report and interview measures; however, the findings from the self-report of symptoms are representative.

The only significant changes observed across pregnancy were increased worries about labour and decreased interest in and satisfaction with sex. Women also reported being more tired in the first trimester. After delivery, women reported significant decreases in most symptoms (e.g. depression, feeling fed-up, irritability, boredom, feeling unwell). Other mood measures were also congruent with these symptom ratings. During the postnatal year, once again, there was little change except for marked increases in sexual interest and satisfaction.

The findings from the Elliott *et al.* (1983) study suggest that women experience relatively stable mood across pregnancy and that mood improves after delivery and remains stable during the first postpartum year. Elliott *et al.* (1983) report that pregnant women do not show symptom levels that are much above the median for normative samples of women who are not pregnant. For example, on the Eysenck Personality Questionnaire (Eysenck and Eysenck, 1975), the pregnant sample was not different from the normative sample on the Neuroticism Scale and they were significantly lower than the normative group on the Psychoticism Scale. Nevertheless, there was significant variability across subjects in the pattern of mood change across pregnancy and the puerperium (Elliott *et al.*, 1983). Although the average mood response to pregnancy and delivery was one of increasingly positive mood, it is clear from much research that a certain proportion of women do not follow this pattern. The task for researchers, of course, is to identify characteristics of women who respond to delivery and the puerperium with depressed mood.

Suicide during pregnancy and the puerperium

During pregnancy women may be especially protected against suicide. Several studies have reported very low rates of suicide for pregnant women. For example, in New York City between 1961 and 1980 only six of the 2437 (0.25%) women of childbearing age who committed suicide were pregnant (Kleiner and Greston, 1984). A similar study from London by Weir found that 66 of the 1686 (3.9%) women of childbearing age who committed suicide were pregnant (Kleiner and Greston, 1984). Overall Kleiner and Greston (1984) reported that in 15 studies since 1950 a total of 119 of the 6454 (1.8%) suicidal women of childbearing age were pregnant.

There is an increased risk of suicide after delivery relative to pregnancy. Barno (1967) found that the risk was 2.5 times greater for a woman after delivery. Nevertheless, over a 15-year period in Minnesota there were only 10 suicides during puerperium following 1 301 745 births (1 in 130 174 births). The data from England and Wales are similar (Kleiner and Greston, 1984). From 1969 to 1975 there were 6 677 211 births and there were 35 suicides in the first year postpartum (1 in 190 777 births). Finally, estimates of percentage of maternal mortality (during pregnancy and the puerperium) due to suicide range from 1% to 5% (Kleiner and Greston, 1984). It is clear, based on a large number of observations, that suicide in the puerperium is thankfully rare.

Summary

Although there is good evidence that following childbirth women are at increased risk for severe mental illness (postpartum psychosis) (Kendell *et al.*, 1976) and periods of mild dysphoria (postpartum blues) (Stein, 1982), there is little evidence that following childbirth women are at increased risk for non-psychotic depression. One of the most adequate studies to date (Kumar and Robson, 1984) did find a much greater rate of depression in the trimester after delivery than in the trimester before pregnancy. However, we have found nearly identical rates of depression in postpartum and control subjects (O'Hara, 1986a). Other researchers (e.g. O'Hara, Neunaber and Zekoski, 1984; Watson *et al.*, 1984) have compared rates of postpartum depression obtained in their studies to rates of depression obtained in other studies. It was noted earlier that these types of comparisons are fraught with difficulties that make the relative rates of depression difficult to compare. More evidence will have to be forthcoming before it can be confidently asserted that the puerperium is a high risk time for non-psychotic depression.

The revelation that depression is no more common after delivery than at other times provides little solace to the puerperally depressed woman. Several studies have documented the long duration of many postpartum depressions (e.g. Cox, Connor and Kendell, 1982; Kumar and Robson, 1984; Watson *et al.*, 1984). These studies also make clear that the woman, her child, and her family suffer as a result of postpartum depression. The long-term effects on the infant of having a depressed mother are significant and they are discussed elsewhere in this volume. It is clear that whatever the relative risk of depression after childbirth; it is a serious problem that must be attended to by the mental health community.

Aetiology

Myriad potential causes of risk factors for postpartum depression have been studied. The findings and methodological features of these studies (except background factors) are summarized in *Table 2.3*. In the sections that follow we will discuss the rationale for the study of various factors, comment briefly on the more adequate or illustrative studies, and summarize the major findings from this research. Factors discussed include obstetrical and gynaecological events, hormones, stressful life events, interpersonal relationships and psychopathology.

Background factors

Many background factors have been studied, although few of these factors have shown any consistent association with postpartum depression. For example, of the 13 studies that reported on the relation between postpartum depression (diagnosis or symptom level) and socioeconomic status (SES), only two studies reported a significant association (Feggetter and Gath, 1981; Playfair and Gowers, 1981). Both studies reported that higher SES was associated with lower levels of depression after delivery. Four studies have incorporated measures of education level and only one found a significant association between education and postpartum depression diagnosis (O'Hara, Neunaber and Zekoski, 1984).

Marital status was found to be significantly associated with postpartum depression in one of 12 studies where it was investigated (Feggetter and Gath, 1981). In this study being unmarried was associated with a higher risk of depression. It should be noted, however, that many studies recruit only married women.

Age and its relation to postpartum depression has been reported in 17 studies and a significant association has been found in five studies. Four studies (Hayworth *et al.*, 1980; Paykel *et al.*, 1980; Feggetter and Gath, 1981; O'Hara, Neunaber and Zekoski, 1984) have found that younger women were more at risk, and one study has found that older primiparae were more at risk (Kumar and Robson, 1984).

A significant relation between parity and postpartum depression has been found in six of 18 studies. In three studies higher parity has been associated with higher levels of postpartum depression (Tod, 1964; Jarrahi-Zadeh *et al.*, 1969; Playfair and Gowers, 1981), and in three studies lower parity was associated with higher levels of postpartum depression (Gordon, 1961; Martin, 1977; Bridge *et al.*, 1985).

Obstetric and gynaecological factors

The majority of the work in this area has been on obstetrical complications which are natural stressors to study in the context of postpartum depression. Yet, the data regarding the relation between obstetrical complications and postpartum depression are puzzling. Several studies have found a significant positive association and several studies have found a significant negative association. These differences may, in large part, be due to how obstetrical complications are defined in various studies. For example, Pitt (1968) studied pregnancy complications such as toxaemia and anaemia, whereas Paykel et al. (1980) studied labour complications. Oakley (1980) studied level of birth technology with interventions such as general anaesthesia and caesarean section receiving the highest ratings. O'Hara, Rehm and Campbell (1982) also defined caesarean section as the highest level in their birth stress score. Despite some degree of similarity between these latter two studies, their findings were directly opposite. Nevertheless, there were differences in depression outcome measures that may have affected their findings. For example, Oakley (1980) tried to identify women who had at least two weeks of depressed mood and at least two other symptoms of depression, whereas O'Hara, Rehm and Campbell (1982) used the Beck Depression Inventory as the outcome measure.

Biological factors

There are two basic perspectives from which to view research on biological factors in postpartum depression. The first perspective views postpartum depression as sharing characteristics fundamental to depressions occurring at other times ('non-specific biological factors'). The biological factors that are studied would include cortisol as well as neurotransmitters such as noradrenaline and neurotransmitter precursors such as tryptophan (for serotonin). The second perspective is more concerned with the special features of postpartum mood disorders and potential hormonal dysfunction ('specific biological factors'). The biological factors of interest are those that show particular changes during pregnancy, e.g. oestrogens, progesterone and prolactin. Regardless of the perspective, most of the work in this area has focused on the postpartum blues rather than depression or psychosis (see Chapter 4). This section will address only those studies that have looked at the association between biological factors and depression occurring after the first 1–2 weeks postpartum.

Non-specific biological factors
Based on evidence in the literature linking low levels of circulating tryptophan with the development of depression and several promising preliminary studies (e.g. Handley et al., 1977), Handley et al. (1980) undertook one of the more adequate studies in this area. In this study 71 subjects responded to four separate rating scales (Blues Symptom Index, Beck Depression Inventory, Multiple Affect Adjective Check List, Visual Analogue Scale). Subjects had to show a significant elevation (80th percentile) on at least one scale to be considered a case. Blood was drawn at 36 and 38 weeks gestation, days 1–5 postpartum, and at six weeks postpartum. A total of 28 subjects met case criteria in the first week after delivery. With respect to total tryptophan, cases (in the first week postpartum) showed a later rise in total tryptophan levels after delivery than non-cases. However, the 16 women who met case criteria at six weeks postpartum did not show the 'later rise in total tryptophan levels after

Table 2.3 Aetiological factors studied in association with increased risk of postpartum depression (diagnosis or symptom level)

Risk factors	Studies that found increased risk	Comments	Studies that found no increase in risk	Comments
Obstetrical and gynaecological factors: Menstrual problems	Jacobson et al. (1965) Pitt (1968) Blair et al. (1970) Playfair and Gowers (1981) Uddenberg (1974)	2,3,4 4,5 3,4,5 3,5 4	Nilsson and Almgren (1975)	4,5
Abortion and miscarriage	Tod (1964) Jacobson et al. (1965) Playfair and Gowers (1981)	3,4 2,3,4 3,4	Blair et al. (1970) Nilsson and Almgren (1970) Paykel et al. (1980) Kumar and Robson (1984) Watson et al. (1984)	3,4 4 4 4 4
Obstetrical complications	Tod (1964) Oakley (1980) Kumar and Robson (1984) Ballinger (1982)	4,5 1,4 4 3,4	Jacobson et al. (1965) Pitt (1968)[a] Dalton (1971) Martin (1977) Paykel et al. (1980)[a] Playfair and Gowers (1981) Cox et al. (1982) O'Hara et al. (1982)[a] O'Hara (1986b)	2,4 4 2,6 4 4 3 2,3 3 4
Biological factors: Tryptophan (predicted negative association)	Handley et al. (1980)	3,4	Gard et al. (1986)	3,4
Non-esterified fatty acids (NEFA) (predicted positive association)	Gard et al. (1986)	3,4		

Variable	Study	Codes	Study	Codes
Cortisol (predicted positive association)	Handley et al. (1980)	3,4		
Dexamethasone suppression	Greenwood and Parker (1984)	3		
Oestrogens (predicted negative association)	Gard et al. (1986)	3,4		
Protein bound iodine (predicted negative association)	Grimmell and Larsen (1965)	1		
Progesterone (predicted negative association)	Gard et al. (1986)	3,4		
Stressful life events:	Pitt (1968)	2,4,5	Paykel et al. (1980)	2,4
	Kumar and Robson (1984)	4	Playfair and Gowers (1981)	2,3,5
	Hopkins et al. (1986)	2	O'Hara et al. (1982)	2,3
			Cutrona (1983)	2,3
			O'Hara et al. (1983)	2,3,4
			O'Hara et al.(1984)	2
			Hopkins et al. (1986)	2
Interpersonal relationships: Poor marital relationship	Blair et al. (1970)	3,4,5	Nilsson and Almgren (1970)	2,4,5
			Uddenberg (1974)	2,4,5
			Martin (1977)	2,4,5
			Braverman and Roux (1978)	4,5
			Paykel et al. (1980)	2,4
			Cox et al. (1982)	2,3,4,5
			O'Hara et al. (1983)	2,4
			Kumar and Robson (1984)	4
			Watson et al. (1984)	4
			O'Hara (1986b)	

Table 2.3 (contd)

Risk factors	Studies that found increased risk	Comments	Studies that found no increase in risk	Comments
Poor parental relationship	Nilsson and Almgren (1970) Uddenberg (1974) Kumar and Robson (1984)	4,5 4,5 4	Paykel et al. (1980)	2,4,5
Inadequate social support	Gordon et al. (1965) Blair et al. (1970) Paykel et al. (1980) Feggetter and Gath (1981) O'Hara et al. (1983) Cutrona (1984) O'Hara (1986b)	4,5 3,4,5 2,4 2,4 3 2,4	Hopkins et al. (1986)	2
Psychopathology/personality disturbance: Neuroticism	Pitt (1968) Watson et al. (1984)	2,4 4	Kumar and Robson (1984)	4
High prenatal anxiety	Dalton (1971) Watson et al. (1984)	4,5,6 4	Pitt (1968) Playfair and Gowers (1981)	4 3,5
Dysfunctional cognitions	O'Hara et al. (1982) Cutrona (1983) O'Hara et al. (1984)	3 3 3	Manly et al. (1982)	3

Psychiatric history	Tod (1964)	4,5	Pitt (1968)	4,5
	Jacobson et al. (1965)	2,3,4,5	Blair et al. (1970)	3,4,5
	Nilsson and Almgren (1970)	4	Dalton (1971)	2,5,6
	Uddenberg (1974)		Kumar and Robson (1984)	6
	Martin (1977)	2,4,5		
	Paykel et al. (1980)	2,4,5		
	Playfair and Gowers (1981)	3,5		
	O'Hara et al. (1983)	2,4		
	O'Hara et al. (1984)			
	Watson et al. (1984)	4		
Family psychiatric history	Nilsson and Almgren (1970)	4,5	Kumar and Robson (1984)	4
	O'Hara et al. (1984)			
	Watson et al. (1984)	4		

(a)Studies that found significant decrease in risk.

Comments:
1 Small sample size (fewer than 40 subjects).
2 Retrospective assessment (possible bias on part of subject or investigator due to predictor variable and postpartum depression being measured at about the same time).
3 Self-report of symptoms.
4 Problems with multiple tests of statistical significance.
5 Question regarding reliability or validity of measurement of construct.
6 Excessive subject loss.

delivery' that was associated with the blues cases in the first week after delivery. Nevertheless, women who sought medical care for mood problems in the first six months postpartum ($n = 9$) did show the 'later rise in total tryptophan levels after delivery', although there were no significant differences in free tryptophan. A later study by Handley's group (Gard *et al.*, 1986) found no association between free and total tryptophan levels after delivery and the presence of depressive symptoms lasting two weeks or more in the first nine months postpartum. They did find that the level of non-esterified fatty acids (NEFA) (which compete with tryptophan for albumin binding) at three days postpartum was associated with the presence of postpartum depression.

Dysregulation in the HPAC (hypothalamic–pituitary–adrenocorticoid) system is thought to be related to vulnerability to depression. Pregnant women show high levels of unbound cortisol, especially late in pregnancy, sometimes approaching levels of mild Cushing's syndrome (Burke and Roulet, 1970). Most of the large increase in plasma cortisol during pregnancy is accommodated by the rather large increase in CBG (corticosteroid-binding globulin). Nevertheless, the possibility of dysregulation following childbirth and the rather clear relationship of corticosteroids and depression suggest that study of the role of cortisol in postpartum depression may be fruitful.

In the Handley *et al.* (1980) study described earlier, cortisol levels were found to be unrelated to help-seeking in the first six months postpartum. Dexamethasone suppression in postpartum depression was evaluated in a group of 45 women (Greenwood and Parker, 1984). A very high percentage of subjects had an abnormal dexamethasone response (usually reflecting dysregulation in the HPAC system) in the first week postpartum. However, there was no relation between dexamethasone response and depression symptom level at six weeks postpartum. One problem with all of the cortisol studies is that only total cortisol is being measured. Given the large changes occurring in plasma levels and the large increase in CBG levels, it is probably important to measure levels of free cortisol (which is biologically active). Interestingly, Railton (1961) published a report describing good results treating and preventing postpartum depression using the corticoid prednisolone (16 controls and 16 treated with prednisolone).

Hamilton's (1962) hypothesis that hypothyroidism after delivery may contribute to postpartum mental illness, including depression, was tested in a study by Grimmell and Larsen (1965). They compared three groups of 11 women each which included: (a) patients who were confused and depressed in the first six months postpartum, (b) non-postpartum depressed patients, and (c) non-postpartum non-depressed women. They predicted that the postpartum and non-postpartum depressed patients would show thyroid hypoactivity, as measured by lowered serum protein bound iodine (PBI) and elevated cholesterol levels compared with the normal subjects; however, there were no differences among the groups. When additional non-postpartum depressed patients and normal controls were added and the postpartum and non-postpartum groups were combined and compared to the normal controls, there were significant differences between the groups in the predicted direction for PBI.

Specific biological factors

There has been a great deal of theoretical speculation on the role of hormones such as the oestrogens, progesterone, and prolactin in postpartum depression. The two principal reasons for this interest are:

(1) These hormones show rather dramatic changes in concentration over a very short period of time around delivery; and
(2) These hormones also show marked shifts at other times when many women experience mood disturbance (e.g. premenstrual disorders).

Steiner (1979) has suggested that postpartum depression is due to high levels of prolactin and low levels of oestrogen and progesterone. Also, Dalton (1980) has linked low levels of progesterone to both premenstrual dysphoria and postpartum depression. Despite this theorizing, only one study (Gard *et al.*, 1986) has investigated the association between levels of progesterone, oestradiol and oestriol and postpartum depression. These investigators found no significant relations between any of these hormones and depression occurring between two weeks and nine months postpartum.

In one of the few therapy studies in this area, Dalton (1980) treated a sample of 27 women who had at least one previous episode of postpartum depression (42 episodes/60 pregnancies) with 100 mg i.m. progesterone for seven days, followed by 400 mg progesterone suppositories twice a day for 60 days. She reported no cases of postpartum depression within six months of delivery. Although these data are encouraging, this trial was uncontrolled and many factors other than the administration of progesterone may have accounted for the results.

In an indirect study of hormonal factors in postpartum depression the relations among breast feeding and the use of oral contraceptives after delivery and postpartum depression were studied in a group of 89 women (Alder and Cox, 1983). The investigators found that women who were taking oral contraceptives during the puerperium were more likely to be depressed 3–5 months postpartum. Moreover, within the group of women not taking oral contraceptives, those women who were total breast feeders were more likely to be depressed. The women at lowest risk for depression after delivery were those who were most likely to have normal levels of endogenous hormones, i.e. the non-pill taking partial breast feeders (Alder and Cox, 1983).

Stressful life events

Pregnancy and birth are often regarded as stressful life events in their own right, and the stressfulness of these events may lead to depression (Holmes and Rahe, 1967). However, a few groups of researchers have studied the effects of additional stressful life events that women experience during pregnancy and the puerperium. These events, thought to reflect additional stress at a time during which women are vulnerable, may play a causal role in postpartum depression. Moreover, the link between stressful life events and depression that women experience at other times has been well documented (Brown and Harris, 1978; Paykel, 1979).

The first study to have stressful life events as a focus was conducted by Paykel *et al.* (1980). They found in a retrospective study that negative life events of the moderate to severe variety were associated with increased probability of being rated in the clinical depression range on the Raskin Three Area Depression Scale (Raskin *et al.*, 1970). Their depressed group ($n = 24$) experienced a mean of 1.92 moderate to severe negative life events in the previous 11 months. Their non-depressed group ($n = 80$) experienced a mean of 0.50 moderate to severe life events over the same period.

O'Hara, Rehm and Campbell (1982, 1983) found that high levels of life events from the beginning of pregnancy until about 11 weeks postpartum were associated with higher levels of depressive symptomatology and a greater likelihood of receiving a diagnosis of postpartum depression. In a second study (O'Hara, Neunaber and Zekoski, 1984) an association was also found between stressful life events since the beginning of pregnancy and self-report of depressive symptoms ($r = 0.204$) and diagnosis of postpartum depression ($r = 0.245$). Cutrona (1983) reported that higher levels of childcare-related stressors were associated with higher levels of depressive symptomatology. Playfair and Gowers (1981) reported that experiencing external stress after birth was associated with higher levels of postpartum depression symptoms. Finally, Hopkins, Campbell and Marcus (1986) found that having a difficult baby or a baby with neonatal complications was associated with a diagnosis of postpartum depression. However, they found no association between other types of life events and postpartum depression. Also, at least two other studies have not been supportive of the association between stressful life events and postpartum depression (Pitt, 1968; Kumar and Robson, 1984).

Interpersonal relationships

There is little doubt that the social context in which a woman functions at the time of the birth of a child is an important influence on her mental health. Several studies have addressed issues related to a woman's relationship with her husband/partner, child, parents and close friends.

Marital relationship

A number of studies have found an association between postpartum depression or high levels of depressive symptoms and poor marital relationship (*see Table 2.3*). However, only a few have provided clear evidence that the poor marital relationship preceded the postpartum depression. Braverman and Roux (1978) found that women who reported marital problems during pregnancy were more likely to have higher levels of symptoms after delivery. Kumar and Robson (1984) found that women experiencing prenatal marital conflict were more at risk for a postpartum depression. O'Hara (1986b) reported that women who reported less marital satisfaction on the Dyadic Adjustment Scale (Spanier, 1976) during pregnancy had a greater likelihood of being diagnosed with postpartum depression. Watson *et al.* (1984) also found, based on a semi-structured interview with couples during pregnancy, that women experiencing dysfunctional marital relationships were more likely to experience a postpartum depression. However, Hopkins, Campbell and Marcus (1986) found no association between marital satisfaction and diagnosis of postpartum depression.

Mother-infant bonding failure
Mother-infant bonding failure may be an aetiological factor in postpartum depression (Margison, 1982). Evidence exists which suggests that depressed mothers are less attached to their babies than non-depressed mothers. Margison (1982) found that non-psychotic depressed mothers more frequently expressed ideas of rejection toward the baby than women with postpartum psychosis. In addition, Robson and Kumar (1980) reported that mothers who were depressed at three months postpartum were more likely to express feelings of dislike or indifference to the baby than non-depressed mothers. Livingood, Dean and Smith (1983) reported that mothers with high scores on the Beck Depression Inventory 2–3 days postpartum were rated by observers as providing lower levels of unconditional positive regard than low scoring mothers. Other researchers (Davenport *et al.*, 1984; Gaensbauer *et al.*, 1984) have found deficiencies in the behaviour of both depressed mothers and their infants.

Parental relationship
Parental relationships may be important for at least two reasons. First, particularly for primiparous women, the birth of a child represents a transition to parenthood. If conflicts have existed for a long period of time with a woman's parents, the mother in particular, the woman may have ambivalent feelings herself that could interfere with postpartum adjustment. Second, parents can be an important source of social support to a woman who has recently delivered. Not unexpectedly, several studies have found that a poor relationship with the mother, in particular, was associated with increased risk for postpartum depression (*see Table 2.3*). However, Paykel *et al.* (1980) found that depressed women did not report any more disturbance in their childhood or present relationships with their mother or father than non-depressed women.

Loss of parents
Although parental loss and, in particular, loss of the mother at a young age has been implicated as a vulnerability factor for depression (Brown and Harris, 1978), few postpartum depression studies have reported a relation between parental loss and depression. Kumar and Robson (1984) reported that women who had been separated from their fathers in childhood were more likely to experience a postpartum depression. However, Paykel *et al.* (1980) and Watson *et al.* (1984) found no relation between postpartum depression and childhood loss or separation from either parent.

Social support
The provision of social support by friends and relatives to individuals experiencing psychosocial stress is thought to reduce the chances of depression occurring (Mueller, 1980). Several studies have evaluated the role of social support in reducing the chances of postpartum depression. O'Hara, Rehm and Campbell (1983) reported on a study of the relation between perceived social support and postpartum depression. They found that depressed women reported that their spouse was deficient on a number of dimensions of social support (e.g. instrumental and emotional support) after delivery. However, these women did not identify their spouse as being less supportive during pregnancy any more than did

non-depressed women. To a somewhat lesser degree, the confidants and parents of depressed women were also perceived as being less supportive during the puerperium, but not during pregnancy. A second study (O'Hara, 1986b) confirmed the results. After delivery, spouses were perceived by depressed women to be less supportive than the spouses of non-depressed women. However, these differences were not present during pregnancy based on the social support interview done in the second trimester. Interestingly, there were no differences between depressed and non-depressed women after delivery in the perceived supportiveness of the woman's closest confidant. Finally, Cutrona (1984) reported that several dimensions of perceived social support assessed during pregnancy were predictive of the level of postpartum depressive symptoms. Surprisingly, the strongest predictor concerned the availability of companionship and feeling of belonging to a group of similar others, rather than the quality of intimacy with the husband. Several other, largely retrospective studies have obtained results similar to those reported above (*see Table 2.3*). In contrast to these positive findings, a recent study found no association between several measures of social support after delivery and diagnosis of postpartum depression (Hopkins, Campbell and Marcus, 1986).

Psychopathology and personality

Is postpartum depression related to personality disturbance, psychopathology occurring at other times, or to psychopathology in the family? A number of studies have addressed these issues and they will be reviewed in the following sections.

Neuroticism/anxiety

Tod (1964) reported that women experiencing puerperal depression had previous inadequte personality disorder. Pitt (1968) found that women with postpartum depression were more neurotic and less extroverted than non-depressed women, based on the Maudsley Personality Inventory (Eysenck, 1952). Watson *et al.* (1984), using the Eysenck Personality Questionnaire (EPQ) (Eysenck and Eysenck, 1975), found that women who later developed postpartum depression were more neurotic during pregnancy than were women who did not become depressed. However, several of the women experiencing depression after delivery were already depressed during pregnancy. With respect to neuroticism, Kumar and Robson (1984) reported that depressed and non-depressed women after delivery did not differ on neuroticism as measured by the EPQ during pregnancy.

Dalton (1971) was the first to note that anxiety during pregnancy was predictive of postpartum depression. However, Dalton did not use a standardized measure of anxiety. Using the Delusions-Symptoms-States Inventory (Bedford, Foulds and Sheffield, 1976) Hayworth *et al.* (1980) found that anxiety measured during pregnancy was related to level of postpartum depressive symptomatology. Watson *et al.* (1984) also found that women who were depressed after delivery showed more anxiety (on the Crown-Crisp Experiential Index) during pregnancy than women who were not depressed after delivery. Playfair and Gowers (1981) found that anxiety assessed during pregnancy (no details on the measure) predicted the level of depressive symptoms at 12 weeks postpartum. However, Pitt (1968) found no differences on anxiety during pregnancy between postpartum depressed and non-depressed women.

Dysfunctional cognitions

A few studies have tested hypotheses derived from psychological theories of depression. Attributional style, which refers to the characteristic way individuals perceive causes of events, e.g. feeling responsible versus not responsible for the occurrence of an event (Abramson, Seligman and Teasdale, 1978), has been studied as a predictor of postpartum depression symptom level in several studies. O'Hara, Rehm and Campbell (1982) and Cutrona (1983) both found that attributional style assessed during pregnancy predicted depression symptom level after delivery. However, Manly et al. (1982) and O'Hara, Neunaber and Zekoski (1984) did not find that attributional style measured during pregnancy predicted the level of depressive symptoms after delivery.

O'Hara, Rehm and Campbell (1982) and O'Hara, Neunaber and Zekoski (1984) studied the relationship between self-control attitudes (Rehm, 1977) assessed during pregnancy and depression symptom level after delivery. They found that self-control measured by the Self-Control Questionnaire (SCQ) (Rehm et al., 1981) was significantly correlated with postpartum depression level. However, in the latter study (O'Hara, Neunaber and Zekoski, 1984), the SCQ was not found to be a significant predictor of postpartum depression diagnosis.

Psychiatric history

Many studies have found that women who have experienced a psychiatric disorder in the past (often depression) are at increased risk for a postpartum depression (see Table 2.3). In two studies (O'Hara, Rehm and Campbell, 1983; O'Hara, 1986b) it was found that women who were diagnosed as having a postpartum depression reported having more previous depressions. Depressed women ($n = 11$) in the 1983 study had a mean of 1.82 previous episodes of depression, whereas the non-depressed women ($n = 19$) had a mean of 0.16 previous episodes of depression. The comparable figures for O'Hara (1986b) were 2.25 previous episodes for the depressed women ($n = 12$) and 0.75 for the non-depressed women ($n = 87$). In the first study these assessments were made at the time of the postpartum depression interview. However, in the O'Hara (1986b) study a history of depression was assessed during pregnancy by means of the RDC.

Watson et al. (1984) reported that women who had received care for psychiatric problems were more likely to experience a postpartum depression. Kumar and Robson (1984) in a carefully conducted prospective study found no evidence of increased psychiatric history among women experiencing postpartum depression, as did a few other studies (see Table 2.3).

Family psychiatric history

Only a few studies have reported on the relationship between postpartum depression and family psychiatric history. Nilsson and Almgren (1970) found that higher symptom levels in the subject's mother were related to higher symptom levels after delivery. O'Hara (1986b) found that 66.7% of women ($n = 12$) with postpartum depression compared to 20.7% of women ($n = 87$) without postpartum depression had at least one first degree relative who had been depressed. Watson *et al.* (1984) reported a trend ($P = 0.07$) toward women with postpartum depression reporting during pregnancy that a first degree relative had received psychiatric care. However, Kumar and Robson (1984) reported no association between the diagnosis of postpartum depression and family psychiatric history (not defined but presumably 'received psychiatric care').

Summary

Factors unique to the puerperium (e.g. obstetrical and hormonal) do not show a strong association with postpartum depression, although few adequate studies have been done to test hypotheses related to the role of obstetrical and hormonal factors in postpartum depression. The aetiological factors that have received more support are those that have demonstrated associations with depressions occurring at other times (e.g. life events, social support, personal and family history of psychopathology). What might be suggested from all of the research on aetiological factors is that women at 'risk' by virtue of past personal or family history of psychopathology and poor social support (particularly from spouse) who experience a high level of negative life events in conjunction with childbirth are likely to experience a postpartum depression. Nevertheless, it has only been in the past few years that methodologically adequate aetiological research has been done and it is likely that when more of these studies are completed, a more precise analysis of causal factors will be possible.

Relationship among the postpartum affective disorders

Arbitrariness of classification

Although there is general agreement that there are three types of postpartum affective disorders (Brockington and Kumar, 1982; Cutrona, 1982; Hopkins, Marcus and Campbell, 1984; Kendell, 1985), there seems to be little to distinguish the blues, postpartum depression, and postpartum depressive psychosis other than the severity of the disorder or variables related to severity of disorder, e.g. family and personal history of depression*. Need for treatment, especially hospitalization, has often been used to distinguish mild postpartum depression from more serious postpar-

---

*Brockington on pp. 4–5 of this volume makes the point that postpartum psychoses cluster in the first two weeks postpartum; postpartum depressions show no such clustering.

tum reactions such as puerperal illness (Dean and Kendell, 1981; Paffenbarger, 1982) or puerperal psychosis (Thuwe, 1974; Whalley et al., 1982). However, inspection of the characteristics of two recently reported samples (Brockington et al., 1981; Dean and Kendell, 1981) of women hospitalized for postpartum psychiatric problems illustrates several difficulties when treatment is used as an implicit criterion for diagnosis.

Brockington et al. (1981) reported on 56 women who were hospitalized in a special Mothers and Babies Unit. The authors implied, although they did not say, that all women admitted to their unit were in the midst of a psychotic episode. This unusual occurrence may have been possible because specialized units would be likely to take the most severe cases from surrounding communities. This group of patients was severely impaired and probably could be distinguished readily from samples of women identified in the community as experiencing a postpartum depression but not needing treatment. In contrast, Dean and Kendell (1981) reported on a sample of women hospitalized within 90 days of delivery. This group was apparently characterized by a rather wide range of severity (or impairment in functioning). For example, 23% of the sample received the RDC diagnosis of minor depression while others received diagnoses of schizoaffective disorder, unspecified functional psychosis, and major depression. Of course, even within the RDC diagnosis of major depression, a patient may have rather severe impairment, i.e. psychosis, or she may have rather less impairment but still meet criteria. The point is that even among women who are hospitalized for postpartum psychiatric disorders, there is a fair degree of heterogeneity in terms of symptom presentation and degree of impairment (see Meltzer and Kumar, 1985).

Severity and functional impairment

It is clear that women experience a range of affective reactions following the birth of a child. Some women experience no change in their prevailing mood state, a relatively positive mood state that has persisted through pregnancy and the puerperium (perhaps 20–30%). Other women experience relatively brief periods of dysphoria lasting from a few hours to a week (perhaps 40–50%). Still other women experience mood disturbances that are more substantial, that persist for a week or more, and that cause some impairment in functioning (perhaps 8–20%). A small group of women are so depressed that they require treatment on an inpatient or outpatient basis (perhaps 3–7%). Finally, there is a very small group of women who become psychotic after delivery and require rather intensive inpatient care (perhaps 0.1–0.2%).

It may be that women experiencing auditory hallucinations or paranoid delusions in the context of a severe depression have a disorder that is different from women who have a severe (endogenous) depression without psychotic features*. Within the non-psychotic postpartum affective disturbances, there is little that distinguishes women with various types of postpartum mood disturbance other than severity of symptoms and

*It may be that hallucinations and delusions, rather than marking a disorder that is different from, for example, non-psychotic depression, are markers of very severe depression.

severity of impairment in functioning. What we are proposing, then, is that postpartum mood disturbances range along a continuum of severity from no disturbance to severe endogenous non-psychotic depression. We suggest that there are no natural dividing points for distinguishing between various subtypes of postpartum affective disorders. Although one can devise criteria for one diagnosis or another, women at the boundaries will be very similar to each other. This view is consistent with an emerging perspective on the distinction between endogenous and non-endogenous depression (Lewis, 1938; Zimmerman, Coryell and Pfohl, 1986). The distinction may be a valid one, but many of the results that distinguish endogenous and non-endogenous depression can be attributed to differences in severity of disturbances in the two groups.

One implication of this perspective is that studies of postpartum psychiatric disorders should include sensitive measures of impairment in functioning in addition to symptom inventories and structured interviews to assess diagnostic criteria for various disorders. If we developed a better taxonomy of impairment in functioning, we would be better able to determine the extent to which the postpartum period represents a time of particular social disability for some women. Moreover, we could more accurately determine the proportion of women who need various levels of treatment resources, ranging from family support to inpatient hospitalization. Other salutary effects of this strategy would be the ability objectively to determine the typical level of impairment of women who use treatment resources in the puerperium. The question might be asked, are some women being hospitalized inappropriately? Researchers interested in aetiological factors may also be better served by studying level of impairment as an outcome.

At least two measures are currently available and relevant to the postpartum period. The Social Adjustment Scale self-report (Weissman and Bothwell, 1976; Cooper et al., 1982) was developed to measure social dysfunction due to depression in a number of areas (work in and out of home and relationship with spouse, family and friends). Perhaps more relevant is the Maternal Adjustment and Maternal Attitudes Scale (MAMA) (Kumar, Robson and Smith, 1984). This measure assesses functioning in five domains (body image, somatic symptoms, marital relationship, attitudes toward sex, and attitudes toward pregnancy/baby). These measures represent a good beginning on measuring adjustment problems of recently delivered women. Nevertheless, both measures are somewhat lacking with respect to specifically assessing behavioural dysfunction related to child care, household responsibilities, or marital relationship. The MAMA, for example, assesses the attitude of women toward these domains rather than specific impairment in functioning.

Treatment and prevention

There have been very few studies on the treatment or prevention of postpartum depression. Rather, studies have focused on general adaptation to pregnancy and the early postpartum period.

Gordon and Gordon (1959) reported on two groups of postpartum psychiatric patients, those treated between 1953 and 1954 ($n = 24$) and those treated between 1956 and 1957 ($n = 36$). The chief difference between these two groups was that a more active social intervention was added to a dynamic psychotherapy for the latter patients. Typical interventions included obtaining help from other women experienced in the care of infants, encouraging the husband to provide increased emotional and practical support, and encouraging the maintenance of some leisure time activities. The authors found that patients exposed to the more directive therapy required briefer treatment and were less likely to require hospitalization than patients receiving only dynamic psychotherapy. However, this study was not a controlled trial and many factors other than the addition of an active treatment may have contributed to the differences in the two groups of patients.

Gordon and Gordon (1960) later reported a controlled study aimed at prevention of postpartum emotional distress. Women were assigned to one of two conditions during pregnancy. In the experimental condition women were exposed to instruction regarding ways to prevent emotional distress after delivery. The important points from this paper included the following:

(1) The responsibilities of being a mother (and not a martyr) are learned, hence get help and advice.
(2) Make friends of other couples who are experienced with young children.
(3) Don't overload yourself with extra, less important tasks.
(4) Don't move too soon after the baby arrives.
(5) Don't be too concerned with appearances when other things are more important.
(6) Get plenty of rest and sleep.
(7) Don't be a nurse to elderly relatives at this period.
(8) Confer and consult with husband, family, and experienced friends and discuss your plans and worries.
(9) Don't give up your outside interests, but cut down the responsibilities and rearrange your schedules.
(10) Arrange for babysitters in advance.
(11) Learn to drive a car.
(12) Get a family doctor now.

In the experimental condition some husbands attended the two sessions with their wives ($n = 54$); however, many women attended alone ($n = 31$). In the control condition women were exposed to the routine classes for parents (if their husband participated, $n = 38$) or for mothers (if their husband did not participate, $n = 38$).

All participants were rated on a four-point scale of emotional distress by their obstetrician ($n = 50$) 6–8 weeks after delivery. All obstetricians were blind to the treatment condition of their patients. Experimental subjects (15%) were significantly less likely to experience emotional distress than control subjects (37%), $P < 0.01$. Within the experimental conditions women who attended with their husband (11%) experienced fewer emotional problems than women who attended alone (23%). Although the measures used in this study were rather crude, it is clear that a rather brief prenatal intervention (two 40-minute sessions) was quite effective in reducing future emotional distress.

Halonen and Passman (1985) randomly assigned 48 pregnant women who had completed labour-specific relaxation training to one of four groups: (a) additional relaxation training, (b) extended relaxation training that emphasized possible postpartum stressors, (c) exposure only to postpartum stressors, and (d) a control discussion of their awareness about postpartum distress. The Beck Depression Inventory, an elation rating scale, and a frequency of crying measure were administered one month prepartum, the first nine postpartum days, and one month postpartum. They found that both relaxation groups were significantly less distressed than the non-relaxation groups during the first nine postpartum days. During this time, women in the relaxation groups also cried less frequently.

The two groups exposed to postpartum stressors were significantly less elated postpartum than the two groups that received no exposure. Halonen and Passman suggested that women in the exposure groups might have become sensitized to negative postpartum events and thus experienced less elation than the other women. Consequently, they advocated the use of non-specific relaxation training which extends beyond delivery to the postpartum period. Major benefits of such treatment include its cost effectiveness and its generalizability to other stressful situations.

As stated earlier, Shereshefsky and Yarrow's group (Liebenberg, 1973; Shereshefsky and Lockman, 1973) focused on general adaptation to pregnancy and the postpartum period. Based on the early work of Caplan (1957) and Bibring et al. (1961), these investigators viewed pregnancy as a period of disequilibrium, during which the pregnant woman was more susceptible to therapeutic intervention. Half of their 60 subjects were assigned to a prenatal counselling group while the other half served as a non-counselled control group. Although the prepartum counselling was primarily ego-supportive therapy, it actually consisted of three separate treatment groups. The first treatment technique focused on the clarification of feelings and interpersonal relationships, particularly the marital relationship. The second technique employed was insight-oriented psycho-dynamic therapy. The third technique used was anticipatory guidance, which attempted to prepare the woman for postpartum stressors by exposing her to them ahead of time. Thus, this treatment is analogous to the exposure treatment used by Halonen and Passman (1985) and to general stress inoculation techniques (Meichenbaum, 1985).

Shereshefsky and Lockman (1973) performed both between-groups and within-groups analyses on outcome measures. They found that the counselled group did not differ from the control group on measures of maternal adaptation or infant adaptation. In a comparison of marital adjustment during the first trimester and at six months postpartum, they found that the marital relationship of the control group had deteriorated while the marital relationship of the counselled group remained at the prepartum level. In a within treatment groups analysis, anticipatory guidance resulted in the highest level of maternal adaptation; however, as noted by the authors, this result is probably attributable to counsellor effects.

Consistent with the results of the Shereshefsky and Lockman (1973) investigation, Broussard (1976) found that observing a videotape of a programme designed to help women anticipate child care problems had a positive effect on a mother's perception of her infant. In contrast, Neumann (1978) found no differences between couples receiving anticipatory guidance and a control group on measures of anxiety, depression, marital satisfaction, self-esteem, and attitude toward pregnancy. Thus, empirical support for the use of anticipatory guidance is equivocal.

Social support researchers (Wandersman, Wandersman and Kahn, 1980) have also focused on general adaptation to pregnancy. Wandersman's group studied the effects of social support on a group of primiparous parents (18 fathers and 23 mothers) who attended parenting groups and on a comparison group of 23 fathers and 24 mothers who did not attend parenting groups. The parenting groups began meeting at 6–10 weeks postpartum and met for six weeks. The results indicated that membership in a parenting group did not play a significant role in postpartum adjustment; however, numerous methodological problems may have contributed to these findings.

In summary, the few treatment studies on postpartum depression have almost all focused on prevention rather than direct intervention. Due to major differences in methodology and outcome measures comparisons among studies is difficult. It appears that prepartum preventive intervention may be effective in keeping postpartum distress at a minimal level; however, what constitutes the most beneficial treatment remains unclear.

Recommendations for future research

Although research on postpartum depression has advanced considerably in the last 10 years, there is much work to do. Part of this work reflects the need to improve the methodology of past research and part of this work reflects the need to address new problems.

Measures of constructs

One of the problems of past postpartum depression research was that constructs were not measured well or, if they were, the reports contained insufficient information. For example, many studies have used one item to characterize a construct such as marital satisfaction rather than using a recognized scale. It is clear that constructs of importance in postpartum depression research must be measured adequately. Moreover, psychometric characteristics of both self-report (questionnaire) and clinical assessments should be provided in research reports so that the precision with which measurements are made can be known.

A related problem is that of validating measures for use with pregnant/ postpartum subjects. Many researchers have expressed concern about the adequacy of widely used self-report measures of depression during the puerperium (O'Hara, Neunaber and Zekoski, 1984; Cox, Holden and Sagovsky, 1987). There have been some recent developments, particularly by Cox and his colleagues (1987) in developing depression measures that are both sensitive and specific to depression in the puerperium. Similar efforts should be directed toward the adequacy of diagnostic criteria (e.g. DSM-III, RDC) commonly used in studies of postpartum depression.

In addition to the development of depression measures suitable for use in the puerperium, the development of a measure of social adjustment specific to the puerperium would seem warranted. While there are social adjustment scales that have been used in depression research (Weissman and Bothwell, 1976), a measure designed specifically for the postpartum period would emphasize behavioural performance in a limited number of relevant roles for the new mother (*see* Kumar, Robson and Smith, 1984). Routine use of a valid postpartum social adjustment measure would go a long way toward illuminating the true level of disability associated with postpartum depression. Moreover, the use of a standard measure would allow better comparison of samples of subjects across studies. In sum, if advances are to continue to be made in understanding the aetiology of postpartum depression, our measures must be both reliable and valid for the purposes of our research.

Theoretically based research

Few investigators have tested a specific model of postpartum depression. There will always be a need for descriptive research on postpartum depression; however, further advances await testing of clearly formulated hypotheses that have a basis in some theory of psychopathology. A few examples of theoretically based research in the current literature include the work on life events by Paykel *et al.* (1980) and our own work on testing the multiple influences of psychological, environmental and heritable factors on postpartum depression (O'Hara, Rehm and Campbell, 1982; O'Hara, Neunaber and Zekoski, 1984). Also, many of the biological studies have a theoretical basis, for example those addressing predictions from the more general depression literature (Handley *et al.*, 1980), or those testing hormonal theories of postpartum depression (Gard *et al.*, 1986). Certainly, most postpartum depression researchers have either explicit or implicit theories regarding the aetiology of postpartum depression. These theories need to be formulated into testable hypotheses and subjected to empirical scrutiny.

Studies of multiple factors

Biological and psychological/environmental studies of postpartum depression have typically been conducted in isolation from each other. Although this strategy is understandable given limited resources and expertise to carry out multifactorial studies, the interaction of the biological and psychological/environmental variables will be impossible to determine unless they are investigated in a single study. For example, it might be that hormonal factors are only important in postpartum depression if certain social stressors are in place, e.g. poor marital relationship, or if a woman is otherwise vulnerable, e.g. personal or family history of psychopathology. Of course this example could be turned around just as easily. Larger scale studies should be conducted that incorporate both the biological and psychological/environmental variables that based on past research are most likely to be causally related to postpartum depression. Testing models that include multiple variables will demand increased statistical sophistication on the part of investigators and the use of techniques such as hierarchical multiple regression (Pedhazur, 1982) and structural modelling with latent variables (Bentler, 1980).

Treatment and prevention research

Until recently there has been very little treatment or prevention research in the area of postpartum depression, the work of the Gordons being the most striking exception (Gordon and Gordon, 1959, 1960). Several studies in this area are underway (Rickel and Smith, 1984; Leverton and Elliott, 1985) or recently completed (e.g. Halonen and Passman, 1985). Of course, there have been many studies aimed at preventing general postpartum adjustment problems (Shereshefsky and Yarrow, 1973). Despite the work that is currently underway, more research in this area is needed.

There are several directions this work might take. One possible strategy is that adopted by Gordon and Gordon (1960) which was to provide a brief intervention during pregnancy to all women to prepare them and their spouses for the rigours of the postpartum period. Although it would be necessary to provide these interventions to women who would have no problems in any event, they could be easily integrated into most types of childbirth preparation classes, thus reducing their cost. The advantage of interventions done in this way is that they carry little stigma, i.e. women are not being singled out for special psychological or psychiatric attention.

A second strategy is to identify women during pregnancy who are at risk for postpartum depression and provide a more intense intervention for them during pregnancy (Leverton and Elliott, 1985). This strategy pre-supposes that risk factors for postpartum depression are known. Unfortunately, there is no set of risk factors that is both sensitive and specific to postpartum depression. Thus, researchers adopting this strategy will probably treat many women in no real need of treatment and miss many women who will go on to have a postpartum depression.

The third strategy is to screen women on single or multiple occasions after delivery and treat them while they are depressed. This strategy has the value of economy of effort and it is widely used for postpartum psychosis but has not been used for postpartum depression. The new postpartum depression measure developed by Cox, Holden and Sagovsky (1987) might be particularly useful as a way of identifying women after delivery who are in need of treatment.

Follow-up studies

A major issue with respect to postpartum depression is its long-term effects on the mental health of the woman and its effects on the family, most particularly the child (Uddenberg and Englesson, 1978; Wolkind, Zajicek and Ghodsian, 1980; Ghodsian, Zajicek and Wolkind, 1984; Kumar and Robson, 1984; Wrate et al., 1985). These studies have shown that women who experience postpartum depressions are likely to continue to experience extended or frequent depression in the future. Moreover, there is some (though not overwhelming) evidence that children of women with postpartum depression have behavioural problems later on. Specifically, what is needed are studies that assess potential emotional, cognitive and social deficits in the children of mothers who have experienced postpartum depression. It may be that women who experience postpartum depression are those women who are generally vulnerable to depression (Watson *et al.*, 1984; O'Hara, 1986b). Nevertheless, it is important to determine whether having a postpartum depression conveys a special risk for future depressions beyond what might be expected based on past personal and family history of psychopathology.

Postpartum depression and public policy

One of the most striking features of postpartum depression is that so few women who experience it seek professional treatment. This fact is surprising given the clear evidence that these women are impaired, though not incapable, in carrying out responsibilities as wives, mothers and workers. Moreover, there is also clear evidence that many women experience depressions that are quite lengthy. Many studies have shown that children of depressed mothers are at risk for cognitive and social disability (Rolf, 1972; Weissman *et al.*, 1984); similar findings have now been described in 4-year-olds whose mothers had experienced early postpartum depressions (Cogill *et al*, 1986; Caplan *et al.*, 1988). Although there is evidence that non-psychotic depressions show an increased incidence after delivery relative to pregnancy, there is very little evidence that the incidence of depression after delivery is elevated relative to non-childbearing times. Finally, suicide is rare both during pregnancy and after delivery. Given this state of affairs, what should the response be of researchers, mental health professionals and government policy makers?

First of all, there is little question that research into postpartum depression must continue. Only in the last few years have well controlled studies of postpartum depression been published (Cox, Connor and Kendell, 1982; Kumar and Robson, 1984; O'Hara, Neunaber and Zekoski, 1984; Watson *et al.*, 1984). Many questions remain regarding aetiological factors, prevalence of postpartum depression in relation to prevalence of depression in comparable non-puerperal samples, and the relation of postpartum depression to the blues and psychosis. Moreover, because a large proportion of postpartum depressions occur within the first three months after delivery, investigators have a natural laboratory for the prospective study of many theories of depression.

For mental health professionals the issue is the extent to which aggressive efforts into primary prevention and case finding should be instituted. Certainly, many women who experience postpartum depression do seek out professional services and benefit from them. Moreover, excellent treatment facilities have been established to care for the more severely impaired mother, particularly in the UK. Current research does not substantiate the need for extensive independent efforts in primary prevention and case finding given other pressing mental health needs in most communities. Nevertheless, some prevention and treatment efforts could be integrated into existing prenatal and postnatal social and medical services. For example, following the model of Gordon and Gordon (1960), brief preventive interventions could be coupled with childbirth preparation classes. In addition, during the puerperium, postpartum depression screening measures (Cox, Holden and Sagovsky, 1987) could be administered routinely to women during postnatal visits to the obstetrician and paediatrician. Women who, on the basis of psychometric assessment appear to be experiencing a significant depression, could be referred for a more thorough evaluation. Much of this preventive and case finding work can be carried out, with only a little extra training, by the same individuals who provide routine prenatal and postnatal care.

Government policy makers must decide where to allocate scarce resources for maximal public good. Two points have been made that bear on the allocation of resources. First, continued research into postpartum depression and allied disorders is important. Second, preventive and case finding efforts for postpartum depression can be undertaken at relatively low cost to the health care system. Nevertheless, it is still the community, in communicating its wishes to policy makers, that must decide how important is the problem of postpartum depression.

Final comment

This chapter and other chapters in this volume make clear that postpartum depression is a serious problem for mother, child and family. Nevertheless, this chapter also makes clear that there is little convincing evidence that the rate of non-psychotic depression is elevated during the puerperium. Moreover, aetiological factors directly related to childbearing such as obstetrical stressors and changing hormone levels are only weakly associated with the presence of postpartum depression. The term postpartum depression, then, would appear to reflect the coincidental occurrence of the puerperium and depression rather than reflecting a causal relation between childbearing and depression.

Acknowledgements

The writing of this chapter was suppported in part by National Institute of Mental Health Grant MH39283 to Michael W. O'Hara. This chapter was written while Michael O'Hara was on a developmental assignment supported by the Department of Psychology, University of Iowa.

The authors gratefully acknowledge the comments by Carolyn E. Cutrona, Jane Engeldinger and Ellen Wright.

References

ABRAMSON, L. Y., SELIGMAN, M. E. P. and TEASDALE, J. D. (1978). Learned helplessness in humans: critique and reformulation. *Journal of Abnormal Psychology*, **87**, 49–74

ALDER, E. M. and COX, J. L. (1983). Breast feeding and post-natal depression. *Journal of Psychosomatic Research*, **27**, 139–144

AMERICAN PSYCHIATRIC ASSOCIATION (1980). *Diagnostic and Statistical Manual of Mental Disorders*, 3rd Edition. Washington: American Psychiatric Association

BALLINGER, C. B. (1982). Emotional disturbance during pregnancy and following delivery. *Journal of Psychosomatic Research*, **26**, 629–634

BARNO, A. (1967). Criminal abortion deaths, illegitimate pregnancy deaths, and suicides in pregnancy. Minnesota, 1950–1965. *American Journal of Obstetrics and Gynecology*, **98**, 356–363

BEBBINGTON, P., HURRY, J., TENNANT, C., STURT, E. and WING, J. K. (1971). Epidemiology of mental disorders in Camberwell. *Psychological Medicine*, **11**, 561–597

BECK, A. T., WARD, C. H., MENDELSON, M., MOCK, J. and ERBAUGH, J. (1961). An inventory for measuring depression. *Archives of General Psychiatry*, **4**, 561–569

BECK, A. T., WARD, C. H., MENDELSON, M., MOCK, J. E. and ERBAUGH, J. K. (1962). Reliability in psychiatric diagnoses: 2. A study of consistency in clinical judgments and ratings. *American Journal of Psychiatry*, **119**, 351–357

BEDFORD, A., FOULDS, G. A. and SHEFFIELD, B. F. (1976). A new Personal Disturbance Scale (DSSI/SAD). *British Journal of Social and Clinical Psychology*, **15**, 387–394

BENTLER, P. M. (1980). Multivariate analysis with latent variables: causal modeling. In: *Annual Review of Psychology,* Volume 31, (M. R. Rosenzweig and L. W. Porter, eds), pp. 419–456. Palo Alto, CA: Annual Reviews Inc.

BIBRING, G. L., DYWER, T. F., HUNTINGTON, P. S. and VALENSTEIN, A. F. (1961). A study of the psychological processes in pregnancy and of the earliest mother-child relationship. In: *The Psychoanalytic Study of the Child*, Volume XVI, (R. S. Eissler, A. Freud, H. Harmann and M. Kris, eds). pp. 9–72. New York: International Universities Press

BLAIR, R. A., GILMORE, J. S., PLAYFAIR, H. R., TISDALL, M. W. and O'SHEA, M. W. (1970). Puerperal depression: a study of predictive factors. *Journal of the Royal College of General Practitioners*, **19**, 22–25

BRAVERMAN, J. and ROUX, J. F. (1978). Screening for the patient at risk for postpartum depression. *Obstetrics and Gynecology*, **52**, 731–736

BREEN, D. (1975). *The Birth of a First Child: Towards an Understanding of Femininity*. London: Tavistock Publications

BRIDGE, L. R., LITTLE, B. C., HAYWORTH, J., DEWHURST, J. and PRIEST, R. G. (1985). Psychometric predictors of post-natal depressed mood. *Journal of Psychosomatic Research*, **29**, 325–331

BROCKINGTON, I. F. and KUMAR, R. (eds) (1982). *Motherhood and Mental Illness*. London: Academic Press

BROCKINGTON, I. F., WINOKUR, G. and DEAN, C. (1982). Puerperal psychosis. In: *Motherhood and Mental Illness*, (I. F. Brockington and R. Kumar, eds), pp. 37–69. London: Academic Press

BROCKINGTON, I. F., CERNIK, K. F., SCHOFIELD, E. M., DOWNING, A. R., FRANCIS, A. F. and KEELAN, C. (1981). Puerperal psychosis: phenomena and diagnosis. *Archives of General Psychiatry*, **38**, 829–833

BROUSSARD, E. R. (1976). Evaluation of televised anticipatory guidance to primiparae. *Community Mental Health Journal*, **12**, 203–210

BROWN, G. W. and HARRIS, T. (1978). *Social Origins of Depression: A Study of Psychiatric Disorder in Women*. New York: The Free Press

BROWN, G. W. and SHERESHEFSKY, P. M. (1973). Seven women: a prospective study of postpartum psychiatric disorders. In: *Psychological Aspects of a First Pregnancy and Early Postnatal Adaptation*, (P. M. Shereshefsky and L. J. Yarrow, eds), pp. 181–207. New York: Raven Press

BURKE, C. W. and ROULET, F. (1970). Increased exposure of tissues to cortisol in late pregnancy. *British Medical Journal*, **i**, 657–659

CAPLAN, G. (1957). Psychological aspects of maternity care. *American Journal of Public Health*, **47**, 25–31

CAPLAN, H. L., COGILL, S. R., ALEXANDRA, H., ROBSON, K. M. and KUMAR, R. (1988). The effect of maternal postnatal depression on the emotional development of the child. *British Journal of Psychiatry* (in press)

COGILL, S. R., CAPLAN, H. L., ALEXANDRA, H., ROBSON, K. M. and KUMAR, R. (1986). Impact of maternal postnatal depression on cognitive development of young children. *British Medical Journal*, **292**, 1165–1167

COOPER, P., OSBORN, M., GATH, D. and FEGGETTER, G. (1982). Evaluation of a modified self-report measure of social adjustment. *British Journal of Psychiatry*, **141**, 68–75

COX, J. L. (1976). Psychiatric morbidity and childbirth: a prospective study from Kansagati Health Centre, Kampala. *Proceedings of the Royal Society of Medicine*, **69**, 221–222

COX, J. L. (1983). Postnatal depression: a comparison of African and Scottish women. *Social Psychiatry*, **18**, 25–28

COX, J. L., CONNOR, Y. and KENDELL, R. E. (1982). Prospective study of the psychiatric disorders of childbirth. *British Journal of Psychiatry*, **140**, 111–117

COX, J. L., HOLDEN, J. M. and SAGOVSKY, R. (1987). Detection of postnatal depression: Development of the 10-item Edinburgh Postnatal Depression Scale. *British Journal of Psychiatry*, **150**, 782–786

COX, J. L., CONNOR, Y. M., HENDERSON, I., McGUIRE, R. J. and KENDELL, R. E. (1983). Prospective study of the psychiatric disorders of childbirth by self-report questionnaire. *Journal of Affective Disorders*, **5**, 1–7

COX, J. L., ROONEY, A., THOMAS, P. F. and WRATE, R. W. (1984). How accurately do mothers recall postnatal depression? Further data from a 3-year follow-up study. *Journal of Psychosomatic Obstetrics and Gynaecology*, **3**, 185–189

CUTRONA, C. E. (1982). Nonpsychotic postpartum depression: a review of recent research. *Clinical Psychology Review*, **2**, 487–503

CUTRONA, C. E. (1983). Causal attributions and perinatal depression. *Journal of Abnormal Psychology*, **92**, 161–172

CUTRONA, C. E. (1984). Social support and stress in the transition to parenthood. *Journal of Abnormal Psychology*, **93**, 378–390

DALTON, K. (1971). Prospective study into puerperal depression. *British Journal of Psychiatry*, **118**, 689–692

DALTON, K. (1980). *Depression after Childbirth*. Oxford: Oxford University Press

DAVENPORT, Y. B., ZAHN-WAXLER, C., ADLAND, M. L. and MAYFIELD, A. (1984). Early child-rearing practices in families with a manic-depressive parent. *American Journal of Psychiatry*, **141**, 230–235

DEAN, C. and KENDELL, R. E. (1981). The symptomatology of puerperal illnesses. *British Journal of Psychiatry*, **139**, 128–133

ELLIOTT, S. A., RUGG, A., J., WATSON, J. P. and BROUGH, D. I. (1983). Mood changes during pregnancy and after the birth of a child. *British Journal of Clinical Psychology*, **22**, 295–308

ENDICOTT, J. and SPITZER, R. L. (1978). A diagnostic interview: the schedule for affective disorders and schizophrenia. *Archives of General Psychiatry*, **35**, 837–844

EYSENCK, H. J. (1952). *The Scientific Study of Personality*. London: Routledge and Kegan Paul

EYSENCK, H. J. and EYSENCK, S. G. B. (1975). *Manual of the Eysenck Personality Questionnaire*. London: Hodder and Stoughton

FEGGETTER, P. and GATH, D. (1981). Non-psychotic psychiatric disorders in women one year after childbirth. *Journal of Psychosomatic Research*, **25**, 369–372

GAENSBAUER, T. J., HARMON, R. J., CYTRYN, L. and McKNEW, D. H. (1984). Social and affective development in infants with a manic-depressive parent. *American Journal of Psychiatry*, **141**, 223–229

GARD, P. R., HANDLEY, S. L., PARSONS, A. D. and WALDRON, G. (1986). A multivariate investigation of postpartum mood disturbance. *British Journal of Psychiatry*, **148**, 567–575

GHODSIAN, M., ZAJICEK, E. and WOLKIND, S. (1984). A longitudinal study of maternal depression and child behaviour problems. *Journal of Child Psychology and Psychiatry and Allied Disciplines*, **25**, 91–109

GOLDBERG, D. (1972). *The Detection of Psychiatric Illness by Questionnaire*. London: Oxford University Press

GOLDBERG, D., COOPER, B., EASTWOOD, M. R., KEDWARD, H. B. and SHEPARD, M. (1970). A standardized psychiatric interview for use in community surveys. *British Journal of Preventative and Social Medicine*, **24**, 18–23

GORDON, R. E. (1961). *Prevention of Postpartum Emotional Difficulties*. Ann Arbor, Michigan: University Microfilms Inc.

GORDON, R. E. and GORDON, K. K. (1959). Social factors in the prediction and treatment of emotional disorders of pregnancy. *American Journal of Obstetrics and Gynecology*, **77**,

1074–1083

GORDON, R. E. and GORDON, K. K. (1960). Social factors in the prevention of postpartum emotional problems. *Obstetrics and Gynecology*, **15**, 433–438

GORDON, R. E., KAPOSTINS, E. E. and GORDON, K. K. (1965). Factors in postpartum emotional adjustment. *Obstetrics and Gynecology*, **25**, 158–166

GREENWOOD, J. and PARKER, G. (1984). The dexamethasone suppression test in the puerperium. *Australian and New Zealand Journal of Psychiatry*, **18**, 282–284

GRIMMELL, K. and LARSEN, V. L. (1965). Postpartum and depressive psychiatric symptoms and thyroid activity. *Journal of the American Medical Women's Association*, **20**, 542–546

HALONEN, J. S. and PASSMAN, R. H. (1985). Relaxation training and expectation in the treatment of postpartum distress. *Journal of Consulting and Clinical Psychology*, **53**, 839–845

HAMILTON, J. A. (1962). *Postpartum Psychiatric Problems*. St. Louis: C. V. Mosby

HANDLEY, S. L., DUNN, T. L., BAKER, J. M., COCKSHOTT, C. and GOULD, S. (1977). Mood changes in puerperium, and plasma tryptophan and cortisol concentrations. *Britsh Medical Journal*, **ii**, 18–22

HANDLEY, S. L., DUNN, T. L., WALDON, G. and BAKER, J. M. (1980). Tryptophan, cortisol and puerperal mood. *British Journal of Psychiatry*, **136**, 498–508

HAYWORTH, J., LITTLE, B. C., CARTER, S. B., RAPTOPOULOS, P., PRIEST, R. G. and SANDLER, M. (1980). A predictive study of post-partum depression: some predisposing characteristics. *British Journal of Medical Psychology*, **53**, 161–167

HOLMES, T. H. and RAHE, R. H. (1967). The social readjustment rating scale. *Journal of Psychosomatic Research*, **11**, 213–218

HOPKINS, J., CAMPBELL, S. B. and MARCUS, M. (1986). The role of infant-related stressors in postpartum depression. *Journal of Abnormal Psychology*, **96**, 237–241

HOPKINS, J., MARCUS, M. and CAMPBELL, S. B. (1984). Postpartum depression: a critical review. *Psychological Bulletin*, **95**, 498–515

JACOBSON, L., KAIJ, L. and NILSSON, A. (1965). Post-partum mental disorders in an unselected sample: frequency of symptoms and predisposing factors. *British Medical Journal*, **i**, 1640–1643

JARRAHI-ZADEH, A., KANE, F. J. Jr., VAN DE CASTLE, R. C., LACHENBRUCH, P. A. and EWING, J. A. (1969). Emotional and cognitive changes in pregnancy and early puerperium. *British Journal of Psychiatry*, **115**, 797–805

KENDELL, R. E. (1985). Emotional and physical factors in the genesis of puerperal mental disorders. *Journal of Psychosomatic Research*, **29**, 3–11

KENDELL, R. E., WAINWRIGHT, S., HAILEY, A. and SHANNON, B. (1976). The influence of childbirth on psychiatric morbidity. *Psychological Medicine*, **6**, 297–302

KENDELL, R. E., RENNIE, D., CLARKE, J. A. and DEAN, C. (1981). The social and obstetric correlates of psychiatric admission in the puerperium. *Psychological Medicine*, **11**, 341–350

KLEINER, G. J. and GRESTON, W. M. (1984). Overview of demographic and statistical factors. In: *Suicide in Pregnancy*, (G. J. Kleiner and W. M. Greston, eds), pp. 23–40. Littleton, Massachusetts: John Wright

KUMAR, R. and ROBSON, K. M. (1984). A prospective study of emotional disorders in childbearing women. *British Journal of Psychiatry*, **144**, 35–47

KUMAR, R., ROBSON, K. M. and SMITH, A. M. R. (1984). Development of a self-administered questionnaire to measure maternal adjustment and maternal attitudes during pregnancy and after delivery. *Journal of Psychosomatic Research*, **28**, 43–51

LEIFER, M. (1977). Psychological changes accompanying pregnancy and motherhood. *Genetic Psychology Monographs*, **95**, 55–96

LEVERTON, T. and ELLIOTT, S. (1985). Prevention of postnatal depression: intervention in the antenatal clinic. Paper presented at the Annual Meeting of the Marcé Society, London.

LEWIS, A. (1938). States of depression: their clinical and aetiological differentiation. *British Medical Journal*, **ii**, 875–878

LIEBENBERG, B. (1973). Techniques in prenatal counselling. In: *Psychological Aspects of a First Pregnancy*, (P. M. Shereshefsky and L. J. Yarrow, eds), pp. 123–151. New York: Raven Press

LIVINGOOD, A. B., DAEN, P. and SMITH, B. D. (1983). The depressed mother as a source of stimulation for her infant. *Journal of Clinical Psychology*, **39**, 369–375

MANLY, P. C., McMAHON, R. B., BRADLEY, C. F. and DAVIDSON, P. O. (1982). Depressive attributional style and depression following childbirth. *Journal of Abnormal Psychology*, **91**, 245–254

MARCÉ L. V. (1858). *Traité de la Folie des Femmes Enceintes, des Nouvelles Accouchées et des Nourrices*. Paris: Baillière

MARGISON, F. (1982). The pathology of the mother–child relationship. In: *Motherhood and Mental Illness*, (I. F. Brockington and R. Kumar, eds), pp. 191–222. London: Academic Press

MARTIN, M. E. (1977). A maternity hospital study of psychiatric illness associated with childbirth. *Irish Journal of Medical Science*, **146**, 239–244

MEICHENBAUM, D. (1985). *Stress Inoculation Training*. New York: Pergamon.

MELTZER, E. S. and KUMAR, R. (1985). Puerperal mental illness, clinical features and classification: a study of 142 mother-and-baby admissions. *British Journal of Psychiatry*, **147**, 647–654

MUELLER, D. P. (1980). Social networks: a promising direction for research on the relationship of the social environment to psychiatric disorder. *Social Science and Medicine*, **14a**, 147–161

MYERS, J. K., WEISSMAN, M. M., TISCHLER, G. L. et al. (1984). Six-month prevalence of psychiatric disorders in three communities. *Archives of General Psychiatry*, **41**, 959–967

NEUGEBAUER, R. (1983). Rate of depression in the puerperium. *British Journal of Psychiatry*, **143**, 421–422

NEUMANN, G. L. (1978). Beyond pregnancy and childbirth: the use of anticipatory guidance in preparing couples for postpartum stress. *Dissertation Abstracts International*, **38**, 5582B

NILSSON, A. (1970). Para-natal emotional adjustment: a prospective study of 165 women, Part I. *Acta Psychiatrica Scandinavica, Supplementum*, **220**, 1–61

NILSSON, A. and ALMGREN, P. E. (1970). Para-natal emotional adjustment: a prospective investigation of 165 women, Part II. *Acta Psychiatrica Scandinavica, Supplementum*, **220**, 62–141

NOTT, P. N. (1982). Psychiatric illness following childbirth in Southampton: a case register study. *Psychological Medicine*, **12**, 557–561

OAKLEY, A. (1980). *Women Confined—Towards a Sociology of Childbirth*. Oxford: Martin Robertson

OFFER, D. and SABSHIN, M. (1966). *Normality: Theoretical and Clinical Concepts of Mental Health*. New York: Basic Books

OFFER, D. and SABSHIN, M. (1984). Preface. In: *Normality and the Life Cycle: A Critical Integration*, (D. Offer and M. Sabshin, eds), pp. ix–xiii. New York: Basic Books

O'HARA, M. W. (1986a). Psychological and biological factors in postpartum depression. Paper presented at the Biennial Meeting of the Marcé Society, Nottingham, England.

O'HARA, M. W. (1986b). Social support, life events, and depression during pregnancy and the puerperium. *Archives of General Psychiatry*, **43**, 569–573

O'HARA, M. W., NEUNABER, D. J. and ZEKOSKI, E. M. (1984). A prospective study of postpartum depression: prevalence, course, and predictive factors. *Journal of Abnormal Psychology*, **93**, 158–171

O'HARA, M. W., REHM, L. P. and CAMPBELL, S. B. (1982). Predicting depressive symptomatology: cognitive-behavioural models and postpartum depression. *Journal of Abnormal Psychology*, **91**, 457–461

O'HARA, M. W., REHM, L. P. and CAMPBELL, S. B. (1983). Postpartum depression: a role for social network and life stress variables. *Journal of Nervous and Mental Disease*, **171**, 336–341

PAFFENBARGER, R. S. (1982). Epidemiological aspects of mental illness associated with childbearing. In: *Motherhood and Mental Illness*, (I. F. Brockington and R. Kumar, eds), pp. 21–36. London: Academic Press

PAYKEL, E. W. (1979). Recent life events in the development of depressive disorders. In: *The Psychobiology of the Depressive Disorders*, (R. Depue, ed.), pp. 245–262. New York: Academic Press

PAYKEL, E. S., EMMS, E. M., FLETCHER, J. and RASSABY, E. S. (1980). Life events and social support in puerperal depression. *British Journal of Psychiatry*, **136**, 339–346

PEDHAZUR, E. J. (1982). *Multiple Regression in Behavioural Research: Explanation and Prediction*, 2nd Edition. New York: Holt, Rinehart and Winston

PITT, B. (1968). 'Atypical' depression following childbirth. *British Journal of Psychiatry*, **114**, 1325–1335

PITT, B. (1973). 'Maternity blues'. *British Journal of Psychiatry*, **122**, 431–433

PLAYFAIR, H. R. and GOWERS, J. I. (1981). Depression following childbirth—a search for predictive signs. *Journal of the Royal College of General Practitioners*, **31**, 201–208

RAILTON, I. E. (1961). The use of corticoids in postpartum depression. *Journal of American Medical Women's Association*, **16**, 450–452

RASKIN, A., SCHULTERBRANDT, J., REATIG, N. and McKEAN, J. (1970). Differential response to chlorpromazine, imipramine, and placebo. *Archives of General Psychiatry*, **23**, 164–173

REES, W. D. and LUTKINS, S. G. (1971). Parental depression before and after childbirth: an assessment with the Beck Depression Inventory. *Journal of the Royal College of General Practitioners*, **21**, 26–31

REHM, L. P. (1977). A self-control model of depression. *Behaviour Therapy*, **8**, 787–804

REHM, L. P., KORNBLITH, S. J., O'HARA, M. W., LAMPARSKI, D. M., ROMANO, J. M. and VOLKIN, J. (1981). An evaluation of the major elements in a self-control therapy program for depression. *Behaviour Modification*, **5**, 459–489

RICKEL, A. U. and SMITH, R. L. (1984). Directions for research in postpartum depression. Paper presented at the Annual Meeting of the American Psychological Association, Toronto

ROBSON, K. M. and KUMAR, R. (1980). Delayed onset of maternal affection after childbirth. *British Journal of Psychiatry*, **136**, 347–353

ROLF, J. E. (1972). The social and academic competence of children vulnerable to schizophrenia and other behaviour pathologies. *Journal of Abnormal Psychology*, **80**, 225–243

ROSSI, A. (1968). Transition to parenthood. *Journal of Marriage and the Family*, **30**, 26–39

RUTTER, M. (1976). Research report. Isle of Wight Studies, 1964–1974. *Psychological Medicine*, **6**, 313–332

RYLE, A. (1961). The psychological disturbances associated with 345 pregnancies in 137 women. *Journal of Mental Science*, **107**, 279–286

SHERESHEFSKY, P. M. and LOCKMAN, R. F. (1973). Comparison of counselled and non-counselled groups. In: *Psychological Aspects of a First Pregnancy*, (P. M. Shereshefsky and L. J. Yarrow, eds), pp. 151–163. New York: Raven Press

SHERESHEFSKY, P. M. and YARROW, L. J. (1973). *Psychological Aspects of a First Pregnancy and Early Postnatal Adaptation*. New York: Raven Press

SPANIER, G. B. (1976). Measuring dyadic adjustment: new scales for assessing the quality of marriage and similar dyads. *Journal of Marriage and the Family*, **38**, 15–28

SPITZER, R. L., ENDICOTT, J. and ROBINS, E. (1978). Research diagnostic criteria: rationale and reliability. *Archives of General Psychiatry*, **36**, 773–82

STEIN, G. (1982). The maternity blues. In: *Motherhood and Mental Illness*, (I. F. Brockington and R. Kumar, eds), pp. 119–154. London: Academic Press

STEINER, M. (1979). Psychobiology of mental disorders associated with childbearing. *Acta Psychiatrica Scandinavica*, **60**, 449–464

THUWE, I. (1974). Genetic factors in puerperal psychosis. *British Journal of Psychiatry*, **125**, 378–385

TOD, E. D. M. (1964). Puerperal depression: a prospective epidemiological study. *Lancet*, **ii**, 1264–1266

TURNBULL, J. M. (1969). Mental illness in the puerperium. *Canadian Psychiatric Association Journal*, **14**, 525–526

UDDENBERG, N. (1974). Reproductive adaptation in mother and daughter. A study of personality development and adaptation to motherhood. *Acta Psychiatrica Scandinavica, Supplementum*, **254**

UDDENBERG, N. and ENGLESSON, I. (1978). Prognosis of post partum mental disturbance: a prospective study of primiparous women and their 4 1/2-year-old children. *Acta Psychiatrica Scandinavica*, **58**, 201–212

WANDERSMAN, L., WANDERSMAN, A. and KAHN, S. (1980). Social support in the transition to parenthood. *Journal of Community Psychology*, **8**, 332–342

WATSON, J. P., ELLIOTT, S. A., RUGG, A. J. and BROUGH, D. I. (1984). Psychiatric disorder in pregnancy and the first postnatal year. *British Journal of Psychiatry*, **144**, 453–462

WEISSMAN, M. M. and BOTHWELL, S. (1976). Assessment of social adjustment by patient self-report. *Archives of General Psychiatry*, **33**, 1111–1115

WEISSMAN, M. M. and MYERS, J. K. (1978). Affective disorders in a U.S. urban community: the use of the Research Diagnostic Criteria in an epidemiological survey. *Archives of General Psychiatry*, **35**, 1304–1311

WEISSMAN, M. M., PRUSOFF, B. A., GAMON, G. D., MERIKANGAS, K. R., LECKMAN, J. F. and KIDD, K. K. (1984). Psychopathology in the children (ages 6–18) of depressed and normal parents. *Journal of the American Academy of Child Psychiatry*, **23**, 8–84

WHALLEY, L. J., ROBERTS, D. F., WENTZEL, J. and WRIGHT, A. F. (1982). Genetic factors in puerperal affective psychoses. *Acta Psychiatrica Scandinavica*, **65**, 180–193

WING, J. K., COOPER, J. E. and SARTORIUS, N. (1974). *The Measurement and Classification of Psychiatric Symptoms*. Cambridge: Cambridge University Press

WOLKIND, S., ZAJICEK, E. and GHODSIAN, M. (1980). Continuities in maternal depression. *International Journal of Family Psychiatry*, **1**, 167–182

WRATE, R. M., ROONEY, A. C., THOMAS, P. F. and COX, J. L. (1985). Postnatal depression and child development: a three-year follow-up study. *British Journal of Psychiatry*, **146**, 622–627

YALOM, I. D., LUNDE, D. T., MOOS, R. H. and HAMBURG, D. A. (1968). 'Postpartum blues' syndrome. *Archives of General Psychiatry*, **18**, 16–27

ZIMMERMAN, M., CORYELL, W. and PFOHL, B. (1986). Melancholic subtyping: a qualitative or quantitative distinction? *American Journal of Psychiatry*, **143**, 98–100

Chapter 3

The life event of childbirth: sociocultural aspects of postnatal depression

John L. Cox

Introduction

The recent interest in the puerperal mood disorders shown by health professionals as well as the general public is perhaps somewhat surprising, as such topicality is not fully explained by only limited advances in knowledge of the neurochemistry of these disorders, and there has been no popular breakthrough in treatment. This subject, however, has continued to motivate researchers in at least eight British universities and to arouse the concern of health visitors, community psychiatric nurses and general practitioners, as well as postnatal depression self-help group organizers (Cox, 1986). Furthermore five popular books on this subject have been published in the last 10 years (Pitt, 1978; Welburn, 1980; Dalton, 1980; Dix, 1985; Ball, 1987) and media coverage has brought this topic to the attention of the public.

The explanations for this present interest are complex but, nevertheless, important to understand. There is a marked disparity between the persisting stereotype of a contented mother nursing her cheerful child and the reality for one in 10 women of hardship and depression following childbirth. The front cover of Vivian Welburn's book, for example, has a photograph of a downcast mother and her baby with the caption 'You *have* to go around with that big smile on your face, with people saying "aren't you lucky to have such a dear little baby" and you feel utter despair'; a picture which strikes a chord for many women who recognize, and want an explanation for, the contradiction between the high frequency of postnatal depression and the expectation of society that she should be happy. Health professionals, though usually aware of this stereotype, unwittingly may endorse its validity and are surprised when their clients want information about the causes of postnatal depression, or enquire about the effectiveness of counselling or of progesterone treatment. In Holland doctors are being criticized for withholding 'hormone' therapy and some obstetricians have reluctantly established special postnatal depression clinics (Loendersloot and Hilverlink, 1983).

Another problem is the confusion of terms in the literature; postnatal depression being used not only as a formal psychiatric diagnosis of a depressive illness but also as a 'folk' label to describe any psychological difficulty that occurs after childbirth (*see* Oakley and Chamberlain, 1981).

64

Furthermore, as Oakley (1980) and Calvert (1985) have discussed, the causes of postnatal depression are closely linked to the change in role for women in present-day society and a complete understanding of this disorder may require a full recognition of feminist issues. Some authors such as Arms (1975) and Shaw (1974) have even suggested that postnatal depression is a disorder restricted to Western society and is not likely to be found in societies where issues of sexism are less fully expressed.

It is the purpose of this chapter to illustrate these sociocultural facets of postnatal depression with particular reference to cross-cultural observations and to my own research in Africa, and to highlight some of the methodological problems of rating childbirth as a psychosocial life event. I shall not review the world literature on childbirth customs as this task has been attempted by social anthropologists such as MacCormack (1982), Kitzinger (1982) and Mead and Newton (1967) but shall describe those studies that have specifically made links between postpartum customs and postnatal mood disturbance.

Cross-cultural reports

Pillsbury (1978) has provided one of the most specific accounts of the postpartum Chinese custom 'doing the month', and has shown how in the month following childbirth the mother has many defined rules of behaviour which include the avoidance of washing, not to go outside during the entire month, not to eat any raw or cold food, to eat chicken, not to be blown by the wind or to move about, not to go to another person's home, not to have sexual intercourse and not to read or cry. These proscriptions are still practised in Chinese society, and allow the mother to receive extra assistance from her family as well as to rest. She is in this way rewarded following the effort of childbirth and given the sanction 'to be idle in bed for an entire month'. These Chinese mothers therefore receive far more attention than mothers in the United States, and Pillsbury has concluded that this may prevent Chinese women from having postpartum depression.

Jamaican women have a period of ritual seclusion which is intense for the first nine nights after delivery and Kitzinger (1982) described this separation of the mother from her family as being similar to the seclusion which follows a bereavement; this primary seclusion is followed by a less restricted seclusion for a further 31 nights when the mother remains at home with her baby and is looked after by her own mother. In India, among lower castes in particular, postpartum seclusion lasts for a similar period of time (40 days); the mother is regarded as impure and she must therefore remain alone in confinement. Kelly (1967) likewise described how a Nigerian mother and baby are placed in a special hut within the family compound and remain there for 2–3 months, being cared for by the baby's grandmother. At the end of this period the mother and her baby emerge and a feast is then held in their honour. This custom therefore allows the mother to rest and her baby to get considerable attention; Kelly concludes that these postpartum customs may protect against postpartum depression.

In the UK, Okely's (1975) study of gipsy attitudes to childbirth found that childbirth was regarded as polluting and, to prevent contamination, delivery in hospital was encouraged. Assistance with cooking from other women or from older children was to prevent contamination of the food by the puerperal mother. The study of a Punjabi community in the UK by Homans (1982) found that the extent of the confinement was modified according to the availability of others to help, as well as by the need to obtain employment.

In their comprehensive review article, Stern and Kruckman (1983) put forward the challenging hypothesis that it is the absence of postpartum behavioural constraints in Western society that is important in the causation of postnatal depression. By contrast with many non-Western countries, or with some ethnic minorities, the period of time when special attention is given to the mother in the UK is often no longer than 2–3 days and the mother is discharged from the maternity hospital and then expected to resume full domestic responsibility. This change of environment is associated also with the transition of care-giver from the midwife, who has assisted her in pregnancy and may have delivered her baby, to the health visitor or general practitioner whose main concern may be for the child rather than the mother. Furthermore the other major change in Western society related to the availability of support in the puerperium is the present ambiguity about the role of the partner—whether he should be present at the delivery (traditionally a woman's place), and the extent of his assistance after childbirth. In Sweden this ambiguity is illustrated by the legislation for 'paternity leave', which can be shared with his partner or taken wholly by her, or taken entirely by himself.

In Western society there are therefore only vestigeal remains of the 40-day 'lying-in' period; the postnatal clinic which used to take place at six weeks is only occasionally held and baptisms and the churching of the unclean women (which also took place about 40 days after childbirth) are less frequent ceremonies than formerly. Thus, although family and obstetric rituals still occur (*see* Jones and Dougherty, 1982) they are generally more fragmented, less likely to be enforced and quite often they are ignored altogether.

In what way does this lack of postpartum structure in Western society relate to the increased awareness of depression postpartum? Seel (1986) has addressed this most important question and regards childbirth rituals as linked to a 'rite de passage' which is incomplete. Such rituals are nevertheless not only important for the individual who participates in them but are also expressions of social values. Thus the change in status from that of a childless woman to that of mother is a major change of role which should be marked by a public change in social status, and carrying out an an appropriate 'rite de passage'.

There are three components to the 'rite de passage'; the rite of separation (including cleansing and purifying), the 'liminal' period when there is no status and there may be private humiliation, and the rite of incorporation when the subject moves back to a new status and there is feasting and rejoicing. Seel believes that the first two stages of this rite are highly elaborated in Western obstetrics but there is little or no 'rite of incorporation'.

'We leave the rite of passage unfinished; the new mother and father are left in limbo, having to fend for themselves as best they can. The consequences of this incompleteness may be quite serious for some parents.'

Conflicting advice may be given to the mother as there are no norms as to the amount of domestic activities that should be undertaken, and no consensus as to when sexual relationships, for example, can be resumed. Her status is ambiguous and her role as 'mother' is perhaps less valued by society than formerly. Her husband's role is also uncertain which makes it difficult for him to determine what type of support to give his wife.

The absence of these routine behaviours and rituals may relate to the onset of depression in several ways by lowering the mother's self-esteem, causing uncertainty about the availability of social support, increasing the likelihood of physical fatigue, as well as by stressing the relationship with her husband. Furthermore as the lack of ritual structure postpartum represents the ambivalence of society about the status to be attached to mothering, this uncertainty exacerbates her role conflict and increases the threat to her self-esteem.

It is therefore likely that the ideas and observations of medically informed anthropologists will lead to a better understanding of the psychiatric disorders associated with childbearing and further research directed to testing these ideas may be very productive. Thus, evaluating the effectiveness of re-establishing such rites of incorporation, for example, could be undertaken and Seel has suggested that the health visitor could provide more continuity throughout the childbearing period and that collaboration of the church, mosque, temple and local self-help group with such 're-entry' could be encouraged. Jansson (1987), in a most thorough review of the transcultural literature, has particularly emphasized that these rituals could assist to define delivery as being something worth celebrating, although Seel's suggestion that the mother is given a medal, a bouquet of flowers or a congratulations card appear to be rather too simplistic. These hypotheses could, however, be tested in communities with, and without, postnatal rituals and a comparison of the rates of postnatal depression in a Westernized and traditional Asian community, or between a cohesive urban environment (such as the Potteries) with a deprived inner city area would be worthwhile. Prevalence studies of postnatal depression in the Chinese, Asian and Nigerian communities, for example, would also indicate how well these sociocultural hypotheses (e.g. that depression is rare in these communities) are upheld.

The difficulties of carrying out such studies are, nevertheless, considerable and as yet there have been few attempts to translate existing self-report scales for postnatal depression into other languages in a way that is culturally sensitive or to develop interview schedules for use with postpartum women in ethnic minorities.

Although these sociocultural hypotheses are consistent with clinical observation they should not suggest that intrapsychic and neurobiological considerations are not important; indeed the African studies that I shall describe have shown that postnatal depression *can* occur in a non-Western society. Furthermore Jimenez and Newton (1979) in their review of 202 traditional societies found that half of them expected a woman to return to full duties within two weeks of childbirth.

Traditional beliefs in Africa

As my earlier research on postnatal depression (carried out in 1972–74 during my appointment to the Department of Psychiatry at Makerere University) was on women who were predominantly from the Ganda tribe in the southern part of Uganda, it was fortunate that a detailed account of their traditional beliefs and practices had been written by Roscoe in 1911 and that the impressive field work of Orley (1970) had provided vital preliminary information about their childbearing customs and their concepts of neurosis.

Roscoe (1911) emphasized that for the Baganda fertility was associated with high social status: 'Every married woman was anxious to become a mother and expected to show signs of maternity within a few weeks of marriage. A woman who had no children was despised and soon became a slave and drudge of the household.' Sterility therefore carried considerable social stigma and was even regarded as an adult form of a traditional illness, 'ekigalanga', in which the mother had abdominal pain and a thin voice. This illness was believed to be caused by a bad spirit having been transferred to the mother from another person (Bennett, 1965). Roscoe provides numerous examples of the Baganda's sense of responsibility for the health of the fetus. The husband, for example, would ask an elderly woman or another relative to look after his pregnant wife and her task was to ensure that taboos, such as forbidding a man to step over her legs and to stop her from stepping over a mat or over the feet of a man, were observed. A pregnant woman should not sit in a doorway when a man entered the house because harm might come to the fetus and its legitimacy could then not be guaranteed. Other taboos included not looking at a weak child or laughing at a lame man, and avoiding protein foods and salt during pregnancy. Any problems experienced in labour were believed to be caused by the mother's immoral behaviour who was urged to confess her faults. For the Baganda the legitimacy of the child was of particular importance and only when this was fully established could the child be named and placed in a family or clan. Illegitimacy was therefore tested before birth when the naked pregnant mother was inspected by members of her husband's clan and repeated the following morning when her husband would jump over her. After birth a second legitimacy ceremony took place when the mother handed the umbilical cord to her mother-in-law who placed it in a vessel containing a mixture of beer, milk and water; if the cord floated the child was declared to be fully legitimate. The midwife could, however, help to ensure the legitimacy of the baby by rubbing the umbilical cord with fat, so assisting it to float.

Amakiro

It was of particular interest to me that a traditional Ganda puerperal mental illness 'Amakiro' had been recognized long before Western doctors came to work in Uganda and brought with them their formal Western classifications of diseases. Roscoe (1911) was the first to describe this illness although he regarded it as an illness of the baby. Orley (1970) and Bennett (1965), on the other hand, said that Amakiro was a puerperal mental illness of the mother. In order to investigate further the contemporary beliefs about Amakiro, 31 women were interviewed by a Ugandan medical student; 28 said they had heard of the illness and 12 had known a mother who had suffered from it (Cox, 1979a). These informants were unanimous that Amakiro was a *mental* illness of the mother that usually followed childbirth but which could also occur during pregnancy. It was a serious illness which sometimes resulted in death of the mother or of her baby. Its symptoms included a disordered relationship between the mother and her baby; for example, the mother might not wish to feed her baby and might wish to eat it. The cause of Amakiro was promiscuity of the mother or of her husband during pregnancy; explanations of how such illicit intercourse might cause Amakiro are shown in *Table 3.1*.

Table 3.1 Possible causes of 'Amakiro'

If mother promiscuous:	*If father promiscuous:*
(1) *Semen* from other men incompatible with that of the husband and so causing damage to the child inside.	(1) *Heat* which is brought by the husband from another woman may be incompatible with the woman's blood and so harm either the mother or her fetus.
(2) One of the men with whom the woman had been promiscuous might have some *infectious disease*.	(2) The *odour* of the other women may not be compatible with that of his wife and so damage the child.
(3) The chest or bones of the fetus could be broken by another man, but not by the father	
(4) 'Incompatible blood'.	
(5) Promiscuity must somehow harm the mother or baby.	

An interview with the traditional healer, Makolo, was carried out with a Luganda speaking medical student and showed clearly that Amakiro was not just a folk illness confined to the belief system of the Ganda women alone but was also well recognized within the nosology of established traditional 'medical' opinion (Asuni, 1986). When asked about the causes of Amakiro, however, the healer told us that promiscuity of the mother during or before pregnancy and not using herbal baths both needed to be considered. In contrast to the explanations given to us by the women themselves, Makolo did not think that promiscuity of the husband was so important.

The symptoms of Amakiro were described by Makolo in the following way: 'Normal understanding is changed. The patient may talk nonsense and the symptoms would range from weakness (to the extent that she may not be able to lift the head off the bed) to violence. There is rejection of the child. The mother does not want to see or even feed the baby and in some cases the mother would go to the extent of wanting to eat it'. Like many Western doctors he was guarded when asked for an opinion about the duration of the illness and said that to give such an estimation would be misleading because he would not know how long the illness would last if it was not treated; if it was treated then the duration would depend on the type of treatment used and on the particular patient.

We were told that the onset occurred after delivery although during pregnancy the mother may have become ill and been vomiting or had general 'bad health'. Makolo said that he had never seen a case of Amakiro where there had been an attempt to eat the baby but had heard that this could happen from others 'who were older than me'. Although he usually treated patients with roots or herbs, the success of a particular remedy for one patient was not a guarantee that it would be so with another.

The traditional illness Amakiro is relevant to our present discussion, not only because the Baganda and their traditional healers have recognized and named this specific postpartum mental illness (with a distinctive aetiology and symptomatology), but because this aetiology may relate to aberrant behaviour by the mother *or* by the father; such concern about extramarital intercourse being a result of the Ganda's need to be certain the legitimacy of the child. Thus, although in Western society marital difficulties are beginning to be recognized as important causes of puerperal mental illness, it is nevertheless uncommon for the *father's* behaviour to be regarded as a cause of his partner's mental illness and it is possible that the Ganda are amongst the first to put forward this most plausible explanation.

Puerperal psychosis

Other African studies of psychiatric disorder following childbirth include those by Swift (1972), Ebie (1972), Collomb, Guena and Diop (1972) and Ifabumuyi and Akindele (1985).

Swift (1972) in his study of 42 Tanzanian women admitted to Muhimbuli Hospital in Dar es Salaam found the most frequent diagnosis was schizophrenia (53%), the second most common was an acute confusional state (37%) and only 5% of women had a depressive psychosis; none were admitted because of a neurotic disorder. A quarter of the women had a previous history of a febrile illness and Swift emphasized the need to exclude a physical cause for a psychosis such as infection, malnutrition or anaemia.

In a study of Nigerian women with a puerperal psychosis, Ebie (1972) also found that a high proportion had schizophrenia or an organic psychosis. Of 62 mothers admitted to University College Hospital, Ibadan, 24% were schizophrenic and 23% had organic confusional states; 8% died in hospital and the poor physical state of the mothers was again emphasized. However, Ifabumuyi and Akindele (1985) in a retrospective case notes study of women admitted to the teaching hospital in Kaduna, Nigeria found that 12% had an organic psychosis, 20% had schizophrenia, 28% had worries and 34% depression. These findings again emphasize the frequency of physical complications in the puerperium—two mothers with organic psychoses died.

In Senegal, Collomb, Guena and Diop (1972) found that a third of women admitted to the mental hospital between 1965 and 1969 had a puerperal psychosis. This very high incidence was explained by the disabling fears of childbearing women in that society as well as by their high fertility rate. On becoming pregnant these authors report that a woman 'enters a world of uncertainties, fears and threats. Her status is very ambiguous. It is rich and strong but it is also vulnerable, fragile and diminished. Quite often anxiety wins out over veneration and contentment'.

Postnatal depression

My own research into postnatal depression was spurred on by the finding of Assael *et al.* (1972) that a quarter of women attending antenatal clinics at Kasangati Health Centre, 10 miles from Kampala, were suffering from 'conspicuous psychiatric morbidity'. This prospective study (Cox, 1979b) was, as far as I am aware, the first controlled study of antenatal depression in Africa, and possibly in Europe or the USA and its findings confirmed those of Assael *et al.* (1972); 17% of the pregnant women were found to have definite psychiatric morbidity, twice the frequency found in the control non-pregnant, non-puerperal sample; such antenatal psychiatric disorder occurred particularly in women with marital problems who were separated from their husbands. 183 women from this antenatal sample were then interviewed for a second time three months after delivery by the author and a Luganda speaking research assistant using the Luganda translation of the standardized semi-structured interview developed by Goldberg *et al.* (1970).

At the postnatal interview, 18 (10%) women were found to have a depressive illness and six were so severely impaired by this disorder that they could not carry out important household tasks. When compared with the Scottish women subsequently studied (Cox, 1983), the Ugandans were less likely to report that they felt personally responsible for their babies or to describe guilt or self-blame. However the frequency of postnatal depression was about the same in the two studies (10% Ugandan, 13% Scottish) and there was no obvious association found between postnatal depression and marital status, method or place of delivery in either study.

In the context of this present chapter, however, the finding that postnatal depression could readily be identified in a semi-rural group of African women provides an appropriate corrective to the assumptions discussed previously that this disorder is confined to Western society, and results from its fragmentary postpartum rituals. Nevertheless, review of the case records of the African depressed mothers shows clearly that many such women were reminded of previous abortions, stillbirths and neonatal deaths and that their obstetric care was therefore far inferior to that available in the UK—factors which would indeed increase the likelihood of depression occurring, and if they had been present in Scotland to the same extent as in Uganda, the frequency of depression in the Scottish mothers would have been substantially in excess of that found in the Africans. The research design did not include any precise measures of postnatal support or assessment of whether postnatal rituals had been violated; the possibility that intact postnatal rituals protected some of the African women from becoming depressed could not therefore be tested.

Childbirth: a life event

It is a strange paradox that despite the extensive literature on the presentation and prevalence of postnatal depression, the specific contribution of childbirth (one of the most predictable and frequent of 'life events') has not yet been fully established nor have its social and biological components been studied in sufficient detail. Thus although the seminal research of Brown and Harris (1978) showed that having young children was a vulnerability factor for depression, their study did not investigate further the nature of the childbirth 'life event' and it did not distinguish between mothers who were pregnant and those who recently had delivered. Nevertheless their finding that depressed women had twice the rate of pregnancy and birth events than non-depressed women would suggest that a relationship may exist between childbirth and depression but that other ongoing problems (such as bad housing and major marital difficulties) were the major triggers for the onset of depression. They conclude that childbirth 'brings home to women the disappointment and hopelessness of her position: aspirations are made distant as she becomes more dependent on an uncertain relationship'.

In a prospective study of postnatal depression Watson *et al.* (1984) did record life events and difficulties using an adaptation of the Brown and Harris interview, and found that of 29 women with episodes of affective disorder before or after childbirth, only three had no obvious *other* life event that could have brought this about. The depressed mothers were classified into five groups depending on the relationships of their depression to life events other than childbirth as well as to long-term difficulties:

(1) Depression was unrelated to pregnancy and childbirth events (e.g. bereavement, housing crisis).
(2) Depression was associated with life events derived from pregnancy and childbirth (e.g. antenatal complications, premature births).
(3) Depressive episodes occurred in response to continuing life difficulties rather than acute life events.
(4) Events which provoked depression in the present pregnancy as well as caused a previous depression (e.g. the death of a previous child).
(5) Those few women whose depression followed the birth event only and had no previous psychiatric history.

Other researchers who have wrestled with these methodological problems of rating the birth event include O'Hara, Rehm and Campbell (1983) who attempted to go beyond a single measure of the birth event and divided the stresses of the childbirth event into:

(1) those occurring during pregnancy;
(2) those related to the actual stress of delivery; and
(3) those related to child care.

These authors emphasized that all three forms of stressful events needed to be assessed to characterize adequately the environmental demands on the childbearing mother. They also used specially adapted life event schedules and recognized that the existing measures of recording life events by self-report, as well as by personal interview, were not able to tease out the precise factors of the childbirth life event. Similarly Barnett, Hanna and Parker (1983) recognized the need to re-think the way in which life events associated with childbirth were recorded and were unable to identify a life event scale which acknowledged the unique aspects of obstetric groups. They therefore constructed a scale of their own and the items were ranked according to their expected distress to the mother. Those items regarded as most distressing were death, separation or unfaithfulness of the husband and the birth of an abnormal baby. This innovative scale nevertheless had some of the limitations that characterized the life event inventory of Holmes and Rahe (1967); the distinction between events independent of childbirth and those which resulted from it was not readily made.

In their prospective study of postnatal depression Kumar and Robson (1984) also included measures of life events, which were divided into four categories:

(1) marital or occupational changes of self or partner;
(2) health;
(3) domestic or social change; and
(4) crisis, such as burglaries, theft or witnessing disturbing events.

The most powerful contribution of events to depression was related to an impaired marital relationship and, in pregnancy, to a previous termination. These authors, however, also concluded that childbearing *per se* did have a 'particular and deleterious effect on the mental health of a substantial proportion of first time mothers'.

Paykel and colleagues (1980), on the other hand, regarded the stress of pregnancy and childbirth as being important only as an *additional* stress in tenuous situations, rather than as a major overwhelming cause. Their findings also pointed to the existence of a small sub-group of depression with primarily a biological cause. However they also aptly underlined that the absence of a control group of non-childbearing mothers in this and other research means that it is not possible to 'assess directly the contribution of pregnancy and childbirth to psychiatric disorder'. This crucial question about the specificity of childbirth stresses remains at the present time unanswered.

The limitations of these studies therefore illustrate the exceedingly complex interaction between sociocultural, psychological and biological factors when considering the aetiology of psychiatric disorder following childbirth. Thus the limitations of any simple rating instruction to record the 'severity', 'negative impact', 'focus', 'exit/entrance' of the childbirth life event is readily apparent and too great an emphasis in the rating instructions may be placed, for example, on an assumption that the amount of stress is related to the number of rooms in the house.

If to these difficulties of measuring the social impact of the birth event are added the uncertain impact of biological changes and a consideration of the unconscious links with earlier half-forgotten events, then the reason for the apparent neglect of this methodological minefield in life event research can be readily understood.

It is this writer's opinion that further advances will only be made if controlled studies are carried out to determine whether the apparent similarity in the frequency of postnatal depression in childbearing women with depression found in community samples (whether or not childbearing) is disguising an *actual* increase of postpartum depression. Furthermore there is also a need to develop life event interview schedules that are designed more specifically for childbearing women and which include precise instructions on how to rate the 'severity' and 'independence' of childbirth events, and also include clinically meaningful examples of 'anchor points'. These revised interview schedules are likely to be optimally developed from a collaboration between primary care health professionals, researchers and the childbearing women themselves.

It seems probable that childbirth acts as a potent vulnerability factor for depression, which can alter the meaning of other current events and difficulties (such as marital separation, bereavement or physical illness) and which may bring to mind earlier loss events (such as a termination or bereavement). However, although the birth event could directly initiate mood disturbance through neurohumoral changes, the constellation of these social and personal factors may cumulatively be sufficient to provoke a major affective illness, without the need to invoke a primary biological cause. Childbirth can usefully be regarded as a combination of several severe 'loss' life events—sometimes including the loss of a 'cherished ambition', and for some parents may also result in an ongoing 'life difficulty' (the baby). These factors give further credence to the possibility that social and psychological sequelae could cumulatively, and alone, account for a greater risk of depression occurring postpartum than in non-childbearing women.

Impact on the family

Although several recent studies (Brown and Harris, 1978; Paykel *et al.*, 1980; Cox, Connor and Kendell, 1982; Kumar and Robson, 1984; Watson *et al.*, 1984; Nettelbladt, Uddenberg and Englesson, 1985) have shown that an important relationship exists between marital disturbance and postnatal depression, the extent to which such marital difficulties result from the depression, or were themselves important initiators of a low mood, is not always clear. As discussed succinctly by Beail and McGuire (1982) and more fully reviewed by Lewis (1986), there tends to be a concentration on mothering with a relative neglect of 'parenting'. Pregnancy, birth and the care of children is often construed as a woman's domain, and fathers are therefore regarded as peripheral to childcare. Furthermore, women's reactions to childbearing and to parenthood tend to be explained in terms of maternal *intra*-psychic processes, the relationship to her partner being largely ignored. However, recent studies have underlined the importance of this relationship and Brown and Harris (1978) have shown that the supportive 'confidant role' of the husband was protective against maternal depression. The father is not only a 'supporter' (or 'assistant') for the mother but he may also provide direct practical care for the baby. Studies from Sweden (Nettelbladt, Uddenberg and Englesson, 1985) and the UK (Lewis, 1986) indicate that many contemporary fathers *are* more involved, but they do not necessarily carry out mothering tasks such as feeding or washing the baby. They are more likely to play with the baby, or to take the children to public entertainments.

The opportunity to investigate paternal postnatal depression and to collaborate with medical anthropologists at the University of Keele is provided by the author's present post in North Staffordshire. In this distinctive Potteries sub-culture families are possibly more cohesive than in other urban areas and it is possible to study the relationship of family support to postnatal depression and to investigate how it may cushion against depression.

Conclusion

In this chapter an attempt has been made to show in what way some aspects of a sociocultural perspective such as the obligations of a marital relationship, the determinants of legitimacy, the process of illness labelling, and the extent of childbirth rituals are closely related to the recognition and treatment of postnatal depression; and to indicate the possibility that the present increased awareness of this disorder in Western society may be a reflection of the major social changes in family life that are taking place. It is certainly a plausible hypothesis that the apparent lack of postnatal taboos in Western society has led to role ambiguity and to the lack of social support for the mother at a time when she, as well as her partner, are most vulnerable and may have experienced an 'exit' event rather than an 'entrance', and a 'loss' rather than a 'gain'.

Furthermore the failure so far to identify any definite neuroendocrine abnormality in puerperal mental illness would suggest that this sociocultural dimension should be explored more energetically and that collaboration with social scientists, such as medical anthropologists, is likely to be most worthwhile.

References

ARMS, S. (1975). *Immaculate Deception: A New Look at Women and Childbirth in America.* Haughton, Boston: San Francisco Book Company

ASSAEL, M. I., NAMBOZE, J. M., GERMAN, G. A. and BENNETT, F. J. (1972). Psychiatric disturbances during pregnancy in rural group of African women. *Social Science and Medicine*, **6**, 387–395

ASUNI, I. (1986). African and Western psychiatry: a comparison. In: *Transcultural Psychiatry*, (J. L. Cox, ed.), pp. 306–321. London: Croom Helm

BALL, J. A. (1987). *Reactions to Motherhood.* Cambridge: Cambridge University Press

BARNETT, B. F. W., HANNA, B. and PARKER, G. (1983). Life event scales for obstetric groups. *Journal of Psychosomatic Research*, **27**, 313–330

BEAIL, N. and MCGUIRE, J. (1982). *Fathers: Psychological Perspectives.* London: Junction Books

BENNETT, F. J. (1965). The social, cultural and emotional aspects of sterility in women in Buganda. *Fertility and Sterility*, **16**, 243–251

BROWN, G. W. and HARRIS, T. (1978). *Social Origins of Depression.* London: Tavistock Publications

CALVERT, J. (1985). Motherhood. In: *Women, the Family and Social Work*, (F. Brook and A. Davis, eds), pp. 51–69. London: Tavistock Publications

COLLOMB, H., GUENA, R. and DIOP, B. (1972). Psychological and social factors in the pathology of childbearing. *Foreign Psychiatry*, **1**, 77–89

COX, J. L. (1979a). Amakiro: a Ugandan puerperal psychosis? *Social Psychiatry*, **14**, 49–52

COX, J. L. (1979b). Psychiatric morbidity and pregnancy: a controlled study of 263 semi-rural Ugandan women. *British Journal of Psychiatry*, **134**, 401–405

COX, J. L. (1983). Postnatal depression: a comparison of Scottish and African women. *Social Psychiatry*, **18**, 25–28

COX, J. L. (1986). *Postnatal Depression—A Guide for Health Professionals*. Edinburgh: Churchill Livingstone

COX, J.L., CONNOR, Y. and KENDELL, R. E. (1982). Prospective study of the psychiatric disorders of childbirth by personal interview. *British Journal of Psychiatry*, **140**, 111–117

DALTON, K. (1980). *Depression After Childbirth*. Oxford: Oxford University Press

DIX, C. (1985). *The New Mother Syndrome*. Garden City: Allen and Unwin

EBIE, J. C. (1972). Psychiatric illness in the puerperium among Nigerians. *Tropical Geographical Medicine*, **24**, 253–256

GOLDBERG, D. P., COOPER, B., EASTWOOD, M.R., KEDWARD, H. B. and SHEPHERD, M. (1970). A standardized psychiatric interview for use in community surveys. *British Journal of Preventive and Social Medicine*, **24**, 18–23

HOLMES, T. H. and RAHE, R. H. (1967?). The social readjustment rating scale. *Journal of Psychosomatic Research*, **11**, 213–218

HOMANS, H. (1982). Pregnancy and birth as rites of passage. In: *Ethnography of Fertility and Birth*, (C. P. MacCormack, ed.), pp. 231–268. London: Academic Press

IFABUMUYI, O. I. and AKINDELE, M. O. (1985). Post partum mental illnesses in Northern Nigeria. *Acta Psychiatrica Scandinavica*, **2**, 63–68

JANSSON, B. (1987). Transcultural aspects of postnatal depression. *Bulletin of Marcé Society*, Summer, 18–26

JIMINEZ, M. H. and NEWTON, N. (1979). Activity and work during pregnancy and the post partum period: a cross cultural study of 202 societies. *American Journal of Obstetrics and Gynaecology*, **135**, 171–176

JONES, A. D. and DOUGHERTY, C. (1982). Childbirth in a scientific and industrial society. In: *Ethnography of Fertility and Birth*, (C. P. McCormack, ed.), pp. 269–290. London: Academic Press

KELLY, J. V. (1967). The influences of native customs on obstetrics in Nigeria. *Obstetrics and Gynaecology*, **30**, 608–612

KITZINGER, S. (1982). The social context of birth: some comparisons between childbirth in Jamaica and Britain. In: *Ethnography of Fertility and Birth*, (C. P. MacCormack, ed.), pp. 181–203. London: Academic Press

KUMAR, R. and ROBSON, K. M. (1984). A prospective study of emotional disorders in childbearing women. *British Journal of Psychiatry*, **144**, 35–47

LEWIS, C. (1986). *Becoming a Father*. Milton Keynes: Open University Press

LOENDERSLOOT, E. W. and HILVERLINK, E. (1983). Management of postpartum depression (PPD) in a special PPD clinic. *Journal of Psychosomatic Obstetrics and Gynaecology*, **2**, 53–58

MACCORMACK, C. P. (ed.) (1982). *Ethnography of Fertility and Birth*. London: Academic Press

MEAD, M. and NEWTON, N. (1967). Cultural patterning of perinatal behaviour. In: *Childbearing—its Social and Psychological Aspects*, (S. A. Richardson and A. F. Guttmacher, eds), pp. 142–243. Baltimore: Williams and Wilkins

NETTLEBLADT, P., UDDENBERG, M. and ENGLESSON, I. (1985). Marital disharmony four and a half years post partum. *Acta Psychiatrica Scandinavica*, **71**, 392–401

OAKLEY, A. (1980). *Women Confined: Towards a Sociology of Childbirth*. Oxford: Martin Robertson

OAKLEY, A. and CHAMBERLAIN, G. (1981). Medical and social factors in post partum depression. *Journal of Obstetrics and Gynaecology*, **1**, 181–187

OKELY, J. (1975). Gipsy women: models in conflict. In: *Perceiving Women* (S. Ardener, ed.), pp. 55–86. London: Dent

O'HARA, M., REHM, L. P. and CAMPBELL, S. B. (1983). Postpartum depression: a role for social network and life stress variables. *Journal of Nervous and Mental Disease*, **171**, 336–341

ORLEY, J. H. (1970). *Culture and Mental Illness; a Study from Uganda*. Makerere Institute of Social Research. East African Publishing House

PAYKEL, E. S., EMMS, E. M., FLETCHER, J. and RASSABY, E. S. (1980). Life events and social support in puerperal depression. *British Journal of Psychiatry*, **136**, 339–346

PILLSBURY, B. L. K. (1978). "Doing the month": confinement and convalescence of Chinese women after childbirth. *Social Science and Medicine*, **12**, 11–22

PITT, B. (1978). *Feelings about Childbirth*. London: Sheldon Press

ROSCOE, J. (1911). *The Baganda—An Account of their Native Customs and Beliefs*. London: Macmillan

SEEL, R. M. (1986). Birth rite. *Health Visitor*, **59**, 182–184

SHAW, N. S. (1974). *Forced Labour: Maternity Care in the United States*. London: Pergamon Press

STERN, G. and KRUCKMAN, L. (1983). Multi-disciplinary perspectives on post partum depression; an anthropological critique. *Social Science and Medicine*, **17**, 1027–1041

SWIFT, C. R. (1972). Psychosis during the puerperium among Tanzanians. *East African Medical Journal*, **49**, 651–657

WATSON, J. P., ELLIOTT, S. A., RUGG, A. J. and BROUGH, D. I. (1984). Psychiatric disorder in pregnancy and the first postnatal year. *British Journal of Psychiatry*, **144**, 453–462

WELBURN, V. (1980). *Postnatal Depression*. London: Fontana Books

Chapter 4

Endocrine and biochemical studies in puerperal mental disorders

Alan George and Merton Sandler

Introduction

Of the major human endocrine-related life events—puberty, pregnancy, childbirth, puerperium and the menopause—the puerperal period is most frequently associated with both mild transient and severe mental disorder. In theory, the search for aetiological factors in puerperal mental illness should be a simple matter of systematically investigating the major hormones involved in pregnancy and correlating any postpartum changes with variations in mood and mentation. Such investigations have been made even simpler by the development of specific radioimmunoassay techniques for steroid and peptide hormones, which allow small quantities of them to be measured accurately. The involvement of biochemical factors in the aetiology of postpartum mental illness has come to the fore only recently, despite the quiet revolution in attitudes to endogenous depression and schizophrenia which have largely undergone a biological reorientation. Even in the face of this late start, biochemical research into postpartum mental illness has provided us with tantalizing glimpses of more interesting results to come.

This chapter reviews current biological research into postpartum mental illness and tries to identify reasons why some of this effort has run into the sands, yielding confusing or, at best, paradoxical results. For ease of reference and analysis the review is divided into endocrine and biochemical aspects. An attempt is made to identify fruitful areas for future biological research in this important but neglected area of psychiatry.

Endocrine factors

Modern biochemical and neurophysiological techniques have revolutionized our approach to endocrinology, revealing not only the nature of hormone action but also the presence of previously unknown hormones and discrete endocrine tissue, particularly in the brain. Hormones may be simply divided into (a) steroids which are fat-soluble and produce their effects mainly by an interaction with the genetic apparatus of the cell nucleus, and (b) peptides, which are water-soluble and produce their effects by binding to cell surface receptors. Examples of steroid hormones are oestradiol, testosterone and cortisol, while insulin, prolactin and growth hormone are examples of peptide hormones. Tissues which are responsive to a particular hormone are termed its target tissue. As well as containing many hormone-releasing structures, various brain areas such as the hypothalamus are target tissues for hormones, in particular the sex hormones and corticosteroids. Numerous studies have shown that particular hormones not only cause biochemical changes in their particular brain target tissue but may induce behavioural changes in animals and mood changes in humans. The large number of hormones which have target tissues in the brain is comprehensively discussed and described in an excellent review by McEwan et al. (1979). Testosterone is known to stimulate libido in male and female primates. In rats this action depends on the conversion of testosterone to oestradiol within the brain. Chronic administration of high doses of glucocorticoids such as cortisol to humans is known to induce feelings of euphoria, while later withdrawal of this steroid may induce depression. For reasons such as this, it has been supposed that hormonal changes occurring during pregnancy and the puerperium may be involved in the aetiology of postnatal mental disorders.

The endocrinology of pregnancy and the puerperium

In the adult woman there are episodic changes in hormone levels throughout the menstrual cycle. The steady rise in plasma oestradiol level after menstruation suddenly changes to a surge which stimulates a synchronous release of luteotrophic hormone (LH) and follicle stimulating hormone (FSH) which trigger ovulation. After ovulation, progesterone levels rise and then fall rapidly to initiate menstruation. Plasma levels of testosterone, androstenedione and prolactin also exhibit a cyclic variation. This change in hormonal status has been associated, in women, with changes in mood, emotional lability and sexuality. If conception occurs, the developing embryo produces a peptide hormone, human chorionic gonadotrophin (hCG) which has an action like LH and maintains ovarian progesterone output. As pregnancy progresses, plasma progesterone levels rise and the maturing placenta contributes progesterone, oestriol and some peptide hormones, human placental lactogen (hPL) and β-endorphin (βEP). In the last 3–4 weeks of pregnancy, prolactin secretion from the anterior pituitary increases, as does the secretion of corticosteroids (mainly cortisol) from the adrenal cortex.

Four weeks before parturition, plasma oestradiol levels begin to rise and progesterone levels to fall. This phenomenon has usually been taken as the probable instigator of childbirth but it also seems that uterine endogenous factors, such as prostaglandins, may be involved. There seems to be little agreement on what initiates childbirth and not all researchers accept that plasma progesterone levels do fall before delivery (Findlay, 1984).

During the puerperium, the plasma concentrations of oestradiol and progesterone gradually return to the pre-pregnancy level. The postpartum reduction in plasma progesterone concentration allows prolactin to stimulate milk secretion from the mammary secretory cells, a process which is glucocorticoid and insulin-dependent. Suckling by the infant promotes prolactin secretion, while in the non-breast feeding mother, plasma prolactin levels decline. Oxytocin secretion is also stimulated by suckling, and this hormone is responsible for milk ejection.

It is tempting to think, therefore, that the massive rise in blood level of many hormones, mounting gradually through pregnancy, to be followed by an abrupt reduction after parturition, results in some kind of 'hormonal' shock. Not all hormone levels, in fact, fall sharply after childbirth; research has concentrated therefore on those that do. Researchers tend to be most concerned with puerperal *concentrations* of hormones rather than hormonal actions and variations in target organ sensitivity. They frequently forget that steroid hormones such as oestradiol and progesterone are able to bind to plasma proteins and, in this form, they are biologically inactive. A more important index of a steroid hormone's activity may therefore be its free concentration in the plasma rather than the total concentration which includes the protein-bound inactive hormone. The percentage of the total plasma oestradiol and progesterone which is unbound is about 2%. The role of the placenta has been little studied. How does the sudden withdrawal of its special secretions such as hPL and βEP affect the maternal central nervous system?

Steroid hormones

Progesterone   Both progesterone and oestrogen (oestradiol and oestriol) concentrations fall quickly after childbirth. Gelder (1978), who reviewed these changes and their implications, suggested that a sudden decrease of this kind after delivery may be a contributory factor to puerperal mental illness. A similar argument was advanced by Dalton (1980) who pointed to progesterone withdrawal as an aetiological cause of postpartum dysphoria. There is a certain amount of clinical evidence to support this view, in particular the apparently successful use of progesterone administration immediately after parturition to counter mood disturbance, as originally claimed by Bower and Altschule (1956) and later by Dalton (1980) and Solthau and Taylor (1982). However, Hatotani, Nishikubo and Kitayama (1979) found that progesterone alone was insufficient to alleviate psychotic puerperal mood disturbance in three cases whom they recorded.

Some corroboration for the progesterone deficit hypothesis in postpartum mood disturbance was provided by Nott *et al.* (1976) who showed that women with high scores on the blues syndrome questionnaire (Pitt, 1968) had lower postpartum progesterone levels than those with low 'Pitt' scores; women with the greatest pre- to postnatal drop were most likely to rate themselves as depressed within 10 days of childbirth. Nott *et al.* did not attempt, however, to measure the actual *rate* of progesterone decline although this factor might be important if it were a precipitating event. Ballinger *et al.* (1982) found no evidence of this difference in progesterone level in their study of the blues. Kuevi *et al.* (1983) even showed, in their own patient group, that the drop in progesterone level was *greater* in those without puerperal mood disturbance (275 ng ml^{-1}) than in those with mood disturbance (152 ng ml^{-1}). At the 36th week of pregnancy, the mean plasma progesterone concentration was 282.7 ng ml^{-1} in the normal group and 158.5 ng ml^{-1} in those with puerperal dysphoria. Mood disturbance was measured here with a self-rating scale (Lubin, 1965). It can be seen that the progesterone concentrations were approximately 130 ng ml^{-1} higher before delivery in the patients not suffering from puerperal symptoms. In the same two groups of patients, progesterone concentration was significantly lower during the first five postpartum days in those noted to have 'mood disturbance'. However, peak mood disturbance scores in each blues patient failed to correlate with their respective lowest progesterone values.

Similarly, Metz et al. (1983) found no difference in progesterone level (7–10 days postpartum) between 'blues' and 'non-blues' sufferers and no significant difference in prepartum progesterone concentrations between the two clinical groups. Nor was there any difference in the rate at which the progesterone levels fell in either group.

In all these studies, the total plasma progesterone concentration has been measured and not the free, biologically active hormone. In the plasma, progesterone normally binds to a protein, cortisol-binding globulin (CBG) and an equilibrium exists between free, biologically active progesterone and that bound to CBG which is inactive. Thus, although the total progesterone concentration at term is sometimes lower than the 36-week level, the free progesterone concentration is unchanged (Anderson, Hancock and Oakey, 1985).

For puerperal depression, Dalton (1980) has advocated the use of progesterone by injection, 100 mg i.m. for the first postpartum week and then 400 mg b.d. by suppository for two or more months postpartum. Solthau and Taylor (1982) have similarly claimed success using this treatment. The drug has been used in this way by Dalton (1980) for the treatment of premenstrual syndrome. However, its therapeutic success in the puerperium has not been substantiated by controlled clinical trials. Thus, there is as yet no straightforward endocrinological explanation of why progesterone therapy should be successful, unless some change in progesterone receptor sensitivity is involved in the aetiology of postpartum mood disturbance. Alternatively, the improvements in mood may be a placebo response. This question obviously needs more rigorous clinical evaluation, coupled with more thorough and frequent analysis of progesterone levels in the first puerperal week and progesterone receptor evaluation.

Oestradiol The increase in oestradiol levels prepartum, succeeded by the rapid fall following parturition, is a prime object of suspicion both for initiating the blues and the more severe puerperal psychoses (Bonnar et al., 1975). However, in two studies where this factor has been investigated in detail, there was no agreement; Nott et al. (1976) showed that pre-delivery oestradiol concentration was correlated significantly with postpartum 'mental instability' while Kuevi et al. (1983) could find no relationship between plasma oestradiol levels and postpartum blues symptoms.

On days 1–11 and 15–28 of the normal menstrual cycle, the ratio of plasma oestradiol to oestrone is approximately 2:1, while on days 12–14 it is 1:1. The pre-ovulatory surge in plasma oestrone concentration is much less pronounced than that for oestradiol. In terms of oestrogenic activity, oestrone is approximately 10 times less potent than oestradiol.

Hatotani, Nishikubo and Kitayama (1979) investigated oestradiol and oestrone levels in several cases of puerperal manic depressive psychosis. Although no clear relationship emerged between total plasma oestrogen concentration and the recorded manic and depressive episodes, they noted a reversal of the normal non-pregnancy oestradiol to oestrone ratio of 2:1 during the follicular phase of the menstrual cycle in three psychotic patients.

In the 'blues' study of Kuevi et al. (1983), the normal ratio of oestradiol to oestrone of 1:1 found during pregnancy and the immediate postpartum period was present in both 'blues' and 'non-blues' sufferers. It is possible that a change in oestrogen to progesterone ratio in the puerperium is responsible for some features of puerperal mental illness but this is not apparent from any of the studies we have reviewed. The oestradiol studies reviewed here involved measurement of total plasma oestradiol concentrations. Since 98% of the total plasma oestradiol is bound to sex hormone-binding globulin and is thus biologically inactive, the same criticism applied to these studies as to the measurements of progesterone discussed previously.

Androgens   In the adult female, the ovary and the adrenal cortex secrete androgens—testosterone and some androstenedione. The ovarian secretion of these androgens shows cyclic variation and is usually at its peak between days 12–14 of the menstrual cycle. Such cyclic variation is absent during both pregnancy and lactation.

Greenblatt et al. (1985) have reviewed several studies in which androgen therapy, usually combined with oestrogen, has restored libido and improved mood in depressed, menopausal women. Perhaps there is a role for similar treatments in postpartum depressive illness (providing the mother refrains from breast feeding). Changes in the levels of serum androgens such as testosterone or androstenedione have been shown to be associated with changes in mood and sexuality in the menstrual cycle (Sanders and Bancroft, 1982). Alder et al. (1986) demonstrated that, in the puerperium, certain aspects of mood such as sociableness, cheerfulness and fatigue significantly correlated with plasma concentrations of androstenedione and testosterone. In women who were lactating, plasma concentrations of these hormones were significantly lower than in women who were not breast feeding. The reduced affect and sexuality in the lactating women was correlated with reduced testosterone and androstenedione levels and was attributed to lactational suppression of ovarian function, resulting in reduced ovarian androgen secretion.

Cortisol   The human adrenal cortex secretes the corticosteroid hormones cortisol and corticosterone. Their biosynthesis and release is stimulated by adrenocorticotrophic hormone (ACTH) produced by the anterior pituitary. ACTH secretion is itself regulated by corticotrophin-releasing factor (CRF) which is secreted by neurones originating in the hypothalamic arcuate nuclei. CRF release is controlled by noradrenergic (noradrenaline-releasing) and serotonergic (5-HT-releasing) neurone systems. CRF and ACTH release are also regulated by the circulating level of cortisol and corticosterone.

In 1956, Bower and Altschule suggested that affective disorder in the puerperium might be related to altered corticosteroid secretion after parturition. Plasma corticosteroid levels rise in pregnancy and reach a peak during labour: such overproduction might induce psychosis in susceptible individuals. Subsequent investigations of this hypothesis have been extensively reviewed by Hamilton (1962) who drew attention to the similarity between psychotic episodes induced by chronic corticosteroid administration and the periodic psychoses sometimes found in the early puerperium. Handley et al. (1977) demonstrated a positive correlation between elation (as measured by the Hildreth (1946) questionnaire) and plasma cortisol in the first week postpartum. However, using a larger number of patients, the same group were unable later to replicate these findings (Handley et al., 1980); they did demonstrate, however, that a raised plasma cortisol from the 38th week of pregnancy was associated with a more severe episode of postpartum blues, perhaps providing the first evidence of prenatal endocrinological predisposition to puerperal mental disturbance.

Ballinger et al. (1982) failed to demonstrate a significant relationship between mood and urinary excretion of 11-hydroxycorticosteroids. Kuevi et al. (1983) were also unable to show any difference between plasma cortisol concentrations in blues and non-blues sufferers. A possible explanation for these discrepancies between different research groups, and even within the groups themselves, may lie in the analytical techniques used. Kuevi et al. (1983) measured cortisol by radioimmunoassay procedures whereas Handley et al. (1977, 1980) used a less sensitive chemical method for both their series. Since abnormalities in cortisol secretion have been well demonstrated in endogenous depression, it is surprising that little evidence of them has so far emerged in postpartum mental disorder. However, plasma cortisol concentrations exhibit a diurnal rhythmicity: higher levels are seen on waking, while the lowest values are present in the late evening. Most investigations cited here have favoured early morning sampling since plasma cortisol levels are higher after waking than in the late evening: it is obvious, however, that evening sampling, in addition, would have provided a clearer impression of the total picture. It may be that differences between controls and psychiatrically disturbed puerperal patients are only detectable when their *daily* cortisol cycles are compared. Sachar et al. (1980) have already demonstrated a difference in diurnal cortisol secretion between endogenous depressives and controls. This aspect of the problem will be discussed more fully in the methodology section on pp. 102–104.

The dexamethasone suppression (of cortisol secretion) test (DST) has now been standardized (Carroll et al., 1981) and detailed analyses of its ability to distinguish and classify depressive patients have been produced (Green and Kane, 1983). Since this test involves a challenge to anterior pituitary, limbic and hypothalamic glucocorticoid receptors, it may represent a better test of the pituitary/adrenocortical system and its CNS control mechanisms than does a mere measurement of plasma cortisol level. When the DST was administered to 45 women 3–5 days postpartum, 82% showed an abnormal response which did not correlate with self-reported feelings of depression (Greenwood and Parker, 1984). The abnormal DST results did not predict depressive or other morbid symptomatology at the end of a six-week follow-up period. In a more detailed study, Singh *et al.* (1986) administered the DST to seven women suffering with puerperal psychosis, to six with postnatal depression and to 19 normal women five days postpartum. A positive DST result, i.e. non-suppression of cortisol secretion, was obtained in 67% of the puerperal depressed group, in 71% of the puerperal psychotic group and in 79% of the control postpartum women. Since the incidence of a positive DST declined to 11.4% in the control group between 5–24 days postpartum, Singh *et al.* (1986) concluded that the immediate postpartum period itself is a confounding factor in the interpretation and application of this test and that the DST cannot by itself be used in the puerperium to discriminate severe depressive from psychotic postpartum patients or, indeed, either of these groups from controls.

The validity of the DST as a diagnostic aid has been challenged also because factors such as stress, duration of hospital admission and weight change may confound the results. The interpretation and validity of DST results and biological tests in general have been reviewed recently by Ross (1986).

Thyroid system

The thyroid gland produces two major hormones, tri-iodothyronine (T_3) and tetra-iodothyronine or thyroxine (T_4), both of which have wide-ranging stimulatory effects on metabolism in nervous and systemic tissue. Secretion of T_3 and T_4 is regulated by thyroid stimulating hormone (TSH), a peptide produced by the anterior pituitary. TSH secretion is itself regulated by thyrotropin releasing hormone (TRH), a peptide hormone which is secreted by neurones originating in the arcuate nucleus of the hypothalamus. TRH release is regulated by central neurotransmitters such as serotonin and noradrenaline and by plasma levels of T_3 and T_4.

Puerperal mood disturbances and even psychoses were attributed by Danowski (1953) to a thyroid hormone imbalance. Further developments of this hypothesis and the results of investigations designed to test it have been evaluated in detail by Hamilton (1962, 1977). A dysfunction of the thyroid system was considered to be a causative agent in puerperal mood disturbance, mainly because the well-documented clinical syndromes of thyrotoxicosis and myxoedema are often accompanied by marked changes in mood, whilst mild, transient hypothyroidism is an occasional feature of the puerperium.

According to Hamilton (1977), however, postpartum psychiatric syndromes of the early puerperium (up to three weeks postpartum) are not associated with thyroid disorder. This view was based on the observation that *free* thyroxine concentrations lie at the normal puerperal level in both depressed and non-depressed subjects at this time. Plasma thyroxine levels then fall in all puerperal women from about the third postpartum week. From this time onwards, Hamilton (1977) claims that therapy with thyroxine is more effective. George and Wilson (1983) showed that plasma TSH levels are unchanged during the first week postpartum in both blues and non-blues sufferers. Perhaps T_3 and T_4 are less effective in those cases quoted by Hamilton resulting from reduced T_3 and T_4 entry into target cells or reduced binding of the two hormones in the cell nucleus. What appears to be required is a thorough clinical investigation of thyroid function in the puerperium, extending up to three months after parturition. This evaluation should include measurements of free and bound T_3 and T_4, and of TSH, in order to demonstrate any subtle changes in thyroid secretion which might otherwise be missed. Tests for autoimmune thyroid disease might also be useful. Based on earlier observations on the usefulness of thyroxine treatment for the depressive phase of bipolar affective disorder, Hatotani, Nishikubo and Kitayama (1979) investigated the possible involvement of the thyroid system in three patients with periodic psychoses. In two of the patients the TSH response to intravenous TRH was abnormally low, pointing to some hypothalamic pituitary disorder involving inadequate production of TSH, defective TRH receptors or some inhibition of TRH access to TSH-containing cells in the anterior pituitary.

Peptide hormones
β-Endorphin

β-Endorphin (βEP) is a peptide consisting of 31 amino acids, with a structure corresponding to the sequence 61–91 of the peptide β-lipotrophin (βLP) which itself consists of 91 residues. βEP has opiate activity, binds with greatest affinity to (E)-opiate receptors and is elaborated by the corticotrophin-producing cells of the pars intermedia and anterior pituitary. *In vivo*, βEP is formed, together with ACTH and melanocyte-stimulating hormone (MSH), from the large pro-opiomelanocortin molecule by enzymatic degradation. This fascinating hormone family and its interrelationships have been reviewed by Bloom (1983).

In 1979, Csontos *et al.* showed that βEP and βLP levels rise in both maternal and neonatal plasma during labour, reaching a peak of 110 pg ml^{-1} in the mother immediately before delivery. Similar observations were made by Fletcher, Thomas and Hill (1980) who demonstrated an increase of βEP through each stage of labour to a plateau of 100 pg ml^{-1} at delivery, noting that a rise in βEP from the prepartum plateau occurs only after labour has been initiated and is paralleled by a similar rise in the neonate. They found no difference between βEP levels in pregnant women before labour had commenced, in comparison with non-pregnant controls. After parturition, plasma levels decline in parallel with a puerperal fall in prolactin and George and Wilson (1982, 1983) showed that by one week postpartum, mean βEP levels had reached 70 pg ml^{-1} in lactating and 52 pg ml^{-1} in non-lactating women. In both these studies there was a significant correlation between plasma concentrations of βEP and prolactin plasma levels and between βEP and certain puerperal neurotic features such as depression, anxiety and tension. Disturbances in each of these psychological measures correlated significantly with βEP concentrations during the first week postpartum in both lactating and non-lactating women.

The pain threshold increases in the last trimester of pregnancy and this increase correlates with an increase in plasma endorphin concentration (Gintzler, 1980). Pancheri *et al.* (1985) measured pain, anxiety and 'stress' subjectively before parturition and during the various stages of labour. They showed that peak βEP concentrations occurred at the expulsive stage of labour and correlated with a levelling out of the previous increases in pain and anxiety. No clear conclusion could be reached on whether the rise in βEP was induced by the mechanism of parturition or by the increased levels of stress and anxiety. The claim that βEP has an analgesic role in parturition is dubious since this hormone does not cross the blood-brain barrier.

Newnham *et al.* (1984) examined circulating βEP 'immunoreactivity' before and during parturition, and at one day postpartum. Plasma βEP levels rose from 632 ng l^{-1} at term to 5738 ng l^{-1} at delivery, declining to 218 ng l^{-1} at one day postpartum. They found no correlation between plasma βEP and anxiety scores or social support but they did report a positive correlation between the 'blues' and the pain of labour (as estimated by the attending midwife). Although there was no correlation between the 'blues' score and βEP concentrations and though, disappointingly, there was no measurement of βEP after the first postpartum day, Newnham *et al.* (1984) also made the interesting speculation that the blues or more severe postnatal disorders might result from the 'withdrawal' of endogenous opiates. Brinsmead *et al.* (1985) have also demonstrated a positive correlation between decreased βEP concentration postpartum and increased symptoms of anxiety, tension and depression. Dysphoric symptoms were also increased in the 38th week of pregnancy but declined significantly by the second day postpartum and this decline correlated significantly with the rise in βEP concentrations. Risch (1982) has shown that plasma βEP levels are raised in endogenous depressive and schizoaffective patients compared with normal controls. Zis *et al.* (1985) have shown that the inhibitory opiate influence on the hypothalamic-pituitary-adrenal axis is significantly reduced in depression. Matthews *et al.* (1986) have shown that there is a diurnal variation in plasma βEP concentration which is disturbed in some patients with endogenous depression and that the secretion of βEP can be suppressed by dexamethasone. In the puerperal studies mentioned above, the fall in βEP concentration might have been due to a general decrease in pituitary activity in the puerperium, although plasma TSH levels remained unchanged, suggesting that a more selective decline in hormone output had occurred (George and Wilson, 1983). Whether βEP has a specific role in normal parturition and whether it contributes to the causation of puerperal mental disturbance still remains to be established.

An interesting finding is that while the puerperal fall in circulating maternal prolactin correlates with the puerperal fall in βEP, suckling induces a rise in the former but not the latter (Genazzini *et al.*, 1982). Thus, two control mechanisms might exist for the regulation of prolactin secretion, whilst βEP involvement in prolactin secretion control might be confined to parturition and the early puerperium. While the studies quoted suggest that βEP concentration correlates with depressive and neurotic symptoms in the puerperium, we still do not know the origin of the βEP in maternal plasma, i.e. whether it is of maternal, placental or fetal origin. A study by Goland *et al.* (1981) suggests that βEP is produced independently in mother and fetus.

Prolactin

In 1937 Karnosh and Hope reviewed the evidence relating to the aetiology of puerperal psychoses. Amongst the causes they listed were loss of liver glycogen stores and the action of 'lactogenic hormone', now called prolactin. They pointed out that the onset of both mild and severe puerperal mental symptoms seemed to be associated with the initiation of lactation and that the lactation suppressant procedures then available were ineffective in relieving mental symptoms.

Despite this early association between prolactin and puerperal psychopathology, it is only recently that studies of this hormone in puerperal mental disorders have been carried out. There used to be difficulties in distinguishing and isolating human PRL from human growth hormone and a specific radioimmunoassay for the former was not developed until 1972.

After parturition, prolactin stimulates milk secretion in the suitably primed mammary gland and it also inhibits ovulation. Its role in the non-pregnant woman and the male is unknown; it may conceivably influence aspects of the ovarian cycle in both non-pregnant and puerperal states (Bohnet and McNeilly, 1979). Many behavioural effects of prolactin have been demonstrated in animals. Specific behaviours in the rat such as grooming and certain conditioned avoidance responses are strongly influenced by this hormone (Drago, Bohus and Mattheij, 1982). The full range of rat behaviour, as influenced by prolactin, is discussed in detail in the excellent monograph of Drago (1982). Prolactin secretion from the anterior pituitary lactotrophic cells is likely to be controlled directly by dopamine-releasing and probably also 5-hydroxytryptamine (5-HT)-releasing neurones (MacLeod and Lehmeyer, 1974; Clemens, Sawyer and Cerimele, 1977). Dopaminergic neurones of the tuberoinfundibular system inhibit prolactin secretion by release of dopamine on to D_1 receptors located in the median eminence or in the anterior pituitary itself. Prolactin appears to have a regulatory effect on dopamine release from these neurones and perhaps from other dopaminergic neurones as well (Drago, Bohus and Mattheij, 1982). Recently, the prolactin response to a challenge by intravenous tryptophan has been used as a measure of 5-HT receptor sensitivity (Heninger, Charney and Sternberg, 1984; Cowen *et al.*, 1986). Thus, measurement of changes in prolactin secretion may indicate general changes in CNS dopaminergic and serotoninergic activity. Basal prolactin levels rise during pregnancy and fall during the puerperium in both lactating and non-lactating women (Bonnar *et al.*, 1975). In 1976, Nott *et al.* measured plasma prolactin concentrations in 'blues' and 'non-blues' sufferers, as distinguished by the Pitt questionnaire (Pitt, 1968) but found no difference between these two groups at any stage postpartum. George, Copeland and Wilson (1980) reported a significant correlation between basal plasma prolactin concentrations and depression, anxiety and tension in 38 patients during the first puerperal week. The basal level was taken as the plasma concentration immediately before each breast feeding. Symptoms were rated using the Present State Examination (PSE) in the simplified version (Cooper *et al.*, 1977) with additional questions relating to maternity and hospital environment. Blood samples were obtained at the outset and immediately before the first breast feed of the day (in the lactating women) so that only the basal prolactin level while *at rest* was recorded. Kuevi *et al.* (1983) found no relationship between prolactin and symptoms of the blues, but like Nott *et al.* (1976), they did not control for ambulation—and did not appear to be measuring *basal* prolactin secretion. Suckling by the child stimulates prolactin secretion causing a wide individual variation in plasma concentrations, depending on the length and frequency of suckling.

Alder *et al.* (1986) found no relationship between plasma prolactin and either mood or sexuality postpartum. They measured plasma prolactin two hours after the last suckling but did not mention controls for ambulation. Exercise, and even slight moving about, cause a rise in plasma prolactin (Dessypris, Karoness and Adlercreutz, 1979). Alder's group attributed dysphoria and reduced sexuality to suppression of ovarian function during lactation but, strangely, found no significant relationship between the behavioural changes and plasma prolactin, given that this is the hormone mainly responsible for ovarian suppression in the puerperium (Bonnar *et al.*, 1975). The behavioural changes were, however, correlated with changes in serum androgen concentrations.

In non-puerperal mental disorders, correlations between the prolactin levels and mood change have been found. Hyperprolactinaemic women have increased anxiety, hostility and depression scores which are reduced when the plasma PRL concentration is lowered (Campbell and Winokur, 1985). Mendlewicz *et al.* (1980) reported an abnormal 24-hour prolactin secretory profile in 10 unipolar and eight bipolar depressives compared with their healthy controls. Halbreich, Gunhaus and Ben-David (1979) found an abnormal prolactin secretory rhythm in seven endogenous depressives compared with healthy controls. These studies demonstrate the importance of measuring hormones several times during the day of study, to allow for circadian changes in concentration.

Stress, such as a surgical operation, increases prolactin secretion and graded increases in stress produced by the Mirror Drawing Test have been shown to produce related increases in plasma prolactin (Noel *et al.*, 1972). However, Mathew *et al.* (1979) could find no relationship between morbid anxiety and prolactin levels and they were unable to demonstrate any reductions after successful anti-anxiety therapy in the same patients. Nesse *et al.* (1980) failed to demonstrate any change in prolactin level in response to flooding therapy for severe anxiety. It may well be that the prolactin response to acute and to chronic stress is different, since Shin (1980) has shown that prolactin secretion which is induced by acute stress is *not* linked to the dopamine-regulated system. Thus, there may be more than one neural pathway by which psychological factors on the one hand and physiological factors on the other stimulate prolactin secretion. In consequence, great care should be taken when designing experiments to measure this hormone during the puerperium so that specific factors such as ambulation, timing of blood sampling before breast feeding and environmental stress can be controlled.

Carroll and Steiner (1978) have proposed that mood change and affective disorders associated with the menstrual cycle may be the result of an interaction between prolactin, and oestradiol and progesterone. However, the ovarian hormones were not determined in any of the studies in which a positive correlation between prolactin concentration and postnatal mood change were demonstrated. Thus, this interesting theory remains unsubstantiated. If increased prolactin secretion is associated with postpartum mood changes, then it is possible that the drug, α-bromocriptine, which inhibits prolactin secretion, might be a useful treatment. α-Bromocriptine is an agonist of dopamine D_2 receptors. Stimulation of these receptors, which are thought to be located on the pituitary lactotrophs or in the hypothalamus, leads to an inhibition of prolactin secretion.

Vasopressin

Arginine vasopressin (AVP) is the major hormone regulating blood osmotic pressure. It is released from the posterior pituitary from nerve terminals, the axons of which originate mainly in the supraoptic nucleus of the hypothalamus. AVP is also a neurotransmitter in certain areas of the brain. Despite evidence that it is associated with and may facilitate certain aspects of memory and learning in rats (Kovacs, Bohus and Versteed, 1974), little attention has been paid to AVP in mental disorders. In one recent study (Raskind et al., 1986), the AVP concentration in the cerebrospinal fluid was found to be significantly reduced in patients with Alzheimer's disease, in whom there was severe memory impairment. In puerperal mental disorders, studies of AVP have been carried out only in association with changes in electrolyte balance (see pp. 100–102).

Oxytocin

This peptide hormone consists of nine amino acids and is structurally similar to AVP. It is released from nerve terminals in the posterior pituitary arising from axons originating in the supraoptic and paraventricular nuclei of the hypothalamus. Considering the crucial importance of oxytocin to parturition and lactation, it is surprising that so little attention has been paid to it by researchers in puerperal mental illness. Oxytocin is essential for promoting the expulsive phase of labour, where it induces synchronous contractions of the uterine muscle. After delivery, oxytocin release instigates milk ejection from the nipples following suckling stimulation by the child. Oxytocin has been shown in animal studies to retard learning and memory (Kovacs, 1986) but in humans there is no association between cerebrospinal fluid oxytocin levels and memory deficits in disorders such as Alzheimer's disease (Raskind et al., 1986).

Growth hormone

This peptide hormone is produced by the anterior pituitary. During pregnancy the placenta produces a hormone, hPL, which has metabolic and growth-stimulating properties similar to growth hormone (GH) and with the lactogenic activity of prolactin. No research on the association between either GH or hPL and puerperal mental disorder has yet been carried out.

GH secretion appears to be influenced in part by α_2-adrenoceptors which are probably situated in the hypothalamus, the anterior pituitary or possibly in part of the limbic system. Changes in the sensitivity of central α_2-adrenoceptors have been associated with endogenous depression (Charney et al., 1981; Checkley et al., 1984). Intravenous administration of the α_2-adrenoceptor agonist, clonidine, produces a dose-dependent increase in plasma GH concentration. This phenomenon has been used as an index of central α_2-adrenoceptor responsiveness (Charney et al., 1981; Checkley et al., 1984).

General comments

We have briefly reviewed recent research into hormonal aspects of puerperal mental illness, and have tried to emphasize both what has been done and what remains to be done. Early studies have tested for possible differences in hormone concentrations between, for example, blues and non-blues sufferers or for changes in hormone levels that might be related to episodes of puerperal psychosis. Many hormonal investigations have been carried out using older, less sensitive assay techniques. Individual hormones have been measured in isolation rather than as part of a spectrum of endocrine change. All steroid hormones bind extensively to plasma proteins and the bound hormone is biologically inactive. No measurements have yet been made of the free, unbound, plasma concentration of these hormones in women with puerperal mental illness. There has been little attempt to categorize puerperal disturbances in terms of underlying or suspected endocrine abnormality. Where little or no difference in hormone level has been found between normal women and those suffering from mood disturbance, no attempt has been made to suggest or investigate why this should be so. Sometimes there may be faulty technique, laboratory or clinical, but it may well be that hormonal concentrations are not as important as the receptors to which they bind and the biochemical events which these receptors influence. There is now much evidence that changes in both neurotransmitter and hormone receptor *numbers* may be implicated in some mental and systemic disorders. Thus, an increase in *post mortem* dopamine receptor density has been claimed in specific brain areas of some patients with schizophrenia, compared with controls (Owen et al., 1978). An increase in central α_2-adrenoceptor sensitivity may be present in patients with endogenous depression (Charney et al., 1981; Checkley et al., 1984) and some studies also indicate that platelet α_2-adrenoceptor numbers are similarly increased (Garcia-Sevilla et al., 1981). A change in insulin receptor sensitivity has been postulated as one aetiological feature of type II diabetes (Montague, 1983). Recently, Gormley et al. (1985) have demonstrated that in unmedicated patients with major depressive disorder, glucocorticoid receptor numbers are significantly reduced compared to controls. It is quite possible that receptor changes may similarly play a role in the aetiology of puerperal mental disorders.

Other biochemical factors

In this section we discuss the non-endocrine factors which have been studied in postpartum mental illness and closely related disorders such as premenstrual tension and endogenous depression. The major part of this discussion involves neurotransmitters, their receptors, metabolizing enzymes and second messenger systems. There are also sections on vitamins and electrolytes.

Neurotransmission

It is now 50 years since the chemical nature of neurotransmission was conclusively established firstly in the peripheral and autonomic nervous systems and then in the central nervous system. The essential features of neurotransmission (the means by which nerve fibres communicate with each other and with other cells) are now well established. It is known that electrical impulses or action potentials pass along the nerve axon and depolarize the nerve terminal, resulting in a release of chemical neurotransmitter. The amount of neurotransmitter released is dependent on the frequency with which action potentials arrive at the nerve terminal. The neurotransmitter passes across the gap between the nerve terminal and the cell with which it is communicating (referred to as the postsynaptic cell) and binds to specific receptor sites on the cell's surface. Stimulation of the receptors by the neurotransmitter leads to an electrophysiological and/or biochemical change in the postsynaptic cell. These changes are often effected within the postsynaptic cell by the release of another chemical called a 'second messenger'. Following stimulation of the receptors, the neurotransmitter is removed, either by being taken up into the nerve terminal (re-uptake) or by enzymatic degradation. In some neurotransmission systems, stimulation of receptors located on the nerve terminal itself (presynaptic receptors) results in a reduction in the amount of neurotransmitter released.

In 1954, the observation that the powerful hallucinogen, lysergide (LSD), was a potent antagonist of the neurotransmitter 5-HT, led to early suggestions that disorders of neurotransmission might be involved in the aetiology of mental disorders. A biochemical theory of affective disorder, adumbrated by Pare and Sandler (1959), was proposed by Schildkraut (1965). Such theories, based on the results of animal models and on the observations of drug treatment in humans, have now been shown to be simplistic (Stone, 1983). The original catecholamine theory of affective disorders (Schildkraut, 1965) proposed that depressive mood disorders in humans were the result of catecholamine neurotransmitter deficiency, particularly in those nerve terminals innervating key brain areas influencing mood and behaviour. It was suggested that depletion of these neurotransmitters would result in reduced neurotransmitter release at their respective synapses, resulting in reduced stimulation of postsynaptic receptors and reduced stimulatory activity of the centres regulating mood and behaviour. The theory was based on the observation that euphoriants such as amphetamine were powerful stimulators of noradrenaline and dopamine release, and that the drug reserpine, which can cause severe depression in humans, brought about loss of noradrenaline and dopamine from their respective nerve terminals. It is now apparent that defects in other neurotransmitter systems e.g. 5-HT, are also associated with affective disorders. In animal studies, chronic administration of antidepressant drugs is associated with changes in neurotransmitter receptor numbers and receptor sensitivity (Stone, 1983). The demonstration of increased dopamine receptor numbers in *post mortem* brain tissue of patients with schizophrenia (Owen *et al.*, 1978) and of decreased α_2-adrenoceptor and 5-HT receptor sensitivity in severely depressed patients (Charney *et al.*, 1981; Charney, Heninger and Sternberg, 1984) has focused researchers' attention on to neurotransmitter receptors rather than on the neurotransmitters or their degradative enzymes.

Indirect techniques currently available for investigating changes in brain neurotransmission include measurement of the concentration of brain neurotransmitters and their metabolites in blood, urine and cerebrospinal fluid. Although noradrenaline and 5-HT are present in the bloodstream, changes in circulating neurotransmitter concentrations show little correlation with mood change in most published studies because much of the noradrenaline and 5-HT present in blood does not originate from the CNS. These amines probably derive peripherally, mainly from sympathetic nerve terminals and intestinal chromaffin cells, respectively. Like the amines themselves, the urinary excretion of their metabolites is not a reliable indicator of central production of the parent neurotransmitter, even though Maas et al. (1972) claimed that the noradrenaline metabolite, 4-hydroxy-3-methoxyphenethyleneglycol (HMPG), was a reliable indicator of central noradrenaline metabolism, a view that has since been hotly disputed (Blombery et al., 1980). Certainly, the excretion of 5-hydroxyindoleacetic acid (5-HIAA), the major metabolite of 5-HT, cannot be taken as a reliable indicator of central 5-HT metabolism (Bertilsson et al., 1982; Linnoila et al., 1983), though changes in cerebrospinal fluid 5-HIAA concentrations may, to some extent, mirror 5-HT metabolism in the brain.

Neurotransmitter receptors are currently investigated by measuring the number and affinity of specific receptors present in a given amount of tissue or by measuring the magnitude of the specific response generated when the receptors are stimulated by the neurotransmitter or one of its chemical analogues (receptor responsiveness). Receptor binding is measured by incubating brain tissue or platelets with increasing concentrations of a radioactive form of either the natural neurotransmitter or a closely related analogue. The degree to which the different concentrations of the radioactive ligand bind to the receptor is determined. The maximum specific binding (B_{max}) is an *estimate* of the number of specific binding sites or receptors present and is expressed per weight of tissue or protein. The affinity (K_D) of the ligand for the receptors is also determined simultaneously.

Apart from Positron Emission Tomography (PET), Single Photon Computed Emission Tomography (SPECT) and Nuclear Magnetic Resonance (NMR) scanning, the direct assessment of changes in brain neurotransmitter receptor binding is only possible using *post mortem* samples, but several indirect methods of receptor measurement are available. Since neurotransmitter receptors regulate the secretion of many pituitary hormones, changes in the rate of secretion of selected hormones have been used as estimates of changes in central neurotransmitter receptor sensitivity. Thus, GH secretion is enhanced by stimulation of central α_2-adrenoceptors by the α_2-adrenoceptor agonist, clonidine (Charney et al., 1981; Checkley et al., 1984). In patients with endogenous depression, the increase in GH secretion induced by clonidine is significantly reduced, indicating a reduction in α_2-adrenoceptor responsiveness (Charney et al., 1981; Checkley et al., 1984). A more controversial indirect estimate of central neurotransmitter receptors is provided by studies using blood platelets. Some biochemical features of the platelet are similar to those of CNS neurones

(Sneddon, 1973). These include the possession of 5-HT_2 receptors, α_2-adrenoceptors, 5-HT uptake, imipramine binding and monoamine oxidase (MAO) activity. The responses to platelet 5-HT_2 and α_2-adrenoceptor stimulation are mediated via separate second messenger systems, the phosphoinositol system and the adenylate cyclase system, respectively. Brain 5-HT_2 receptor and α_2-adrenoceptor responses are also mediated by these sytems. Platelet α_2-adrenoceptor numbers may be increased (Garcia-Sevilla et al., 1981) or may remain unchanged (Stahl et al., 1983) in severe depression, while chronic antidepressant treatment increases platelet 5-HT receptor numbers (Cowen et al., 1986). A defect in platelet 5-HT uptake has been demonstrated in endogeneous depression (Tuomisto and Tukiainen, 1976; Meltzer et al., 1981) which may be connected with the ability to respond to tricyclic antidepressants.

The extrapolation of the results of platelet receptor, uptake and enzyme studies to brain neurones remains controversial, though their use as markers of affective illness may still be valid (Elliott, 1984; Slotkin et al., 1986).

Noradrenaline neurotransmission

Noradrenaline and metabolites   Most studies in this area in women with puerperal mental illness have concentrated on monitoring possible changes in concentrations of monoamines or their precursors. Treadway et al. (1969) claimed to find a relationship between reduced urinary noradrenaline excretion and depressed mood in pregnancy but identified no significant relationship between postpartum mood change and any amine or amine metabolite. Kuevi et al. (1983) demonstrated a drop in plasma noradrenaline and adrenaline concentrations in blues patients on the day before an episode of dysphoria and 'emotional lability'. However, there was no clear difference in the excretion patterns of these hormones in their groups of blues and non-blues sufferers so that no conclusions could be drawn.

Despite earlier claims that urinary 4-hydroxy-3-methoxyphenethylene-glycol (HMPG) excretion is a reliable indicator of central noradrenaline turnover (Maas et al., 1972) and may be employed as a means for differentiating between subcategories of depressive disorder (Schildkraut et al., 1978), recent work suggests that it is a good guide only to *total* body noradrenaline turnover (Linnoila et al., 1983). Even so, this finding does not necessarily preclude its use in the diagnosis and classification of depression. A detailed examination of the methodology and psychopathology of HMPG is provided in a monograph by Maas (1983).

α_2-Adrenoceptors   Several recent studies have demonstrated an apparent defect in both central and platelet α_2-adrenoceptors in endogenous depression (Charney et al., 1981; Garcia-Sevilla et al., 1981, 1986). α_2-adrenoceptors have been studied in blood platelets: in some studies those platelets from untreated endogenous depressives show a significant increase in α_2-adrenoceptor numbers (B_{max}) compared with those from healthy matched controls (Garcia-Sevilla et al., 1981, 1986) while others have shown that α_2-adrenoceptor numbers are unchanged (Stahl et al., 1983). In

the CNS, α_2-adrenoceptors are located presynaptically and postsynaptically (U'Pritchard, 1984). Stimulation of the presynaptic receptors leads to a reduction in noradrenaline release and thus to a reduced stimulation of receptors on the postsynaptic cell (Langer, 1980). In puerperal mental disorders, only platelet α_2-adrenoceptor studies have been carried out, because the measurement of *central* α_2-adrenoceptor activity involves the determination of GH secretion during an intravenous infusion of clonidine (Charney *et al.*, 1981; Checkley *et al.*, 1984) which might be impracticable during the puerperium. Jones *et al.* (1983) reported that platelet α_2-adrenoceptor numbers varied during the menstrual cycle; the highest receptor number occurred at the onset of menstruation and values then fell by 74–79% by the middle of the cycle. However, Sundaresan *et al.* (1985) found no significant difference in platelet α_2-adrenoceptor numbers during various stages of the menstrual cycle. This study was flawed in that full saturation curves for the binding of the antagonist ligand, ^{3}H-yohimbine, were not prepared so that the maximum binding was an estimate and no dissociation constant for the ligand binding could be derived. Roberts *et al.* (1985) found no difference in platelet α_2-adrenoceptor numbers or sensitivity between pregnant and non-pregnant women.

Metz *et al.* (1983) have investigated platelet α_2-adrenoceptor binding in 28 women, both pre- and postpartum, using the antagonist ligand, ^{3}H-yohimbine. They found that α_2-adrenoceptor numbers were higher prepartum compared with non-pregnant controls, dropping in the puerperium, the greatest fall occurring in the period immediately after the first puerperal week. In women who reported maternity blues symptoms, receptor binding capacity, i.e. receptor number, was significantly greater than in women who did not experience the blues. The blues rating was by means of a self-rating questionnaire. In non-blues sufferers, platelet α_2-adrenoceptor binding fell to control non-pregnant levels 10 days postpartum, whereas in the blues group values remained significantly higher than both puerperal non-blues sufferers and non-pregnant controls. Metz *et al.* found no relationship between pre- or postpartum oestradiol and progesterone levels and either platelet α_2-adrenoceptor binding capacity or the blues. They noted that the precipitous postpartum fall in concentrations of both hormones from their prepartum level preceded the decrease in platelet α_2-adrenoceptor binding. In a further study using platelets, Best *et al.* (1985) examined α_2-adrenoceptor binding to intact platelets during the early puerperium. α_2-Adrenoceptor binding, as demonstrated by specific binding of ^{3}H-yohimbine, was significantly reduced at 10 days postpartum compared to the prepartum level, but the prepartum values were not significantly different from those in non-pregnant women.

We may conclude from Metz's work that the increased platelet α_2-adrenoceptor binding in puerperal mental illness may mirror a parallel change in central α_2-adrenoceptor binding. Studies of α_2-adrenoceptors in human platelets are controversial, however, because the demonstrated changes in receptor numbers may depend on whether an agonist or antagonist ligand is used (Elliott, 1984) or whether whole or lysed platelets are studied. In the platelet, α_2-adrenoceptors may not be linked to any functional post-receptor mechanism, and changes in them may also not be linked temporally to changes in their CNS counterparts (Siever *et al.*, 1984). It is also possible that, in the platelet, changes in post-receptor responsiveness may occur without parallel changes in membrane receptor numbers or affinity and that changes in plasma catecholamine concentrations may induce changes in platelet receptor numbers (Kafka and Paul, 1986).

β-*Adrenoceptors*   Both types of β-adrenoceptor (β$_1$ and β$_2$) are present in mammalian CNS neurotransmission systems and these receptors are located mainly on the postsynaptic cell (Sulser, 1984). A reduction in CNS β-adrenoceptor sensitivity has been demonstrated in rats treated chronically with tricyclic antidepressants (Sulser, 1984). Thompson *et al.* (1985) have shown that central β-adrenoceptor sensitivity is increased in patients treated with desipramine, while Healy, Carney and Leonard (1983) noted that lymphocyte β-adrenoceptor binding is increased in depressed patients. No studies of β-adrenoceptors in puerperal mental illness have been carried out. However, Steiner *et al.* (1973) reported that the β-adrenoceptor antagonist, propranolol, is a more effective treatment for postpartum psychosis than chlorpromazine. In a rather limited study, using high dosage, the authors claimed that clinical improvement occurred within three days whereas response to chlorpromazine is often delayed for about a month.

The tyramine conjugation test
Tyramine is a monoamine which can be formed from the amino acid tyrosine. It is structurally similar to noradrenaline and dopamine and is capable of releasing these neurotransmitters from their respective nerve terminals. Tyramine occurs naturally in food products as diverse as cheese, Chianti wine and Marmite.

Sandler and his colleagues have repeatedly demonstrated that patients with depressive illness show a consistent and highly significant decrease in urinary output of sulphate-conjugated tyramine compared with controls, when challenged with an oral tyramine load (Sandler *et al.*, 1975; Bonham Carter *et al.*, 1978a). This finding has now been confirmed by others (Harrison *et al.*, 1984). Although the finding is more clear-cut for tyramine, they have also identified a similar impairment of octopamine and dopamine metabolism in affected subjects (Sandler, Bonham-Carter and Walker, 1983). The nature of the biochemical lesion remains unknown; platelets from depressed patients, for instance, possess their full complement of the sulphate-conjugating enzyme, phenolsulphotransferase (Bonham Carter *et al.*, 1981). Even so, the tyramine conjugation deficit seems likely to be an important trait marker for depressive illness.

The first indication that they might be dealing with a trait marker emerged with the realization that the conjugation deficit persists even after clinical recovery (Bonham Carter *et al.*, 1987a). Thus, it can probably be considered as a marker for predisposition to the illness rather than of the depressive state itself, and used as such as a predictor for vulnerability. A population study of tyramine-conjugating ability performed blind to clinical status showed a significantly higher proportion of subjects with a lifetime history of depressive illness in low compared with high conjugated tyramine excretors (Bonham Carter *et al.*, 1980b). In a recent survey (Hale *et al.*, 1986), the only two control subjects showing values that overlapped with the depressive range also turned out to be the only two controls with a family history of depressive illness. The most convincing evidence on this point to date is that unaffected first degree relatives of probands with endogenous depression, even those thus far clinically unaffected, show a highly significant decrease in tyramine-conjugating ability compared with controls (Hale *et al.*, 1986).

Perhaps the most dramatic finding to emerge is that the deficit is a clean marker for *endogenous* depression (Harrison *et al.*, 1984; Hale *et al.*, 1986). The difference between patients and controls has proved to be very highly significant and so distinct, in fact, that Hale *et al.* are almost confident enough to recommend the investigation as a biochemical test for 'endogenousness'. Patients with non-endogenous (neurotic) depression were not significantly different from controls (Hale *et al.*, 1986). Despite earlier impressions (Sandler *et al.*, 1975), the degree of conjugation deficiency appears to be independent of clinical severity of depression (Hale *et al.*, 1986).

The biochemical lesion is neither an artefact of sulphate deficiency (Bonham Carter *et al.*, 1980a) nor a result of impaired gastrointestinal motility (Bonham Carter *et al.*, 1978b). The number of bipolar patients so far examined by Hale *et al.* (1986) was insufficient to enable them to decide unequivocally whether the marker is also characteristic of this clinical condition. Whilst about half of a small group of patients with acute schizophrenia without apparent depression also manifest a tyramine conjugation deficit (Hale *et al.*, 1986), certain methodological questions related to precise diagnosis, drug status and completeness of urine collection need to be answered before these findings can form the basis of a unitarian hypothesis of functional mental illness.

To what extent can the tyramine conjugation test assist us in the study of postnatal depressive illness? A test such as this, which helps us to identify a predisposition to the illness, may well be of considerable value. If a group of such patients could be identified, they might be given appropriate social support in advance of the development of a depressive episode and, perhaps, even prophylactic drug therapy. However, we must first establish whether childbirth itself is a depression-'triggering' event in patients shown by the tyramine test to possess this 'endogenous' diathesis: in other words, it is necessary to determine whether a greater proportion of patients with a conjugation deficit develop postnatal depression, compared with those without such a deficit. Latest tyramine conjugation findings (to be published) tend to place postpartum depressive illness firmly in the neurotic rather than the endogenous group.

5-Hydroxytryptamine and tryptophan
Nerve terminals which release 5-HT are widely distributed in human brain. 5-HT neurotransmission may be involved in the regulation of many brain functions such as sleep, temperature regulation, feeding, aggression and neuroendocrine secretion (Heninger, Charney and Sternberg, 1984). Many of these functions may be abnormal in depression. 5-HT is synthesized from the essential amino acid, tryptophan, in nerve terminals which release

5-HT. Tryptophan enters the brain by crossing the blood-brain barrier, apparently in competition with other neutral amino acids such as phenylalanine (Moller, 1980). After release, 5-HT is returned to the nerve terminal by an active re-uptake process. Any 5-HT which escapes re-uptake is degraded to the inactive metabolite, 5-HIAA, by the enzyme MAO.

Since the identification of at least two major CNS 5-HT receptor types (Peroutka and Snyder, 1983), the situation has, latterly, become much more complex (*see*, for example Hamon *et al.*, 1986; Murphy, 1986). Two studies have demonstrated reduced 5-HT receptor sensitivity in endogenous depression (Charney *et al.*, 1984; Heninger, Charney and Sternberg, 1984) by measuring the increase in PRL secretion in response to an intravenous tryptophan infusion. Several investigators have revealed an abnormality of platelet 5-HT uptake in endogenous depression (e.g. Tuomisto and Tukiainen, 1976; Meltzer *et al.*, 1981).

Platelet 5-HT uptake   The blood platelet possesses an active 5-HT uptake mechanism similar in some biochemical properties to that found in 5-HT CNS neurones (von Hahn, Honegger and Pletscher, 1980). However, platelets and 5-HT neurones appear to respond differently to chronic antidepressant drug therapy (Slotkin *et al.*, 1986). Castrén and Tuomisto (1983) reported that there was no significant difference in 5-HT uptake between pregnant and postpartum women. This is a surprising result since Ehrenkranz (1976) had demonstrated that physiological concentrations of oestradiol cause a 37% enhancement of 5-HT uptake in platelets *in vitro*. When Peters, Elliott and Grahame-Smith (1979) studied platelet 5-HT uptake in women taking combined oestrogen-progestogen contraceptives, they found that discontinuing the dosage for six days caused a significant decrease in 5-HT uptake compared with controls. In Castrén and Tuomisto's study, hormone levels were determined once in each patient, whereas Peters, Elliott and Grahame-Smith measured 5-HT uptake on three occasions in each of their patients and in controls. Taylor *et al.* (1984), using the Moos scale (Moos, 1968), found that there were symptom changes between the pre- and postmenstrual phases which were associated with changes in 5-HT uptake kinetics. In particular, behaviour, water retention and autonomic effects were highly significantly correlated with changes in affinity (K_m) for 5-HT uptake, while behaviour and, to a lesser extent, dysphoria, were negatively correlated with a change in maximum velocity (V_{max}). In contrast, Chan and Lee (1985) found no correlation between the mood ratings of the Moos scale and platelet 5-HT uptake during the menstrual cycle.

The sensitivity of platelet 5-HT uptake to changes in plasma hormone concentration merits further study in postpartum mental illness, though it must be remembered that for up to 10 days in postpartum women there will be platelets present in the circulation which have been exposed to the high prepartum levels of oestradiol and progesterone.

Platelet imipramine binding   In human platelets (Briley *et al.*, 1980; Paul *et al.*, 1981) and brain tissue (Rehavi *et al.*, 1980), imipramine binds to a 'receptor site' closely associated with, but not identical to, the uptake site for 5-HT. In depressed patients the number of platelet imipramine binding sites is decreased (Paul *et al.*, 1981).

Katona *et al.* (1985) found no significant difference in ^{3}H-imipramine maximum binding (B_{max}) in women during pregnancy compared to women at one, two or six weeks postpartum. There was, also, no significant difference in ^{3}H-imipramine binding (B_{max}) between pregnant and non-pregnant women. However, at seven days postpartum, the affinity of the receptors for ^{3}H-imipramine was reduced (demonstrated by a rise in the dissociation constant (K_D)) as compared to the value at two weeks and six weeks postpartum. None of the reported mood changes was shown to correlate with any of the changes in ligand receptor binding. This study, using lysed platelets, is interesting in that the reported mean maximum binding is some 10 times greater than in the other recent study (Best *et al.*, 1985) in which intact platelets were used. The significance of ^{3}H-imipramine binding studies in affective illness is not clear and some of the conclusions which have been reached are controversial (Elliott, 1984).

Plasma tryptophan   If an abnormality of 5-HT neurotransmission exists in postpartum mental illness, it is possible that it could arise from inadequate 5-HT release resulting from an inadequate supply of the 5-HT precursor, tryptophan. 5-HT synthesis in the CNS is very sensitive to changes in brain tryptophan concentration because tryptophan hydroxylase, the initial enzyme in the biosynthetic sequence converting the precursor to 5-HT, is never fully saturated under physiological conditions. Thus, a rise or fall in brain tryptophan concentration, induced by changes in plasma concentration, would have a direct influence on 5-HT synthesis and release.

In 1976, Stein *et al.* demonstrated a relationship between lowered levels of *free* plasma tryptophan and certain features of depression in 18 puerperal patients. These observations were confirmed by Handley *et al.* (1977) who showed that *free* plasma tryptophan and cortisol correlated significantly with depression. Neither study, however, instituted controls for protein catabolism although both attempted to control for dietary intake of amino acids. When Handley *et al.* (1980) repeated this study with a much larger patient group, they found no differences in *free* plasma tryptophan between blues and non-blues sufferers. Harris (1980) could find no evidence of a reduction in blues symptoms in a prospective double blind trial of tryptophan versus placebo in 55 postpartum women; here again, there was no control for peripheral tryptophan catabolism and tryptophan plasma levels were not determined. The role of this amino acid in the pathogenesis of the blues is thus as controversial as it is in non-puerperal depression. Moller, Kirk and Honoré (1979) showed that neither *free* nor *total* plasma tryptophan concentrations in patients with either bipolar or unipolar affective disorder were significantly different from normal controls and that antidepressant therapy produced no change in tryptophan levels. It is uncertain from these studies which tryptophan fraction, free or total, is relevant to the prediction of brain tryptophan concentrations. Handley *et al.* (1980) have suggested that the blood-brain barrier entry mechanism or membrane carrier of tryptophan and other amino acids might be defective in puerperal depression, an idea originally proposed by Rafaelson (1974) in an attempt to explain affective illness and the cyclic nature of manic depressive psychosis.

Monoamine oxidase (MAO)

MAO is an important enzyme in the catabolism of both catecholamines (noradrenaline and adrenaline) and 5-HT. It is bound to the outer mitochondrial membrane and is found in a wide range of tissues. The existence of two forms of MAO, termed A and B, has been demonstrated on the basis of their differing substrate affinities and inhibitor sensitivities (Johnston, 1968). MAO A oxidizes the classical neurotransmitter monoamines, noradrenaline and 5-HT; MAO B metabolizes a wider range of substrates, including phenylethylamine and other 'trace amines', methylhistamine and benzylamine, while both forms oxidize tyramine and dopamine. MAO in a number of tissues is sensitive to hormonal changes and pathological states and this aspect has been reviewed by Murphy (1976) and by Sandler (1976). An interesting finding is that human endometrial MAO activity rises steeply at about day 21 of a normal menstrual cycle, an event corresponding with peak plasma progesterone level (Southgate, 1972). Treatment of rats with progesterone also causes an increase in endometrial MAO (Collins et al., 1970) and this progesterone-induced increase is confined to MAO A activity (Sandler, 1978). Belmaker et al. (1974) claimed that platelet MAO activity also changes according to the state of the menstrual cycle. They attributed their inability to correlate these changes precisely with the cyclic changes in oestradiol and progesterone levels to the fact that platelets have a 10-day life span so that any platelet sample would contain platelets of different ages. However, they also found that mood variation, as measured by the Moos scale (Moos, 1968), did not correlate with changes in MAO activity either. Redmond et al. (1975) noted a premenstrual MAO decline in platelet samples from rhesus monkeys. Feine et al. (1977), however, found no relationship between the menstrual cycle and platelet MAO activity. George and Wilson (1981a,b) examined platelet MAO activity in 38 women in the first postpartum week, using tyramine as substrate. They showed that the degree of depression constituting 'the blues' was significantly correlated with platelet MAO activity throughout the six-day period under investigation, while loss of concentration and listlessness correlated with MAO activity only on days 2 and 4 of the study. As with the foregoing work, care must be exercised in interpreting these results; with a platelet life of approximately 10 days, some platelets would have been present even at the end of the study (seven days postpartum) which had been influenced by prenatal hormone levels and events. The significance of such work with platelet MAO is that it is possible that platelet enzyme changes reflect corresponding changes in the brain. There is some evidence that both platelet MAO activity and 5-HT uptake resemble their respective CNS counterparts (Sneddon, 1973; von Hahn, Honegger and Pletscher, 1980) but the use of platelet MAO activity for classification or prediction of mental illness remains controversial. These aspects have been reviewed by Coper et al. (1979) and Sandler, Reveley and Glover (1981).

Second messenger systems

The translation of neurotransmitter or peptide hormone receptor stimulation into a response is effected in many cells via a second messenger system. Usually, receptor stimulation is coupled to the increase or decrease in the activity of a membrane-bound enzyme regulating the production of an intracellular 'hormone' or second messenger, which itself can enhance or retard the activity of some of the key enzymes of metabolism in the cell. Two major second messenger systems are associated with neurotransmitter receptors: the cyclic AMP-adenylate cyclase system and the phosphatidyl inositol system. So far, most research on affective disorders and second messengers has concentrated on the cyclic AMP (cAMP) system. The major elements of the phospho-inositol system have been reviewed recently by Downes (1986).

Cyclic AMP   A number of studies have demonstrated an association between mood and cAMP concentrations (Abdullah and Hamadah, 1970; Naylor *et al.*, 1974). Naylor's group demonstrated a variable cAMP level in phase with affective state in a group of patients with manic depressive psychosis, higher values being associated with manic symptoms. Ballinger's group made a detailed assessment of urinary excretion and of plasma and red cell concentration of cAMP during the third trimester of pregnancy and the first 10 days postpartum. There were significant positive correlations between both urinary cAMP excretion and mood elevation, and between whole blood cell cAMP level and mood elevation (Ballinger *et al.*, 1979, 1982). It was not apparent from these studies whether cAMP measurement in the three different tissues were statistically correlated with one another throughout the study period. Precisely what clinical changes cAMP measurements reflect, in any case, is very difficult to say! cAMP does cross cell membrane barriers and its efflux from cells and tissues increases when such preparations are stimulated by certain peptides or catecholamine neurotransmitters (Broadus, 1977). Its formation occurs as part of the second messenger mechanism—the process by which receptor stimulation is translated into biochemical activation inside the cell. Since many hormones are thought to influence cellular events via this cAMP mechanism its quantification can only indicate a *general* increase in hormonal activity and not specific activity of one hormone or hormonal group.

Electrolytes

Some of the earliest work identifying biochemical changes in puerperal mental disorders was concerned with plasma and urinary electrolyte concentrations. Studies of this kind, relating to the 'blues' syndrome, were extensively reviewed by Stein (1982). He indicated that changes in mood may correlate with changes in blood sodium concentration but not with urinary vasopressin (AVP) output (Stein, Marsh and Morton, 1981). However, since collecting-duct receptors for AVP are on the 'blood' rather than the 'urinary' side of the renal tubular cells, measurement of *plasma* AVP concentration may well have shown some relationship to mood and/or plasma sodium. Plasma renin and aldosterone levels were not measured. Stein (1982) also considered the involvement of the renin-angiotensin system in pregnancy and the puerperium in relation to puerperal mood change. Plasma renin levels rise in pregnancy, partly as a result of placental renin secretion (Simpson and MacDonald, 1981), and then fall after parturition. An increase in renin secretion causes a rise in plasma angiotensin II concentration which stimulates the thirst 'centre' in the hypothalamus as part of its complex role in the homeostatic regulation of sodium metabolism and the extracellular fluid volume (Reid, Morris and Ganong, 1977). Stein has recorded many cases of thirst abatement coinciding with depressive symptoms on days 3 and 4 postpartum which might coincide with a reduction in renin secretion. In a further study, Stein *et al.* (1984) demonstrated that a peak period for mood change in the puerperium occurred between the second and seventh days postpartum and that this also correlated with a significant weight loss, an increase in thirst and a rise in urinary sodium excretion. The peak mood change did not correlate, however, with any change in urinary vasopressin concentration. Gjerris *et al.* (1985) measured AVP concentration in the cerebrospinal fluid and plasma of patients with either endogenous or neurotic depression or with mania. They found that cerebrospinal fluid but not plasma AVP concentrations were lower in endogenous and neurotic depressives, but unchanged in mania compared to controls, and suggested that reduced AVP values are associated with depressive illness. Throughout their study, cerebrospinal fluid AVP levels were correlated with plasma AVP concentrations and neither variable was related to cerebrospinal fluid or plasma osmolality. Even allowing for a separate role for centrally released non-pituitary AVP, these results are physiologically difficult to interpret and the role of AVP in affective disorders remains interesting but enigmatic. Stein *et al.* (1984) explained these findings on the basis of a possible increase in vasopressin hydrolysis during pregnancy. Thus, further work on these phenomena or electrolyte and body water changes should measure blood and urinary vasopressin concentration and the activity of peptidases which hydrolyse vasopressin. The aetiology of this phenomenon might be explained by the observation that stress, induced by competitive mental tasks, brings about reduced sodium and fluid excretion in young volunteers (Light *et al.*, 1983). Thus, the observation of Stein might be explained in terms of the stress of parturition which may then be an aetiological factor in puerperal mood disorders.

Riley (1979) has suggested that increased plasma calcium is important in determining the onset of puerperal mental disorders in women without a genetic background of mental illness. However, although the patients she described had a raised plasma calcium in relation to mood change, values were still within the normal range for puerperal women.

Recently, Riley and Watt (1985) examined the plasma ionized calcium and plasma total 'corrected' calcium (i.e. corrected for individual variation in serum albumin concentration) in the puerperium. They found that puerperal psychiatric patients without a previous history of mental illness had a significantly higher mean total serum calcium and ionized calcium concentration than those with a previous history. The mean ionized calcium concentration was also significantly higher in the group without previous psychiatric symptoms than in both a control group with non-puerperal psychiatric illness and a symptom-free puerperal group. However, psychiatric symptom ratings correlated only with the total serum calcium in the patients with no previous symptoms. The ionized calcium concentration showed no significant correlation with psychiatric symptoms in any of the patient groups studied. A clearer result might have been obtained if the calcium concentration had been measured by a more accurate method such as atomic absorption spectroscopy or electrochemistry. These results are of interest in suggesting an apparent biochemical distinction between puerperal psychiatric patients either with or without a previous psychiatric history. The plasma parathyroid hormone (PTH) concentration rises during pregnancy (Watney and Rudd, 1974) but the physiological activity of PTH is antagonized by the high circulating levels of oestradiol present (Tan, Raman and Sinnathray, 1972). Riley and Watt (1985) therefore suggested that the rapid decline in plasma oestradiol after parturition might permit an increased PTH activity, and coupled with the absence of fetal demand for calcium, might lead to hypercalcaemia in some women whose calcium homeostatic mechanisms were slow to adapt.

It is possible that mania is associated with an abnormality of calcium ion influx in cells. Dubovsky *et al.* (1986) have reported that verapamil, a potent inhibitor of calcium ion influx into cells, has a significant anti-manic action compared to placebo. Perhaps there is a role for verapamil and other calcium ion antagonists in the treatment of postpartum mania.

Vitamins

Although Livingston, Macleod and Applegarth (1978) found no evidence for vitamin B_6 (pyridoxine) deficiency in women suffering from postpartum depression, some success has been claimed in alleviating puerperal depression with pyridoxine administration: according to Riley (1982) daily administration of 100 mg of pyridoxine for 30 days postpartum causes a statistically significant decrease in depressive mood scores in blues sufferers. Blood pyridoxine concentration was not measured in these patients and it is thus uncertain whether a deficiency of this vitamin was present at the outset of the study. Since vitamin B_6 is necessary for the decarboxylation step in the formation of 5-HT from tryptophan, a deficiency might be responsible for disturbances in the 5-HT/tryptophan neurotransmitter system.

Methodology

Whenever conflicting results are obtained from analysis of what appears to be the same set of clinical phenomena, we must first consider the likelihood of differences in the population under scrutiny. Another equally important cause of variation, however, must be differences in methodology. A difference in assay technique or, perhaps, in the method of psychiatric assessment, may turn out to be the main source of discrepancy. The range of rating scales in the papers reviewed here is very wide and some are obviously inappropriate to maternal mental illness. Some standardization in this area would be helpful. A standardized scale developed specifically for childbearing women such as the Maternal Adjustment and Maternal Attitude Scale (MAMA) (Kumar, Robson and Smith, 1984) and measures of depressive symptoms such as the Edinburgh Postnatal Depression Scale (Cox, Holden and Sagovsky, 1987) or the modified General Health Questionnaire proposed by Nott and Cutts (1982) might prove to be more generally useful. The greatest variations in endocrine and biochemical measurements appear to occur in times of blood and urine sampling and in mode of assay.

In certain endocrine studies, although blood sampling took place at a fixed time on each occasion, this was often at an inappropriate time of the day for the particular hormone in question. For example, Nott *et al.* (1976) measured plasma PRL concentrations between 9.00 am and 12.00 noon on the day of their study, apparently without taking into account when breast feeding had occurred and whether the woman had been active or at rest immediately before the sample had been taken. Although Kuevi *et al.* (1983) also limited their blood sampling to a particular time of day, they performed this task immediately after breast feeding when PRL levels would have been rising as a result of suckling. Again, in this study the degree of ambulation did not appear to have been taken into account, even though it is known to affect PRL levels. Another reason for discrepancies is the sensitivity and specificity of the various assays performed. Most steroid and polypeptide hormones can now be accurately measured by competitive binding radioimmunoassay procedures using relatively small plasma samples. Kuevi *et al.* (1983) have illustrated what can be done by measuring seven hormones simultaneously in postpartum women. The data from modern studies of this sort often conflict with earlier work performed by less specific chemical methods.

The appropriate timing for blood sampling should be worked out in a pilot study of the circadian rhythmicity of the hormone involved. Such investigations have been carried out for plasma cortisol in order to determine optimal timing for the dexamethasone suppression test (Green and Kane, 1983). Most endocrine studies have thus concentrated on comparing hormone levels obtained at a certain time of day between patient groups rather than comparing the circadian rhythmicity of the hormone on a particular day between patient groups. Seasonal variations of hormone secretion and any effect of activity should also be taken into account, as should drug administration. Some drug effects on hormone secretion, such as enhancement of PRL secretion by neuroleptics, are well known.

In biochemical studies, the investigators should ask themselves: 'Are we measuring an indicator of something physiologically important? What does it relate to?' Most clinicians would like such measurements to be a direct index of some central event. Urinary amine metabolite excretion measurements, in particular, are a quicksand for the unwary researcher (Koslow *et al.*, 1983) and before the urinary excretion of any material of this kind is measured, a study of its day-to-day variation in normal individuals should be carried out.

Because of its accessibility, the blood platelet has been intensively studied in CNS research because, in mammals at least, MAO B activity, 5-HT uptake and drug binding sites are similar to those found in central monoaminergic neurones (Sneddon, 1973; von Hahn, Honegger and Pletscher, 1980). Despite the widespread use of platelet studies in endogenous depression, only two recent investigations have been performed involving measurement of MAO activity (George and Wilson, 1981a, b) and three on ligand receptor binding (Metz *et al.*, 1983; Best *et al.*, 1985; Katona *et al.*, 1985). Such MAO and receptor binding studies are easily performed and the methodology is readily available—*see*, for example, Tipton and Youdim (1976) for MAO assay procedure. As for uptake studies, several uptake processes exist in the platelet membrane but it is possible that the rapid uptake carrier (i.e. the one exhibiting maximum uptake velocity at a given substrate concentration after only 10 s incubation) is that most closely associated with affective abnormalities. Its kinetics can be measured by the method of Gordon and Olverman (1978). Receptor studies and their pitfalls are well described by Bennett (1978) and platelet receptor studies have recently been reviewed by Elliott (1984) and Kafka and Paul (1986).

Implications

The results of endocrine research in puerperal mental illness are not encouraging. Despite a profound feeling that hormones 'have something to do with it', there are few positive data. Pituitary failure giving rise to Sheehan's syndrome, with associated psychiatric changes, provides an obvious endocrine cause of mental illness. Even so, this syndrome is a rarity and obviously cannot be the basis of every case of postpartum psychosis. Hamilton (1962, 1977) has recorded cases of puerperal depression with low circulating thyroxine levels where thyroxine therapy relieved psychotic symptoms. It is evident from these and other observations that there may well be a number of separate endocrine syndromes presenting as puerperal mental illness. Thus, it is unlikely that investigation of one system will shed much light on the endocrine mechanisms of puerperal mental illness in general. It seems likely that multiple hormone assays would provide more information in this area. In this way, an endocrine classification of postpartum mental illness might be built up.

We need to know what effects any of the hormonal changes we observe are having on the CNS, particularly on enzyme activity and neuronal receptors. As a precedent, Drago (1982) has shown that prolactin can influence dopamine release in the tubero-infundibular system while Gordon, Borison and Diamond (1980) have demonstrated dopamine receptor modulation by oestrogen. Oestradiol increases MAO turnover in rat brain (Luine and McEwen, 1977) and it also influences MAO activity in the endometrium (Collins *et al.*, 1970). It is well known that anterior pituitary hormone secretion is controlled by systems involving hypothalamic releasing/inhibitory factors which are themselves controlled by neurotransmitters. Prolactin release may be under the control of both dopamine-releasing and 5-HT-releasing neurones (Quattrone *et al.*, 1979). It is thus difficult to know where in the chain of events the aetiological process of postpartum psychiatric disturbance begins.

Changes in thyroid activity as such are probably not associated with the blues since they usually occur 3–4 weeks postpartum; in one study, TSH levels were the same in blues and non-blues partients during the first puerperal week (George and Wilson, 1983). Some (e.g. Dalton, 1980) have attributed symptoms of the blues to a drop in progesterone secretion after parturition. However, four studies (Nott *et al.*, 1976; Ballinger *et al.*, 1982; Kuevi *et al.*, 1983; Metz *et al.*, 1983) have shown no difference in progesterone levels between blues and non-blues sufferers. It may be the *rate* of fall that is important but appropriate multiple daily measurements to check this possibility have not been carried out. Progesterone receptor characteristics in women susceptible to the blues have not so far been investigated. Metz *et al.* (1983) noted a reduction in α_2-adrenoceptor density after the postpartum drop in progesterone level which was much less pronounced in blues sufferers. Thus, they were similar to patients with endogenous depression studied by Garcia-Sevilla *et al.* (1981), i.e. they possessed greater numbers of α_2-adrenoceptors compared with their respective healthy controls. It is tempting to speculate on the possible role of progesterone and oestradiol in the mechanism of 'down-regulation' of α_2-adrenoceptors, although the levels of other hormones do fall as well in the immediate postpartum period.

Careful clinical and laboratory studies are obviously the key to the further unravelling and classification of puerperal illness. Technological advances have provided us with the tools for multiple biochemical assessments. Whether the measurements we are now able to make are the appropriate ones is a matter for the future to decide.

References

ABDULLAH, Y. H. and HAMADAH, K. (1970). 3,'5'-Cyclic adenosine monophosphate in depression and mania. *Lancet*, **i**, 378–381

ALDER, E. M., COOK, A., DAVIDSON, D., WEST, C.and BANCROFT, J. (1986). Hormones, mood and sexuality in lactating women. *British Journal of Psychiatry*, **148**, 74–79

ANDERSON, P. J. B., HANCOCK, K. W. and OAKEY, R.E.(1985). Non-protein-bound oestradiol and progesterone in human peripheral plasma before labour and delivery. *Journal of Endocrinology*, **104**, 7–15

BALLINGER, C. B., BUCKLEY, D. E., NAYLOR, G. J. and STANSFIELD, D. A. (1979). Emotional disturbance following childbirth: clinical findings and urinary excretion of cyclic AMP (adenosine 3,'5'-cyclic monophosphate). *Psychological Medicine*, **9**, 293–300

BALLINGER, C. B., KAY, D. S. G., NAYLOR, G. J. and SMITH, A. H. W. (1982). Some biochemical findings during pregnancy and after delivery in relation to mood change. *Psychological Medicine*, **12**, 549–556

BELMAKER, R. H., MURPHY, D. L., WYATT, R. J. and LORIAUX, L. (1974). Human platelet monoamine oxidase changes during the menstrual cycle. *Archives of General Psychiatry*, **31**, 553–556

BENNETT, J. P. (1978). Methods in binding studies. In: *Neurotransmitter Receptor Binding*, (H. I. Yamamura, S. J. Enna and M. J. Kuhar, eds), pp. 65–84. New York: Raven Press

BERTILSSON, L., TYBRING, G., BRAITHWAITE, R., TRASKAN-BENDZ, L. and ÅSBERG, M. (1982). Urinary excretion of 5-hydroxyindole acetic acid—no relationship to the level in the cerebrospinal fluid. *Acta Psychiatrica Scandinavica*, **66**, 190–198

BEST, N. R., COWEN, P. J., ELLIOTT, J. M., FRASER, S., GOSDEN, B. and STUMP, K. (1985). Changes in imipramine and α_2-adrenoceptor binding sites in the early puerperium. *British Journal of Clinical Pharmacology*, **19**, 555P

BLOMBERY, P. A., KOPIN, I. J., GORDON, E. K., MARKEY, S. P. and EBERT, M. H. (1980). Conversion of MHPG to vanillylmandelic acid. *Archives of General Psychiatry*, **37**, 1095–1098

BLOOM, F. E. (1983). The endorphins: a growing family of pharmacologically pertinent peptides. *Annual Review of Pharmacology and Toxicology*, **23**, 151–170

BOHNET, H. G. and MCNEILLY, A. S. (1979). Prolactin: assessment of its role in the human female. *Hormone and Metabolic Research*, **11**, 533–546

BONHAM CARTER, S. M., SANDLER, M., GOODWIN, B. L., SEPPING, P. and BRIDGES, P. K. (1978a). Decreased urinary output of tyramine and its metabolites in depression. *British Journal of Psychiatry*, **132**, 125–132

BONHAM CARTER, S. M., SANDLER, M., SEPPING, P. and BRIDGES, P. K. (1978b). Decreased conjugated tyramine output in depression: gastro-intestinal factors. *British Journal of Clinical Pharmacology*, **5**, 269–272

BONHAM CARTER, S. M., GOODWIN, B. L., SANDLER, M., GILLMAN, P. K.and BRIDGES, P. K. (1980a). Decreased conjugated tyramine output in depression: the effect of oral L-cysteine. *British Journal of Clinical Pharmacology*, **10**, 305–308

BONHAM CARTER, S. M., REVELEY, M. A., SANDLER, M. *et al.* (1980b). Decreased urinary output of conjugated tyramine is associated with lifetime vulnerability to depressive illness. *Psychiatry Research*, **3**, 13–31

BONHAM CARTER, S. M., GLOVER, V., SANDLER, M., GILLMAN, P. K. and BRIDGES, P. K. (1981). Human platelet phenolsulphotransferase: separate control of the two forms and activity range. *Clinica Chimica Acta*, **117**, 333–344

BONNAR, J., FRANKLIN, M., NOTT, P. N. and MCNEILLY, A. S. (1975). Effect of breast feeding on pituitary-ovarian function after childbirth. *British Medical Journal*, **iv**, 82–84

BOWER, W. H. and ALTSCHULE, M. D. (1956). Use of progesterone in the treatment of postpartum psychosis. *New England Journal of Medicine*, **254**, 157–162

BRILEY, M. S., LANGER, S. Z., RAISMAN, R., SECHTER, D. and ZARIFIAN, E. (1980). Tritiated imipramine binding sites are decreased in platelets of untreated depressed patients. *Science*, **209**, 303–304

BRINSMEAD, M., SMITH, R., SINGH, B., LEWIN, T.and OWENS, P. (1985). Peripartum concentrations of beta-endorphin and cortisol and maternal mood states. *Australian and New Zealand Journal of Obstetrics and Gynaecology*, **25**, 194–197

BROADUS, A. E. (1977). Clinical cyclic nucleotide research In: *Advances in Cyclic Nucleotide Research*, Vol. 8, (P. Greengard and G. A. Robison, eds), pp. 509–548. New York: Academic Press

CAMPBELL, J. L. and WINOKUR, G. (1985). Post-partum affective disorders: selected biological aspects In: *Recent Advances in Post-partum Psychiatric Disorders*, (D. G. Inwood, ed.), pp. 19–40. Washington: American Psychiatric Press.

CARROLL, B. J. and STEINER, M. (1978).The psychobiology of premenstrual dysphoria. The role of prolactin. *Psychoneuroendocrinology*, **3**, 171–180

CARROLL, B. J., FEINBERG, F., GREDEN, J. F. *et al.* (1981). Standardisation of the dexamethasone suppression test for the diagnosis of melancholia. *Advances in Biological Psychiatry*, **7**, 1–13

CASTRÉN, E. and TUOMISTO, J. (1983). Influence of the hormonal balance of late pregnancy on the active uptake of 5-hydroxytryptamine by human blood platelets. *Medical Biology*, **61**, 168–171

CHARNEY, D. S., HENINGER, G.R. and STERNBERG, D. E. (1984). Serotonin function and mechanism of action of antidepressant treatment. *Archives of General Psychiatry*, **41**, 359–365

CHARNEY, D. S., HENINGER, G. R., STERNBERG, D. E. *et al.* (1981). Presynaptic adrenergic receptor sensitivity in depression. *Archives of General Psychiatry*, **38**, 1334–1340

CHECKLEY, S. A., GLASS, I. B., THOMPSON, C., CORN, T. and ROBINSON, P. (1984). The GH response to clonidine in endogenous as compared with reactive depression. *Psychological Medicine*, **14**, 773–777

CLEMENS, J. A., SAWYER, B. D. and CERIMELE, B. (1977). Further evidence that serotonin is a neurotransmitter involved in the control of prolactin secretion. *Endocrinology*, **100**, 692–698

COLLINS, G. G. S., PRYSE-DAVIES, J., SANDLER, M. and SOUTHGATE, J. (1970). Effect of pre-treatment with oestradiol, progesterone and dopa on monoamine oxidase activity in the rat. *Nature*, **226**, 642–643

COOPER, J. E., COPELAND, J. R. M., BROWN, G. W., HARRIS, T. and GOURLAY, A. J. (1977). Further studies on interviewer training and inter-rater reliability of the Present State Examination (PSE). *Psychological Medicine*, **7**, 517–523

COPER, H. FAHNDRICH, E. and GEBERT, A. *et al.* (1979). Depression and monoamine oxidase. *Progress in Neuro-Psychopharmacology*, **3**, 441–463

COWEN, P. J., GEANEY, D. P., SCHACHTER, M., GREEN, A. R. and ELLIOTT, J. M. (1986). Desipramine treatment in normal subjects. *Archives of General Psychiatry*, **43**, 61–67

COX, J. L., HOLDEN, J. M. and SAGOVSKY, R. (1987). Detection of postnatal depression: development of the 10-item Edinburgh Postnatal Depression Scale. *British Journal of Psychiatry*, **150**, 782–786

CSONTOS, K., RUST, M., HOLLT, V., MAHR, W., KROMER, W. and TESCHEMACHER, H. J. (1979). Elevated plasma β-endorphin levels in pregnant women and their neonates. *Life Sciences*, **25**, 835–844

DALTON, K. (1980). *Depression after Childbirth*. Oxford: Oxford University Press

DANOWSKI, T. A. (1953). Is pregnancy followed by relative hypothyroidism? *American Journal of Obstetrics and Gynecology*, **65**, 77–80

DESSYPRIS, A., KARONESS, S. L. and ADLERCREUTZ, H. (1979). Marathon run effects on plasma prolactin and growth hormone. *Acta Endocrinologica, Suppl.*, **225**, 187–194

DOWNES, C. P. (1986). Agonist-stimulated phosphatidylinositol 4,5-bisphosphate metabolism in the nervous system. *Neurochemical International*, **9**, 211–230

DRAGO, F. (1982). Prolactin and behaviour. FIDIA Research Laboratories, Albano Terme

DRAGO, F., BOHUS, B. and MATTHEIJ, J. A. M. (1982). Endogenous hyperprolactinaemia and avoidance behaviours of the rat. *Physiology and Behavior*, **28**, 1–4

DRAGO, F., CANONICO, P. L., BITETTI, R. and SCAPAGNINI, U. (1980). Systemic and intraventricular prolactin induces excessive grooming. *European Journal of Pharmacology*, **65**, 457–458

DUBOVSKY, S. L., FRANKS, R. D., ALLEN, S. and MURPHY, J. (1986). Calcium antagonists in mania: a double blind study of verapamil. *Psychiatry Research*, **18**, 309–320

EHRENKRANZ, J. R. L.(1976). Effects of six steroids on serotonin uptake in blood platelets. *Acta Endocrinologica*, **83**, 420–428

ELLIOTT, J. M. (1984). Platelet receptor binding studies in affective disorders. *Journal of Affective Disorders*, **6**, 219–239

FEINE, R., BELMAKER, R. H., RIMON, R. and EBSTEIN, R. P. (1977). Platelet monoamine oxidase in women with premenstrual syndrome. *Neuropsychobiology*, **3**, 105–110

FINDLAY, A. L. R. (1984). *Reproduction and the Foetus*. London: Edward Arnold

FLETCHER, J. E., THOMAS, T. A. and HILL, R. G. (1980). β-Endorphin and parturition. *Lancet*, **ii**, 310

GARCIA-SEVILLA, J. A., ZIS, A. P., HOLLINSWORTH, P. J., GREDEN, J. F. and SMITH, C. B. (1981). Platelet α₂-adrenergic receptors in major depressive disorder. *Archives of General Psychiatry*, **38**, 1327–1333

GARCIA-SEVILLA, J. A., GUIMON, J., GARCIA-VELLEJO, P and FUSTER, M. J. (1986). Biochemical and functional evidence of supersensitive platelet α₂-adrenoceptors in major affective disorders. *Archives of General Psychiatry*, **43**, 51–57

GELDER, M. (1978). Hormones and post partum depression. In: *Mental Illness in Pregnancy and the Puerperium*, (M. Sandler, ed.), pp. 80–90. Oxford: Oxford University Press

GENAZZINI, A. R., FACHINETTI, F., PARRINI, D. *et al.* (1982). Puerperal breast feeding does not stimulate circulating opioids in humans. *Journal of Endocrinological Investigation*, **5**, 367–371

GEORGE, A. J. and WILSON, K. C. M. (1981a). Monoamine oxidase activity and the puerperal blues syndrome. *Journal of Psychosomatic Research*, **25**, 409–413

GEORGE, A. J. and WILSON, K. C. M. (1981b). Puerperal mood changes and platelet monoamine oxidase activity. *British Journal of Clinical Pharmacology*, **11**, 415–416

GEORGE, A. J. and WILSON, K. C. M. (1982). Maternal β-endorphin/β-lipotrophin immunoreactivity correlates with maternal prolactin in the first postpartum week. *British Journal of Clinical Pharmacology*, **14**, 146–147

GEORGE, A. J. and WILSON, K. C. M. (1983). β-Endorphin and puerperal psychiatric symptoms. *British Journal of Pharmacology*, **80**, 493P

GEORGE, A. J., COPELAND, J. R. M. and WILSON, K. C. M. (1980). Serum prolactin and the post partum blues syndrome. *British Journal of Pharmacology*, **70**, 102–103

GINTZLER, A. R. (1980). Endorphin mediated increases in pain threshold during pregnancy. *Science*, **210**, 193–195

GJERRIS, A., HAMMER, M., VENDSBORG, P., CHRISTENSEN, N. J. and RAFAELSON, O. (1985). Cerebrospinal fluid vasopressin—changes in depression. *British Journal of Psychiatry*, **147**, 696–701

GOLAND, R. S., WARDLAW, S. L., STARKE, R. I. and FRANTZ, A. G. (1981). Human plasma β-endorphin during pregnancy, labor and delivery. *Journal of Clinical Endocrinology and Metabolism*, **52**, 74–78

GORDON, J. H., BORISON, R. L. and DIAMOND, B. I. (1980). Modulation of dopamine receptor sensitivity by estrogen. *Biological Psychiatry*, **15**, 389–396

GORDON, J. L. and OLVERMAN, H. J. (1978). 5-Hydroxytryptamine and dopamine transport by rat and human blood platelets. *British Journal of Pharmacology*, **62**, 219–226

GORMLEY, G. J., LOWY, M. T., REDER, A. T., HOSPELHORN, V. D., ANTEL, J. P. and MELTZER, H. Y. (1985). Glucocorticoid receptors in depression: relationship to the dexamethasone suppression test. *American Journal of Psychiatry*, **142**, 1278–1284

GREEN, H. S. and KANE, J. M. (1983). The dexamethasone suppression test in depression. *Neuropharmacology*, **6**, 7–24

GREENBLATT, R. B., CHADDHA, J. S., TERAN, A. Z. and NEZHAT, C. H. (1985). Aphrodisiacs. In: *Psychopharmacology: Recent Advances and Future Prospects*, British Association for Psychopharmacology Monograph No. 6, (S. D. Iversen, ed.), pp. 290–302. Oxford: Oxford University Press

GREENWOOD, J. and PARKER, G. (1984). The dexamethasone suppression test in the puerperium. *Australian and New Zealand Journal of Psychiatry*, **18**, 282–284

HALBREICH, U., GUNHAUS, L. and BEN-DAVID, M. (1979). Twenty-four hour rhythms of prolactin in depressive patients. *Archives of General Psychiatry*, **36**, 1183–1186

HALE, A. S., WALKER, P. L., BRIDGES, P. K. and SANDLER, M. (1986). Tyramine conjugation deficit as a trait-marker in endogenous depressive illness. *Journal of Psychiatric Research*, **20**, 251–261

HAMILTON, J. A. (1962). *Post Partum Psychiatric Problems*. St. Louis: Mosby

HAMILTON, J. A. (1977). Puerperal psychoses. In: *Gynaecology and Obstetrics*, Vol. 2, pp. 1–8. Hagerston: Harper Row

HAMON, M., COSSERY, J. M., SPAMPINATO, M. and GOZLAN, H. (1986). Are there specific ligands for $5HT_{1A}$ and $5HT_{1B}$ receptor binding sites in the brain? *Trends in Pharmacological Science*, **7**, 336–337

HANDLEY, S. L., DUNN, T. L., BAKER, J. M., COCKSHOTT, C. and GOULD, S. (1977). Mood changes in puerperium and plasma tryptophan and cortisol concentrations. *British Medical Journal*, **ii**, 18–22

HANDLEY, S. L., DUNN, D. L., WALDRON, S. and BAKER, J. M. (1980). Tryptophan, cortisol and puerperal mood change. *British Journal of Psychiatry*, **136**, 498–508

HARRIS, B. (1980). Prospective trial of L-tryptophan in maternity blues. *British Journal of Psychiatry*, **137**, 233–235

HARRISON, W. M., COOPER, T. B. and STEWART, J. W. *et al.* (1984). The tyramine challenge test as a marker for melancholia. *Archives of General Psychiatry*, **41**, 681–685

HATOTANI, N., NISHIKUBO, M. and KITAYAMA, I. (1979). Periodic psychoses in the female and the reproductive process. In: *Psychoneuroendocrinology in Reproduction*, (L. Zichella and P. Panchevi, eds), pp. 55–68. Amsterdam: North Holland-Elsevier

HEALY, D., CARNEY, P. A. and LEONARD, B. E. (1983). Monoamine-related markers of depression: changes following treatment. *Journal of Psychiatric Research*, **17**, 251–260

HENINGER, G. R., CHARNEY, D. S. and STERNBERG, D. E. (1984). Serotonergic function in depression. *Archives of General Psychiatry*, **41**, 398–402

HILDRETH, H. M. (1946). A battery of feeling and attitude scales for clinical use. *Journal of Clinical Psychology*, **2**, 214–221

JOHNSTON, J. P. (1968). Some observations upon a new inhibitor of monoamine oxidase in brain tissue. *Biochemical Pharmacology*, **17** 1285–1297

JONES, S. B., BYLUND, D. B., RIESER, C. A., SHEKIN, W. O., BYER, J. A. and CARR, G. W. (1983). α_2-Adrenergic receptor binding in human platelets. Alterations during the menstrual cycle. *Clinical Pharmacology and Therapeutics*, **34**, 90–96

KAFKA, M. S. and PAUL, S. M. (1986). Platelet α_2-adrenergic receptors in depression. *Archives of General Psychiatry*, **43**, 91–95

KARNOSH, L. J. and HOPE, J. M. (1937). Puerperal psychoses and their sequelae. *American Journal* of Psychiatry, **94**, 537–550

KATONA, C. L. E., THEORODOROU, A. E. and MISSOURIS, C. G. et al. (1985). Platelet ^{3}H-imipramine binding in pregnancy and the puerperium. *Psychiatry Research*, **14**, 33–38

KOSLOW, S. H., MAAS, J. W., BOWDEN, C. L., DAVIS, J. M., HANIN, I. and JAVAID, J. (1983). C.S.F. and urinary biogenic amines and metabolites in depression and mania. *Archives of General Psychiatry*, **40**, 999–1010

KOVACS, G. L. (1986). Oxytocin and behaviour. In: *Neurobiology of Oxytocin*, (D. Ganten and D. Pfaff, eds), pp. 91–128. Berlin: Springer

KOVACS, G. L., BOHUS, B. and VERSTEED, P. H. G. (1974). Facilitation of memory consolidation by vasopressin mediation of terminals of the dorsal noradrenergic bundle. *Brain Research*, **172**, 73–85

KUEVI, V., CARSON, R. and DIXSON, A. F. et al. (1983). Plasma amine and hormone changes in "postpartum blues". *Clinical Endocrinology*, **19**, 39–46

KUMAR, R., ROBSON, K. M. and SMITH, A. M. P. (1984). Development of a self administered questionnaire to measure material adjustment and maternal attitude during pregnancy and after delivery. *Journal of Psychosomatic Research*, **28**, 43–51

LANGER, S. Z. (1980). Presynaptic regulation of the release of catecholamines. *Pharmacological Reviews*, **32**, 337–362

LIGHT, K. C., KOEPKE, J. P., OBRIST, P. A. and WILLIS, P. W. (1983). Psychological stress induces sodium and fluid retention in men at risk for hypertension. *Science*, **220**, 429–431

LINNOILA, M., KAROUM, F., MILLER, R. and POTTER, W. Z. (1983). Reliability of urinary monoamine and metabolite output measurements in depressed patients. *American Journal of Psychiatry*, **140**, 1055–1057

LIVINGSTON, J. E., MACLEOD, P. M. and APPLEGARTH, D. A. (1978). Vitamin B_6 status in women with post partum depression. *American Journal of Clinical Nutrition*, **31**, 886–891

LUBIN, B. (1965). Adjective check lists for measurement of depression. *Archives of General Psychiatry*, **12**, 57–62

LUINE, V. N. and MCEWAN, B. S. (1977). Effect of oestradiol on turnover of type A monoamine oxidase in brain. *Journal of Neurochemistry*, **28**, 1221–1227

MAAS, J. W. (1983). *MHPG: Basic Mechanisms and Psychopathology*. New York: Academic Press

MAAS, J. W., DEKIRMENJIAN, H., GARVER, D., REDMOND, D. E. and LANDIS, D. H. (1972). Catecholamine metabolite excretion following intraventricular injection of 6-OH-dopamine. *Brain Research*, **41**, 507–511

MACLEOD, R. M. and LEHMEYER, J. E. (1974). Studies on the mechanism of the dopamine-mediated inhibition of prolactin secretion. *Endocrinology*, **94**, 1077–1085

MATHEW, R. J., HO, B. T., KRALIK, P. and CLAGHORN, J. L. (1979). Anxiety and serum prolactin. *American Journal of Psychiatry*, **136**, 1322–1326

MATTHEWS, J., AKIL, H. and GREDEN, J. et al. (1986). β-Endorphin/β-lipotrophin immunoreactivity in endogenous depression. *Archives of General Psychiatry*, **43**, 374–381

MCEWAN, B. S., DAVIS, P. G., PARSONS, B. and PFAFF, D. W. (1979). The brain as a target for steroid hormone action. *Annual Review of Neuroscience*, **2**, 65–112

MELTZER, H. Y., ARORA, R. C., BABER, R., and TRICOU, B. L. (1981). Serotonin uptake in blood platelets of psychiatric patients. *Archives of General Psychiatry*, **38**, 1322–1326

MENDLEWICZ, J., VAN CAUTER, E., LINKOWSKI, P., L'HERMITE, M. and ROBYN, C. (1980). The 24 hour profile of prolactin in depression. *Life Sciences*, **27**, 2015–2024

METZ, A., COWEN, P. J., GELDER, M. G., STUMP, K., ELLIOTT, J. M. and GRAHAME-SMITH, D. G. (1983). Changes in platelet α_2-adrenoceptor binding post-partum: possible relation to maternity blues. *Lancet*, **ii**, 495–498

MOLLER, S. E. (1980). Evaluation of the relative potency of individual competing amino acids to tryptophan transport in endogenously depressed patients. *Psychiatry Research*, **3**, 141–150

MOLLER, S. E., KIRK, L. and HONORÉ, P. (1979). Free and total plasma tryptophan in endogenous depression. *Journal of Affective Disorders*, **1**, 69–76

MONTAGUE, W. (1983). *Diabetes and the Endocrine Pancreas*. London: Croom Helm

MOOS, R. H. (1968). The development of a menstrual distress questionnaire. *Psychosomatic*

Medicine, **30**, 853–867

MURPHY, D. L. (1976). Clinical, genetic, hormonal and drug influences on the activity of human platelet monoamine oxidase. In: *Monoamine Oxidase and its Inhibition*, Ciba Foundation Symposium No. 39, (G.E.W. Wolstenholme and J. Knight, eds), pp. 341–352. Amsterdam: Elsevier-Excerpta Medica-North Holland.

MURPHY, D. L. (1986). Serotonin neurochemistry: a commentary on some of its quandaries. *Neurochemical International*, **8**, 161–163

NAYLOR, G. J., STANDFIELD, D. ., WHYTE, S. F. and HUTCHINSON, F. (1974). Urinary excretion of adenosine 3,'5'-cyclic monophosphate in depressive illness. *British Journal of Psychiatry*, **125**, 275–279

NESSE, R. M., CURTISS, G. C., BROWN, G. M. and RUBIN, R. T. (1980). Anxiety induced by flooding therapy for phobia does not elicit prolactin secretory response. *Psychosomatic Medicine*, **42**, 25–31

NEWNHAM, J. P., DENNETT, P. M., FERRON, S. A. *et al*. (1984). a study of the relationship between circulating β-endorphin-like immunoreactivity and post-partum 'blues'. *Clinical Endocrinology*, **20**, 169–177

NOEL, G. L., SUH, H. K., STONE, J. G. and FRANTZ, A. G. (1972). Human prolactin and growth hormone release during surgery and other conditions of stress. *Journal of Clinical Endocrinology and Metabolism*, **35**, 840–851

NOTT, P. N. and CUTTS, S. (1982). Validation of the 30 item General Health Questionnaire in post partum women. *Psychological Medicine*, **12**, 409–413

NOTT, P. N., FRANKLIN, M., ARMITAGE, C. and GELDER, M. G. (1976). Hormonal changes in mood in the puerperium. *British Journal of Psychiatry*, **128**, 379–383

OWEN, F., CROSS, A. J., CROW, T. J., LONGDEN, A., POULTER, M. and RILEY, G. J. (1978). Increased dopamine-receptor sensitivity in schizophrenia. *Lancet*, **ii**, 223–226

PANCHERI, P., ZICHELLA, L., FRAIOLI, F. *et al*. (1985). ACTH, beta-endorphin and met-enkephalin: peripheral modifications during the stress of human labor. *Psychoendocrinology*, **10**, 289–301

PARE, C. M. B.and SANDLER, M. (1959). A clinical and biochemical study of a trial of iproniazid and the treatment of depression. *Journal of Neurology, Neurosurgery and Psychiatry*, **22**, 247–251

PAUL, S. M., REHAVI, M., SKOLNICK, P.and GOODWIN, F. (1981). Depressed patients have decreased binding of tritiated imipramine to platelet serotonin transporter. *Archives of General Psychiatry*, **38**, 1315–1317

PEROUTKA, S. J. and SNYDER, S. H. (1983). Multiple serotonin receptors and their physiological significance. *Federation Proceedings*, **42**, 213–217

PETERS, J. R., ELLIOTT, J. M. and GRAHAME-SMITH, D. G. (1979). Effect of oral contraceptives on platelet noradrenaline and 5HT receptors and aggregation. *Lancet*, **ii**, 933–936

PITT, B. (1968). "Atypical" depression following childbirth. *British Journal of Psychiatry*, **114**, 1325–1335

QUATTRONE, A., SCHETTINI, G., DIRENZO, G. F. and PREZIOSI, P. (1979). Pharmacological evidence of an interaction between serotonergic and dopaminergic neurons in the control of prolactin secretion in male rats. *Archives Internationales de Pharmacodynamie et de Thérapie*, **238**, 42–49

RAFAELSON, O. J. (1974). Manic depressive psychosis of manic melancholic mode. *Danish Medical Bulletin*, **21**, 81–87

RASKIND, M. A., PESKIND, E. R., LAMPE, T. H., RISSE, S. C., TABORSKY, G. H. and DORSA, D. (1986). Cerebrospinal fluid vasopressin, oxytocin, somatostatin and β-endorphin in Alzheimer's disease. *Archives of General Psychiatry*, **43**, 382–388

REDMOND, D. E., MURPHY, D. L., BAULU, J., ZIEGLER, M. G. and LAKE, C. R. (1975). Menstrual cycle and ovarian hormone effects on plasma and platelet monoamine oxidase (MAO) and plasma dopamine β-hydroxylase (DBH) activities in the Rhesus Monkey. *Psychosomatic Medicine*, **37**, 417–428

REHAVI, M., PAUL, S. M., SKOLNICK, P. and GOODWIN, F. K. (1980). Demonstration of specific high affinity binding sites for ^{3}H-imipramine in human brain. *Life Sciences*, **26**, 2273–2279

REID, I. A., MORRIS, B. J. and GANONG, W. F. (1977). The renin-angiotensin system. *Annual Review of Physiology*, **40**, 377–398

RILEY, D. M. (1979). A study of serum calcium in relation to puerperal psychiatric illness. In: *Emotion and Reproduction*, Proceedings of Serono Symposium, Vol. 20B, (A. Carenza and V. Zichella, eds), pp. 829–836. London: Academic Press.

RILEY, D. M. (1982). Double blind trial of pyridoxine in the prevention of depressive symptoms in the first post-partum month. Proceedings of Marcé Society Symposium on Motherhood and Mental Illness. London: Institute of Psychiatry

RILEY, D. M. and WATT, D. C. (1985). Hypercalcaemia in the etiology of puerperal psychosis. *Biological Psychiatry*, **20**, 479–488

RISCH, S. C. (1982). β-Endorphin hypersecretion in depression: possible cholinergic mechanisms. *Biological Psychiatry*, **17**, 1071–1079

ROBERTS, J. M., LEWIS, V., MIZE, N., TSUCHIYA, A. and STARR, J. (1985). Human platelet α-adrenergic receptors and responses during pregnancy. No change except that with differing hematocrit. *American Journal of Obstetrics and Gynecology*, **154**, 206–210

ROSS, C. J. (1986). Biological tests for mental illness: their use and misuse. *Biological Psychiatry*, **21**, 431–435

SACHAR, E. J., NATHAN, R. S., ASMIS, G., HALBREICH, U., TABRIZI, M. A. and HALPERN, F. (1980). Neuroendocrine studies of major depressive disorder. *Acta Psychiatrica Scandinavica*, **61**, Suppl. 280, 201–209

SANDERS, D. J. and BANCROFT, J. (1982). Hormones and the sexuality of women. The menstrual cycle. *Clinical Endocrinology and Metabolism*, **7**, 639–659

SANDLER, M. (1976). Variations in monoamine oxidase activity in some human disease states. In: *Monoamine Oxidase and its Inhibition*, Ciba Foundation Symposium No. 39, (G. E. W. Wolstenholme and J. Knight, eds), pp. 327–340. Amsterdam: Elsevier-Excerpta Medica-North Holland

SANDLER, M. (1978). Some biological correlates of mental illness in relation to childbirth. In: *Mental Illness in Pregnancy and the Puerperium*, (M. Sandler, ed.), pp. 9–24. Oxford, Oxford University Press

SANDLER, M., BONHAM CARTER, S. M. and WALKER, P. L. (1983). Tyramine conjugation deficit as a trait-marker in depression. *Psychopharmacology Bulletin*, **19**, 501–502

SANDLER, M., REVELEY, M. A. and GLOVER, V. (1981). Human platelet monoamine oxidase activity in health and disease: a review. *Journal of Clinical Pathology*, **34**, 292–302

SANDLER, M., BONHAM CARTER, S. M., CUTHBERT, M. F. and PARE, C. M. B. (1975). Is there an increase in monoamine oxidase activity in depressive illness? *Lancet*, **i**, 1045–1049

SCHILDKRAUT, J. (1965). The catecholamine hypothesis of affective disorder. *American Journal of Psychiatry*, **112**, 509–522

SCHILDKRAUT, J. J., ORSULAK, R. J., SCHATZBERG, A. F. et al. (1978). Toward a biochemical classification of depressive disorders. *Archives of General Psychiatry*, **35**, 1427–1433

SHIN, S. H. (1980). Physiological evidence for the existence of a prolactin releasing factor: stress-induced prolactin secretion is not linked to dopaminergic receptors. *Neuroendocrinology*, **31**, 375–379

SIEVER, L. J., KAFKA, K. S., TARGUM, S. and LAKE, C. R. (1984). Platelet alpha adrenergic binding and biochemical responsiveness in depressed patients and controls. *Psychiatry Research*, **11**, 287–302

SIMPSON, E. R. and MACDONALD, P. C. (1981). Endocrine physiology of the placenta. *Annual Review of Physiology*, **43**, 163–188

SINGH, B., GILHOTRA, M., SMITH, R., BRINSMEAD, M., LEWIN, T. and HALL, C. (1986). Post partum psychoses and the dexamethasone suppression test. *Journal of Affective Disorders*, **11**, 173–177

SLOTKIN, T. A., WHITMORE, W. L., DEW, K. L. and KILTS, C. D. (1986). Uptake of serotonin into rat platelets and synaptosomes: comparative structure-activity relationships, energetics and evaluation of the effects of acute and chronic nortriptyline administration. *Brain Research Bulletin*, **17**, 67–73

SNEDDON, J. M. (1973). Blood platelets as a model for monoamine containing neurones.

Progress in Neurobiology, **1**, 151–198

SOLTHAU, A. and TAYLOR, R. (1982). Depression after childbirth. *British Medical Journal*, **284**, 980–981

SOUTHGATE, J. (1972). Endometrial monoamine oxidase: the effect of sex steroids. In: *Monoamine Oxidase—New Vistas*, (E. Costa and M. Sandler, eds), pp. 263–270. New York: Raven Press

STAHL, S. M., LEMOINE, P. M., CIARANELLO, R. D. and BERGER, P. A. (1983). Platelet alpha$_2$-adrenergic receptor sensitivity in major depressive disorder. *Psychiatry Research*, **10**, 157–164

STEIN, G. (1982). The maternity blues: In: *Motherhood and Mental Illness*, (I. Brockington, and R. Kumar, eds), pp. 119–154. London: Academic Press

STEIN, G., MARSH, A. and MORTON, J. (1981). Mental symptoms, weight changes and electrolyte excretion in the first post partum week. *Journal of Psychosomatic Research*, **25**, 395–408

STEIN, G., MILTON, F., BEBBINGTON, P., WOOD, K. and COPPEN, A. (1976). Relationship between mood disturbance and free and total plasma tryptophan in post partum women. *British Medical Journal*, **ii**, 457–459

STEIN, G., MORTON, J., MARSH, A., HARTSHORN, J., EBELING, J. and DESAGA, U. (1984). Vasopressin and mood during the puerperium. *Biological Psychiatry*, **19**, 1711–1718

STEINER, M., LAK, A., BLUM, I., ATSMOR, A. and WIJSENBECK, M. (1973). Propranolol versus chlor-promazine in the treatment of psychoses associated with childbearing. *Psychiatria, Neurologia, Neurochirurgia*, **76**, 421–426

STONE, E. A. (1983). Problems with current catecholamine hypotheses of antidepressant agents: speculations leading to a new hypothesis. *Brain Behaviour Science*, **6**, 535–577

SULSER, F. (1984). Regulation and function of noradrenaline receptor systems in brain. *Neuropharmacology*, **23**, 255–261

SUNDARESAN, P. R., MADAN, M. K., KELVIE, S. L. and WEINTRAUB, M. (1985). Platelet α_2-receptors and the menstrual cycle. *Clinical Pharmacology and Therapeutics*, **37**, 337–342

TAM, W. Y. K., CHAN, M-Y and LEE, P. H. K. (1985). The menstrual cycle and platelet 5HT uptake. *Psychosomatic Medicine*, **47**, 352–362

TAN, C. M., RAMAN, A. and SINNATHRAY, T.A. (1972). Serum ionic calcium levels in pregnancy. *Journal of Obstetrics and Gynaecology of the British Commonwealth*, **79**, 694–697

TAYLOR, D. L., MATHEW, R. J., HO, B. T. and WEINMAN, M. L. (1984). Serotonin levels and platelet uptake during premenstrual tension. *Neuropsychobiology*, **12**, 16–18

THOMPSON, C., MEZEY, G. and CORN, T. *et al.* (1985). The effect of desipramine upon melatonin and cortisol secretion in depressed and normal subjects. *British Journal of Psychiatry*, **147** 389–393

TIPTON, K. and YOUDIM, M. B. H. (1976). Assay of monoamine oxidase. In: *Monoamine Oxidase and Its Inhibition*, Ciba Foundation Symposium No. 39, (G. E. W. Wolstenholme and J. Knight, eds), pp. 393–403. Amsterdam: Elsevier-Excerpta Medica-North Holland

TREADWAY, C. R., KANE, F. J., JARRAHI-ZADEH, A. and LIPTON, M. A. (1969). A psychoendocrine study of pregnancy and puerperium. *American Journal of Psychiatry*, **125**, 1380–1386

TUOMISTO, J. and TUKIAINEN, E. (1976). Decreased uptake of 5-hydroxytryptamine in blood platelets from depressed patients. *Nature*, **262**, 586–590

U'PRICHARD, D. (1984). Biochemical characteristics and regulation of brain α_2-adrenoceptors. In: *Presynaptic Modulation of Postsynaptic Receptors in Mental Diseases*, (A. I. Salama, ed.). *Annals of the New York Academy of Sciences*, **430**, 55–76

VON HAHN, H. P., HONEGGER, C. G. and PLETSCHER, A. (1980). Similar kinetic characteristics of 5-hydroxytryptamine binding in blood platelets and brain membrane of rats. *Neuroscience Letters*, **20**, 319–322

WALKER, P. L. and SANDLER, M. (1987). The analysis of urinary meta- and para-tyramine using gas chromatography with electron-capture detection. *Annals of Clinical Biochemistry* **25**, 304–309

WATNEY, P. J. M. and RUDD, B. T. (1984). Calcium metabolism in pregnancy and the newborn. *Journal of Obstetrics and Gynaecology of the British Commonwealth*, **81**, 210–219

ZIS, A. P., HASKETT, R. T., ALBALA, A. A., CARROLL, B. J. and LOHR, N. E. (1985). Opioid regulation of hypothalamic-pituitary-adrenal function in depression. *Archives of General Psychiatry*, **42**, 383–386

Chapter 5

Relevance of hormone–CNS interactions to psychological changes in the puerperium

J. F. W. Deakin

Introduction

The marked hormonal changes of the early postnatal period result in lactation and amenorrhoea. In addition, animal studies suggest a possible hormonal role in the elaboration of maternal behaviour. More speculatively, the normal emotional lability of mothers in the first postnatal week (the 'blues') may be a psychological consequence of puerperal changes in the hormonal milieu. Puerperal psychoses are rare but the fact that nearly all cases begin in the first two postnatal weeks has led to suggestions that hormonal changes are involved in the aetiology. These possibilities have received almost no sustained research interest. We are left with temporal associations between behavioural and hormonal changes which are intriguing but not compelling. These associations are intriguing because reproductive hormones have a variety of influences upon the central nervous system (CNS) in experimental animals. However, there is considerable variation between species and much less is known about CNS influences of reproductive hormones in humans. Furthermore, there are major practical and ethical difficulties with experimental manipulations in humans, especially in the postnatal period. Hence there is, as yet, no compelling evidence for a major hormonal role in psychological changes of the postnatal period.

This chapter examines the interactions between reproductive hormones and the central nervous system which may be relevant to the psychological changes of the puerperium. It begins with a brief account of the control of the hormones of reproduction and lactation. The hormonal changes of the puerperium are described next and this is followed by a selective review of hormonal influences on the CNS which have behavioural or psychiatric significance. The chapter concludes with an evaluation of the evidence that puerperal hormonal changes are involved in the elaboration of parental behaviour.

The hypothalamico-pituitary-ovarian system

Ovarian steroids

The ovaries secrete oestrogens and progesterone which control the cyclical changes in the endometrium and cervix (*Figure 5.1*). In the first half of the

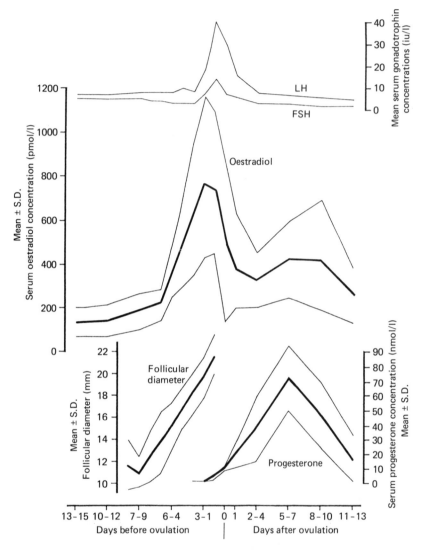

Figure 5.1 Hormonal events of the menstrual cycle. Follicular development monitored by ultrasound scans in 58 normal women. Thick lines depict means and thin lines ±1 S.D. Note the considerable variability in oestradiol concentrations. Reproduced by courtesy of Killick (1986).

menstrual cycle a single follicle develops to produce the ovum. The follicle secretes increasing amounts of oestrogens which peak on the day of ovulation when the follicle ruptures to release the ovum. The second half of the menstrual cycle is the luteal phase in which the corpus luteum secretes progesterone and oestrogens. Menstruation occurs when progesterone and oestrogen concentrations decline at the end of the menstrual cycle. Secretion of ovarian hormones is controlled by gonadotrophic hormones secreted by the anterior pituitary.

Pituitary gonadotrophins (FSH and LH)

The anterior pituitary secretes follicle stimulating hormone (FSH) which induces maturation of an ovarian follicle and the secretion of oestrogen in the first half of the menstrual cycle. A large surge in luteinizing hormone (LH) secretion occurs at mid-cycle, triggering ovulation and the formation of the corpus luteum. Gonadotrophin secretion occurs in pulses in response to pulses of gonadotrophin releasing hormone (GnRH) arriving at the anterior pituitary from the hypothalamus.

Ovarian steroids exert feedback effects on anterior pituitary gonadotrophin secretion. In the first half of the menstrual cycle oestrogens inhibit gonadotrophin release but when increasing oestrogen concentrations exceed a threshold a positive feedback effect is seen triggering the mid-cycle surge in gonadotrophin secretion which results in ovulation and the formation of the corpus luteum. It has recently been demonstrated that ovarian follicles produce a peptide hormone, inhibin, which inhibits pituitary secretion of FSH.

Gonadotrophin releasing hormone (GnRH)

GnRH is released from nerve terminals into capillaries in the median eminence (*Figure 5.2*). These capillaries drain into the portal veins and carry GnRH and other releasing factors to the anterior pituitary. Pulses of GnRH induce anterior pituitary gonadotrophs to secrete pulses of FSH and LH which vary in amplitude and frequency through the menstrual cycle.

GnRH-containing neuronal cell bodies are located in two main groups—the medial preoptic area and the arcuate nucleus (*Figure 5.2*; Silverman and Krey, 1978). A variety of direct or indirect neuronal influences on the activity of GnRH neurones have been demonstrated and include facilitatory noradrenergic and inhibitory dopaminergic, gabaergic and opioid peptide inputs (Sarkar, 1983). Animal experiments suggest that ovarian steroids act on these inputs to modulate the pattern of GnRH secretion throughout the menstrual cycle.

The elegant experiments of Knobil and colleagues (Knobil, 1980) indicate that variations in the pattern of pulsatile GnRH release are not necessary to explain the cyclical changes in gonadotrophin and ovarian steroid secretion of the menstrual cycle in the primate. In these experiments hypothalamic GnRH neurones were destroyed and the animals received unvarying regular pulses of GnRH infusion. Normal menstrual cycles were produced. Thus reciprocal interactions between pituitary and ovary are sufficient to produce the hormonal changes of the menstrual cycle when the pituitary is driven by a constant frequency of GnRH pulses. However, in intact animals and probably in humans GnRH release varies through the menstrual cycle in response to CNS influences.

Opioid peptides and gonadotrophin releasing hormone

In the follicular phase, pituitary gonadotrophin secretion occurs in increasingly frequent pulses as ovulation is approached. In the luteal phase, gonadotrophin pulses are infrequent and this may in part be due to

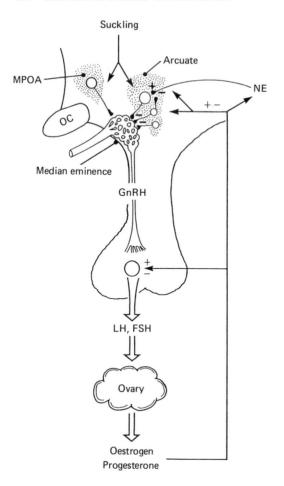

Figure 5.2 Schematic diagram of the hypothalamico-pituitary-ovarian axis. Large neurones depict GnRH-containing neurones with terminals on portal capillaries. Small bipolar neurone depicts β-endorphin-containing neurone. Small unipolar neurone depicts dopamine-containing neurone. The synaptic arrangements are schematic since the actual arrangements in humans are not established. MPOA = medial preoptic area; OC = optic chiasm; NE = noradrenaline projection to hypothalamus.

inhibition of hypothalamic GnRH neurones by an opioid peptide (Ferin, 1984). Infusions of naloxone, an opiate receptor antagonist, induce large pulses of gonadotrophin secretion when administered in the luteal phase. In the early to mid-follicular phase naloxone has little effect. In the immediate postnatal period there is a lack of LH pulsatility and, as in the luteal phase, naloxone infusions induce LH release (Ishizuka, Quigley and Yen, 1984). This suggests that increased CNS opioid inhibition of GnRH release contributes to the amenorrhoea of the period.

It has been suggested that the high circulating concentrations of oestrogens and progesterone in the luteal phase and late pregnancy induce opioid inhibition of GnRH release and result in loss of pulsatile pituitary gonadotrophin release.

Primate studies suggest that the opioid peptide involved in inhibition of GnRH release is β-endorphin (Wehrenberg *et al*, 1982). This seems plausible since β-endorphin-containing neurones are located together with GnRH neurones in the arcuate nucleus of the hypothalamus (*Figure 5.2*). Whether opioid peptides act directly to inhibit GnRH neurones or via some other neurotransmitter input is not known.

Hormonal changes of the early puerperium

In late pregnancy the placenta secretes large quantities of chorionic gonadotrophin, oestrogens and progesterone. With delivery of the placenta there is a rapid clearance of placental steroids whose concentrations reach their nadir by 3–7 days postpartum and remain depressed until resumption of ovarian follicular activity. Oestrogen and progesterone concentrations are over 200 times lower by the end of the first postnatal week than in late pregnancy (e.g. Bonnar *et al.*, 1978; Kuevi *et al.*, 1983).

Prolactin concentrations are increased in late pregnancy and decline rapidly in non-lactating women although normal non-pregnant concentrations are not reached until the second or third postpartum week (Bonnar *et al.*, 1978). In breast feeders prolactin concentrations remain increased for several weeks although they eventually decline even if suckling frequency is maintained.

Circulating β-endorphin concentrations increase in late pregnancy, reaching very high levels during delivery, and decline rapidly within a few hours of delivery (Newnham *et al.*, 1984). These authors found subjective ratings of labour pain to be inversely correlated with β-endorphin concentration measured 24 h later but not at 36 weeks or delivery. They speculate that β-endorphin may have an analgesic role during labour. However, circulating β-endorphin does not cross the blood-brain barrier and does not reflect CNS β-endorphin release. Furthermore, radioimmunoassay does not distinguish between active and the predominant inactive forms of β-endorphin.

Significant concentrations of chorionic gonadotrophin remain detectable in the maternal circulation for two weeks postpartum. This interferes with LH radioimmunoassay because the antibodies partially crossreact.

Neuroendocrine mechanisms of puerperal amenorrhoea are incompletely understood but all levels of the hypothalamico-pituitary-ovarian axis appear to be involved (*Table 5.1*).

Hypothalamic release of GnRH is thought to be suppressed in the puerperium since concentrations of FSH and LH are low and non-pulsatile. Pituitary sensitivity to GnRH is normally maintained by GnRH itself. Pituitary gonadotrophs lose their receptors for GnRH when deprived of GnRH and priming with GnRH restores them. In the puerperium administration of GnRH fails to stimulate FSH and LH secretion (Jeppsson *et al.*, 1977), suggesting that gonadotrophs have lost their receptors for GnRH because endogenous GnRH release is absent or reduced.

There is evidence that opioid peptides contribute to inhibition of GnRH release in the postnatal period—naloxone infusions cause increased release

Table 5.1 Mechanisms of puerperal amenorrhoea

Inhibition of hypothalamic GnRH release:
  Opioid peptides
  Prolactin?
  Suckling?

Inhibition of pituitary FSH and LH release:
  Loss of GnRH receptors
  Reduced GnRH release
  Prolactin?
  Increased negative feedback effects of oestrogen

Inhibition of ovarian steroid release:
  Reduced FSH and LH release
  Inhibition of steroid synthesis by prolactin

of FSH and LH (Ishizuka, Quigley and Yen, 1984). These authors suggest that high circulating oestrogen concentrations in pregnancy increase opioid inhibition of GnRH release and that this influence carries over into the postnatal period.

In non-lactating subjects, basal FSH concentrations begin to increase from about two weeks and oestradiol from about three weeks, indicating follicular development (Bonnar et al., 1978). From about two weeks postpartum FSH responses and, somewhat later, LH responses to exogenous GnRH return (Jeppsson et al., 1977). The return of pituitary responsiveness to GnRH is probably brought about by increasing secretion of GnRH and the appearance of GnRH receptors on pituitary gonadotroph cells.

Positive feedback effects of oestrogen upon gonadotrophin secretion, indicating late follicular development, are seen from about five weeks postpartum in non-lactating subjects (Glass et al., 1981).

Lactation delays the return of normal menstrual cycles. Despite rising FSH concentrations, oestrogen secretion remains reduced in breast feeders. This may be because the pituitary is more sensitive to negative feedback effects of oestrogen suppressing further gonadotrophic stimulation of the ovary (Glass et al., 1981). Furthermore, increased prolactin concentrations may interfere directly with ovarian responsiveness to gonadotrophins (McNeilly et al., 1982). Prolactin and/or the suckling stimulus may interfere with hypothalamic-pituitary control of pulsatile LH secretion (Glasier, McNeilly and Howie, 1984).

The hormonal changes of the puerperium recapitulate those of menstruation. Both involve decreasing steroid concentrations and increasing opioid inhibition of GnRH release. Brockington et al. (1988) have identified eight patients with puerperal psychoses who recovered and then relapsed with florid symptoms just prior to menstruation. Some patients had several premenstrual relapses. There are occasional reports of non-puerperal psychoses linked to the menstrual cycle. Such patients strengthen the case that the hormonal changes of the puerperium are, at least sometimes, causally involved in the aetiology of puerperal mental illness.

Neurotransmitters, hormones and puerperal mental states

Endogenous opioid peptides

As discussed earlier, opioid peptides (β-endorphin) inhibit GnRH release in the second half of the menstrual cycle and in the puerperium. Perhaps β-endorphin projections to other parts of the CNS also become more active at these times. Facchinetti *et al.* (1983) have reported that the LH releasing effects of naloxone in the late luteal phase are reduced in women who suffer with the premenstrual syndrome (PMS). Their results suggest that the normal increase in hypothalamic opioid function of the luteal phase decays more rapidly in women with the PMS. Assuming that a more rapid decay also occurs in other parts of the nervous system, the authors speculate that the symptoms of the PMS are analogous to opiate withdrawal symptoms. These results have yet to be replicated.

The main extra-hypothalamic projection of β-endorphin-containing cells of the arcuate nucleus is to noradrenergic cells in the locus coeruleus (Bloom *et al.*, 1978). Noradrenergic systems have been implicated in the aetiology of depression and anxiety and in the production of opiate withdrawal symptoms. The demonstration of increased hypothalamic opioid activity in the postnatal period (*see* above; Ishizuka, Quigley and Yen, 1984) raises the possibility that dysfunction in opioid systems could be a mechanism by which abnormal puerperal mental states arise. However, too little is known about the behavioural roles of opioid and noradrenergic systems to generate clear hypotheses. Nevertheless, an interesting first step might be to compare pulsatile patterns of LH secretion in women with and without psychological symptoms in the postnatal period. Different patterns would at least be indirect evidence of disturbed CNS influences on GnRH release in the psychologically disturbed.

GnRH: Extra-hypothalamic projections

Immunohistochemical studies in the rodent have demonstrated that GnRH neurones project to various limbic forebrain structures including the amygdala and septum, and to the pons, particularly the ventral tegmental area (VTA) (Silverman and Krey, 1978). It is intriguing that the VTA contains the cell bodies of the mesolimbic dopamine system which has been implicated in the aetiology of the psychoses and as a site of antipsychotic action of neuroleptic drugs. However, it is not known whether GnRH influences dopamine neurotransmission. Receptors for GnRH show a striking localization to specific layers in the rat hippocampus (Reubi and Maurer, 1984).

Central administration of GnRH to male and female experimental animals has marked effects in enhancing sexual behaviour (Moss, and McCann, 1973). Effects on other behavioural functions such as fear, stress, motivation, etc. have not been investigated. Thus GnRH is likely to have behavioural functions in humans but whether dysfunction in CNS GnRH systems might be a candidate mechanism in the pathogenesis of abnormal puerperal mental states is a matter of conjecture. This possibility cannot be investigated experimentally at present since GnRH cannot be measured in the systemic circulation. As discussed in the previous sections, detailed measurement of the pattern of pituitary gonadotrophin (FSH, LH) release may be an indirect way of measuring GnRH release but in view of the many factors controlling GnRH release, any abnormalities found in puerperal patients would have many potential explanations that would be difficult to disentangle. Pituitary gonadotrophins themselves are unlikely to be involved in the pathogenesis of abnormal mental states since they have no known CNS actions.

CNS effects of oestrogens and progesterone

As discussed above, ovarian steroids exert feedback effects on the CNS control of the menstrual cycle. Sex steroid binding sites can be demonstrated using the technique of autoradiography in which brain sections are incubated with tritiated steroid and the distribution of radioactivity, and thus of binding sites, is revealed by pressing the sections against tritium-sensitive photographic emulsion. Many neurones in the CNS contain binding sites for sex steroids. Steroid binding proteins are located in the cytoplasm in contrast to neurotransmitter binding sites which are associated with neuronal membranes. However, membrane-bound steroid receptors may also exist (*see* McEwan, 1985 for review). Some steroid receptors are associated with the cell nucleus and effects of sex steroids upon transcription of DNA have been described in the periphery, pituitary and CNS.

Autoradiographic studies reveal a widespread distribution of oestrogen and progesterone binding sites in limbic forebrain structures and a striking localization to brain stem monoamine-containing cell body groups. Noradrenergic cells occur in six main clusters in the brain stem. Some noradrenergic neurones in each of the six groups also take up tritiated oestradiol (Sar and Stumpf, 1981). Oestrogen receptors have not been found in dopamine-containing cells of the substantia nigra/VTA but are present in dopamine-containing and other cells of the arcuate nucleus. Some of the feedback effects of oestrogens upon GnRH release may be mediated by oestrogen effects on arcuate dopamine-containing cells and noradrenergic nerve terminals (Sarkar, 1983).

The presence of sex steroid receptors in limbic forebrain areas and monoamine cells suggests likely influences on behaviour and on monoamine function. In female rodents, sexually receptive behaviour is reliably induced by a combination of oestrogen and progesterone treatment (*see* McEwan, 1985 for reference). Full expression of female sexual receptiveness (lordosis response) requires 18–24 h of continuous or intermittent oestrogen priming; progesterone injections then induce lordosis within 4 h. Either treatment alone or in the reverse order is ineffective. Thus oestrogen priming renders the animals sensitive to progesterone. It is known that oestrogen treatment induces the appearance of progesterone receptors in the hypothalamus.

Sex steroids and noradrenergic function
Several effects of oestrogens upon noradrenergic function have been described within and outside the hypothalamus. Oestrogens induce a surge

in LH secretion in rats which is dependent upon increased hypothalamic noradrenaline release (Sarkar, 1983). Oestrogen effects on noradrenaline release, turnover, synthesis and receptors have been described, mostly within the hypothalamus. However, no firm or unifying statement about the overall influence of oestrogens upon noradrenergic neurotransmission can be made especially as the doses and duration of oestrogen treatment vary so widely.

Some of the postsynaptic effects of noradrenaline are mediated by β-adrenoceptors which induce the formation of cyclic AMP in the post-synaptic cell (*Figure 5.3*). It is possible to measure numbers of β-adrenoceptors (or other receptors) in brain areas using radioactively labelled drugs which bind strongly to β-adrenoceptors (radioligand binding) in brain membrane preparations. In three studies oestrogen treatment decreased β-adrenoceptor binding in rat cerebral cortex (Wagner, Crutcher and Davis, 1979; Wagner and Davis, 1980, Biegon *et al.*, 1983). It is intriguing that repeated treatment with antidepressant drugs or ECT has the same effect. Indeed, delayed reductions in the number ('down-regulation') of β-adrenoceptors has been proposed as a unified mechanism of antidepressant action (Sulser *et al.*, 1983). The abrupt postnatal decline in oestrogen concentration to very low levels could thus increase vulnerability to depression by removing an antidepressant-like neurochemical action of oestrogen.

α-Noradrenergic receptors have also been implicated in the aetiology of depression although the evidence is confusing. Two types of α-noradrenergic receptors exist in the brain (*Figure 5.3*): α₁-adrenoceptors are postsynaptic; some α₂-adrenoceptors are also postsynaptic but other α₂-adrenoceptors are presynaptic and located on noradrenergic neurones themselves. Presynaptic α₂-adrenoceptors regulate noradrenaline release.

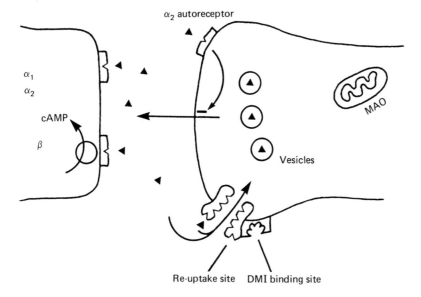

Figure 5.3 Schematic diagram of noradrenergic synapse

α_2-Adrenoceptors have been studied in humans by measuring the effect of the agonist clonidine on growth hormone (GH) secretion (a postsynaptic response) and on blood pressure (a presynaptic effect). There is consistent evidence that the GH response is blunted in depression whereas the blood pressure is unchanged (Checkley et al., 1986). These studies suggest reduced postsynaptic hypothalamic α_2 sensitivity in depression with no change in presynaptic α_2 function. However, many antidepressant drugs induce a gradual decrease in presynaptic α_2-adrenoceptor function (Sugrue, 1983). Whether this effect of drugs would oppose the deficit in postsynaptic α_2-adrenoceptor function in depression is debatable.

Curiously, circulating blood platelets have many of the properties of neurones and they may share a common embryological origin. Platelets have α_2-adrenoceptors and there has been considerable interest in the possibility that neurochemical parameters in platelets may shed light on central processes. This seems unlikely but, whether or not this is so, no consistent changes in platelet α_2-adrenoceptor binding have been reported in depressed patients (Braddock et al., 1986).

Platelet α_2 binding sites are reduced in postmenopausal women and they decline following childbirth but there is no direct evidence that this is caused by reductions in circulating oestrogen concentration or that there are corresponding changes in brain α_2 sites. In experimental animals oestrogen treatment does influence α_2 binding sites but the direction of the change is different in different species and tissues (uterus, platelet, hypothalamus, other CNS areas; Bloomfield, Elliott and Rutterford, 1985; Johnson et al., 1985). In women with maternity blues, platelet α_2-receptor numbers are greater than in those without the blues at 7–10 days postpartum and it may be that falling oestrogen concentrations postpartum trigger changes in α_2 function which predispose some women to puerperal mood changes (Metz et al., 1983).

Sex steroids and 5-hydroxytryptamine (5-HT)
Abnormalities in 5-HT neurotransmission have been implicated in the aetiology of depression and, in older literature, in the mechanism of action of hallucinogenic drugs. There are scattered reports of disparate effects of sex steroids upon 5-HT function.

The role of 5-HT in the aetiology of depression is obscure (Deakin and Crow, 1986). Several lines of evidence suggest that depression is associated with reduced function in 5-HT neurones as indicated by studies of 5-HT metabolism in blood, cerebrospinal fluid and *post mortem* brains of depressed patients. The synaptic actions of 5-HT are terminated by re-uptake channels in 5-HT neurones (*Figure 5.4*) which suck back 5-HT after it has been released. Some antidepressant drugs selectively block the 5-HT re-uptake site thus potentiating the synaptic actions of 5-HT and reversing the putative deficit of 5-HT.

There is evidence that oestrogens influence the 5-HT re-uptake site. 5-HT re-uptake sites can be measured in brain membrane preparations by measuring the binding of radioactive imipramine—a re-uptake blocker. In one study, removal of the ovaries from rats led to a 200% increase in the number of imipramine binding sites (Stockert and De Robertis, 1985). Confusingly, another study found that imipramine binding sites increased in male rats treated with oestrogen (Ravizza *et al.*, 1985). Clearly further studies are needed to clarify the influence of sex steroids on the 5-HT re-uptake site. The functional significance of a change in the number of 5-HT uptake sites is far from understood. Nevertheless, a strong influence of sex steroids upon the 5-HT uptake mechanism would have interesting implications for theories of puerperal mood disorders.

Little is known about sex steroid effects on the synthesis and release of 5-HT outside the hypothalamus but interactions with postsynaptic receptors have been described. Recent years have seen a resurgence of interest in the classification of receptors and multiple subtypes have been described. For present purposes there are two main families—5-HT_1 and 5-HT_2 (Peroutka, Lebovitz and Snyder, 1981). Both types are postsynaptic and some 5-HT_1 receptor subtypes are also presynaptic and regulate 5-HT release (*Figure 5.4*).

Antidepressant drugs have a shared ability to decrease 5-HT_2 receptor binding sites when repeatedly administered for two weeks or more. Since this effect parallels the time course of the clinical effect, 5-HT_2 receptor down-regulation has been proposed as a common mechanism of anti-depressant action (Peroutka and Snyder, 1980). It has been reported that ovariectomy prevents antidepressant-induced 5-HT_2 receptor down-regulation in cerebral cortex and that administration of oestradiol restores the antidepressant effects on 5-HT_2 receptors (Kendall, Stancel and Enna, 1981). Low circulating concentrations of oestrogen in the postnatal period might therefore reduce responsiveness to antidepressant drugs in women who become depressed. This question has not been investigated clinically and at present such generalizing from animal experiments to the human postnatal period is distinctly speculative.

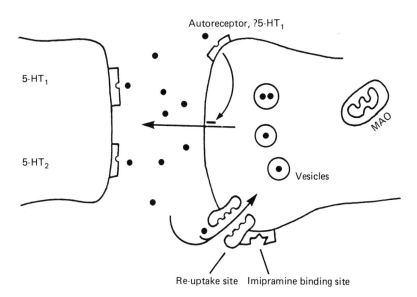

Figure 5.4 Schematic diagram of 5-HT synapse

It can be seen that sex steroids influence some neurochemical parameters related to 5-HT systems but, as with all neurochemical effects of drugs, it is important to know whether the neurochemical change is translated into a functional effect. This is the purpose of experiments in which a behavioural output is measured in response to administration of drugs which act on the neurochemical system of interest. Only one study bears directly on the question of whether sex steroids affect functional 5-HT neurotransmission. O'Connor and Feder (1985) reported that the myoclonus which follows administration of the 5-HT precursor 5-hydroxytryptophan (5-HTP) in ovariectomized guinea pigs is enhanced by pretreatment with oestrogen. However, it was not established whether oestrogen enhanced 5-HTP myoclonus by increasing 5-HT synthesis or release, by increasing 5-HT receptor sensitivity or by acting on a different neurotransmitter system which modifies 5-HT neurotransmission. These results suggest the hypothesis that in humans the postnatal decline in oestrogen concentration reduces functional 5-HT neurotransmission which increases vulnerability to early puerperal depression.

Sex steroids and dopamine

Excessive dopamine neurotransmission has been implicated in the aetiology of functional psychoses, largely on the basis of drug actions (Crow and Deakin, 1985). Amphetamine increases dopamine release and exacerbates or precipitates schizophrenia-like states. Neuroleptics exert their antipsychotic effects by blocking postsynaptic dopamine (D_2) receptors.

Post mortem brain and *in vivo* imaging studies suggest that schizophrenics have increased numbers of postsynaptic dopamine (D_2) receptors and this could be a mechanism for increased dopamine neurotransmission. The issue of whether the *post mortem* increases in D_2 receptor number are part of the disease process or a consequence of neuroleptic treatment in life will probably be resolved by new *in vivo* imaging techniques. These techniques enable radio ligand binding studies of receptors to be carried out in patients during their first illness before they have ever received neuroleptic drugs. Preliminary indications are that D_2 receptors are not increased in patients who have never received drugs and thus that increased D_2 receptors are not involved in the pathogenesis of schizophrenia (Farde *et al.*, 1986; but see Wong *et al.*, 1986; Crawley *et al.*, 1986). If these findings are confirmed, the dopamine theory will face a severe crisis because most other ways in which increased dopamine function could come about have been excluded in *post mortem* brain studies of schizophrenia.

Neuroleptic drugs are also effective in the treatment of manic illnesses and probably ameliorate psychotic symptoms in depression. A problem for the dopamine theory of schizophrenia is that much of the evidence also applies to manic depressive illness. Indeed, excessive dopamine neurotransmission could underlie psychotic symptoms irrespective of clinical diagnosis. If so, some other mechanism is necessary to explain the form of psychosis.

The clinical features of puerperal psychotic states suggest they are usually related to bipolar affective disorder rather than to schizophrenia (*see* Brockington and Roper, Chapter 1). Puerperal psychoses are usually treated with neuroleptic drugs but this treatment has never been the subject of a controlled clinical trial. Nevertheless, dopaminergic mechanisms are clearly of considerable interest in the search for the aetiology of puerperal psychoses.

Oestrogens, progesterone and prolactin undoubtedly influence dopamine release from hypothalamic dopamine neurones involved in the control of prolactin and probably GnRH secretion. In contrast, hormonal effects on limbic and basal ganglia dopamine systems, which are probably more relevant to psychological symptoms in the puerperium, are less clear cut. There is an extensive literature which is well reviewed by Van Hartesveldt and Joyce (1986).

Dopamine-containing cell bodies in the pons probably do not contain oestrogen receptors and any effects of sex steroids on dopamine neurones are likely to be indirect. Most studies find no effect on dopamine turnover although reduced dopamine concentrations in striatum and mesolimbic areas have been described following oestrogen administration (Dupont et al., 1981; Di Paolo et al., 1982). In view of these considerations it is puzzling that, in electrophysiological studies, rapid changes in the firing rate of substantia nigra dopamine neurones followed intravenous oestradiol administration (Chiodo and Caggiula, 1983). However, some neurones responded with increases and others with decreases in firing rates and these opposed effects may explain the apparent lack of effect of oestrogen upon biochemical indices of striatal dopamine turnover.

Several studies have assessed the effects of oestrogen on nigro-striatal dopamine function by observing effects on behavioural stereotypies evoked by the dopamine agonist drugs amphetamine and apomorphine. Conflicting results have been obtained but Gordon (1980) suggested a possible resolution. Oestrogen administration suppresses the effects of dopamine agonists for up to 24 h after administration, but 48 h or longer after oestrogen, enhanced behavioural responses to dopamine agonists are seen. Since this pattern is seen with apomorphine which acts directly on dopamine receptors, the results suggest oestrogen acts upon dopamine receptors or beyond to change responses to apomorphine. Receptor binding studies suggest the receptors themselves are involved. At 24 h or more after the final dose of oestrogen, tritiated neuroleptic binding reveals increased dopamine receptor numbers (e.g. Hruska and Silbergeld, 1980; Di Paolo et al., 1982). There are no clues as to the mechanism of oestrogen effects upon dopamine receptors and a recent study failed to find consistent or marked effects of various oestrogen treatments on dopamine turnover or receptor binding (Simpson, 1986).

The positive results suggest that withdrawal from high circulating concentrations of oestradiol may be associated with increased dopamine receptor sensitivity. Withdrawal from high circulating concentrations of oestrogen occurs in the immediate postnatal period and it is tempting to speculate that increased dopamine receptor sensitivity may be the trigger for puerperal psychotic states. However, little is known about the influence of progesterone upon dopaminergic mechanisms and postnatal changes in progesterone concentrations and other hormones might substantially modify the effects of oestrogen withdrawal upon dopamine receptor function.

Hormones of lactation

Prolactin

Prolactin is secreted by lactotroph cells of the anterior pituitary. Secretion of prolactin is inhibited by dopamine which is released from nerve terminals in the median eminence and is transported in the portal blood. In the pituitary, dopamine acts on D_2 receptors on the lactotrophs to inhibit prolactin release. This inhibitory effect is antagonized by neuroleptic drugs which block D_2 receptors. This is the mechanism of the hyperprolactinaemia which is induced by all neuroleptic drugs. Prolactin secretion is modulated by a number of neurotransmitters (5-HT, GABA) and peptides (TRH, somatostatin, VIP). The subject is reviewed by Tuomisto and Mannisto (1985).

Prolactin binding sites are present in mammary tissue and the most salient function of prolactin is to initiate and maintain lactation (Voogt, 1978). Prolactin receptors are also present in brain but are confined to areas which lie outside the blood-barrier, e.g. the choroid plexus, arcuate nucleus, median eminence and subfornical organ (Walsh, Rosner and Brawer, 1978). However, circulating prolactin does have behavioural effects in animals. Increased circulating prolactin concentrations induced by implantation of pituitary grafts enhances rat grooming behaviour in novel situations. This behavioural effect of peripheral prolactin is reported to be antagonized by intraventricular administration of prolactin antibodies (Drago et al., 1986). The significance of these behavioural effects of prolactin in rats and whether they apply in humans is not clear. Prolactin-secreting tumours are not associated with conspicuous psychiatric morbidity. The possible involvement of prolactin in maternal behaviour is discussed in the next section.

Prolactin exerts feedback effects on hypothalamic dopamine release; increasing prolactin concentration increases dopamine release which inhibits further prolaction release (e.g. Perkins and Westfall, 1978). There has been considerable interest in the possibility that prolactin influences neurotransmission in the major forebrain dopamine systems. Most interest has centred on reports that prolactin increases dopamine function by increasing the number of dopamine receptors. The dopamine receptor agonist apomorphine induces behavioural stereotypies in rats which were enhanced by experimentally-induced hyperprolactinaemia (Drago et al., 1981). One explanation of this result was that prolactin caused an increase in the number of dopamine receptors, thus increasing the behavioural effects of apomorphine. In one study, hyperprolactinaemia increased striatal dopamine receptor binding sites (Hruska et al., 1982). This group has also presented evidence that increases in D_2 receptors which occur during long-term treatment with neuroleptics are due to the associated hyperprolactinaemia. Preventing the hyperprolactinaemia by removing the pituitary prevented the increase in D_2 receptors. However, in a series of careful studies, Simpson, Jenner and Marsden (1986a,b) showed that experimental hyperprolactinaemia failed to affect striatal dopamine receptor binding sites and hypophysectomy did not prevent neuroleptic-induced dopamine receptor supersensitivity.

Oxytocin

Oxytocin is released from nerve terminals in the posterior pituitary directly into the circulation. Oxytocin is a peptide which differs in only two amino acids from vasopressin—the other posterior pituitary hormone. Oxytocin and vasopressin-containing nerve terminals in the posterior pituitary originate from magnocellular neurones in the supraoptic and paraventricular nuclei of the hypothalamus. Scattered parvocellular oxytocin-containing neurones are found in other hypothalamic areas.

Oxytocin is synthesized as part of a larger precursor peptide which is enzymatically cleaved to produce oxytocin and other peptide fragments including a neurophysin. Oxytocin-related neurophysin has a longer half life and is easier to assay than oxytocin in the circulation. Administration of a single dose of oestrogen to male or female humans is followed by an increase in circulating oxytocin and associated neurophysin concentrations (Amico, Said and Robinson, 1981). The possibility of using neurophysin responses to oestrogen administration as an index of oestrogen receptor sensitivity in puerperal mental illness is under investigation (Bearn, Fairhall and Checkley, 1986).

Oxytocin secretion increases during pregnancy and has well known roles in initiating uterine contractions and causing milk ejection in response to suckling. The suckling stimulus to oxytocin secretion is transmitted by sensory nerve fibres from the nipple to the brain stem and relayed along ascending projections to the magnocellular oxytocin neurosecretory neurones of the hypothalamus (see Lincoln and Paisley, 1982). Various neurotransmitters including noradrenaline and opioid peptides modulate oxytocin release in subhuman species.

Oxytocin-containing nerve terminals are found in several CNS areas (Sofroniew, 1983). Highest concentrations of oxytocin are found in monoamine nuclei—substantia nigra, ventral tegmental area, locus coeruleus and raphe nuclei. Significant amounts are also present in amygdala and hippocampus.

Little is known about possible influences of oxytocin on monoamine neurotransmission; there is some evidence for actions on noradrenaline turnover and on functional dopamine neurotransmission (Heuven-Nolsen, DeKloet and Versteeg, 1984). Furthermore, it is not known whether release of oxytocin in the CNS parallels release from the posterior pituitary, for example, during suckling; the two may be quite independent.

There are few studies of possible behavioural functions of oxytocin. A possible role in the induction of maternal behaviour is discussed below. Contrasting effects of oxytocin and vasopressin on learning, extinction and retention of conditioned avoidance behaviour have been described (Bohus et al., 1978) but it has recently been questioned whether memory mechanisms are directly involved in the effects (Saghal and Wright, 1984).

In a prospective study (Whalley, Robinson and Fink, 1982), one mother who developed a puerperal psychosis had markedly raised circulating oxytocin concentrations during pregnancy. However there was some uncertainty as to whether the patient's apparently increased oxytocin concentrations were in fact due to crossreacting placental oxytocinase, an oxytocin degrading enzyme. Another hint that oxytocin may be relevant to the aetiology of affective disorder is the observation that of the various hormonal responses to ECT, greater oxytocin-associated neurophysin responses predict a better outcome (Scott *et al.*, 1986).

Hormones and maternal behaviour

Most mammalian neonates require a considerable period of postnatal development to achieve an independent existence. During this period a variety of parental behaviours nurture the offspring, e.g. retrieval, warming, feeding, cleaning, nest building. There has been considerable interest in the plausible possibility that maternal behaviours are released by the hormonal changes of pregnancy and lactation. This possibility has largely been investigated in the rat. Things may be very different in primates and humans. For example, rat behaviour is heavily influenced by olfactory cues whereas the visual modality is much more developed in the primate. In the primate, parity appears to be an important influence. Multiparous female primates show a full range of maternal behaviours and breast development when presented with a test infant (Capitanio, Weissberg and Reite, 1985). Under some conditions nulliparous females fail to show spontaneous maternal behaviour. Perhaps the first infant causes learning or imprinting of maternal behaviour in the primate and it may be that lactational and placental hormones play a permissive role in this process. It is equally possible that learning maternal behaviour is a social process in the primate and depends on being reared in a normal group with other animals of various ages.

Virgin female rats will eventually display maternal behaviours when housed with a litter of rat pups for several days. The onset of maternal behaviour is accelerated by treatment with oestrogen which induces virgin rats to build nests, retrieve and clean the pups, and lie on them. There is evidence that the eventual spontaneous appearance of maternal behaviour in untreated virgin female rats is due to endogenous oestrogen and in these experiments progesterone appeared to have an antagonistic role (Gonzalez and Deis, 1986). The ability of sex steroids to induce maternal behaviour may be indirect as hypophysectomy eliminated steroid-induced maternal behaviour (Bridges *et al.*, 1985). These authors demonstrated that implantation of prolactin-secreting pituitary grafts reinstated the ability of steroids to induce maternal behaviour in hypophysectomized rats. They suggest that sustained high concentrations of prolactin are necessary for steroids to evoke maternal behaviour and point out that this obtains during pregnancy.

Intraventricular administration of oxytocin induces maternal behaviour within one hour in ovariectomized and oestrogen-primed virgin female rats (Pedersen *et al.*, 1982).

Fahrbach, Morrell and Pfaff (1985) suggest that oestrogen evokes maternal behaviour by its ability to release endogenous oxytocin (*see* above). They found that oxytocin antiserum and antagonists reduced oestrogen-induced maternal behaviour. However, it is possible that oxytocin-induced maternal behaviour may be due to more general effects of oxytocin on responsiveness to stimuli, pups being particularly salient stimuli (Fahrbach, Morrell and Pfaff, 1986).

There is no evidence which bears directly on the question of whether the hormonal changes of pregnancy and lactation are concerned with human maternal behaviour or mother-infant bonding. In bottle feeding mothers, concentrations of prolactin and oxytocin decline postnatally yet they show normal bonding and maternal behaviour. However, this does not rule out the possibility suggested above that sustained high concentrations of prolactin and oxytocin during late pregnancy are necessary for normal human maternal behaviour. If an appropriate hormonal milieu is a necessary pre-condition for the full expression of human maternal behaviour and mother-infant bonding, then hormonal dysfunction could give rise to difficulties in the mother-infant relationship resulting in secondary symptoms of guilt and depression which in turn maintain the mother-infant difficulties.

Little is known about the biology of paternal behaviour but Dixon and George (1982) reported that circulating prolactin concentrations increased markedly in a male primate when handling its infant and not in other situations. They speculate that prolactin may have a role in mediating paternal behaviour in primates.

References

AMICO, J. A., SAID, M. S. and ROBINSON, A. G. (1981). Neurophysin and stimulation with oestrogen. *Journal of Clinical Endocrinology and Metabolism*, **52**, 988–993

BEARN, J., FAIRHALL, S. and CHECKLEY, S. (1986). A new marker for estrogen sensitivity with potential application to post partum depression. Proceedings of Third International Conference of the Marcé Society (abstract)

BIEGON, A., RECHES, A., SNYDER, S. L. and McEWAN, B. S. (1983). Serotonergic and noradrenergic receptors in the rat brain: modulation by chronic exposure to ovarian hormones. *Life Sciences*, **32**, 2015–2021

BLOOM, F., BATTENBERG, E., ROSSIER, J., LING, N. and GUILLEMIN, R. (1978). Neurons containing enkephalin; immunocytochemical studies. *Proceedings of the National Academy of Sciences of the USA*, **75**, 1591–1595

BLOOMFIELD, J. G., ELLIOTT, J. M. and RUTTERFORD, M. G. (1985). Changes in ^{3}H-yohimbine binding in rabbits associated with oestrogen/progesterone treatment and pregnancy. *British Journal of Pharmacology*, **85**, 323P

BOHUS, B., URBAN, I., VAN WIMERSMA GREIDANUS, Tj.B. and DE WEID, D. (1978). Opposite effects of oxytocin and vasopressin on avoidance behaviour and hippocampal theta rhythm in the rat. *Neuropharmacology*, **17**, 239–247

BONNAR, J., FRANKLIN, M., NOTT, P. N. and McNEILLY, A. S. (1978). Effect of breast feeding on pituitary function after childbirth. *British Medical Journal*, **ii**, 82–84

BRADDOCK, L., COWEN, P. J., ELLIOTT, J. M., FRASER, S. and STUMP, K. (1986). Binding of yohimbine and imipramine to platelets in depressive illness. *Psychological Medicine*, **16**, 765–773

BRIDGES, R. S., DI BISSE, R., LOUNDES, D. D. and DOHERTY, P. C. (1985). Prolactin stimulation of maternal behaviour in female rats. *Science*, **227**, 782–784

BROCKINGTON, I. F., KELLY, A., HALL, P. and DEAKIN, J. F. W. (1988). Premenstrual relapse of puerperal psychosis. *Journal of Affective Disorders*, **14**, 287–292

CAPITANIO, J. P., WEISSBERG, M. and REITE, M. (1985). Biology of maternal behaviour: recent findings and implications. In: *The Psychobiology of Attachment and Separation*, (M. Reite and T. Field, eds), pp. 51–92. New York: Academic Press

CHECKLEY, S. A., CORN, T. H., GLASS, I. B., BURTON, S. W. and BURKE, C. A. (1986). The responsiveness of central α_2 adrenoceptors in depression. In *The Biology of Depression*, (J. F. W. Deakin, ed.), pp. 100–120. London: Gaskell

CHIODO, L. A. and CAGGIULA, A. R. (1983). Substantia nigra dopamine neurones: alterations in basal discharge rate and auto receptor sensitivity induced by oestrogen. *Neuropharmacology*, **22**, 593–599

CRAWLEY, J. C. W., CROW, T. J., JOHNSTONE, E. C. *et al.* (1986). Uptake of ^{77}Br-spiperone in the striata of schizophrenic patients and controls. *Nuclear Medicine Communications*, **7**, 599–607

CROW, T. J. and DEAKIN, J. F. W. (1985). Neurohormonal transmission, behaviour and mental disorder. In: *Handbook of Psychiatry*, Vol. 5, (M. Shepherd, ed), pp. 137–182. Cambridge: Cambridge University Press

DEAKIN, J. F. W. and CROW, T. J. (1986). Monoamines, rewards and punishments: the anatomy and physiology of the affective disorders. In: *The Biology of Depression*, (J. F. W. Deakin, ed.), pp. 1–25., London: Gaskell

DI PAOLO, T., BEDARD, P. J., DUPONT, A., POGET, P. and LABRIE, F. (1982). Effects of oestradiol on intact and denervated striatal dopamine receptors and on dopamine levels: a biochemical and behavioural study. *Canadian Journal of Physiology and Pharmacology*, **60**, 350–357

DIXON, A. F. and GEORGE, L. (1982). Prolactin and parental behaviour in a male new world primate. *Nature*, **299**, 551–553

DRAGO, F., VAN REE, J. M., BOHUS, B. and DE WEID, D. (1981). Endogenous hyperprolactinaemia enhances amphetamine and apomorphine-induced stereotypy. *European Journal of Pharmacology*, **72**, 249–253

DRAGO, F., BOHUS, B., BITETTI, K., SCAPAGNINI, U., VAN REE, J. M. and DE WEID, D. (1986). Intra-cerebroventricular injection of anti-prolactin serum suppresses excessive grooming of pituitary homografted rats. *Behavioural and Neural Biology*, **46**, 99–105

DUPONT, A., DI PAOLO, T., GAGUE, B. and BARDEN, N. (1981). Effects of chronic oestrogen treatment on dopamine concentrations and turnover in discrete brain nuclei of ovariectomized rats. *Neuroscience Letters*, **22**, 69–74

FACCHINETTI, F., NAPPI, G., PETRALGIA, F., VOLPE, A. and GENAZZANI, A. R. (1983). Oestradiol/progesterone imbalance and the premenstrual syndrome. *Lancet*, **ii**, 1302

FAHRBACH, S. E., MORRELL, J. I. and PFAFF, D. W. (1985). Possible role for endogenous oxytocin in oestrogen—facilitated maternal behaviour in rats. *Neuroendocrinology*, **40**, 526–532

FAHRBACH, S. E., MORRELL, J. I. and PFAFF, D. W. (1986). Effect of varying the duration of pre-test cage habituation on oxytocin induction of short-latency maternal behaviour. *Physiology and Behaviour*, **37**, 135–139

FARDE, L., HALL, H., EHRIN, E. and SEDVALL, G. (1986). Quantitative analysis of D_2 dopamine receptor binding in the living human brain by PET. *Science*, **231**, 258–261

FERIN, M. (1984). Endogenous opioid peptides and the menstrual cycle. *Trends in the Neurosciences*, **7**, 194–196

GLASIER, A., McNEILLY, A. S. and HOWIE, P. W. (1984). Pulsatile secretion of LH in relation to the resumption of ovarian activity post-partum. *Clinical Endocrinology*, **20**, 415–426

GLASS, M. R., RUDD, B. T., LYNCH, S. S. and BULL, W. R. (1981). Oestrogen-gonadotrophin feedback mechanisms in the puerperium. *Clinical Endocrinology*, **14**, 257–268

GONZALEZ, D. E. and DEIS, R. P. (1986). Maternal behaviours in cyclic and androgenized female rats: role of ovarian hormones. *Physiology and Behaviour*, **38**, 789–793

GORDON, J. H. (1980). Modulation of apromorphine-induced stereotypy by oestrogen: time course and dose response. *Brain Research Bulletin*, **5** , 679–682

HEUVEN-NOLSEN, D. VAN, DEKLOET, E. R. and VERSTEEG, D. H. G. (1984). Oxytocin affects utilization of noradrenaline in distinct limbic forebrain regions of the rat brains. *Neuropharmacology*, **23**, 1373–1377

HRUSKA, R. E. and SILBERGELD, E. K. (1980). Estrogen treatment enhances dopamine receptor sensitivity in the rat striatum. *European Journal of Pharmacology*, **61**, 367–400

HRUSKA, R. E. PITMAN, K. T., SILBERGELD, E. K. and LUDMER, L. M. (1982). Prolactin increases the density of striatal dopamine receptors in normal and hypophysectomized male rats. *Life Sciences*, **30**, 547–553

ISHIZUKA, B., QUIGLEY, M. E. and YEN, S. S. C. (1984). Post partum hypogonadotrophinism: evidence for increased opioid inhibition. *Clinical Endocrinology*, **20**, 573–578

JEPPSSON, S., RAMEVIK, G., THORELL, J. I. and WIDE, L. (1977). Influence of LH/FSH releasing hormone (LRH) on the basal secretion of gonadotrophinism: relation to plasma levels of oestradiol, progesterone and prolactin during the post-partum period of lactating and in non-lactating women. *Acta Endocrinologica*, **84**, 713–728

JOHNSON, A. E., NOCK, B., McEWAN, B. and FEDER, H. H. (1985). Estradiol modulation of α_2-noradrenergic receptors in guinea pig brain assessed by tritium-sensitive film autoradiography. *Brain Research*, **336**, 153–157

KENDALL, D. A., STANCEL, G. M. and ENNA, S. J. (1981). Imipramine: effect of ovarian steroids on modifications in serotonin receptor binding. *Science*, **211**, 1184–1185

KILLICK, S. R. (1986). Ultrasonographic studies of ovarian follicular development in normal, oral contraceptive and luteinized unruptured follicle cycles. M.D. Thesis, University of Manchester

KNOBIL, E. (1980). The neuroendocrine control of the menstrual cycle. *Recent Progress in Hormonal Research*, **36**, 53–88

KUEVI, V., LAWSON, R., DIXSON, A. F. et al. (1983). Plasma amine and hormone changes in post-partum blues. *Clinical Endocrinology*, **19**, 39–46.

LINCOLN, D. W. and PAISLEY, A. C. (1982). Neuroendocrine control of milk ejection. *Journal of Reproduction and Fertility*, **65**, 571–586

McEWAN, B. S. (1985). Steroids and brain function. *Trends in Pharmacological Sciences*, January, 22–26

McNEILLY, A. S., GLASIER, A., JONASSEN, J. and HOWIE, P. (1982). Evidence for direct inhibition of ovarian function by prolactin. *Journal of Reproduction and Fertility*, **65**, 559–569

METZ, A., STUMP, K., COWAN, P. S., ELLIOTT, J. M., GELDER, M. G. and GRAHAME-SMITH, D. G. (1983). Changes in platelet α_2-adrenoceptor binding post-partum: possible relation to maternity blues. *Lancet*, **i**, 495–498

MOSS, R. L. and McCANN, S. M. (1973). Induction of mating behaviour in rats by luteinizing hormone-releasing factor. *Science*, **181**, 177–179

NEWNHAM, J. P., DENNETT, P. M., FERRON, S. A. et al. (1984). A study of the relationship between circulating beta-endorphin-like immunoreactivity and post partum 'blues'. *Clinical Endocrinology*, **20**, 169–177

O'CONNOR, L. H. and FEDER, H. H. (1985). Estradiol and progesterone influence L-5-hydroxytryptophan-induced myoclonus in male guinea pigs: sex differences in serotonin–steroid interactions. *Brain Research*, **330**, 121–125

PEDERSEN, C. A., ASCHER, J. A., MONROE, J. L. and PRANGE, A. J. (1982). Oxytocin induces maternal behaviour in virgin female rats. *Science*, **216**, 648–650

PERKINS, N. A. and WESTFALL, T. C. (1978). The effect of prolactin on dopamine release from rat striatum and medial basal hypothalamus. *Neuroscience*, **3**, 59–63

PEROUTKA, S. J. and SNYDER, S. H. (1980). Long-term antidepressant treatment decreased spiroperidol-labelled serotonin receptor binding. *Science*, **210**, 88–90

PEROUTKA, S. J., LEBOVITZ, R. M. and SNYDER, S. H. (1981). Two distinct central serotonin receptors with different physiological functions. *Science*, **212**, 827–829

RAVIZZA, L., NICOLETTI, F., POZZI, O. and BARBACCIA, M. L. (1985). Repeated daily treatments with estradiol benzoate increase the [^{3}H] imipramine binding in male rat frontal cortex. *European Journal of Pharmacology*, **107**, 395–396

REUBI, J. C. and MAURER, R. (1984). Visualisation of LH-RH receptors in the rat brain. *European Journal of Pharmacology*, **106**, 453–454

SAGHAL, A. and WRIGHT, C. (1984). Choice as opposed to latency measures in avoidance suggests that vasopressin and oxytocin do not affect memory in the rat. *Neuroscience Letters*, **48**, 299–304

SAR, M. and STUMPF, W. E. (1981). Central noradrenergic neurones concentrate ^{3}H-oestradiol. *Nature*, **289**, 500–504

SARKAR, D. K. (1983). Does LH-RH meet the criteria for a hypothalamic releasing factor. *Psychoneuroendocrinology*, **8**, 259–275

SCOTT, A. I. F., WHALLEY, L. J., BENNIE, J. and BOWLER, G. (1986). Oestrogen-stimulated neurophysin and outcome after electroconvulsive therapy. *Lancet*, **i**, 1411–1414

SILVERMAN, A. J. and KREY, L. C. (1978). The luteinizing hormone releasing hormone (LH-RH) neuronal networks of the guinea pig brain. 1. Intra- and extra-hypothalamic projections. *Brain Research*, **157**, 233–246

SIMPSON, M. D. C. (1986). Hormonal regulation of forebrain dopamine systems in the rat. PhD Thesis, University of London

SIMPSON, M. D. C., JENNER, P. and MARSDEN. C. D. (1986a). Hyperprolactinaemia does not alter specific striatal ^{3}H-spiperone binding in the rat. *Biochemical Pharmacology*, **35**, 3203–3206

SIMPSON, M. D. C., JENNER, P. and MARSDEN, D. C. (1986b). Hypophysectomy may non-selectively alter pharmacokinetic parameters to enhance the ability of haloperidol to increase striatal dopamine receptor binding density in the rat. *Biochemical Pharmacology*, **37**, 3501–3506

SOFRONIEW, M. W. (1983). Vasopressin and oxytocin in the mammalian brain and spinal cord. *Trends in the Neurosciences*, **6**, 467–472

SUGRUE, M. F. (1983). Chronic antidepressant therapy and associated changes in the central monoaminergic receptor functioning. *Pharmacology and Therapeutics*, **21**, 1–33

STOCKERT, M. and DE ROBERTIS, E. (1985). Effect of ovariectomy and estrogen on [^{3}H] imipramine binding to different regions of rat brain. *European Journal of Pharmacology*, **119**, 255–257

SULSER, F., JANOWSKY, A. J., OKADA, F., MANIER, P. H. and MOBLEY, P. L. (1983). Regulation of recognition and action function of the norepinephrine (NE) receptor-coupled adenylate cyclase system in brain: implications for the therapy of depression. *Neuropharmacology*, **22**, 425–432

TUOMISTO, J. and MANNISTO, D. (1985). Neurotransmitter regulation of anterior pituitary hormones. *Pharmacological Reviews*, **37**, 249–331

VAN HARTESVELDT, C. and JOYCE, J. N. (1986). Effects of estrogen on the basal ganglia. *Neuroscience and Biobehavioural Reviews*, **10**, 1–14

VOOGT, J. L. (1978). Control of hormone release during lactation. *Clinics in Obstetrics and Gynaecology*, **5**, 435–457

WAGNER, H. R., CRUTCHER, K. A. and DAVIS, J. N. (1979). Chronic estrogen treatment decreases beta-adrenergic responses in rat cerebral cortex. *Brain Research*, **171**, 147–151

WAGNER, H. R. and DAVIS, J. N. (1980). Decreased beta-adrenergic responses in the female rat brain are eliminated by ovariectomy: correlation of ^{3}H-dihydroalprenolol binding and catecholamine-stimulated cyclic AMP levels. *Brain Research*, **201**, 235–239

WALSH, R. S., ROSNER, B. I. and BRAWER, J. R. (1978). Prolactin binding sites in the rat brain. *Science*, **201**, 1041–1043

WEHRENBERG, W. B., WARDLAW, S. L., FRANTZ, A. G. and FERIN, M. (1982). Beta-endorphin in hypophyseal portal blood: variations throughout the menstrual cycle. *Endocrinology*, **111**, 879–881

WHALLEY, L. T., ROBINSON, I. C. A. F. and FINK, G. (1982). Oxytocin and neurophysin in post-partum mania. *Lancet*, **ii**, 387–388

WONG, D. F., WAGNER, H. N., TUNE, L. E. *et al.* (1986). Positron emission tomography reveals elevated D$_2$ dopamine receptors in drug-naive schizophrenics. *Science*, **234**, 1558–1563

Chapter 6

The development of an integrated community-orientated service for severe postnatal mental illness

Margaret Oates

Introduction

The fascination of psychiatrists with the most severe form of postnatal mental illness, often called puerperal psychosis, dates back at least to the early part of the last century and is evident in the writings of Esquirol and Marcé. However, it is relatively recently that the special needs of this group of patients have excited attention and interest. At about the same time that the work of Bowlby (1953) was beginning to have an impact on the practice of separation of mothers from their hospitalized children, the first facilities for the admission of babies together with their mentally ill mothers became available. Amongst the first hospitals to have such joint admissions were the Cassel Hospital in London and psychiatric units in Banstead (Surrey) and St. Nicholas's Hospital (Newcastle). By the 1970s there were a wide variety of admission facilities for mentally ill mothers and their babies throughout the country. Some of these facilities were in separate Mother and Baby Units, for example in Manchester, the Bethlem Royal Hospital, and in Shenley (Margison and Brockington, 1982).

Other facilities were in modified annexes in general psychiatric admission wards, for example in Sheffield, Nottingham and Leicester. In the absence of any special facilities, puerperal psychosis may result in the admission of a mother and baby pair to a general psychiatric ward. Despite the fact that the admission of babies with their severely mentally ill mothers is now common practice in the UK, it is by no means universal and probably fewer than half of these patients have the opportunity to be admitted with their babies when it is necessary. It is still very unusual in the rest of the world for such facilities to be available. British attitudes towards the management of mentally ill mothers and their babies excite interest and some incredulity at international meetings. The underlying philosophy of mother and baby admission is that prolonged separation of mothers from their infants is potentially damaging to the mother/infant relationship. It is very much in keeping with the now almost universal practice in the UK of allowing parents to stay with their sick children when in hospital and the 'rooming-in' policies of almost all British maternity units. It is presumed that keeping a mother and baby together during the treatment of her mental illness improves the chances of developing successful parenting skills and facilitates the rehabilitation of the patient with her family, if not the treatment of her condition as well (Bardon *et al.*, 1968). However, both these suppositions remain to be proven by clinical trials.

Despite the growth of District General Hospital psychiatric units over the past 20 years, the majority of psychiatric care in the UK is still provided by large Victorian mental hospitals, often remote from the community they serve. For many patients, particularly patients who have recently had a baby, there is a reluctance to be admitted to mental hospitals, and the distance involved in treatment often involves disruption to the family and to neighbourhood links and this can cause problems with rehabilitation. This is one of the reasons why there has been a tremendous growth of community care in psychiatry over the past 15 years. There has been a development of more local services, alternatives to admission, and consequently fewer and shorter in-patient admissions. These changes will inevitably affect the development of care for severe postnatal mental illness. Until the 1980s, the interest of psychiatrists (with a few exceptions, e.g. Tod, 1964; Pitt, 1968) had mainly been in those few patients who were ill enough to be admitted to hospital following childbirth, approximately two for every 1000 live births. The interest of the lay public has, on the other hand, been in the milder and much commoner conditions, probably at least 15% of all deliveries (Cox, Connor and Kendell, 1982). Few of these patients are ever seen by a psychiatrist (Kumar and Robson, 1984). Very little is known of the group of seriously mentally ill women who are referred for psychiatric care but who are not admitted to hospital. Despite the growth of professional and lay interest in postnatal mental illness, few women in the UK have the advantage of being referred to a consultant psychiatrist who has special experience in the subject. There has been only one consultant appointment in the UK with special responsibility for obstetric liaison and postnatal mental illness (Riley, 1986), although special clinics for such women have been developed in some areas of the country.

Nottingham and its psychiatric services

Nottingham is the eighth largest city in the UK and is the commercial, administrative and educational centre of the East Midlands, with a large campus University and a Medical School. Within its defined city boundaries it has a population of 400 000, but the population is 600 000 if the immediate suburbs are included. This conurbation is set within the larger county of Nottinghamshire, which apart from a few mining towns is predominantly rural. The population of the county of Nottingham is close to 1 000 000 people.

Nottingham's main industries are light engineering, textiles, electronics, tobacco and pharmaceuticals. This marked diversity of occupations has led to relative industrial resilience and prosperity and a stable population with little migration in or out of the city, apart from the arrival of two ethnic minority groups from the West Indies and Pakistan in the 1950s and 1970s. Nottingham's sociodemographic composition is typical of the rest of the UK and it has its share of inner urban problems (Giggs and Mather, 1983).

Prior to the last reorganization of the National Health Service in 1982, the Nottingham Health District served the smaller urban population of

400 000 to whom there were approximately 5500 births a year. Its psychiatric services until that time were provided from a Victorian mental hospital (Mapperley), which was also the base of the University Department of Psychiatry. This hospital has had a long, liberal tradition and a strong community orientation to its psychiatric services (Wing and Brown, 1961). Since the reorganization of the Health Service a new larger health district has been created, which now includes the wider catchment area of the City of Nottingham and its immediate suburbs, a population of 600 000 with an annual birth rate of approximately 7500 (*see Figure 6.1*). Since

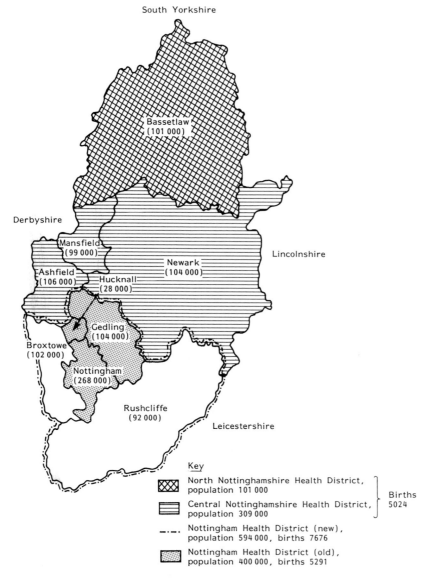

Figure 6.1 The county of Nottinghamshire Health District and district councils. Population figures for the district councils are given in brackets.

1984, the new Nottingham Health District has been served by a unified psychiatric service based upon the University Hospital (on the University campus) and Mapperley Hospital. The district is served by a single maternity unit (based on two general hospital sites), which delivers about 10 000 babies a year, 7500 of whom are from the Health District. Both psychiatric and maternity services are comprehensive and it is rare for patients to seek care out of Nottingham. This is also true for all other medical services. Private medical care plays little part in the provision of services to the population of Nottingham Health District.

Since 1975 all contacts with the psychiatric services have been recorded on the computerized psychiatric Case Register. Its coverage of the population was increased to include the new expanded Health District. The Case Register records sociodemographic information, patients' diagnoses, the manner and source of presentation, the utilization of services and the duration of the episode of care. Since 1982 the Case Register has also recorded, for female patients, the presence of children under the age of five years and one year in the family. All women who present to psychiatric services with a new episode of mental illness within a year of childbirth, are given a subsidiary ICD-9 diagnosis of 648.4 (complications of childbirth). This allows the subsequent retrieval of this patient group from the Case Register. Since the ninth version of the ICD was introduced in 1979, there has been no separate diagnostic code for postnatal mental illness. The Registration Form used for new patients is shown in *Figure 6.2*.

The history of management of postnatal mental illness in Nottingham

In 1970 a new Medical School was created at the University of Nottingham and in 1973 its clinical Department of Psychiatry was established. One of its members developed a special interest in postnatal mental illness and created, in 1974, the first joint admission facility for mentally ill mothers and their new babies. Two side-rooms on the academic acute psychiatric admission ward at Mapperley Hospital were modified to provide a daytime nursery and sitting room for the mothers and their babies, immediately adjacent to the nursing station to allow for easy observation. Because of the internal architecture of this old hospital, at night the mothers slept separately in a dormitory and their babies in a night nursery. These two mother and baby beds were soon constantly occupied but were sufficient only for half of those mothers requiring psychiatric admission; the remainder were admitted alone. Over the new few years, links were built up with the obstetricians and paediatricians and the clinical academic team saw an increasing number of referrals from these two sources, not all of whom required admission. In 1980 the admission facility was increased to four beds and cots (still on the acute psychiatric general admission ward), and further modifications were made to the existing premises to allow for a larger daytime nursery, mothers' sitting room and laundry facilities. The same clinical academic consultant assumed responsibility for these four beds. The aim of the academic unit was now to provide in-patient facilities for all mothers and babies requiring psychiatric admission in the puerperium. The number of postnatally mentally ill women seen by the Depart-

NOTTINGHAM HEALTH AUTHORITY

NEW CONTACT REGISTRATION FORM   N.F. 4/4

To be completed for:—

A first attendance at an Out-patient clinic or
A return to an Out-patient clinic after 6 months out of contact and
Every Ward and domiciliary visit and unarranged contact

SURNAME	PSYCHIATRIC UNIT No.	DATE SEEN
	SOUTH NOTTM UNIT No.	**CONTACT NOT MADE** ☐ CANCELLED
FORENAME	NORTH NOTTM. UNIT No.	☐ DNA, FURTHER APPOINTMENT ☐ DNA, NO ACTION
SECOND 3RD INITIAL	DATE OF BIRTH	**RESPONSIBLE CONSULTANT** (Sector allocated or Dr. on duty in cases of emergency)
PREVIOUS/MAIDEN SURNAME	SEX	
ADDRESS	☐ MALE ☐ FEMALE	**ALLOCATED TO MEMBER OF SECTOR TEAM** ☐ S.W. ☐ O.T. ☐ PSYCHOLOGIST ☐ C.P.N.
	MARITAL STATUS ☐ SINGLE ☐ MARRIED	
SECTOR	☐ WIDOWED ☐ DIVORCED ☐ SEPARATED	**WHERE SEEN**
BIRTHPLACE		
G.P.	**PREVIOUS PSYCHIATRIC CARE** ☐ MAPPERLEY GROUP	**TICK IF APPROPRIATE** ☐ DOMICILIARY VISIT – EMERGENCY
DR.	☐ SAXONDALE ☐ ELSEWHERE ☐ NONE	☐ COMMUNITY HOME VISIT ☐ FORENSIC – CIVIL ACTION (i.e. Compensation) ☐ FORENSIC – CRIMINAL
ADDRESS	**DIAGNOSIS**	☐ WARD VISIT – PARASUICIDE ☐ WARD VISIT – OTHER
OCCUPATION 1. Give occupation of patient only if male or unmarried female (or last occupation if currently unemployed)	1	☐ SEEN IN CASUALTY–PARASUICIDE ☐ SEEN IN CASUALTY–OTHER
....	2	☐ OTHER CONTACTS – PLEASE SPECIFY
2. Give occupation of father/husband for child or student/married woman.	PHYSICAL	**SOURCE OF REFERRAL** If multiple, mark the last agency only. ☐ SOCIAL SERVICES
.... Employer	If no psychiatric illness, mark **NPD**	☐ G.P. ☐ NON PSYCH. HOSPITAL
Status of employee in firm	**DISPOSAL**	☐ OTHER PSYCH. HOSPITAL OUTSIDE NOTTINGHAM HEALTH AUTHORITY
Employment status of patient at time of contact ☐ UNEMPLOYED ☐ RETIRED	☐ I.P. PSYCH. CARE ☐ DAY HOSPITAL	☐ OWN FAMILY ☐ POLICE
☐ HOUSEWIFE ☐ STUDENT ☐ EMPLOYED	☐ O.P. CARE **SECTOR TEAM**	☐ OTHER LEGAL (COURTS, PRISON) ☐ OTHER LAY (ie. neighbour)
☐ NUMBER OF CHILDREN	☐ SOCIAL WORKER ☐ PSYCHOLOGIST	☐ NOTTINGHAM MENTAL ILLNESS UNIT
☐☐☐☐☐☐ DATE OF BIRTH IF CHILD UNDER ONE YEAR	☐ COMM. NURSE ☐ G.P. ONLY	**LIKELY ETHNIC ORIGIN** ☐ AFRO CARIBBEAN
☐ CHILD OVER ONE BUT UNDER FIVE YEARS ☐ PATIENT PREGNANT	☐ NO FURTHER CONTACT	☐ INDO ASIAN ☐ OTHER

.... SIGNATURE OF MEDICAL OFFICER COMPLETING FORM

FILE TOP COPY IN THE CASE NOTES. SEND CARBON COPY TO MEDICAL RECORDS AS SOON AS POSSIBLE.

Figure 6.2 New Contact Registration Form used for new patients in the Nottinghamshire Health District.

ment was increasing steadily and many were being referred by consultant psychiatric colleagues.

In 1982, using the Psychiatric Case Register, all women presenting to the psychiatric services with a new episode of mental illness within a year of childbirth were identified for the purposes of clinical audit and research. By 1982 all such women requiring admission were admitted with their babies. At this stage, all members of the psychiatric team, both doctors and nurses, were still involved in general psychiatric work, but a special outpatient clinic was set up. Later in 1982 there was the first appointment of a full-time community psychiatric nursing sister in postnatal mental illness, initially to assist in the rehabilitation of in-patients. From 1983 to 1984, the clinical management of postnatal mental illness was continued with the same resources at the same hospital, Mapperley.

However, a major reorganization of the local psychiatric services was occurring in anticipation of the opening of a new District General Hospital Psychiatric Unit which was due to take place in July 1984. In 1984, a specialist postnatal mental illness service was created, with its base at the new University Hospital, which provided in-patient facilities for six mothers and babies in a specially modified annexe to a new general psychiatric admission ward. The population it served was now larger—600 000 and an annual birth rate of 7500—and its staff was proportionately increased. Apart from the medical members of the team, the other members—nurses, community psychiatric nurses and social worker—were now full-time specialists in the field.

These events are set out in *Table 6.1*.

Background to the study

The study described in this chapter preceded the most recent development in the management of postnatal mental illness in Nottingham, and took place between March 1983 and February 1984.

Clinical experience over the preceding 10 years had suggested that there were enough patients manifesting psychiatric morbidity following childbirth to occupy a substantial amount of the clinical workload of a consultant psychiatrist and the multidisciplinary team. The special needs of mentally ill mothers and their small babies were very apparent. The team needed special skills and sensitivities in handling the mother/infant pair and it was important to have close working links with obstetricians, midwives and paediatricians, as well as close contacts with members of the primary health care team. The psychiatric team had to respond to the needs of each mother, her baby and the rest of the family as well. The need to estimate the potential workload of the new expanded health district led to the setting up of the study. Its purpose was to estimate the total referred psychiatric morbidity in relation to childbirth in the defined old Nottingham Health District catchment area, and to examine the requirements of this group of patients in terms of the numbers of admission beds, staffing levels and facilities in order to extrapolate the findings to the new larger catchment area and to plan an adequate postnatal mental illness service for them. The study also set out to compare the postnatal psychiatric population with all other men and women from the same age group referred to the

Table 6.1 Development of postnatal mental illness unit

Old Health District

1970	Nottingham Medical School opens.
1974	Two Mother and Baby beds at Mapperley. Links with Maternity and Paediatric Services established.
1978	Liaison service to Maternity Unit.
1980	Four Mother and Baby beds under single consultant responsibility.
1982	Over 90% women within year of childbirth admitted to psychiatric hospital are now admitted with their babies. Establishment of multidisciplinary team. Postnatal outpatient clinic. Appointment full-time community psychiatric nurse, and half-time equivalent psychiatric social worker.
1982	Reorganization National Health Service. Psychiatric Case Register includes data on childbirth.
1983	Experimental project to replace admission of seriously ill mothers by intensive community nursing. Research project to examine need for specialist service. 90% admissions of mothers, and 60% of all referrals now managed by multidisciplinary team.

New Health District

1984	Move to new District General Hospital Psychiatric Unit. Establishment of Postnatal Mental Illness Service. New in-patient facility. Six beds and cots with separate facilities and specialist nursing staff on acute admission ward. Consultant Psychiatrist and supporting junior staff designated half-time equivalent specialists in postnatal mental illness and obstetric liaison. Two community psychiatric nurses. Psychiatric social worker full-time.
1985	Three outpatient clinics per week.
1986	Research project to evaluate impact new service on patterns referral and service uptake.
1988	New in-patient unit independently staffed and separate from general acute admission ward.

psychiatric services. If there were distinctive features in terms of diagnosis, patterns of referral and service uptake, this might suggest a different organization of services for postnatal mental illness than that appropriate for other psychiatric patients. The establishment of a specialist postnatal mental illness service with the appointment of full-time staff and the allocation of resources and consultant sessions would be further supported by evidence of a substantial workload.

Methods

For a period of one year from March 1983 to February 1984, Case Register data collection forms were scrutinized for women of reproductive age who had a new episode of psychiatric contact in the year following childbirth. A new episode of psychiatric contact is either a first-ever contact with psychiatric services or a contact made by a patient who has been out of contact with the psychiatric services or who has been well for the previous six months. A system of cross-checking with outpatient returns and the follow-up of incomplete forms ensured that this method of monitoring was both accurate and complete. Information was obtained from the Case Register and the patient's case notes in order to check the reliability of the diagnoses. The Case Register was used to obtain equivalent data on all other women and men between the ages of 16 and 50 (reproductive age) who presented with a new psychiatric contact during the same one-year period. The information used for the study for both the postnatal and the two control groups was their ICD-9 diagnosis, their mode of presentation and subsequent level of care. A hierarchical system was used to describe the level of care reached by the patients in the three months following their first contact. This system allows the patient to be described in terms of the highest level of care received, i.e. admission, day care, four or more subsequent outpatient appointments, between one and three outpatient appointments and no further contact made after the initial contact. The hierarchical nature of the system means that patients were not counted twice.

Incidence of referred postnatal illness and its implications for the organization of services

During the year from March 1983 to February 1984, the population of Nottingham Health District was 390 000 and during this year there were 5200 live births. One hundred and twelve women were referred to the psychiatric services within a year of childbirth; 87 (78%) of these women came from the catchment area giving an administrative (referred) incidence of postnatal mental illness of 16 per 1000 live births. During this year 1280 women were referred who were not in the year following childbirth and there were 1177 men. Approximately 25% of patients in all three groups came from outside the catchment area. Almost 10% of all women between the ages of 16 and 50 who were referred to the psychiatric services with a new episode of illness had a child under the age of one year. A further 15% of women ($n = 284$) had a child aged between one and five years.

At the same time as this study was carried out, each consultant psychiatrist in Nottingham was responsible, on average, for a population of 50 000 patients, generating 200 new episodes of psychiatric care and 1500 total patient contacts in this year. It can be seen that the number of new referrals from a population of 5200 women with a child under the age of one is about half the number of general adult patients who are referred to the average full-time general psychiatrist responsible for a population of 50 000. The number of patients included in this study ($n = 112$) substantially underrepresents the total number of referrals related to childbirth. The study team also managed women who were pregnant or who were experiencing peri-reproductive problems, for example those relating to perinatal death or women whose children were older than one year.

This figure also does not take account of the cumulative morbidity in the postnatal group. The total number of patients with pregnancy-related disorders was in excess of 200 and the total number of patient contacts during this year was 1200. This approximates to the sector workload of a full-time general psychiatric consultant in Nottingham. The psychiatric workload generated by childbirth would therefore appear to be one justification for the services of a consultant psychiatrist with at least a half-time special interest in postnatal mental illness, with supporting resources.

The diagnoses of the postnatal group

Table 6.2 shows the diagnostic distribution of the women who presented in the year following childbirth compared with all other women and men within the age range of 16–50. The women who did not have a child under the age of one and the men resembled each other in diagnoses, except that women had more depression (lines 4,5,6) but the diagnostic distribution of the postnatal group was different. A significantly higher proportion of the postnatal women were diagnosed as suffering from manic depressive illness, both mania and depression. They had also less schizophrenia and related disorders although the numbers were small. Of all the postnatal women, 40% were suffering from a severe or psychotic mental illness (lines 1–4) as compared with only 17% of the other women and 23% of the men. Depressive illness of all types (lines 4–6) accounted for 43% of the postnatal women, but only 26% of the other women and 14% of the men. Psychotic mental illness appears to be twice as common in patients referred within a year of childbirth as in other patients, as does depressive illness of all varieties. There are, however, no such significant differences in the distribution of other neurotic disorders. It is therefore evident that there are some conditions that present less frequently after childbirth than in men and women of the same age. In line 8 of *Table 6.2* it can be seen that 34% of women within a year of childbirth present with other diagnoses, as compared with over 50% of the control groups. These other diagnoses are mainly accounted for by alcoholism, personality disorder and no psychiatric diagnosis.

Table 6.2 Diagnoses of the postnatal group and two control groups

ICD code	Diagnostic term	Women with child under one year		Women without child under one year		Men	
		n	%	n	%	n	%
(1) 295, 297 298.3–.9	Schizophrenia and allied states	5	5	110	9	188	16
(2) 296.0, 296.2	Manic depression, manic	11	10	26	2	20	2
(3) 296.4, 298.1	Mixed affective state	3	3	3	0.2	2	0.2
(4) 296.1, 296.3 298.0	Manic depression, depressed	24	22	81	6	64	5
(5) 300.4	Neurotic depression	19	17	176	14	75	6
(6) 311	Depression NOS	4	4	72	6	38	3
(7) 300 (other)	Non-depressive neurotic	5	5.	178	14	107	9
(8)	All other diagnoses + no psychiatric diagnosis	41	34	634	50	683	58
Total		112		1280		1177	
		C1		C2		C3	

C1 v. C2: χ^2 = 83.13; df = 7; $P<0.001$.
C1 v. C3: χ^2 = 118.64; df = 7; $P<0.001$.

Initial contact with the psychiatric services

The type of contact by which the three groups presented to psychiatric services is shown in *Table 6.3*. No women in the postnatal group started their psychiatric care by direct admission or daycare. This manner of presentation (following a telephone consultation) is obviously unusual for all patients. Twenty-nine women were first seen on a general hospital ward (27 on the postnatal ward, i.e. within 3–10 days of childbirth). In contrast, only 8% of the non-postnatal women and men were referred from general hospital wards. Almost a third of the postnatal group were first seen as emergency referrals at home (domiciliary visit), compared with less than 10% of the other women and men. Taking lines 2 and 3 together, it can be seen that 55% of all postnatal patients make their first contact with the psychiatric services as an emergency, and are seen within 24 h either on a domiciliary visit or on a postnatal ward. This compares with only 17% of other women who make such first contact and 13% of men, despite the community orientation of all general psychiatric teams and their readiness to see patients at home. Fewer women in the postnatal period first presented as overdoses than other women. The acute nature of postnatal

Table 6.3 Initial contact with psychiatric services

Type of first contact	Women with child under one year		Women without child under one year		Men	
	n	%	n	%	n	%
(1) Admission/daycare	0	0	58	4	94	8
(2) Emergency domiciliary visit	33	29	114	9	87	7
(3) Ward referral (non-AS)	29	26	98	8	69	6
(4) Attempted suicide	12	11	203	16	109	9
(5) Outpatient contact	38	34	807	63	818	69
Total	112		1280		1177	
C1 v. C2: χ^2 = 99.9; $P<0.001$	C1		C2		C3	

referrals is further reflected in the small proportion (34%) of these patients who were first seen as outpatients in scheduled clinics, compared with the majority of other women and men (between 60% and 70% first saw a psychiatrist in this situation).

Levels of psychiatric care received following presentation

The severity of postnatal mental illness indicated by the diagnoses of the postnatal women and their mode of presentation is further demonstrated by the levels of care received in the three months following first contact which is shown in *Table 6.4*. A significantly higher proportion (27%) of women presenting in the year following childbirth were admitted to hospital than other women and men. However, it is interesting that 40% of the severely ill women were not admitted. The overwhelming majority of postnatal women received further psychiatric care for at least three months after first presentation. Only 13% had no further contact with psychiatric services, in contrast to almost half of the two control groups. It can also be seen from *Table 6.4* that the frequency of outpatient contacts was greater

Table 6.4 Level of care reached in the three months following the first episode of care from March 1983 to February 1984

	Women with child under one year		Women without child under one year		Men	
	n	%	n	%	n	%
Admission	30	27	116	9	113	10
Day care	–	–	32	3	43	4
4+ outpatient contacts	53	47	61	5	40	3
1–3 outpatient contacts	14	13	478	38	401	34
No further contact	15	13	593	46	580	49
Total	112		1280		1177	
C1 v. C2: χ^2 = 289.97; df = 3; $P<0.001$.	C1		C2		C3	

in the postnatal group, with almost half of the postnatal women being seen on more than four occasions in the outpatients clinic as compared with only 5% of other women and men. Three-quarters of the postnatal group were either admitted or in frequent contact in the three months following presentation, whereas three-quarters of the other two groups had either only one or no further contact with the psychiatric services.

The relationship between diagnosis, type of first contact and level of care

Of the total postnatal group, 40% were suffering from a severe or psychotic mental illness, all but five of them from manic depressive illness. *Table 6.5* shows that nine out of the 11 women who were manic were first seen on a postnatal ward, all of them within 10 days of childbirth, emphasizing the very early onset of this condition in relation to childbirth. Of the 24 women who were suffering from a depressive psychosis, only a third (7) presented on the postnatal ward within 10 days of childbirth, two-thirds of them being seen at home on a domiciliary visit (5), or in outpatients or Accident and Emergency (12). None of the neurotic illnesses or other diagnoses presented on the postnatal wards. Eleven of the 19 women with neurotic depressions were seen first on a domiciliary visit, the rest in outpatients, and taking all depressive illnesses together, only seven out of the 48 cases of depressive illness presented on the postnatal wards.

It is uncommon in Nottingham for a mother who has had an uncomplicated vaginal delivery to be detained in hospital for longer than five days. Those patients remaining on a postnatal ward for up to 10 days have usually had either operative delivery or other complications of childbirth. The fact that the majority of the manic patients and one-third of the patients with depressive psychoses were seen on the postnatal wards confirms the findings of other authors (Dean and Kendell, 1981) that the most acutely disturbed postnatal mental illnesses arise in close proximity to childbirth and that there is an association with caesarean section (Kendell *et al.*, 1981). Two-thirds of depressive psychoses and all forms of depressive illness were first seen at home or in the outpatient clinic, i.e. later in the puerperium, again confirming the findings of Dean and Kendell (1981).

Table 6.6 shows that women who were first seen on the postnatal wards were the most likely to be admitted. Sixteen of the 27 women who were first seen on a postnatal ward were transferred to a psychiatric inpatient bed. In contrast, only four out of the 33 women first seen on a domicilary visit and only six out of the 21 women first seen in outpatients were admitted. Only half of the women with depressive psychoses (12) were admitted and none of the women suffering with neurotic depression. Almost half of the remaining women with psychotic depressions and the majority of those with neurotic depressions were managed at home.

Conclusions

Of all women between the ages of 16 and 50 presenting to psychiatric services with a new episode of mental illness, 25% have a child under five years of age; 10% of all such women have a child under the age of one

Table 6.5 Relationship between diagnoses, presentation and highest level of care

ICD-9	Diagnosis	No.	Emergency referral Ward	Emergency referral Home	Admission	Community care	Outpatient only	No further contact
295	Schizophrenia	5	2	1	3	2	0	0
296.0 296.	Mania	11	9	2	9	2	0	0
296.4 298.1	Mixed affective	3	0	0	2	0	1	0
296.1 296.3	Depressive psychosis	24	7	5	12	10	1	1
300.4	Neurotic depression	19	0	11	0	14	4	1
300 other	Non-depressive neurotic	5	1	3	0	2	3	0
308.9	Adjustment disorder	21	4	5	0	12	1	8
	Other	24	4	6	4	3	7	10
	Total	112				30	45	17
							112	

Mode of presentation v. diagnosis: $\chi^2 = 12.02$; df = 1; $P<0.001$.
Highest level of care v. diagnosis: $\chi^2 = 46.09$; df = 1; $P<0.001$.

Table 6.6 Presentation to psychiatric services source by outcome

	No.	Inpatient	Outpatient with CPN	Outpatient	No further contact
Postnatal wards	27	16	7	1	3
Outpatients	33	6	19	2	6
Domiciliary visit	21	4	12	4	1
Other	31	4	15	2	10
Total	112	30	53	9	20

$\chi^2 = 19.45$; df = 3; $P<0.001$.
CPN = Community Psychiatric Nurse.

year. Considerable attention therefore needs to be paid to the impact of maternal illness on the family. This study suggests that women who present in the year following childbirth are more severely ill than men and women in the same age group and are much more likely to be suffering from manic depressive illness. Other authors (Dean and Kendell, 1981; Katona, 1982) have already commented that these women are more likely to have a psychotic mental state on examination and are likely to be more deluded and hallucinated than age-matched controls who have the same diagnosis. Within the group of postnatal patients there would seem to be a strong association between early presentation on the postnatal wards, i.e. within 10 days of childbirth, and the subsequent development of mania or a schizophrenia-like condition. As none of these patients presented within 72 h of childbirth—the usual duration of postnatal stay—it would seem likely that these early presentations are associated with complications of childbirth, most notably caesarean section which necessitates a longer stay in hospital. The majority of these women received inpatient psychiatric care as their initial method of treatment, suggesting that these were the most profoundly disturbed women.

Two-thirds of the depressive psychoses and all of the depressive neuroses presented after discharge from hospital, suggesting that these women either delivered vaginally and were therefore discharged from hospital within 72 h, or presented later in the puerperium. These women, having first been seen at home, tended to be managed at home.

The size of the population of the Health District at the time of the study was 360 000. Its sociodemographic features, face-to-face contact rate of its population of 1.7% that year, and a birthrate of approximately 12 per 1000 of its population, make Nottingham typical of the rest of the UK. The referred psychiatric morbidity in the postnatal population was seen to be sufficient to justify the services of a half-time consultant with a special interest in postnatal mental illness and because Nottingham is representative of the rest of the country, it may be reasonable to generalize these findings to other, similarly sized Health Districts. The distinctive features of this group of patients in terms of the severity of their illnesses, the manner in which they present to the services and their use of services subsequent to presentation, suggest that a special service for these patients could be justified. This service should be organized in such a way as to provide a rapid response to patients at home and on postnatal wards. For this population, an admission facility of four beds and cots is required, providing intensive psychiatric care for a group of severely disturbed women and their babies. Of the psychotic women, 40% will not be admitted, so community psychiatric nurses will be required to nurse these women at home in addition to providing a supportive service for other postnatal patients. For all postnatal patients, whatever their diagnosis and initial method of treatment, frequent outpatient clinics will be needed because they receive more frequent psychiatric contact, both at home and in outpatient clinics than that received by the rest of the psychiatric population. The fact that so many of the postnatal women are both very ill and have very small babies, suggests that it is essential that both the community and hospital psychiatric staff maintain close links with the local obstetric and paediatric services and with the primary care health team. The staff of the postnatal mental illness service must possess the special skills necessary for the management of these profoundly ill patients and their small babies.

Intensive community nursing as an alternative to admission

Background to the clinical project

We had found that, despite the availability of mother and baby facilities, many profoundly ill women and their families were reluctant to accept admission. This seemed to be particularly common amongst women who had other children and did not want to be separated from them and amongst women who were first seen at home. Many families reluctantly accepted admission after fruitless attempts had been made to manage the mother's illness at home. It was often found that, when severely ill women were managed at home, the thin line between help and interference was crossed, many women's autonomy with their babies being inadvertently undermined by well-meaning relatives who 'took over' the care of the child. We also became aware of another group of women who were initially admitted, but whose constant pleas for discharge seriously interfered with their treatment and progress whilst on the ward, and dominated all therapeutic interactions.

For these reasons a pilot study was initiated in 1982 with two patients. The first was a manic patient who had been admitted to the psychiatric unit 24 h previously with a six-day-old baby and who angrily refused to leave her baby for even a few seconds and was demanding to return home with her baby to her older child and husband. The second patient had a schizoaffective illness which presented 11 days after a caesarean section. She was first seen at home. Her husband was finding it extremely difficult to cope with her but the couple were very distressed and resistant to the idea of admission. These two women were managed at home at a time when their mental states and levels of disturbance would normally have indicated admission. The community psychiatric nurse spent a number of hours every day in their homes and the health visitors and midwives visited daily on a rota basis. The close collaboration with the primary health care team in both cases involved frequent visits from the general practitioners.

The successful management of these two patients led to the setting up of a larger experimental project to see whether intensive community psychiatric nursing could form a viable alternative to admission for a large group of seriously disturbed women whose mental state and behavioural disturbance would otherwise have merited admission.

Methods

During the study year March 1983 to February 1984, all those patients presenting to the psychiatric services with a diagnosis of manic depressive illness or schizophrenia ($n = 43$) were managed by the study team; 26 of these women were admitted and 17 were not (*Table 6.5*).

The study involved two groups of women. The first group ($n = 20$), the majority of whom were initially seen on a postnatal ward, were admitted to the psychiatric Mother and Baby Unit but were discharged home at a time when their psychiatric state would have warranted a continuing stay in hospital. The second group ($n = 11$) were seen initially on a domiciliary visit and managed completely at home, thus avoiding admission. Both of these groups of women ($n = 31$) were nursed intensively at home as a substitute for admission. These cases were examined in terms of their diagnoses and level of disturbance at the time when the treatment was instigated and the duration of the levels of care that they received. The length of time to clinical recovery was noted, as was the frequency and reasons for re-admission and any behaviour that might have been a risk to the safety of the patient or her child.

The postnatal mental illness study team consisted of three medical members, a consultant, a senior registrar and a registrar and, in addition, a psychologist and a social worker. These members all had other clinical commitments but devoted about half of their clinical work to postnatal patients. During the community nursing project, the team also included two full-time community psychiatric nurses who had no other commitment and who worked only with postnatal patients. The team also had the services of a group of Homestart volunteers. Homestart is a national voluntary organization which was started in the East Midlands 15 years ago and now has a group of volunteers in many towns in the UK. The volunteers are all mothers who support other mothers at home with children under the age of five years. The volunteers, after selection, receive a six-week intensive training which includes a contribution from the study team on the emotional problems of mothers with small children and postnatal mental illness. They receive regular supervision from their leader, who is a trained social worker and counseller. Volunteers receive only their expenses but their premises and their leader are financially supported by the local town Social Services Department. We had been involved in their training programme for a number of years and had worked with their volunteers before. In 1983 this link was formalized and a group of six volunteers received extra training from us and worked with us in managing severely mentally ill mothers at home. They had close contact with community psychiatric nurses and received regular supervision as a group with members of the study team.

Frequent communication and close collaboration with the primary health care team was essential to this project. We worked closely with the midwives (when the baby was under 28 days old) and health visitors, meeting with them frequently to avoid giving the patient conflicting advice. Rota systems for visiting and support were worked out to avoid too many professionals visiting on any particular day.

Three levels of intensive community nursing were used for these patients:

Level 1
The nurse spent 8 h a day in the patient's home, leaving the home only when a reliable family member took over the care. A psychiatrist visited the house on alternate days.

Case example 1   Mrs A., a 26-year-old lady married to a miner living in comfortable circumstances with two children. This was her fourth illness: she had been admitted twice with mania before having the children and had had a manic illness starting on the fifth day after the birth of her first child which necessitated an in-patient stay. She had recovered from all her illnesses within four weeks and was known to be a caring and competent mother of her first child. She was admitted on the sixth day postpartum in a state hallmarked by insomnia, motor overactivity, flight of ideas and pressure of speech. She was noisy, restless, angry and argumentative towards staff and refused to move from the nursery or be separated from her baby for even a few minutes. Despite her disturbed mental state she was affectionate and caring towards her baby. She was continuously demanding to go home and refused all medication. Her husband felt that she would settle at home and would be more amenable to treatment in that environment. However, he did not feel that he could manage her on his own and there were no other family members available to help. The patient's mental state continued unchanged for four days before she was sent home with intensive community nursing.

From 7 am to 8 pm there was continuous nursing presence in the home for seven days. The psychiatrist and the midwife visited daily. She immediately cooperated with her medication, her behaviour settled, and she assumed responsibility for the baby, although caring for it always in the presence of another person. On the eighth day the nursing presence was reduced to two visits for two hours each day from 7 am to 9 am when the husband left for work and from 4 pm until 6 pm when the husband returned from work. In the third week the visits were reduced to alternate days at a time when clinical recovery occurred and in the fourth week the visits were reduced to weekly, with the patient attending the hospital outpatient clinic. Negotiations with the husband's employer resulted in his being allowed to work regular shifts during this period of nursing care.

Case example 2   Miss J. B., a 19-year-old woman, cohabiting with a 19-year-old unemployed man. They had poor living circumstances and major financial problems. They had strained and unsupportive relationships with their families and were socially isolated with no friends.

The patient was readmitted to the Maternity Unit on the tenth postpartum day because of feeling unwell and unable to cope with her first baby. On the fourteenth day she developed hypochondriacal and nihilistic delusions about herself and the baby. They were transferred to the Psychiatric Mother and Baby Unit, where she stayed for three weeks. Her family did not visit her. They were hopeless about her prognosis as her mother was a long stay in-patient in a mental hospital. She remained agitated and deluded and very distressed and was constantly running away. All interactions with the staff were dominated by her pleas for discharge. She was concerned and affectionate towards her baby but frightened of handling her. Level 1 nursing care was instigated, the community nurse staying in the patient's home from 8 am to 7 pm for 10 days. The psychiatrist visited three times and the nurse, together with the assistance of the social worker, improved the home and settled the financial problems. The patient's distress and confidence with the baby rapidly improved and the nurse gained her cooperation and trust. She was admitted over the first weekend (her nurse was on leave) and then went home again when she agreed to have ECT, the nurse transporting her to and from the hospital and staying for the remainder of the day. Level 2 nursing was continued for a further four weeks, the nurse visiting morning and evening. Clinical recovery occurred during the fourth week. Level 3 care, the nurse visiting on alternate days, was continued for a further four weeks by which time the patient was a competent and caring mother. She was then transferred to outpatient clinic and orthodox weekly community nursing visits for a further six months before her discharge.

Level 2

The nurse paid a minimum of two visits a day to the patient's home, each visit lasting at least 2 h. During her absence from the house either a family member, another health professional (health visitor, midwife or a Home-start volunteer) was present. A psychiatrist visited twice a week.

Case example 3   Mrs J., a 21-year-old lady, married to a miner, living in comfortable surroundings with her first baby. This was her first illness. She was readmitted to the Maternity Hospital on the 12th postpartum day because she was weepy and not coping. After a three-day admission she was referred to the study psychiatrist when she was found to be suffering from a mixed affective disorder. She was restless, suffering from insomnia, had pressure of speech and flight of ideas but also had depressive ideation and was very tearful. Both she and her family were very distressed at the idea of a psychiatric admission. She had a supportive mother living close by. Intensive home nursing was instigated from the onset.

Week 1—the community psychiatric nurse visited twice a day from 7 am until 9 am and from 4 pm until 6 pm, coinciding with her husband leaving for, and returning from work. The nurse was relieved by the patient's mother. Week 2—the patient's mental state changed. She became profoundly depressed with marked psychomotor retardation and diurnal variation of mood. ECT was started, the community nurse transporting the patient to hospital twice weekly and returning with her, where she stayed for the rest of the day. During weeks 3 and 4 she steadily improved, receiving six ECT treatments and after a brief hypomanic episode lasting 48 h, had made a clinical recovery by the end of the fourth week. She was then seen on alternate days for a further two weeks (Level 3) before transferring to orthodox community psychiatric nursing support and the outpatient clinic. This patient has subsequently had a second baby followed by a depressive puerperal psychosis starting on the tenth postpartum day. This illness, too, has been managed with a combination of Level 2 community psychiatric nursing and the therapeutic assistance of the patient's mother.

Level 3
The community nurse visited the home on alternate days, alternating her care with either family members or other health professionals. The psychiatrist visited weekly.

No more than one intensive nursing project at level 1 would be carried out at a given time, no more than three at level 2, and no more than six at level 3. With all levels of nursing care a medical member of the team could be summoned to the house immediately. A bed was available for the community nurse to admit the patient immediately without reference to the medical staff, and all forms of physical treatment were available in the home, the nurse transporting the patient, if necessary, to hospital for ECT and returning with her. A community psychiatric nurse was available by telephone 24 h a day, seven days a week, and the family had direct access to the Mother and Baby Unit in an emergency. The services of the team social worker and psychologist were also available when required.

The study patients selected to be managed at home fulfilled the following criteria:

(1) They were suffering from a new episode of manic depressive illness or a schizophrenia-like illness.
(2) They required nursing observation and treatment to the extent that would normally warrant admission. This (with one exception) meant that these patients were psychotic at the instigation of treatment, i.e. they had hallucinations and/or delusions and impaired reality testing as well as considerable personal disability requiring help and supervision with personal and childcare.
(3) The patient and her family positively wished her to remain at home and were prepared to accept both the nature of her illness and that this illness required treatment. The patient and her family were prepared to allow free access to the home by a community psychiatric nurse and other members of the team.
(4) The patient and her family understood that if the home management was not possible, she would be admitted.
(5) The general practitioner, health visitor and midwife agreed to the patient being managed at home.
(6) The patient lived within the defined catchment area or within a 20 minute car journey to the hospital.
(7) Another responsible adult lived in the home of the patient.

Results

Table 6.7 shows that all the patients were suffering from either manic depressive illness or schizophrenia and with one exception all these women were psychotic on mental state examination at the initiation of home nursing. One third of the patients were manic—a condition not usually managed at home. The diagnostic configuration of all three groups of women was broadly similar but the manic and schizophrenic patients, the majority of whom had been transferred from the postnatal wards and initially admitted (*Table 6.7*), received the most intensive levels of daily home nursing (levels 1 and 2). They also had the youngest babies (under three weeks old) and were undoubtedly the most disturbed women. Level 2 nursing rather than level 1 was indicated for this group if a relative was able to stay with the patient all day and if the patient's mental state and behaviour was stable and predictable during the few hours' absence of the community nurse. Over half of the patients managed with level 3 nursing had not been admitted, the majority having been seen initially on a domiciliary visit (*Table 6.7*). They had older babies and the choice of level 3 nursing was indicated by the continuous presence of a family member and clinical state that was stable and predictable over a 24 h period.

Table 6.7 Intensive community nursing project

ICD-9 code	Diagnosis	No.	Baby under 3 weeks old	Previous episode	Initial admission	Highest level community nursing		
						1	*2*	*3*
295.7 295.9	Schizophrenia-like conditions	3	3	1	3	1	2	0
296.0 296.4	Mania	10	9	5	9	4	2	2
296.1	Depressive psychosis	18	9	11	8	2	2	14
Total		31	21	17	20	7	8	16

Tables 6.8, 6.9 and *6.10* show the duration in each level of care and the next level of care reached. The decision to change the level of care was made jointly by the study team and reflected clinical change, particularly the stability and predictability of the patient's mental state and behaviour and the family resources. The majority of patients in levels 1 and 2 moved on to a lower order of intensive nursing, and only three were re-admitted. The majority nursed at level 3 moved on to conventional outpatient care and community psychiatric nursing with only two admissions and one day hospital admission. However, it can be seen that a change of nursing level to a higher mode, that is to say admission, only occurred on three occasions (one from level 2 and two from level 3), because of a major relapse in the patient's condition. The other reasons were that on two occasions the

Table 6.8 Level 1 intensive nursing

Patient	ICD-9	Diagnosis	Duration initial admission	Duration level 1	Duration next level	Re-admission	Relapse
1	295.9	Schizophreniform psychosis	10 days	7 days	2–3 days	No	No
2	296.0	Mania	4 days	7 days	2–7 days 3–14 days	No	No
3	296.0	Mania	3 weeks	10 days	2–14 days 3–4 weeks	No No	No No
4	296.0	Mania	2 weeks	7 days	2–3 weeks	No	No
5	296.4	Mixed affective psychosis	6 weeks	7 days	2–4 weeks 3–4 weeks	No	No
6	296.1	Depressive psychosis	3 weeks	10 days	2–4 weeks 3–4 weeks	Yes (w/e)	No
7	296.1	Depressive psychosis	None	10 days	2–2 weeks 3–4 weeks	Yes (w/e)	No

Table 6.9 Level 2 intensive nursing

Patient	ICD-9	Diagnosis	Duration initial admission	Duration level 2	Duration next level	Re-admission	Relapse
1	295.7	Schizoaffective disorder	7 weeks	7 weeks	3–8 weeks	No	No
2	295.9	Schizophreniform psychosis	2 weeks	14 days	3–2 weeks	No	No
3	296.0	Mania	6 days	14 days	3–2 weeks	No	No
4	296.0	Mania	7 days	7 days	3–4 weeks	No	No
5	296.0	Mania	6 days	14 days	3–7 days	No	No
6	296.4	Mixed affective psychosis	0	21 days	3–3 weeks	No	No
7	296.1	Depressive psychosis	0	14 days	Admission	Yes	Yes
8	296.1	Depressive psychosis	4 weeks	10 days	3–4 weeks	No	No

Table 6.10 Level 3 intensive nursing

Patient	ICD-9	Diagnosis	Duration initial admission	Duration level 3	Duration next level	Re-admission	Relapse
1	296.0	Mania	11 days	2 weeks	Outpatients	No	No
2	296.0	Mania	4 days	2 weeks	Outpatients	No	No
3							
4							
5	296.1	Depressive psychosis	3–4 weeks	2 weeks	Outpatients	No	No
6							
7							
8							
9							
10							
11	296.1	Depressive psychosis	0	4 weeks	Outpatients	No	No
12							
13							
14	296.1	Depressive psychosis	0	3 months	Day hospital	No	Yes
15	296.1	Depressive psychosis	0	10 days	Admission	Yes	No
16	296.3	Manic depressive psychosis (depressed)	2 weeks	7 days	Admission	Yes	Yes

community nursing care was not available over a weekend and on one occasion the patient wished to be admitted. None of the manic patients required re-admission. All three admissions were of patients suffering from a depressive psychosis. It can also be seen that all of the patients requiring intensive nursing on a continuous basis ceased to be nursed in this way within 10 days. In level 2, all patients except one had finished this level of nursing by two weeks, the one exception lasting for three weeks. In level 3 all patients had finished this level of nursing within four weeks, except for one patient who was nursed for three months before transfer to a psychiatric day hospital.

The patients included in this study represented 66% of all the postnatal patients referred to the psychiatric services with a new episode of psychotic illness and 76% of all those admitted.

The diagnoses and parity of the study patients differed from those of the patients admitted and managed conventionally: 91% of all cases of mania, the majority of women suffering from psychosis who had more than one child, and all those women who had had a previous episode of postnatal illness treated in hospital chose this form of treatment.

Nursing the mentally ill mother at home

The philosophy of care is to achieve the bespoke management of an individual patient deploying the resources of the community, the family and the psychiatric team flexibly in order to preserve continuity of the mother/infant relationship and to minimize the effects of the maternal mental illness on other members of the family. Each nursing project is designed to meet the needs and problems of a particular patient and her family. The community psychiatric nurses are members of a multidisciplinary team and key workers for those patients who are managed at home. Despite the individual nature of each nursing project, there are general principles which apply to all patients.

Assessment
The community psychiatric nurse is closely involved in the initial assessment of the patient and the design of the management plan. An essential part of this procedure is the community nurse's assessment of the patient's home and social circumstances, the supports available and her observation of the patient within her home. Her views on the feasibility of the community nursing project are paramount. The community nurse knows that she has access to medical advice and support at all times and that she may admit the patient to an available bed in the Mother and Baby Unit should she feel it necessary.

Relief of symptoms
The community nurse continually assesses the mental state and monitors the medication. All forms of physical treatment are possible in the community, including transportation to the hospital for ECT if necessary. She is able to instil hope and optimism in the patient by reassuring her that her symptoms are familiar and that her recovery will be complete.

Maternal autonomy and self-esteem
A great deal of nursing effort is devoted to the task of increasing the mother's self-confidence and her feelings of mastery and pleasure in her relationship with her baby. To this end, she works alongside the mother, ensuring that the baby's needs, both emotional and physical, are met, but at the same time relieving her of those tasks which she is unable to complete by virtue of her impaired concentration or restlessness and agitation. As far as possible, all nursing involvement with the baby takes place in the presence of the mother and with her permission. As the mother's state gradually improves she is gently encouraged to initiate and continue with all childcare tasks, but at a rate which prevents the mother from becoming agitated and flustered and therefore suffering from a lowering of self-esteem. The nurse also has an important role to play in supporting the husband and other key relatives in order that they can facilitate a recovery of maternal self-confidence. This often means advising the relatives not to take over the care of the baby but to help with other aspects of household management.

Individuality
The nurse helps the mother to create her own individual style of mothering which may bear little resemblance to the mother's preconceived ideas and expectations. Some mothers need help to develop more flexibility and a more natural and spontaneous style with less preoccupation with rules and routines, whilst others may need to develop more organization and more consistency.

Universality
Many mothers are distressed and guilty because they have experienced feelings of ambivalence, irritation and other unpleasant emotions. These feelings of alienation will be significantly reduced by the nurse helping them to understand how many of these feelings they have in common with other mothers.

Realism
Many of these mothers have idealized and unrealistic expectations of themselves and motherhood. The failure of both mother and baby to achieve these ideals leads to a feeling that the mother is inadequate and that the baby's essentially normal behaviour is a manifestation of her inadequacy. Information given by the nurse about the wide range of normal infant behaviour and the spectrum of normal maternal emotions is an essential step in the development of realistic expectations, both of self and baby. In the early stages of treatment this information comes during relationship between the nurse and the patient. However, later on the encouragement to attend the Infant Welfare clinics and to discuss the development of the child with health visitor and GP ensures that this acquisition of knowledge is an ongoing process.

Socialization and group identity
Ultimately, these lessons are best learned from other mothers. Later in the treatment process the mothers are actively encouraged by the nurse to

establish neighbourhood links, join Mother and Toddler groups and to attend the health visitor's clinics. Some will attend professionally run group sessions for mothers recovering from postnatal depressive illness.

The patients who could not be nursed at home

During the study year only those patients who expressed a positive wish to be nursed at home when given the alternative between intensive home nursing and admission were managed in this way. However, there were four patients who wished to be managed at home but could not be included in the project for the following reasons:

(1) One patient lived too far away from the base hospital to be easily reached in an emergency.
(2) One patient lived alone and there was no other responsible adult available to live in the home with whom the community psychiatric nurse could share her care.
(3) One patient was suitable for home nursing at a time when the community psychiatric nurses were already engaged in the maximum number of intensive nursing projects that they could initiate at any given time.
(4) One patient was not able to accept the nature of her illness and that treatment with medication was necessary.

No member of the multidisciplinary team would suggest the management of the patient at home if the baby was involved in the psychotic process or if the mother was engaging in potentially hazardous behaviour towards the baby.

Discussion

Intensive home nursing, together with the support and resources of a specialist multidisciplinary team and the back-up of a Mother and Baby Unit, can form a viable alternative to admission either in part or in whole. Thorough assessment and careful selection is essential; we did not attempt to manage the actively suicidal or infanticidal mother in the community, nor those mothers who lived alone without anyone who could stay with them. The patients must live within a 20 minute car journey from the base hospital. This method of management appears to be particularly effective in manic conditions as well as in severe depressive illness. Women with older children and those who have had a previous episode of puerperal psychosis appear to have welcomed this form of treatment. Used judiciously, it does not expose the mother or infant to risk. Anxieties about the patient's welfare only gave rise to admission on three occasions. All three of these patients were depressed but only one was admitted because of suicidal behaviour (she took an overdose of her antidepressants). None of the manic or schizophrenic patients required admission because their behaviour was hazardous to themselves or their babies. None of the mothers in the study injured their babies, nor did any of them engage in behaviour that was neglectful of the infant's emotional or physical well being that could not be easily and quickly overcome by the support and assistance of the community nurse and the patient's family. The inability of seriously mentally ill women to provide consistent and adequate levels of care for their babies is inevitably impaired in the early stages of illness. This is one of the most important reasons for either admission or intensive home nursing and in all cases a mother's ability independently to care for her child returned when her mental state became normal. Intensive home nursing does not limit the range of treatments available to the patient, which are the same as if she were admitted; neither does it merely delay admission. It minimizes disruption to the family and facilitates an early resumption of maternal autonomy and self-esteem. The clinical recovery of those 17 patients in the study who had been admitted for a previous episode of puerperal psychosis was the same with intensive home nursing. Interestingly, most of these patients thought that they had recovered more quickly when they were managed at home with their second episode.

References

BARDON, D., GLASER, Y., PROTHERO, D. and WESTON, D. H. (1968). Mother and Baby Unit. Psychiatric survey of 115 cases. *British Medical Journal*, **ii**, 755–758

BOWLBY, J. (1953). *Child Care and the Growth of Love.* Harmondsworth; Pelican Books

COX, J. L., CONNOR, Y. M. and KENDELL, R. E. (1982). Prospective study of the psychiatric disorders of childbirth. *British Journal of Psychiatry*, **140**, 111–117

DEAN, C. and KENDELL, R. E. (1981). The symptomatology of puerperal illness. *British Journal of Psychiatry*, **139**, 128–133

GIGGS, J. A. and MATHER, P. M. (1983). Perspectives on mental health in urban areas. Nottingham Monographs in Applied Geography, No. 3. University of Nottingham

KATONA, C. L. E. (1982). Puerperal mental illness; comparison with non-puerperal controls. *British Journal of Psychiatry*, **141**, 447–452

KENDELL, R. E., RENNIE, D., CLARK, J. A. and DEAN, C. (1981). The social and obstetric correlates of psychiatric admission in puerperium. *Psychological Medicine*, **11**, 351–359

KUMAR, R. and ROBSON, K. M. (1984). A prospective study of emotional disorders in child bearing women. *British Journal of Psychiatry*, **144**, 35–47

MARGISON, F. and BROCKINGTON, I. F. (1982). Psychiatric mother and baby units. In: *Motherhood and Mental Illness*, (I. F. Brockington and R. Kumar, eds), pp. 223–238. London: Academic Press

PITT, B. (1968). Atypical depression following childbirth. *British Journal of Psychiatry*, **144**, 1325–1335

RILEY, D. (1986). An audit of obstetric liaison psychiatry in 1984. *Journal of Reproductive and Infant Psychology*, **4**, 99–115

TOD, E. D. M. (1964). Puerperal depression: a prospective epidemiological study. *Lancet*, **ii**, 1264–1266

WING, J. K. and BROWN, G. W. (1961). Social treatment of chronic schizophrenia. A comparative survey of three mental hospitals. *Journal of Mental Science*, **107**, 847–861

Chapter 7

Effects of postnatal depression on infant development: direct studies of early mother-infant interactions

Lynne Murray

Introduction

This chapter outlines the effects of parental depression on children of school age, and then examines evidence for the impact of maternal depression in the postnatal period on infants. Since no direct longitudinal evidence of the impact of maternal depression is available for early infancy, recent observational and experimental studies of normal mother-infant interactions during the first year are described that help to clarify the role of maternal support in infant development.

Effects of parental depression on school-age children

In marked contrast to the considerable volume of research that has been carried out with the children of schizophrenic parents, relatively little work has been done to examine the impact on the child of having a parent who suffers from depression. However, the few studies that have been carried out (and these have tended to look at children of school age) consistently report adverse effects, for example on measures of psychiatric disturbance, IQ, success in attention and problem-solving tasks, and strategies for solving them (Weissman, Paykel and Klerman, 1972; Gamer et al., 1977; Cohler et al., 1977; Welner et al., 1977; Grunebaum et al., 1978; McKnew et al., 1979; Weissman et al., 1984; —see Chapter 8 for a fuller discussion of this evidence). Moreover, contrary to some initial expectations, such effects are reported to be more pronounced than those occurring in schizophrenics' children (Cohler et al., 1977; Grunebaum et al., 1978).

Indirect studies of the effects of maternal postnatal depression

If little is known about the impact on children of parental depression in general, even less is known about the possible effects on infant development of maternal affective disorders occurring in the puerperium. This omission is striking for several reasons. Firstly, and most obviously, because it is in the postnatal period and the ensuing months, more than at any other time, that the infant's primary environment will, in all probability, be the mother herself. Secondly, it has been suggested that many depressed mothers provide distorted environments for their infants. Weissman and Paykel (1974), on the basis of clinical observations and records of women admitted as consecutive cases to a clinic for the treatment of acute depression, describe their predicament thus:

> Helpless and overwhelmed by the care required by the newborn infant, they often became over indulgent, over protective and compulsive mothers. Their unreasonably high standards left them feeling inadequate to cope . . . . inability to cope with their new infants was seen in their tendency to overfeed the infants, in their fear of doing psychological damage to them, and in their anxiety on holding or leaving them. Aware of their difficulties, these women expressed considerable guilt and inadequacy over their performance.

Alternatively, if not overconcerned, helpless and guilty, the depressed mother could be directly hostile. The final cause for concern lies in the scale of the problem, with estimates of the prevalence of depressive disorders in the puerperium consistently around 10–15% (Pitt, 1968; Cox, Connor and Kendell, 1978; Kumar and Robson, 1984).

A few prospective studies have been reported recently of the effects on infants and young children of maternal affective disorders occurring in the months following childbirth; some of these studies, however, suffer from severe methodological limitations, and there are also inconsistencies in the results. Both Zajicek and de Salis (1979) and Uddenberg and Englesson (1978) found that mothers who had suffered from psychiatric disorders in the postnatal period gave more negative descriptions of their children at two and four years respectively than did control mothers. (The Zajicek and de Salis study looked at mothers who had been depressed postpartum, and that of Uddenberg and Englesson examined mothers four months postpartum, who had 'very painful mental symptoms', emotional disturbance resulting in definite deterioration of social and interpersonal functioning, and 'obvious signs of mental disturbance'.) Williams and Carmichael (1985), in a study of infant health and development in a multi-ethnic economically disadvantaged population in Melbourne, also found that depressed mothers who had only one child reported more behavioural problems in their infants (feeding, sleeping, crying and mood) than non-depressed controls. However, if there were other children in the family, no increase in perceived infant problems was found in the depressed group. Ghodsian, Zajicek and Wolkind (1984), although finding that maternal depression at 14 months was associated with child behaviour problems at 42 months, did not find such a relationship between child behaviour and postnatal depression at an earlier period. Wrate et al. (1985) found more maternal reports of child disturbance at three years from women who had been mildly depressed postpartum (their 'symptom' group) than from control women, but no increase for children of mothers who had had more long-standing and marked postnatal depression. Finally, Cogill et al. (1986) found that maternal depression in the first three months postpartum was associated with poorer performance on the McCarthy scales of cognitive functioning at four years. However, it is important to note that in some of these studies the conclusions must be qualified: thus with the exception of Uddenberg and Englesson's observation of the child at play at four years of age, and Cogill et al.'s assessments of cognitive function, all the data on the children were derived indirectly from maternal reports, and there is evidence that these are liable to be coloured by the mother's current emotional state (Fergusson *et al.*, 1985).

Direct studies of older infants

Recently a few studies have been published which, while not having a prospective design—since assessment of the mother's affective state was not made in the puerperium—nevertheless have included some mothers who were judged to have been depressed during the postnatal period, and have the advantage that direct assessments were made of the children not too far beyond infancy.

Radke-Yarrow *et al.* (1985) report the first part of an investigation of the interpersonal and affective behaviour of 2–3-year-old children whose mothers were classified as either 'normal', or as unipolar, bipolar or minor depressives. They found differences in the quality of attachment which related to maternal diagnosis. Children with mothers suffering from major affective disorders (and particularly those of the bipolar group) showed a pattern of insecure attachment, involving avoidance of, and resistance to, the mother when reunited with her after brief periods of separation in Ainsworth's Strange Situation (Ainsworth and Wittig, 1969). A rather different pattern of results has been reported in a Swedish study by Persson-Blennow *et al.* (1984). They found that, at one year, infants of mothers who had a cycloid or affective non-organic psychosis (including postpartum affective cases) did not differ from controls (matched for maternal parity, age and social class) on a modified version of Ainsworth's Strange Situation. Infants of schizophrenic mothers, however, showed more signs of anxious attachment than controls.

The Swedish researchers (Persson-Blennow *et al.* 1984) also observed the mothers and their 3-day-old infants during feeding on the postnatal ward. At this time the schizophrenic, and also the cycloid groups, differed from their controls (there was less harmony in feeding, less social contact and more tension and uncertainty in the case group mothers), but again no differences were found between controls and mothers with a history of depressive or postpartum psychosis.

Pound *et al.* (1985) and Mills *et al.* (1985), together studied 2–3-year-olds and their depressed or well mothers. Like Zajicek and de Salis (1979), Pound *et al.* found that depressed mothers reported more behaviour problems (assessed using Richman and Graham's Behaviour Screening Questionnaire) in their children than did control mothers. Mills *et al.* (1985) observed interactions in the home between these same children and their mothers, and identified a quality of relationship in the depressed group (applying particularly where the child showed marked behaviour problems) which they termed 'poor meshing'; this was a lack of responsiveness by the child to the mother's attempts to sustain a dialogue between them. Mills *et al.* (1985) suggested that the underlying problem was the mother's failure to recruit, sustain and expand the young child's concentration and attention in their interactions.

Although this quality characterized the relationships of depressed mothers taken as a group, Mills *et al.* make the interesting observation that distinct subgroups existed within the depressed population, and that each was accompanied by a different child profile. There were, on the one hand, women who had a history of personality disorder and/or extensive previous depression: these mothers tended to show little emotion and did not have fun with the child, rather, they would stare into space, leaving the child unoccupied, making few 'links' with the child's activity, or alternatively, they would be over-controlling: these mothers tended to have children with behaviour problems. On the other hand there was a group of depressed mothers who were highly sensitive to their children, entering into their play and providing emotional containment, thus indirectly meeting the child's cognitive needs, and it seems that these children were problem-free.

Pound *et al.* also refer to such clearly identifiable subgroups within this population—that is, women where the depression was part of a long-standing psychiatric disturbance, or else women whose depression seemed to have been precipitated by recent stressful life events such as bereavement. For the latter group, where the depression appeared to be a realistic response to specific adversity but nevertheless reached clinical proportions, the woman's experience of being a mother seemed to be left intact, the child escaped from the focus of her despair, and consequently, these researchers claim, suffered little impact.

This impression is also conveyed in Williams and Carmichael's study: they note on the basis of clinical observations that for some of their depressed mothers 'the infant seemed to be the one joy and comfort in their otherwise sad, drab, lives'. Conversely, for women with more long-standing difficulties, depression after childbirth may constitute a more serious threat to the child's development. In these latter cases it seems possible that childbirth is a provoking factor, not merely because additional life stresses are operative, but, perhaps more importantly, because the particular quality of the demands of the helpless infant stir up previously unresolved problems, e.g. dependency, that are then directly brought into play in relation to the infant. Dynamics of this kind are suggested both by Brown and Harris (1978) and Frommer and O'Shea (1973), who showed that early loss of a parent acts as a vulnerability factor, and by findings that the woman's poor evaluation of, or relationship to, her own mother correlated with the presence of depression after childbirth (Kumar and Robson, 1984; Pound *et al.*, 1985). Recently, Main (1985) has argued from interview material analysed for its coherence and consistency, that resolution of a mother's own experience of maternal rejection is critical in predicting whether or not she will reject her own child: this evidence thus reinforces and refines the general picture of intergenerational correlations, with their impact on the quality of the current mother-child relationship.

Weissman and Paykel (1974) have demonstrated from detailed, structured interview material, in which marital, family and social relationships are assessed (the Social Adjustment Scale) that in women with longstanding problems, significant deficits in relation to their children persist, even when depressive symptomatology has remitted: communication continues to be inhibited, and friction persists. From his reviews of the effects of parental psychiatric disorder on children, Rutter considers that it is just such direct involvement of the child with long-term disturbed parental communication, irrespective of psychiatric diagnosis, that poses the key threat to the child's stability (Rutter, 1966; Rutter and Quinton, 1984).

The picture of continued impairments—despite symptomatic improvement—in those with a history of depression, has received some further support recently from a study carried out by Stein (Stein et al., 1986, unpublished and personal communication). Stein is currently analysing the development and interpersonal relationships of 19-month-old children of mothers recruited in the postnatal period who, at the time of the child assessments, fell into three groups: (a) those who had been depressed before the child's first birthday but had recovered by 19 months; (b) those who remained depressed, and (c) controls without any depression. Preliminary analysis of his assessments, made uninformed as to the mother's clinical status, revealed differences not only between currently depressed and control mothers, but also some modest differences between the *recovered* and control groups. Although the amount of time spent interacting with their children did not differ between the last two groups, the quality of their contacts did d'ffer, with the control mothers facilitating the children's activity to a greater extent than mothers who had recovered. Furthermore, in addition to effects that distinguished the children of control and currently depressed groups (for example, results suggest that children in the latter may have had an expressive language delay), Stein identified a number of differences between the children of control and recovered groups: children of recovered depressives showed, for example, less sharing of emotion with their mothers and poorer concentration than the children of women in the control group.

As in the studies of Mills et al. (1985), Pound et al. (1985) and Williams and Carmichael (1985), Stein too identified important differences within the depressed population. Thus, within the entire index group (i.e. all mothers who had been postnatally depressed, whether or not they had recovered) a subgroup of women existed who experienced severe chronic difficulties (marital, housing, financial). These mothers and their children differed on a number of measures when compared with the other index dyads, the mothers showing less facilitation, and their children less emotional sharing. Indeed, it seemed that much of the difference between the index and control populations at 19 months could be accounted for by this subgroup who had experienced both postnatal depression and severe chronic problems.

This brief review of studies of children whose mothers have been depressed at some point in the year or so following childbirth answers, but also raises, several questions. Firstly, the research provides consistent evidence of differences in children aged 19 months to four years which are related to maternal emotional state. Secondly, the description of subgroups within depressed populations adds an important refinement to the overall finding of adverse effects, and may go some way to explain apparent inconsistencies in the results of some of the previous studies where this distinction has not been recognized (*see* above, p. 160). It also argues that in future research assessment should be made, not simply of depressive symptomatology, but also of the quality of communication and of the focus of depression, i.e. whether centred on some specific recent event, chronic problems or the particular demands of the infant. Stein's finding of differences between the children in his control and recovered groups is of particular interest since it indicates that differences that have been found between the different child populations cannot be said to be purely a function of *current* depressive symptoms—a point which has not been addressed specifically in the other direct studies.

However, the crucial question of just how these adverse effects might be mediated remains: Stein's finding of deficits in the communication of recovered depressives raises the question whether the adverse effects on the child, while not a consequence of current depressive symptoms, nevertheless reflect long-term impaired communication in the mother-child relationship. This interpretation might suggest that child problems at 2–3 years need not bear a *direct* relationship to the earlier period postpartum when the mother had been actively depressed, and would find its place among current theories that claim that development is not linear—with one stage inevitably leading to another—but discontinuous (*see* Clarke and Clarke, 1976; Kagan, 1980, 1982). Alternatively, the evidence to date is consistent with models that assume that the major and significant disruption may have been the presence of maternal depressive symptoms early on. Such models would allow for immediate and direct effects of postpartum depression on the infant (such as the infant's withdrawal and unresponsiveness) provoking behaviour in the mother that may in turn, even though she is no longer depressed, have further negative consequences for the child with a vicious spiral of impaired communication being set up. Nevertheless, these models would assert the possibility of a critical disruption having been constituted by maternal depression occurring during a formative, or sensitive, period of infant development, affecting some fundamental organization of the infant's psychological functioning and experience with irrevocable long-term consequences, which, though they might be mitigated by later, more adequate environments, nevertheless would persist. These latter views are, of course, fundamental tenets of psychoanalytical theory. They are most evident with respect to early infant experience in the work of Winnicott (Winnicott, 1958, 1965) and Klein (Klein *et al.*, 1952). They also appear in the work of ethologists and attachment theorists, and in Stern's recent integration of the clinical insights of psychoanalytical theory with evidence from current developmental research (Stern, 1985).

In order to answer questions about the aetiology of pathological outcome in the child, it is necessary to obtain direct, detailed and longitudinal evidence about the developing relationship between infants and their postnatally depressed mothers in the first year. Until such evidence is available, it is certainly fruitful to consider what is now known about 'normal' infant development in the first year. Some recent research is therefore described that has examined the infant's interpersonal behaviour and emotional responses, and this is considered in the light of descriptions of the environment provided for the infant by the depressed mother.

Interpersonal and emotional development in the first year

Early infant sensitivity to persons: 0–6 weeks

Over the past 15 years meticulous descriptions, greatly facilitated by advances in video and film technology, have been made of unstructured mother-infant interactions throughout the first year or so of the child's life. Typically, mother and infant are settled in an observation room, sitting opposite each other, and the mother is asked to chat to, or play with her baby, as she might at home. The infant is placed in a specially designed chair that gives support, yet allows maximum freedom of limb movement. Full-face images of mother and infant can be obtained by the use of two cameras, and the two images can be shown alongside each other on the split screen of a television monitor. Alternatively one camera may be used in combination with a mirror (*see Figure 7.1*). In addition the time in, for example, tenths of a second can be superimposed on the television image, allowing the researcher to analyse the timing of one partner's actions in relation to the other's in fine detail. If a one-way mirror is installed the recording can be made from a next door room so as to minimize disturbance. Although the situation is clearly in one sense artificial and constrained, it is possible to create a relaxed atmosphere by letting the mother feed and change the infant before filming starts. Mothers usually appear quite unperturbed, and a wide range of individual differences can be revealed.

These methods of recording 'natural history' have been accompanied by the development of increasingly refined and elegant experimental procedures for presenting the world to very young infants, coupled with subtle and detailed examination of infant responses. Acts that occur fairly frequently and that are under early voluntary control—like sucking, gazing and head-turning—can be used to examine the infant's preferences and capacities to discriminate. For example, a pressure transducer fitted into the nipple of a dummy can be made to start up some environmental event such as the tape recording of a voice when the infant sucks. Once the infant has learned the association, different sucking rates produced in response to different sounds can be used to monitor infant preferences. Powers to discriminate can be investigated by examining whether the infant's pattern of gaze will alter with a change in visual presentation, e.g. a change from one facial expression to another. More cognitive capacities in the infant in relation to properties of objects, e.g. expectations about their solidity, have been tested by the ingenious devising of situations that entail critical disruptions, e.g. the creation of a 3D image of an object (a 'virtual' object) that has no substance (Bower, 1974). The infant's expression of startle or surprise upon encountering the disruption is then used to infer that an expectation was present. These two complementary lines of research, the experimental and observational, have brought about considerable advance in our knowledge of the scope and limitations of early infant perceptual sensitivities and expressive capacities, and of the way in which these are regulated in relation to the environment.

One conclusion to emerge from this work is that from a very early age infants are selectively responsive to *human* qualities. Relevant findings include a demonstration (Fantz, 1963) of the preference of two-month-olds

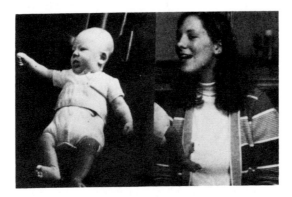

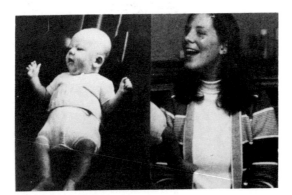

Figure 7.1 Seven-week-old baby girl in communication with her mother. The pair sit opposite each other, and the mother's image is shown reflected in a mirror placed alongside her daughter. The infant shows mouth shaping ('prespeech') and gestures.

for face-like rather than scrambled visual arrays, since confirmed for newborn infants by Goren, Sarty and Wu (1975). Neonates not only seem to be attracted to faces, or face-like stimuli; they are also capable of discriminating and reproducing specific facial movements, for example tongue protrusion (Meltzoff and Moore, 1977) and different expressions of emotion (Field et al., 1982; Field, 1985). By one month, infants respond to complex and more abstract qualities of facial arrays like animation (Sherrod, 1981).

A predisposition to respond to the sound of the human voice has been demonstrated by Alegria and Noirot (1978) who observed selective orientation to the source of gentle human speech in infants 1 h old. Preferences for speech rather than non-human sounds of the same pitch and volume, and for the sound of the female rather than male human voice, has been reported in neonates by Friedlander (1970) and by Eisenberg (1975). Eimas (Eimas et al., 1971; Eimas, 1985) has shown that infants less than two weeks old can distinguish between categories of consonant-vowel syllables (e.g. between 'bah' and 'pah') that differ by only 20–50 ms in 'voice-onset time' (the interval between the release of air and the onset of voicing). It is noteworthy that those boundary points of voice-onset time that specify distinctive categories in adult speech from all languages—and these represent but a very limited selection from the scale of potential sound distinctions—are just those that are identified categorically by infants at this early age. This, and other related findings, have led Eimas to conclude that infants 'are richly endowed with innate perceptual mechanisms, well adapted to the characteristics of human language' (Eimas, 1985).

Leslie has shown that six-month-old infants discriminate *human* action in relation to objects from equivalent physical effects created by objects (Leslie, 1984). This has been confirmed for infants as young as 15 weeks in pilot studies (A. M. Leslie, personal communication). Such findings suggest that the infant's selective responsiveness to persons cannot be reduced to a simple attraction for certain salient physical features like movement, light or noise. Rather, it appears that the infant is innately disposed to respond to human qualities as special categories of experience.

Research has also shown that young infants rapidly develop preferences for the particular characteristics of the person who consistently cares for them. Preference for the infant's own mother's face seems to be established shortly after birth (Field, 1985), for her voice by 1–2 days (De Casper and Fifer, 1980), and by one month infants will suck a dummy to produce their mother's voice, but only if the intonation is normal (Mehler, Bertoncini and Barniere, 1978). McFarlane (1975) has shown that, by six days, infants prefer the smell of their own mother's breast pad to that of another woman. By two weeks they will discriminate between their mother and a strange woman picking them up in silence and in the dark, showing head, neck and whole body postural adjustments that indicate 'moulding' and relaxation with their mother to a significantly greater extent than with the stranger (Widmer-Robert Tissot, 1981).

On the expressive side, in addition to the imitation of specific facial movements, the newborn infant's facial musculature can be coordinated in complex patterns to produce the majority of facial expressions shown by adults (Oster and Ekman, 1977). This capacity conveys a vivid impression of the infant's humanness, an impression that is particularly enhanced by the form of neonatal gaze patterns which have been described as 'almost indistinguishable in form, velocity and frequency from those of an adult' (Trevarthen, Murray and Hubley, 1981).

The attributes of newborn infants—the attraction to humans, their own expression of personal qualities, the rapid development of preferences for those involved in their care—all indicate an adaptation to a human environment of consistent care from birth. In addition, the infant's capacity actively to seek, and then to regulate, input from the environment, mean that as well as the contribution made by the mother's own motivation which brings her into personal relationship with her baby, even the newborn infant plays an active role in bringing about contact with, and experience of, other people.

This experience is, of course, important for the infant's physical survival, but findings of the kind described above indicate that the complementary involvement of another person is just as much a component of the newborn's psychological structure. Evidence of this requirement for a human environment is perhaps particularly striking when identified in neonates, but the principle applies throughout infant development: observations of mother-infant interactions in the first year show that as the infant develops, so different forms of complementary personal care are necessary to facilitate this progress.

Mother-infant interactions: 6 weeks–3 months

At a time when he is largely ineffective in relation to the world of physical objects (reaching and grasping not being properly established before 18 weeks), the infant will, in states of satisfaction and alertness, be captivated intensely, for prolonged periods, by a partner who is attentive and solicitous. This phase is regarded by many researchers in the field as the most exclusively social in infancy, being termed by Trevarthen the period of 'Primary Intersubjectivity' (Trevarthen, 1979), and by Stern that of 'core relatedness' (Stern, 1985), since communication between mother and infant typically has no other focus but the feelings and intentions of the two participants, and each partner's experience of being in relation to the other appears to exist as an end in itself. On the mother's side, a particular motivational state has been supposed to operate from late pregnancy—'Primary Maternal Preoccupation' (Winnicott, 1956)—that permits, *inter alia*, the delicate adaptations manifest in these contacts.

Characteristics of mother-infant interactions in this period have been reported extensively in the literature, for example by Brazelton (Brazelton, Koslowski and Main, 1974), Trevarthen (Trevarthen, 1979), and Stern (Stern, 1977, 1985). These researchers have described the interactions as having a conversation-like form. As in exchanges between two adults, the mother-infant contacts involve subtle, moment-to-moment transformations in the balance of initiative that, in spite of the obvious asymmetry in roles, are nevertheless mutually regulated (Murray and Trevarthen, 1986). There are thus moments when one partner attends intently while being 'addressed' by the other, followed by a joint shift in focus. The infant 'addresses' his mother with smiles or grimaces, and what Trevarthen has termed 'prespeech' where form (movements of lip and tongue coupled with fine finger posturing or large arm gestures as in *Figure 7.1*) and timing in relation to maternal activity together convey the impression that the infant is trying to communicate. Indeed, mothers frequently make comments such as 'Oh, that's a nice story you're telling me', or 'What's that you're saying then?' in response to this activity. Mothers and infants of this age show a closer congruence in form and in time in their actions than do adults (Beebe *et al.*, 1985). Such episodes, in which the two partners appear to experience a common 'state of mind', seem to arise from the mother's tendency to follow infant expressions closely, and to render them back in exaggerated fashion, and this 'mirroring' process by the mother has attracted particular attention (Spitz, 1957; Winnicott, 1967; Lacan, 1977; Stern, 1985). The infant's gaze is finely tuned to the state of joint engagement, and at points when, with maternal support and encouragement, his level of excitement becomes intense, he may turn away, resuming eye contact when his arousal has subsided: in so doing the intensity of his own, but also of his mother's, affects is regulated.

Maternal behaviour in these interactions is finely adjusted to infant sensitivities: the mother will position her face so that it is at the optimal focal distance for the infant, so facilitating eye-to-eye contact (Schoeztau and Papousek, 1977). The pitch of voice is raised in baby talk to the range that infants prefer, head movements and facial expressions are exaggerated, and these displays are prolonged and slow in build up and decline.

It is hard when observing interactions at this stage to identify features of maternal behaviour that contribute to their harmonious character, and to estimate the importance of the quality of maternal response for the infant. For, as Winnicott stated, 'The infant and the maternal care together form a unit . . . . at the earliest stages the infant and maternal care belong to each other and cannot be disentangled' (Winnicott, 1960).

The contribution of perturbation studies
One solution to this problem is to examine the morphology of maternal acts even more closely. For example, Trevarthen (1985) has shown how the analysis of mother and infant behaviour to within fractions of a second can clarify which acts stimulate behaviour in the other partner, and which are more responsive. Another approach has been to study the effects of selective interferences or 'perturbations' that are deliberately introduced into the interaction. Perhaps the ealiest study of this kind is that reported by Darwin (1877) who used mild perturbations played out with his infant son to trace the progress of emotional and interpersonal development. Darwin relates how, in the course of his investigation into the emergence of fear in his son who was about four months old:

> I approached with my back towards him and then stood motionless: he looked very grave and much surprised, and would soon have cried, had I not turned round; then his face instantly relaxed into a smile.

From such experiments in the nursery he was led to conclude:

> An infant understands to a certain extent, and as I believe at a very early period, the meaning or feelings of those who tend him, by the expression of their features.

During the period when research was focused on infant learning capacities, a number of conditioning studies were published that, unintentionally, had involved perturbations to adult communication with the infant. Infant responses to these disruptions were so dramatic that, in spite of their peripheral relevance to the aims of these experiments, they were described in some detail. In a study of the conditioning of smiling in four-month-olds by social reinforcement, Brackbill (1958) observed that in the extinction phase, when the adult presented an immobile and unresponsive face, the infant actively avoided the experimenter. Similarly, in Rheingold's study of the conditioning of vocalizations, similar behaviour by the adult provoked a range of 'emotional responses' that again seemed to be attempts at avoidance (Rheingold, Gewirtz and Ross, 1959). Koch (1967) reported difficulty in conditioning infant head turns to stereotyped presentations of the mother's face and voice: the two-month-old infants became restless and negative and resisted attempts by the experimenter to direct their heads towards the mother.

More recently investigators have employed perturbations with the specific purpose of examining infant sensitivities in social encounters. Wolff (1969) found presentation of a silent nodding face to a fussy baby in the third week provoked crying which stopped when the face withdrew. Carpenter et al. (1970) and Carpenter (1974) also reported distress, as well as gaze aversion, in infants under two months when their mother appeared still-faced before them, and this has since been confirmed in several studies (Brazelton et al., 1975; Tronick et al., 1978; Murray, 1980; Murray and Trevarthen, 1985). Papousek and Papousek (1975) analysed infant responses to distortions in the normal presentation of the mother. They placed a perspex screen with transparent horizontal stripes in front of the mother and this caused the infant to lose interest in her. In the same study it was found that the infant reacted with avoidance if the mother tried to resume contact after 'incomprehensible' absences, such as the room being plunged into darkness whilst she left. But if the mother repeatedly left in sight of the baby, doing so in a natural fashion, no such reaction was seen.

Interpretations of infant response to these disruptions have varied: in some accounts it has been proposed that distress and avoidance arise because the distorted behaviour of the partner presents a degree of *discrepancy* from a standard, built up by the infant on the basis of repeated normal experiences, that exceeds the infant's powers of assimilation (e.g. Koch, 1967; Carpenter, 1974). Other researchers argue that the perturbations violate the expectation of a *contingent* relationship between infant acts and environmental events (Papousek and Papousek, 1975). Over the past few years a more complex motivational structure has been proposed to explain infant respones. Tronick and colleagues (Tronick et al., 1978, Cohn and Tronick 1983), Murray and Trevarthen (Murray, 1980; Murray and Trevarthen, 1985) claim, like Darwin and psychoanalytical theorists such as Winnicott and Klein, that within the first 2–3 months of life, infants are able to perceive the form of the adult partners' expression in terms of its personal and communicative significance, and that their response to perturbations to adult communication reflect complementary adaptations of the same order.

In order to illustrate the basis for these claims in more detail, studies carried out in the Department of Psychology at Edinburgh University are described, in which communication of mothers with their 6–12-week-old infants was perturbed in various ways, and a detailed analysis made of infant responses. In one study two disruptions to the mother's normal face-to-face communication with her infant were brought about: the first, called the 'Interruption Condition' was a natural alteration in behaviour: an adult entered the room where the mother and baby were settled together and engaged the mother in casual conversation for about 30 s during which time the mother turned away from the infant and modified her whole style of interaction.

The second perturbation again required the mother to cease communicating with her infant, but in this case—the 'Blank Face Condition'—the change was quite unnatural: here, at a prearranged signal the mother became still and quite expressionless for a period of 45 s whilst continuing to look at her baby. These two sequences of perturbed maternal behaviour alternated with periods of normal communication. The whole procedure lasted approximately three minutes, and mother and infant were filmed throughout from the adjoining room, a near full-face image of the mother appearing alongside that of the infant by means of a mirror being placed adjacent to the infant chair (*see Figure 7.1*).

In another study the *timing* (not the form) of the mother's acts in relation to the infant's was perturbed by using the Double Closed-Circuit Television Technique (*see Figure 7.2*) (Murray, 1980). In this system mother and infant each sees a full-face life size video image of the other where perfect eye-to-eye contact is possible. When the images are relayed in real or 'live' time the two are able to interact in a normal, mutually responsive fashion. But if the mother's image is replayed to the infant after an interval of some 30 s, the interaction is perturbed; the infant sees and hears the same maternal behaviours that occurred during the Live sequence, but in the Replay sequence the mother's communication is unrelated to her infant's behaviour. The infant was filmed during the Live and Replay sequences, along with the mirror reflection of the video image of the mother.

Infant behaviours, categorized as 'Direction of Attention', 'Communication' and 'Affect' were scored in 0.5 s time blocks by the author, and a 10% random sample by an independent observer. Inter-observer agreement ranged between 87% and 94% on the presence or absence of the different behaviours. The frequency of occurrence of each behaviour was compared between each perturbation period and the preceding Normal or Live condition. *Table 7.1* shows those acts that differed in distribution between Normal, Interruption and Blank Face conditions, *Table 7.2* those that changed between Live and Replay sequences. This analysis shows that each of the three perturbations provoked a different form of infant response.

During the periods of normal interaction, the infant's gaze was directed at the mother's face almost all the time, and the baby made active tonguing movements and wide open shapings of the mouth. The infant smiled at the mother, and the brows were either relaxed or raised (*see Figure 7.1*). In the

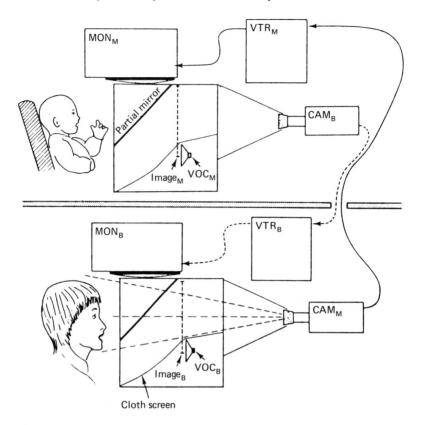

Figure 7.2 The Double Video Technique: mother and infant communicate via a linked video system that permits either live, real-time communication or else a delayed, replayed version to be presented. MON = monitor; VTR = video tape recorder; CAM = camera; VOC = loudspeaker conveying voice of mother or baby.

Interruption Condition when the experimenter entered the room and the mother turned to talk to her, the infant's 'communicative behaviour' subsided, mouthing and tonguing movements and smiling all occurring less frequently. Although the signs of positive excitement were reduced, there was no indication that the Interruption was distressing: although the infant gazed less at the mother, this seemed to arise not as a function of the infant's avoidance of her, but because gaze was focused on the experimenter, and there was no increase in any of the displacement activities—fingering the clothes or face, yawning or biting the lower lip—or in frowning (*see Figure 7.3*).

In contrast, when the mother presented a 'Blank Face' the infant very quickly appeared to be disturbed (*see Figure 7.4*). Frequently a form of response that suggested protest occurred: rather than falling off, as in the Interruption, active mouthing and tonguing movements were at first sustained, if not intensified; frowning increased as did sneering grimaces of the mouth, as well as displacement-type activities. This phase of apparent protest was often followed by one of withdrawal, gaze being averted from the mother's face; at such times the head might droop, or regard would be

Table 7.1 Distribution of infant behaviours in Normal, Interruption and Blank Face conditions. Comparisons between normal and subsequent perturbation condition are by *t*-tests for related samples

Infant acts	Normal		Interruption	Normal		Blank face
Direction of attention:						
Gaze to mother's face	90.2	>	76.9$^{(*)}$	88.8	>	64.5***
Gaze to experimenter	–		14	–		–
Gaze away or down	9.8		8.4	10.1	<	34.2***
Communication:						
Tonguing movements	21.1	>	9.3$^{(*)}$	28.7		23.0
Wide open mouthing	26.0	>	2.4***	22.3		18.0
Relaxed mouth	34.8		38.7	42.2	>	33.2$^{(*)}$
Closed mouth	39.2	<	58.9**	35.4	<	48.7$^{(*)}$
Affect:						
(i) Positive						
Raised brows	32.8		23.9	33.0	>	13.8***
Relaxed brows	49.9		48.1	45.2	>	27.4***
Smiling	31.8	>	3.3***	23.6	>	4.2***
(ii) Negative						
Frowning	5.1		7.1	3.1	<	30.1**
Raised frown	11.9	<	20.9$^{(*)}$	18.7	<	28.8$^{(*)}$
Grimace	0		0.3	0.2	<	10.0***
Chew lower lip	0.1		0.6	0.2	<	2.7$^{(*)}$
Yawn	–		–	0	<	0.4$^{(*)}$
Left hand finger clothes	22.4		27.3	24.4	<	30.7$^{(*)}$
Left hand touch face	0.2		0.8	0	<	1.3$^{(*)}$
Right hand touch face	1.1		1.9	3.9	<	6.1$^{(*)}$

Figures show mean percentage of condition time occupied by each infant act.
$^{(*)}$Trend $P = 0.1$; $^{*}P < 0.05$; $^{**}P < 0.01$; $^{***}P < 0.001$. Some caution is required in considering significance levels due to the interdependency of some behaviours.

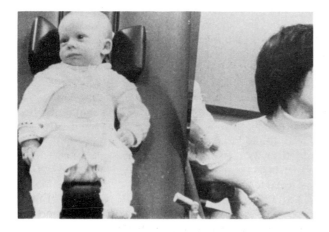

Figure 7.3 An eight-week-old infant boy watches quietly as his mother turns away from him to talk to the experimenter.

Table 7.2 Distribution of infant behaviours in Live and Replay conditions. Statistical comparisons are by *t*-tests for related samples.

Infant acts	Live		Replay
Direction of attention:			
Gaze to mother's face	89.3	>	63.4***
Gaze away or down	9.4	<	35.2***
Communication:			
Tonguing movements	29.2	>	19.5(*)
Wide open mouthing	20.4	>	5.0***
Relaxed mouth	48.3	>	38.7(*)
Closed mouth	31.3	<	36.3***
Affect:			
(i) Positive			
Raised brows	38.3	>	15.6***
Relaxed brows	46.7	>	38.0(*)
Smiling	4.9	>	1.0(*)
(ii) Negative			
Frowning	0.5	<	25.4***
Raised frown	14.5	<	20.9*
Grimace	0.4	<	7.7***
Chew lower lip	0.1	<	1.5(*)
Yawn	0		0.8
Left hand finger clothes	15.9	<	24.6(*)
Left hand touch face	0		2.5
Right hand touch face	0.3	<	1.8(*)

Figures show mean percentage of condition time occupied by each infant act.
(*) trend $P = 0.1$; * $P < 0.05$; ** $P < 0.01$; *** $P < 0.001$. Some caution is required in considering significance levels due to the interdependency of some behaviours.

directed at the infant's own hand. Not only did the overall duration of gazing at the mother's face alter according to maternal behaviour, but its organization in time also varied with changes in maternal response: during normal interaction looks to the mother were usually sustained and continuous, but in the Blank Face condition the proportion of short darting glances to her face (looks of 2.5 s or less) almost doubled (*Figure 7.5*).

Coherence and organization of the infant's behaviour is also evident from the way in which emotional and communicative behaviours were coordinated in time with the direction of gaze (*see Table 7.3*). Gaze to the mother's face was accompanied by tonguing and wide open shaping of the mouth, and by signs of enjoyment in all conditions, whereas the expression was neutral when the infant looked away. Furthermore, in the Blank Face condition the infant tended to show expressions of negative affect (frowning and grimacing) when looking at the mother, suggesting protest or solicitation for her responsiveness.

Coherent behaviour was also seen in the Live and Replay conditions. The infant's behaviour during the Live sequence was very similar to that seen in normal face-to-face interactions, except that the mood appeared

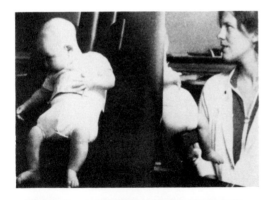

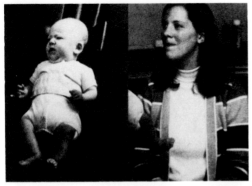

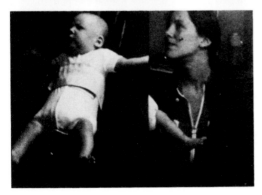

Figure 7.4 Infant girl showing typical response to the 'Blank Face' perturbation: first a period of protest or solicitation with thrashing arms and frowning to the mother (lower frames) and then withdrawal and avoidance.

less exuberant, and was reflected in lower levels of smiling (*Figure 7.6*). Nevertheless, eye contact was maintained in long continuous bouts, and the infant made arm gestures and movements of lips and tongue. When presented with the Replay sequence there was a rapid change in behaviour that in some ways resembled the response to the Blank Face Condition

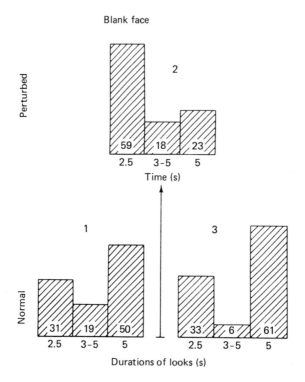

Blank face

Perturbed

Time (s)

Normal

Durations of looks (s)

Figure 7.5 Distribution of different length looking bouts between normal and perturbed conditions, with long continuous looks to the mother's face (>5 s) in normal conditions, short darting glances (<2.5 s) predominating in the Blank Face perturbation.

Table 7.3 Co-occurrence of communicative and emotionally expressive acts with the direction of infant gaze in Normal, Interruption and Blank Face conditions.

	Normal	*Interruption*	*Blank Face*
Acts co-occurring with gaze to mother's face:			
Tonguing movements	0.1	0.01	
Wide open mouthing	0.01		0.1
Raised brows	0.06		0.001
Smiling	0.06	0.03	0.01
Grimace			0.1
Frowning			0.1
Acts co-occurring with gaze away from mother's face:			
Neutral expression	0.06	0.03	0.01
Relaxed brows	0.09		
Mouth closed		0.09	

Statistical analysis by the binomial sign test, comparing expected and obtained frequencie of occurrence. Figures represent *P* values.

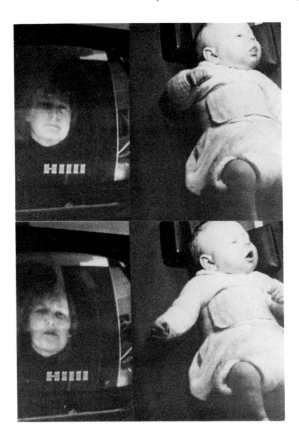

Figure 7.6 Six-week-old infant boy in a Live sequence of the Double Video Experiment, showing prespeech and gesturing to his mother who is reflected in a mirror placed alongside the baby.

(*Figure 7.7*). Gaze was averted from the mother's face, and became organized predominantly in short, darting glances (*Figure 7.8*), and there were also signs of distress such as frowning and grimacing, and fingering of the clothes and face. However, unlike the response to the Blank Face condition, tonguing and wide open mouthing occurred less often, and the impression was not of protest, but rather of puzzlement or confusion. This impression was reinforced by analysis of the simultaneous occurrence of emotional expressions and communicative behaviours with the direction of gaze (*see Table 7.4*); this revealed a strong association between frowning and looking away from the mother in the Replay condition—the converse of the relationship between these measures in the Blank Face condition. In both Live and Replay conditions communicative behaviours and expressions of positive affect accompanied looks to the mother's face, whereas a neutral expression occurred when the infant looked away.

This general description of the infant's response to perturbations fails to do justice to individual differences: these were shown not so much in

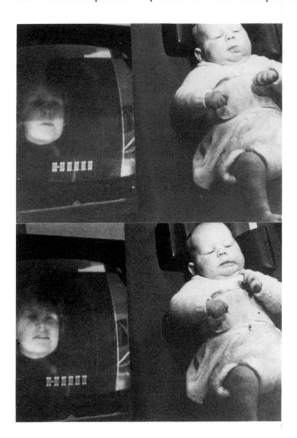

Figure 7.7 The same six-week-old infant as in *Figure 7.6* a few minutes later, when presented with the same sequence of his mother, but in delayed time, showing avoidance and twisted mouth grimaces.

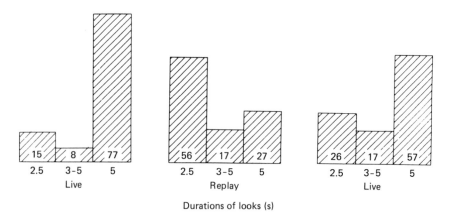

Figure 7.8 Distribution of different length infant looking bouts to the mother's face occurring between Live and Replay conditions in the Double Video Experiment. Long looks predominate in Live conditions, short glances in the Replay.

Table 7.4 Co-occurrence of communicative and emotionally expressive acts with the direction of infant gaze in Live and Replay conditions.

	Live	Replay
Acts co-occurring with gaze to mother's face:		
Raised brows	0.006	0.002
Smiling	0.03	
Eyebrows relaxed		0.04
Wide open mouthing	0.004	
Tonguing movements	0.01	
Acts co-occurring with gaze away from mother's face:		
Mouth closed		0.05
Neutral expression	0.03	
Relaxed brows	0.09	
Frowning		0.004

Statistical analysis by the binomial sign test. Figures represent P values.

unique forms of response as in the balance—some infants would maintain a vigorous protest for some time before subsiding into withdrawal, others would become detached and self-absorbed very quickly. This question of temperamental differences is discussed further below.

The distinctive forms of response to the different perturbations—quiet interest during the Interruption, protest and withdrawal at the Blank Face presentation, and puzzlement or confusion in the Replay sequence—defy explanation in terms of simple response to a disruption of contingency, or to discrepancy from an acquired schema (*see* p. 170 above). Both these elements were present in the Interruption, and yet no distress arose. Although the infant is undoubtedly sensitive to the timing or contingency of the mother's acts, as shown by the response to the Replay sequence, and to the form of her presentation, the infant seems to coordinate such dimensions in higher order structures that specify actions and emotions of personal significance.

Implications for the effects of postpartum depression during this period of development

The results of perturbation studies show how sensitive two- and three-month-old infants are to the quality of their mother's communication. Infants can not only discriminate subtle variations in maternal behaviour, but their distress when the mother behaves inappropriately, and their apparent protests or efforts to solicit communication, are also evidence for a strong motivation for the particular forms of interpersonal engagement that mothers spontaneously provide in normal face-to-face encounters.

What then are the likely consequences for the infant of maternal depression occurring during this period? It is clear from descriptions of the depressed mother that her relations with the infant may fail to show the subtle adaptations to which the infant is so sensitive that are the character-istics of ordinary maternal communication. Case studies (Robertson, 1963; Fraiberg, 1980; Murray, 1980; Stern, 1985), and experimental investiga-tions of the effects of simulated maternal depression (Cohn and Tronick, 1983) show patterns of protest, solicitation, and particularly of withdrawal, that may be elaborations of the response to some of the experimentally produced perturbations described above.

In the normal course of events when disruptions occur in maternal attentiveness the infant's responses may be adaptive. It has been suggested by psychoanalysts such as Klein et al. (1952) and Winnicott (1962) that withdrawal or self-directed behaviours may serve to protect against anxiety. Others, for example Trevarthen, Murray and Hubley (1981) and Murray and Trevarthen (1985), have drawn attention to the communicat-ive significance of infant responses and, in similar vein, Tronick et al. (1978) and Main and Weston (1982) have likened infant responses of gaze avoidance and displacement-type activities to the cut-off postures described by ethologists (Chance, 1962) that act as appeasement signals in situations where there is potential conflict between individuals of the same species, such as in boundary disputes. The potential for infant gaze aversion to regulate and influence the mother's subsequent behaviour is evident from her reaction to the infant's lingering avoidance for the first few seconds after she resumes normal contact following the Blank Face. Here a mother may make comments such as 'Oh, are you in a huff with me now?' with evident sympathy, and become even more solicitous and attentive. Indeed, when the infant protests or makes vigorous efforts to solicit a response, mothers often find it very hard to maintain a Blank Face—they literally become unable to 'keep a straight face' and, in their efforts to comply with the experimenter's request, may avoid the infant's gaze.

However, mechanisms such as these, serving both intra- and interpsychic functions, which are very effective in the context of mild everyday perturbations, may take on a different significance in the face of prolonged exposure to a more seriously pathological environment such as that constituted by maternal depression.

Researchers with strong clinical interests (e.g. Cytryn, 1976; Korner and Grobstein, 1976), have for some time recognized that individual differ-ences exist in the style for coping with environmental stresses and these ideas have received recent experimental support from studies that have shown that even newborns differ in the way they respond to stimuli; some infants, described as 'externalizers' are facially expressive and unreactive autonomically when responding, whereas for others—the 'internali-zers'—the opposite is found (Field, 1985). One of the risks posed by maternal depression is that infant coping mechanisms of whatever kind that are quite appropriate in the immediate context may, in extreme or prolonged circumstances, become persistent and predominant. As Winnicott (1960) stated, 'the personality becomes built on the basis of reactions to environmental impingement'. An infant's adaptation to his depressed mother may become an established and inappropriate pattern of relating to people other than the mother, and to the mother after she has recovered, as Robertson (1963) and Stern (1985) have described in case studies.

Similarly, Field (1984) has found from experimental work that 12-week-old infants of mildly depressed mothers show little discrimination in terms of facial expression (positive, negative and wary) and vocalizations between their mothers' behaviour when acting either depressed or else not depressed, and appear withdrawn throughout (although it should be noted that their mother's behaviour did not vary as much between these two conditions as did the control mothers').

It appears then that two related problems may arise, at least in the short term, for the infant whose mother is depressed during this period of development: in the first instance the infant may be denied the consistent experience of that form of interpersonal contact, precisely adapted to his needs, that mothers ordinarily provide. The infant may become distressed and withdrawn and, as a consequence, a second difficulty may emerge. The infant's pattern of adaptation to this enviromental deficit may become overgeneralized or fixed, thus limiting subsequent experience.

Do such immediate effects have any long-term consequences for development? Longitudinal studies of the developing relationship between depressed mothers and their infants are not yet available, although there is some relevant literature. Stern (1985) has hypothesized that the maternal adaptations normally seen in interactions at an early stage of development play a crucial role in establishing a stable and enduring sense of 'core self'—a sense of self 'that is experienced as a coherent, wilful, physical entity with a unique affective life and history that belong to it'. For example, Stern reports that when a mother responds to her infant's expressive displays she does so along a number of dimensions that are precisely coordinated: thus the speed, intensity and contouring of her head movements match the patterning of her speech. This observation is then set against experimental evidence for the young infant's capacity for 'cross-modal transfer', i.e. the ability to perceive equivalence of form across different sensory modalities (e.g. Meltzoff and Borton, 1979). Stern proposes that when the infant experiences maternal responsiveness in one modality he is already genetically equipped to identify the same form in a second; when that too is presented the infant has 'primitive forms of déjà vu' (Stern, 1985)—experience that is self-affirming and that gives coherence to infant psychological functioning. In the absence of continually presented experiences of this kind—as might be the case where the mother is depressed—Stern suggests that the long-term sense of 'core self' will be weakened.

With regard to the second possible consequence of maternal depression at this stage—the overgeneralization of patterns of adaptation—Trevarthen (1986) has proposed that brain structure and functioning may be influenced by consistent activation of motivational states, and by the quality of experience that arises as a consequence. He has argued from split brain studies that differences in cognitive functioning of the two hemispheres reflect different forms of subjective experience—one interpersonal and one with the outside world. In healthy development the hemispheres are linked in complementary fashion that gives proper scope to both functions. However, brain growth also progresses competitively, and its course is partly regulated by 'rewarding and punishing patterns of motivation that the brain generates in itself'. Just as the development of the kitten's visual cortex requires both patterned visual input and activation of the brain core mediated by neurotransmitters (Singer, 1984), in a similar way, Trevarthen argues, the development of the infant brain is affected by experience obtained from the world and by internal motivational states. His position thus suggests that the infant's adoption, for example, of a withdrawal into a private experience of the world, avoiding interpersonal engagement, may have neurophysiological consequences for later development.

However, the problems of tracing such continuities are complex and manifold. At the level of neurophysiology little is known about the neurophysiological correlates of distortions of the balance of motivational mechanisms, and it should be noted that protective and self-repairing functions may mitigate the effects of earlier damage. A further difficulty, readily acknowledged by Stern in relation to the concept of 'core-self', concerns the establishment of criteria for identifying parallels between earlier and later functioning, since the surface structure of behaviour may be transformed by changes in context and by developmental progress. Even where there is close identity between behaviours occurring at different times, giving evidence for continuity, their later manifestation may be 'swamped' by the impact of other experiences that have further independent effects on development (Bateson, 1978; Hinde and Bateson, 1984). The evidence discussed above (p. 163) for the persistence of maternal communicative problems, despite recovery from depression, compounds still further the difficulty of identifying longer-term phenomena that can be said unequivocably to be direct repercussions of earlier, immediate effects.

With these considerations in mind, it seems less fruitful at the present time to speculate about the relationship between early responses to maternal depression (behavioural or neurophysiological) and effects that have been identified in older children, than to consider the way in which infant development progresses, with maternal support, in the ensuing months.

Mother-infant interactions: 4–9 months

Towards the end of the third month, a change takes place in the quality of mother-infant engagement. Winnicott (1960) describes it thus:

> A change comes with the end of merging . . . as soon as mother and infant are separate, from the infant's point of view, then it will be noted that the mother tends to change in her attitude. It is as if she now realizes that the infant no longer expects the condition in which there is almost magical understanding of need. The mother seems to know that the infant has a new capacity, that of giving a signal so that she can be guided towards meeting the infant's needs.

A growing motivation in the infant for different forms of experience at around 3–4 months has been reported by several researchers (Bruner, 1975; Tronick et al., 1978, 1986; Sylvester-Bradley, 1981; Trevarthen, Murray and Hubley, 1981). At a time when the infant's visual acuity approaches that of adult's (Haith, 1977), and reach and grasp movements start to become effective (White, Castle and Held, 1964), his interest will be readily caught by some attractive object nearby. No longer is he captivated by the form of maternal response that was previously so engaging, and there is a decline in eye-to-eye contact and in smiling to the mother (Ambrose, 1961; Sylvester-Bradley, 1981).

Although the quality of engagement between mother and infant alters, the infant remains dependent on the mother's accurate and sensitive reading of his changing attention and emotions, for these infant expressions can have no impact in themselves on the wider world that has become the subject of his emerging interest. Until he is independently mobile, it is only through the mother that his desire to experience the wider environment can be realized.

Mothers adapt to this development in their infants by following their gaze and expressions of interest (Collis and Schaffer, 1975), and show this adaptation clearly in their baby-talk. This ceases to be 'phatic', i.e. referring only to the intentions and emotions of the two partners (Bruner, 1975), and increasingly refers to the new foci of infant attention (Sylvester-Bradley and Trevarthen, 1978). Mothers also make more use of objects when playing with their babies. Tronick *et al.* (1986) report a five-fold increase in the proportion of time spent by mothers playing with toys or objects from 3–9 months, and they comment that 'the shift to Mother Object Play from Mother Social Attend was the major and singular change in maternal behaviour'.

Even if the mother is not using an object as a focus of joint attention, the change in the infant's psychology normally propels her into adopting a different form of interpersonal contact with the infant that also incorporates some shared referent, which is often part of her own body. Sylvester-Bradley (1981) describes the success of such change in maternal strategy:

> The mother soon found that she could capture Joanna's attention by holding up her hand in Joanna's line of vision and waving her fingers. Joanna would be fascinated by this, looking at the fingers continuously and ceasing all vocal protests.

On the infant's part, he will spontaneously grab at the mother's hair, nose, tongue or fingers; such episodes, and those in which the mother presents herself, become elaborated into 'games of the person', in which both participants may take on an assertive, teasing, albeit asymmetrical, role (Trevarthen, 1980), and which are reiterated in routines of play that draw on conventionalized forms, e.g. 'clap-a-clap-a-handies' or 'peek-a-boo' (Bruner and Sherwood, 1975).

Sensitivity of the infant to maternal behaviour has not been as extensively explored at this later age as during the first three months. At times when the 4–9-month-old infant is absorbed in manipulative or exploratory activity it appears superficially as though he pays little heed to the precise quality of maternal response. For example, Hubley has found that although the infant's attention may be drawn to a locus specified by the mother for infant action upon objects, the details of her activity go unacknowledged (Hubley and Trevarthen, 1979; Hubley, 1984). Bates (1976) has observed that when an infant at this stage wants something that is out of reach, he will not look to the mother's face to direct her action in relation to the desired object, but rather will look and gesture towards the object alone. When the mother executes her infant's desire and brings the object within his grasp, she appears an unrecognized slave to her infant's will. It has been suggested that, at this stage, infant responses to objects are unintegrated with responses to persons (Brazelton, Koslowski and Main, 1974; Trevarthen, 1979; Tronick *et al.*, 1986). However, Stern has recently reported that by at least eight months, an infant who is absorbed in exploration or object play may be distinctly perturbed if his mother is inaccurately attuned to the intensity and quality of his own mood (Stern *et al.*, 1985). It seems, therefore, that although the infant may not explicitly seek or acknowledge a response from his mother when things go smoothly, distortions in maternal support may nevertheless impinge on his experience of even the physical world.

These observations of interactions during the period 4–9 months indicate how infant developmental progress (praxic, cognitive, interpersonal and cultural) is intimately bound up with and facilitated by complementary maternal care. Should maternal care be compromised by depression, or by the inhibited communication and increased friction that have been identified as residual deficits (Weissman and Paykel, 1974), or else if the infant has caused such care to be less available through his own withdrawal, the consequence may be that the range and richness of his experience of the world—both personal and physical—may be markedly reduced.

Mother-infant interactions: 9 months–1 year

Towards the end of the first year, at around 9–10 months, the form of face-to-face encounters between mother and infant is once more recast as important changes in infant psychological functioning take place. This latest restructuring of the relationship is reported widely in the literature (Bruner, 1975; Bates, 1976; Emde *et al.*, 1978; Bretherton and Bates, 1979; Hubley and Trevarthen, 1979; Campos and Sternberg, 1981; Hubley, 1984; Stern, 1985; Tronick *et al.*, 1986). It appears to stem from a new capacity in the infant to perceive others as independent agents with distinct feelings and intentions of their own. Indeed, these feelings and intentions themselves become the focus of infant interest. This development is manifest in several ways; one is in the explicit direction of another's agency vis à vis the world. Bretherton and Bates (1979) and Hubley and Trevarthen (1979) have reported that at this period the infant will look and gesture to the mother to direct her action in relation to objects, and Halliday (1975) has noted that by 10 months the inflection of vocalizations can serve the same instrumental and regulatory purpose.

Secondly, the infant will now expressly seek out and incorporate another's attitudes and intentions to define his own experience. Emde *et al.* (1978) and Campos and Sternberg (1981) have termed this 'social referencing', and describe how the infant will look to and use the mother's emotional expression in an ambiguous situation to guide his behaviour. Just as the infant seeks the mother's definition of events at this time, so in turn does the mother regularly offer an interpretation of the infant's behaviour that carries a cultural significance not initially there for the infant. This function has received particular attention from infant researchers with a sociological orientation, e.g. Richards, (1974) and Shotter, (1974), and has been termed 'scaffolding' by Bruner and Sherwood (1981). It has the effect of enriching the infant's experience, and of making a bridge between personal and wider social worlds. The infant's readiness to take advantage of socially defined meanings, and to appreciate the shared significance of objects, is reflected in their conventional use. Freeman, Lloyd and Sinha (1980) have found that infants at this age, who otherwise fail on tests of object permanence, will pass if the test objects are presented in a way that is consistent with their conventional use.

A further sign of this new 'intersubjective' development is a reciprocity in game playing and in joint activities with objects. Whereas previous games showed an asymmetry in the roles of mother and infant, towards the end of the first year the infant seems to recognize the mother's equivalent status. Bruner and Sherwood (1975) for example, describe how the infant will now play the role of active revealer in 'peek-a-boo'. Hubley (1984) and Trevarthen (1979) have shown how, during this period, infants become increasingly interested in their mothers' actions upon objects, and are more likely to comply with her suggestions. This change in the infant is complemented by the mother who evolves new strategies to negotiate joint activities. By the end of the first year cooperative action in tasks is successful and sustained. A related capacity which emerges with this more conscious appreciation of 'other minds' is the infant's growing sense of his dependency upon the mother. A marked wariness of strangers may be observed, as well as distress provoked by maternal departures. As before, the mother plays a central role in helping the infant to realize his potential as an independent agent, in a world of shared meaning and reciprocal activity.

It is as one reaches this point in the unfolding of infant abilities that one can see how the correlates of maternal depression identified in older children may have evolved from the depressed mother's inability to provide an appropriate environment for infant psychological development. Thus the delay in expressive language, poor concentration, lack of shared affect, and insecurity of attachment, all seen in children of depressed mothers between 19 months and three years (*see* pp. 163–164), bear a close relationship to the interpersonal functions that have been described as emerging towards the end of the first year.

Conclusion

As one charts the progress of development in the first year from the neonate's sensitivity to, and predilection for, human forms, through his motivation for personal engagement in the first three months, then his emergent impulse to experience a wider environment, to the achievement of an intersubjective and cooperative sharing of the world, it is clear that each step requires a particular complementary and facilitating adaptation by another person, usually the mother.

Whether early maternal depression is itself sufficient to impair development or whether the observed adverse effects arise from long-standing problems in maternal communication is an important question, theoretically and clinically. There is a great need for longitudinal studies with repeated direct observations. In the meantime, observational and experimental studies of 'normal' mother-infant interactions can improve our understanding of the role that the mother plays in infant development.

Acknowledgements

The author was funded by the SSRC to carry out her research reported in this chapter. Appreciative thanks are due to the Winnicott Trust, the Camilla Samuel Fund and the Medical Research Council for their current support of this work.

References

AINSWORTH, M. D. S. and WITTIG, B. A. (1969). Attachment and exploratory behaviour in one year olds in a strange situation. In: *Determinants of Infant Behaviour*, Vol. 4, (B. M. Foss, ed.), London: Methuen

ALEGRIA, J. and NOIROT, E. (1978). Neonate orientation behaviour towards the human voice. *Early Human Development*, **1**, 291–312

AMBROSE, J. A. (1961). The development of the smiling response in early infancy. In: *Determinants of Infant Behaviour*, Vol. 1, (B. M. Foss, ed.), London: Methuen

BATES, E. (1976). *Language and Context: The Acquisition of Pragmatics*. New York and London: Academic Press

BATESON, P. (1978). How does behaviour develop? In: *Perspectives in Ethology*, Vol. 3, (P. Bateson and P. H. Klopfer, eds), New York: Plenum

BEEBE, B., JAFFE, J., FELDSTEIN, B., MAYS, K. and ALSON, D. (1985). Interpersonal tuning: the application of an adult dialogue model to mother-infant vocal and kinesic interactions. In: *Social Perception in Infants*, (T. M. Field and N. A. Fox, eds). Norwood, NJ: Ablex

BOWER, T. R. G. (1974). *Development in Infancy*. San Francisco: W. H. Freeman

BRACKBILL, Y. (1958). Extinction of the smiling response in infants as a function of reinforcement schedule. *Child Development*, **29**, 115–124

BRAZELTON, T. B., KOSLOWSKI, B. and MAIN, M. (1974). The origins of reciprocity: the early mother-infant interaction. In: *The Effects of the Infant on its Caregiver*, (M. Lewis and L. A. Rosenblum, eds), New York: Wiley

BRAZELTON, T. B., TRONICK, E. Z., ADAMSON, L., ALS, H. and WISE, S. (1975). Early mother-infant reciprocity. In: *Parent-Infant Interaction*, (M. Hofer, ed.), Amsterdam: Elsevier

BRETHERTON, I. and BATES, E. (1979). Emergence of intentional communication. In: *New Directions for Child Development*, Vol. 4, (I. C. Uzgiris, ed.), San Francisco: Sage

BROWN, G. W. and HARRIS, T. (1978). *Social Origins of Depression: A Study of Psychiatric Disorders in Women*. London: Tavistock

BRUNER, J. S. (1975). The ontogenesis of speech acts. *Journal of Child Language*, **2**, 1–19.

BRUNER, J. S. and SHERWOOD, V. (1975). Peek-a-boo and the learning of rule structure. In: *Play—its Role in Development and Evolution*, (J. S. Bruner, A. Jolley and K. Sylva, eds), Harmondsworth: Penguin.

BRUNER, J. S. and SHERWOOD, V. (1981). Thought, language and interaction in infancy. In: *Social Cognition*. European Monographs in Social Psychology No. 26, (J. P. Forgas, ed.), London: Academic Press

CAMPOS, J. and STERNBERG, C. (1981). Perception and appraisal of emotion: the onset of social referencing. In: *Infant Social Cognition*, (M. E. Lamb and L. Sherrod, eds), Hillsdale, NJ: Erlbaum

CARPENTER, G. C. (1974). Visual regard of moving and stationary faces in early infancy. *Merrill Palmer Quarterly*, **20**, 181–194

CARPENTER, G. C. TECCE, J. S., STECHLER, G. and FRIEDMAN, S. (1970). Differential behaviour to human and humanoid faces in early infancy. *Merrill Palmer Quarterly*, **16**, 91–108

CHANCE, M. R. A. (1962). An interpretation of some agonistic postures: the role of cut-off acts and postures. Symposia of the Zoological Society of London, No. 8. 71–89

CLARKE, A. M. and CLARKE, A. D. B. (1976). *Early Experience: Myth and Evidence*. London: Open Books

COGILL, S. R., CAPLAN, H. L., ALEXANDRA, H., ROBSON, K. M. and KUMAR, R. (1986). Impact of maternal postnatal depression on cognitive development of young children. *British Medical Journal*, **292**, 1165–1167

COHLER, B. J., GRUNEBAUM, H. U., WEISS, J. L., GARNER, E. and GALLANT, D. H. (1977). Disturbance of attention among schizophrenic, depressed and well mothers and their young children. *Journal of Child Psychology and Psychiatry*, **18**, 115–135

COHN, J. F. and TRONICK, E. Z. (1983). Three month-old infants' reaction to simulated maternal depression. *Child Development*, **54**, 185–193

COLLIS, G. M. and SCHAFFER, H. K. (1975). Synchronisation of visual attention in mother-infant pairs. *Journal of Child Psychology and Psychiatry*, **16**, 315–320

COX, J. L., CONNOR, Y. and KENDELL, R. E. (1978). Prospective study of the psychiatric disorders of childbirth. *British Journal of Psychiatry*, **140**, 111–117

CYTRYN, L. (1976). Methodological issues in psychiatric evaluation of infants. In: *Infant Psychiatry: a New Synthesis*, (E. N. Rexford, L. W. Sander and T. Shapiro, eds), Yale: Yale University Press

DARWIN, C. (1877). A biographical sketch of an infant. *Mind* **2**, 285–294

DE CASPER, A. J. and FIFER, W. P. (1980). Of human bonding: newborns prefer their mothers' voices. *Science*, **208**, 1174–1176

EIMAS, P. D. (1985). The perception of speech in early infancy. *Scientific American* **252**, 34–40

EIMAS, P. D., SIQUELAND, E. R., JUSCZYK, P. and VIGORITO, J. (1971). Speech perception in infants. *Science*, **171**, 303–306

EISENBERG, R. B. (1975). *Auditory Competence in Early Life. The Roots of Communicative Behaviour*. Baltimore: University Park Press

EMDE, R. N., KLINGMAN, D. H., REICH, J. H. and WADE, J. D. (1978). Emotional expression in infancy. 1. Initial studies of social signalling and an emergent model. In: *The Development of Affect*, (M. Lewis and L. Rosenblum, eds). New York: Plenum Press

FANTZ, R. L. (1963). Pattern vision in newborn infants. *Science*, **140**, 296–297

FERGUSON D. M., HORWOOD, L. J., GRETTON, M. E. and SHANNON, F. T. (1985). Family life events, maternal depression and maternal and teacher descriptions of child behaviour. *Pediatrics*, **75**, 30–35

FIELD, T. M. (1984). Early interactions between infants and their post partum depressed mothers. *Infant Behaviour and Development*, **7**, 517–522

FIELD, T. M. (1985). Neonatal perception of people: motivational and individual differences. In *Social Perception in Infants*, (T. M. Field and N. A. Fox, eds). Norwood, NJ: Ablex

FIELD, T. M., WOODSON, R., GREENBERG, R. and COHEN, D. (1982). Discrimination and imitation of facial expressions by neonates. *Science*, **218**, 179–181

FRAIBERG, S. (1980). *Clinical Studies in Infant Mental Health. The First Year of Life*. London: Tavistock Publications

FREEMAN, N. H., LLOYD, S. and SINHA, C. G. (1980). Infant search tasks reveal early concepts of containment and canonical usage of objects. *Cognition*, **8**, 243–262

FRIEDLANDER, B. (1970). Receptive language development in infancy. *Merrill Palmer Quarterly*, **16**, 7–51

FROMMER, E. A. and O'SHEA, G. (1973). Antenatal identification of women liable to have problems managing their infants. *British Journal of Psychiatry*, **123**, 149–156

GAMER, E., GALLANT, D., GRUNEBAUM, H. U. and COHLER, B. J. (1977). Children of psychotic mothers. *Archives of General Psychiatry*, **34**, 592–597

GHODSIAN, M., ZAJICEK, E. and WOLKIND, S. (1984). A longitudinal study of maternal depression and child behaviour problems. *Journal of Child Psychology and Psychiatry*, **25**, 91–109

GOREN, C. G., SARTY, M. and WU, P. Y. K. (1975). Visual following and pattern discrimination of face-life stimuli by newborn infants. *Paediatrics*, **56**, 544–549

GRUNEBAUM, H. U., COHLER, B. J., KAUFFMAN, C. and GALLANT, D. (1978). Children of depressed and schizophrenic mothers. *Child Psychiatry and Human Development*, **8**, 219–228

HAITH, M. H. (1977). Visual competence in early infancy. In: *Handbook of Sensory Physiology*, Vol. 8, (R. Held, H. Leibovitz and H. L. Teuber, eds). Berlin: Springer-Verlag

HALLIDAY, M. A. K. (1975). *Learning How to Mean. Explorations in the Development of Language*. London: Arnold

HINDE, R. A. and BATESON, P. (1984). Discontinuities versus continuities in behavioural development and the neglect of process. *International Journal of Behavioural Development*, **7**, 129–143

HUBLEY, P. A. (1984). The development of cooperative action in infants. PhD Thesis, University of Edinburgh

HUBLEY, P. A. and TREVARTHEN, C. B. (1979). Sharing a task in infancy. In: *New Directions for Child Development*, Vol. 4, (I. C. Uzgiris, ed.), San Francisco: Sage

KAGAN, J. (1980). Four questions in psychological development. *International Journal of Behavioural Development*, **3**, 231–241

KAGAN, J. (1982). *Psychological Research on the Human Infant: An Evaluative Summary*. New York: William Grant Foundation

KLEIN, M., HEINMANN, P., ISAACS, P. and RIVIERE, J. (1952). *Developments in Psychoanalysis*. London: Hogarth

KOCH, J. (1967). Conditioned orienting. Reactions in two-month old infants. *British Journal of Psychology*, **57**, 105–110

KORNER, A. F. and GROBSTEIN, R. (1976). Individual differences at birth: implications for mother-infant relationships and later development. In: *Infant Psychiatry: A New Synthesis*, (E. N. Rexford, L. W. Sander and T. Shapiro, eds), Yale: Yale University Press

KUMAR, R. and ROBSON, K. M. (1984). A prospective study of the emotional disorders of child bearing women. *British Journal of Psychiatry*, **144**, 35–47

LACAN, J. (1977). *Ecrits*. New York: Norton

LESLIE, A. M. (1984). Infant perception of a manual pick up event. *British Journal of Developmental Psychology*, **2**, 19–32

MAIN, M. (1985) Growing points of attachment theory and research. In *Monographs of the Society for Research in Child Development*, 50, 1–2 Serial No. 209, (I. Bretherton and E. Waters, eds).

MAIN, M. and WESTON, D. R. (1982). Avoidance of the attachment figure in infancy: descriptions and interpretations. In: *The Place of Attachment in Human Behaviour*, (J. Stevenson-Hinde and C. Murray Parkes, eds), Chapter 2. London: Tavistock Publications

MCFARLANE, J. (1975). Olfaction in the development of social preferences in the human neonate. In: *Parent-Infant Interaction*, (M. Hofer, ed.), Amsterdam: Elsevier

MCKNEW, P. H., CYTRYN, L., EFRON, A. M., GERSHON, E. S. and BUNNEY, W. E. (1979). The offspring of parents with affective disorders. *British Journal of Psychiatry*, **134**, 148–152

MEHLER, J., BERTONCINI, J. and BARNIERE, M. (1978). Infant recognition of mother's voice. *Perception*, **7**, 491–497

MELTZOFF, A. N. and BORTON, W. (1979). Intermodel matching in human neonates. *Nature*, **282**, 403–404

MELTZOFF, A. N. and MOORE, M. K. (1977). Imitation of facial and manual gestures by human neonates. *Science*, **198**, 73–75

MILLS, M., PUCKERING, C., POUND, A. and COX, A. (1985). What is it about depressed mothers that influences their children's functioning? In: *Recent Research in Developmental Psychopathology*, (J. E. Stevenson, ed.), pp. 11–17. Oxford: Pergamon Press

MURRAY, L. (1980). The sensitivities and expressive capacities of young infants in communication with their mothers. PhD Thesis, University of Edinburgh

MURRAY, L. and TREVARTHEN, C. B. (1985). Emotional regulation of interactions between two month olds and their mother's. In: *Social Perception in Infants*, (T. M. Field and N. A. Fox, eds), Norwood, NJ: Ablex

MURRAY, L. and TREVARTHEN, C. B. (1986). The infant's role in mother-infant communication. *Journal of Child Language*, **13**, 15–29

OSTER, H. and EKMAN, P. (1977). Facial behaviour in child development. In: *Minnesota Symposium on Child Development*, Vol. 11, (A. Collins, ed.), New York: J. A. Crowell.

PAPOUSEK, H. and PAPOUSEK, M. (1975). Cognitive aspects of preverbal social interaction between human infants and adults. In: *Parent-Infant Interaction*, (E. Hofer, ed.), Amsterdam: Elsevier.

PERSSON-BLENNOW, I. NÄSLUND, B., McNEIL, T. F., KAIJ, L. and MALMQVIST-LARSSON, A. (1984). Offspring of women with non-organic psychosis: mother-infant reaction at three days of age. *Acta Psychiatrica Scandinavica*, **70**, 149–159

PITT, B. (1968). Atypical depression following childbirth. *British Journal of Psychiatry*, **114**, 1325–1335

POUND, A., COX, A., PUCKERING, C. and MILLS, M. (1985). The impact of maternal depression on young children. In: *Recent Research in Developmental Psychopathology*, (J. E. Stevenson, ed.), Oxford: Pergamon Press

RADKE-YARROW, M., CUMMINGS, E. M., KUCZYNSKI, L. and CHAPMAN, M. (1985). Patterns of attachment in two and three year olds in normal families and families with parental depression. *Child Development*, **56**, 884–893

RHEINGOLD, H. L., GEWIRTZ, J. F. and ROSS, H. (1959). Social conditioning of vocalizations in the infant. *Journal of Comparative and Physiological Psychology*, **52**, 68–73

RICHARDS, M. P. M. (1974). First steps in becoming social. In: *The Integration of a Child into a Social World*, (M. P. M. Richards, ed.), Cambridge: Cambridge University Press

ROBERTSON, J. (1963). Mother-infant interaction from birth to 12 months: two case studies. In: *Determinants of Infant Behaviour*, Vol. 3, (B. M. Foss, ed.). London: Methuen

RUTTER, M. (1966). *Children of Sick Parents*. Maudsley Monographs 16. London: Oxford University Press

RUTTER, M. and QUINTON, D. (1984). Parental psychiatric disorder: effects on children. *Psychological Medicine*, **14**, 873–880

SCHOEZTAU, A. and PAPOUSEK, H. (1977). Mutterliches verhalten bei der Aufnahme von Blickkontakt mit dem Neugeboren. *Zeitschrift fur Entwicklungs Psychologie und Paedagogische Psychologie*, **9**, 1088–1089

SHERROD, L. R. (1981). Issues in cognitive-perceptual development. The special case of social stimuli. In: *Infant Social Cognition*, (M. E. Lamb and L. R. Sherrod, eds), Hillsdale, NJ: Erlbaum

SHOTTER, J. (1974). The development of personal powers. In: *The Integration of a Child into a Social World*, (M. P. M. Richards, ed.), Cambridge: Cambridge University Press

SINGER, W. (1984). Learning to see: mechanisms in experience dependent development. In: *The Biology of Learning*, (D. Marler and H. S. Terrace, eds). Berlin: Springer

SPITZ, R. (1957). *No and Yes: On the Genesis of Human Communication*. New York: Inter University Press.

STERN, D. N. (1977). *The First Relationship: Infant and Mother*. Cambridge: Harvard University Press

STERN, D. N. (1985). *The Interpersonal World of the Infant. A View from Psychoanalysis and Developmental Psychology*. New York: Basic Books

STERN, D. N., HOFER, L., HAFT, W. and DORE, J. (1985). Affect attunement: the sharing of feeling states between mother and infant by means of intermodal fluency. In: *Social Perception in Infants*, (T. M. Field and N. A. Fox, eds). Norwood, NJ: Ablex

SYLVESTER-BRADLEY, B. (1981). Negativity in early infant adult exchanges and its developmental significance. In: *Communication in Development*, (P. Robinson, ed.), London: Academic Press

SYLVESTER-BRADLEY, B. and TREVARTHEN, C. B. (1978). Baby talk as an adaptation to the infants' communication. In: *The Development of Communication*, (N. Waterson and C. Snow, eds), London: Wiley.

TREVARTHEN, C. B. (1979). Communication and cooperation in early infancy: a description of primary intersubjectivity. In: *Before Speech*, (M. Bullows, ed.). Cambridge: Cambridge University Press

TREVARTHEN, C. B. (1980). The foundations of intersubjectivity: development of interpersonal and cooperative understanding in infants. In: *The Social Foundations of Language and Thought. Essays in Honor of J. S. Bruner*, (D. K. Olson, ed.). New York: Norton

TREVARTHEN, C. B. (1985). Facial expressions of emotion in mother-infant interaction. *Human Neurobiology*, **4**, 21–32

TREVARTHEN, C. B. (1986). Brain science and the human spirit. *Zygon*, **21**, 161–200

TREVARTHEN, C. B., MURRAY, L. and HUBLEY, P. A. (1981). Psychology of infants. In: *Scientific Foundations of Paediatrics*, 2nd Edition, (J. A. Davis and J. Dobbing, eds). London: Heinemann

TRONICK, E. Z., ALS, H., ADAMSON, L., WISE, S. and BRAZELTON, T. B. (1978). The infants' response to entrapment between contradictory messages in face-to-face interaction. *Journal of the American Academy of Child Psychiatry*, **17**, 1–13

TRONICK, E. Z., KRATCHUCK, E., RICKS, M., COHN, J. and WINN, S. (1986). Mother-infant face-to-face interaction at 3, 6 and 9 months. Content matching. *Child Development* (paper submitted for publication)

UDDENBERG, N. and ENGLESSON, I. (1978). Prognosis of postpartum mental disturbance. A prospective study of primiparous women and their 4 year-old children. *Acta Psychiatrica Scandinavica*, **58**, 201–212

WEISSMAN, M. M. and PAYKEL, E. S. (1974). *The Depressed Woman*. Chicago and London: University of Chicago Press

WEISSMAN, M. M., PAYKEL, E. S. and KLERMAN, G. L. (1972). The depressed woman as a mother. *Social Psychiatry*, **7**, 98–108

WEISSMAN, M. M., PRUSOFF, B. A., GAMMON, G. D., MERINKANGAS, K. R., LECKMAN, J. F. and KID, K. K. (1984). Psychopathology in the children (6–18) of depressed and normal parents. *Journal of the American Academy of Child Psychiatry*, **23**, 78–84

WELNER, Z., WELNER, A., DONALD, M., McCRANY, B. A. and LEONARD, M. A. (1977). Psychopathology in children of inpatients with depression. *Journal of Nervous and Mental Disease*, **164**, 408–413

WHITE, B. L., CASTLE, P. and HELD, R. (1964). Observation on the development of visually directed reaching. *Child Development*, **35**, 349–364

WIDMER-ROBERT TISSOT, C. (1981). Les modes de communication du bébé: postures, mouvements et vocalisés. In: *Actualités Pédagogiques et Psychologiques*, (Delachaux and Niestlé, eds), Paris: Neuchâtel

WILLIAMS, H. and CARMICHAEL, A. (1985). Depression in mothers in a multi-ethnic urban industrial municipality in Melbourne. Aetiological factors and effects on infants and pre-schoolchildren. *Journal of Child Psychology and Psychiatry*, **26**, 277–288

WINNICOTT, D. W. (1956). Primary maternal preoccupation. In *Through Paediatrics to Psychoanalysis*, (M. Masud and R. Khan, eds). London: Hogarth Press

WINNICOTT, D. W. (1958). Collected papers. In: *Through Paediatrics to Psychoanalysis*, (M. Masud and R. Khan, eds). London: Hogarth Press

WINNICOTT, D. W. (1960). The theory of the parent-infant relationship. In: *The Maturational Process and the Facilitating Environment*, (J. D. Sutherland, ed.). London: Hogarth Press

WINNICOTT, D. W. (1962). Ego integration in child development. In *The Maturational Process and the Facilitating Environment*, (J. D. Sutherland, ed.). London: Hogarth Press

WINNICOTT, D. W. (1965). *The Maturational Process and the Facilitating Environment*, (J. D. Sutherland, ed.). London: Hogarth Press

WINNICOTT, D. W. (1967). Mirror role of mother and family in child development. In: *Playing and Reality*. London: Tavistock Publications

WOLFF, P. H. (1969). The natural history of crying and other vocalizations in early infancy. In: *Determinants of Infant Behaviour*, Vol. 4, (B. M. Foss, ed.). London: Methuen

WRATE, R. M., ROONEY, A. C., THOMAS, P. F. and COX, J. L. (1985). Postnatal depression and child development: a 3-year follow-up study. *British Journal of Psychiatry*, **146**, 622–627

ZAJICEK, E. and de SALIS, W. (1979). Depression in mothers of young children. *Child Abuse and Neglect*, **3**, 833–835

Chapter 8

Maternal mental illness and the mother-infant relationship

E. C. Melhuish, Carol Gambles and R. Kumar

Introduction

This chapter is divided into two sections. First we review some of the major clinical problems that arise in the management of puerperal mental illness with particular reference to the mother-infant relationship. The second part of the chapter is a review of studies of mothers and infants together, suggesting ways in which such research can begin to address questions that were posed in the first part of the review. Murray (Chapter 7) has given a full account of her own very detailed studies of mothers and infants and she has focused on investigations of depressed mothers. Our review, which complements Murray's chapter, contains a more general examination of strategies used in existing research and for future research as they may apply to a wide range of puerperal mental illnesses.

The clinical problem

Postpartum psychosis

Timing of the mother's illness
Psychiatric illness in childbearing women is normally classified in terms of predominant symptomatology, but it is also useful to group such illnesses by their time of onset. There are, as yet, no reported investigations of severe puerperal mental illnesses which are phenomenologically similar but which may, because of their timing, have different consequences for the developing child and for the mother-infant relationship. Is the outcome likely to be very different in cases where pre-existing chronic psychiatric disorders are complicated by pregnancy, as opposed to those cases in whom the illness is a sequel to childbirth? In whom will there be the greatest disruption of attachment and towards whom should most re-sources and interventions be channelled? Are mothers with chronic illnesses most at risk? It may be a mistake automatically to assume so, because they, their partners and others, may have made many personal and social adaptations to the presence of persisting psychiatric problems. Such adaptation may turn out to have 'protective' functions after the baby is born. Resources such as 'home helps', day nurseries, support from

relatives and friends may have been primed because the mother's vulnerability was already known. The mother herself may be psychologically
better prepared because she has been able to confront in her mind some of
the problems which may arise if her illness recurs or becomes worse. In
contrast, a new mother who unexpectedly becomes ill for the first time in
her life will be in unknown territory and her attachment to her infant may
be doubly disrupted because she may see the baby as the cause of her
condition. Similarly, partners and others often find that it takes weeks or
months before they are able to cope adequately with the aftermath of an
unexpected postnatal illness. Inadequate or inappropriate support for the
mother may increase the strain on her relationship with her baby.

It may be fruitful, therefore, when studying the consequences of
maternal mental illnesses to place mothers into subgroups, e.g.

(1) Those whose illnesses antedate the pregnancy, e.g. women with
histories of schizophrenia, manic depressive illness, neurotic disorders
and severe personality disturbances. In such cases the mother's mental
condition can be considered to be complicated by pregnancy and
childbirth. Complications can also occur in the opposite direction
because obstetric outcome may be influenced by factors related to the
mother's illness.

(2) Those mothers who become psychiatrically ill *during* pregnancy for the
first time in their lives. The incidence of mental illness during
pregnancy is far less than after childbirth (Brockington, Winokur and
Dean, 1982; Kumar, 1982) and slightly less than at times unrelated to
childbirth. Comparisons of outcome of illnesses arising in pregnancy as
opposed to postnatally (Cogill *et al.*, 1986) suggest that only illnesses
which persist into the puerperium are likely adversely to affect the
developing child.

(3) The third group are those mothers whose psychiatric disorders begin
after childbirth. These illnesses mainly take two forms:
(a) postpartum psychosis, and
(b) postnatal depression.
The common, mild and transient 'maternity blues' is not an illness (*see*
Stein, 1982) and will therefore be disregarded here.

Links between the nature and timing of maternal psychopathology and
putative disturbances of the mother-child relationship cannot meaningfully
be studied in isolation from the personal, social and clinical context. Many
factors may play a part in shaping the mother-infant relationship: they
include the mother's age, parity, medical history and current health, her
personality, past family background, present domestic and marital circumstances, occupation, exposure to life stresses, access to support, her
partner's health and supportiveness, the presence of personal or marital
conflicts about wanting the pregnancy, the infant's health and temp-
ment, the presence of siblings and their health and reactions to the new
baby. It will be obvious that most of these listed variables, and others too
numerous to catalogue here, may also play some part in causing the mother
to become ill in the first place. The putative dependent variable (mother-
infant relationship) is therefore subject to many influences, among which
are the nature and time course of maternal psychopathology. Discerning

how such influences intermingle and change over time is a little like trying to analyse patterns in a three-dimensional spider's web. The prey is the developing child and so there is strong motivation to persist with the analysis.

Method of management of mothers who are severely ill
One factor which is not already listed, but which may have far reaching consequences, is the way in which the mother's illness is managed. About one in every 500 newly delivered women is admitted to a psychiatric hospital within a few months of childbirth and about half of these patients become ill within the first four weeks (Brockington, Winokur and Dean, 1982). Most of the acute, early onset illnesses can be categorized as affective psychoses (Brockington *et al.*, 1981; Dean and Kendell, 1981; Meltzer and Kumar, 1985) with an about equal representation of predominantly manic or depressive subtypes. 'Mixed' affective and schizoaffective syndromes are also seen, but it is uncommon to find schizophrenia arising *de novo* in the early puerperium. Thus, there are about 1000 mothers each year in England and Wales who become severely mentally ill following childbirth and about two-thirds of them will have had their first child and their first ever psychotic breakdown. The treatments that are prescribed are the same as for non-puerperal psychoses, i.e. neuroleptic and anti-depressant drugs, lithium and ECT. In general the prognosis is favourable with most mothers making good clinical recoveries and returning to their families after about 6–12 weeks.

The UK is unique among Western countries in that, more often than not, babies are admitted with their mothers into psychiatric hospitals (Margison and Brockington, 1982). A recent survey of the South East Thames Health Region of England (Kumar *et al.*, 1986) gave a picture that was broadly representative of the country as a whole. The total population of this region (South East London, Kent and East Sussex) was 3.5 million, with an annual live birth rate of about 45 000. In this part of England there was only one specialized Mother and Baby Unit which had separate facilities and its own staff team; this unit could take up to eight mothers and their babies. There were 11 other psychiatric hospitals or units within general hospitals which took between one and four mothers and babies, using mainly extemporized facilities and no specialized staff. There were undoubtedly other mothers who were admitted into general psychiatric wards *without* their babies, but their number could not be ascertained because of current confusion over the way in which 'cases' of puerperal mental illness are classified and notified to the Department of Health (Meltzer and Kumar, 1985). Another method of management has been pioneered in Nottingham by Oates (*see* Chapter 6), and this is mainly domiciliary care of psychotic mothers. The impression gained by Kumar *et al.* (1986) was that in the South East Thames Region none, or very few, psychotic mothers were managed at home with their infants.

The rationale for joint admission of mother and baby is that, despite severe mental and behavioural disorganization, separating a mother from her infant may have both short and long-term adverse effects upon their relationship and upon the psychological development of the child. On the distaff side there is a small, but always worrying, risk that a mother may harm or kill her child (D'Orban, 1979; Margison, 1982); there is also a concern about the possible undesirable impact on the developing infant of being with a severely disturbed mother. Finally, it may also be the case that placing a young baby in an institution where, inevitably, there are many 'caregivers' to help or 'take over' from the mother, of itself may have some lasting influence on the child's development. There are, as yet, no reports of studies of child development or of parent-child relationships looking at the possible consequences of different kinds of maternal mental illness. There are also no reliable ways of predicting which infants are most likely to be 'at risk' of harm from their mothers whether through impulse to harm or through neglect. Schizophrenic patients (Da Silva and Johnstone, 1981) and sometimes manic or psychotically depressed women (Margison, 1982) do rarely kill their children, but clinical staff urgently need more sensitive indicators of potential risk.

Aside from the mother's mental condition *per se*, there are many other related factors which may affect her behaviour and the relationship with her infant; she may be heavily sedated by medication, she may have to discontinue breast feeding and access to her infant may be limited by staff because they are concerned about risk to the child, or because of the nature of the facilities. Some hospitals encourage 'rooming-in', others have nurseries adjacent to the wards and in others the child may be looked after in a paediatric ward at some distance from the mother (Kumar *et al.*, 1986). Systematic studies of outcome have yet to be done which examine not only the impact of the mother's illness, but also the context in which this is managed. From a purely clinical point of view, we need more reliable ways of making observations of mentally ill mothers and their infants. Anecdotal and narrative accounts by doctors and nurses are always informative, but by themselves they may not provide a reliable basis for measuring change or for predicting immediate or future problems. On the other hand, very detailed ratings and observations of behavioural interactions are only feasible in research settings. Methods of assessment are, therefore, needed that are clinically relevant, perceived as appropriate by ward staff and yet which incorporate some form of graded evaluation of different aspects of mother-infant interaction. Such measures should be sensitive and specific, reliable, valid and capable of accurately reflecting change. They should provide both an index of clinical outcome as well as a means of predicting problems such as 'risk' to the child. Ideally, such measures should also give warning of longer term problems reflecting characteristics such as maternal indifference, lack of affection or impaired caregiving ability, all of which are critically important when the child's interests must be considered separately from the mother's, e.g. in the context of care proceedings.

In a small but important group of mothers it is necessary to take steps to protect the short and the long-term interests of the child, e.g. by care proceedings, fostering, adoption and wardship. Except in extreme cases, surprisingly little is known about social, personal and clinical character-istics which can reliably predict whether or not such interventions will be required in the first month or two of the child's life. There is a large literature on child abuse which is outside the scope of this review. We are concerned mainly with the early weeks and months after delivery.

Severe breakdown of the mother-infant relationship

Infanticide   The literature on mothers who kill their babies has been recently reviewed by Margison (1982). English law (Infanticide Act 1938) dates back to the mid-nineteenth century and it springs from cases such as one heard in 1847 at the Essex Assizes (Lancet, 1848) when a mother who had killed her newborn infant was acquitted of murder on the grounds of insanity. In England, infanticide is treated as manslaughter provided that the act occurs within the first year after delivery and that it can be shown that the balance of the mother's mind was disturbed by reason of her not having fully recovered from the effect of giving birth to the child or by reason of the effect of lactation consequent upon the birth of the child. A number of surveys (*see* review by Margison, 1982) point to the presence of psychiatric disorder in a proportion of such mothers, most commonly depression with associated suicidal ideation (West, 1965; Gibson, 1975; D'Orban, 1979) and, more rarely, schizophrenia (Gregger and Hoffmeyer, 1969; Da Silva and Johnstone, 1981). Women with manic illnesses may also place their children at extreme risk, for example through the belief that they have supernatural powers (Margison, 1982). Some women may be tortured by obsessional impulses to harm their infants (Chapman, 1959) but in keeping with this condition they rarely act on their impulses. There are no clear guidelines for assessing 'risk' and Margison advocates paying particular attention to mothers with a previous history of violent behaviour. Other empirically useful warning signs are the presence of delusions of nihilism, of possession and of unusual powers vested in either the mother or the child. Many mothers with such severe abnormalities do not harm their infants and it is not possible as yet to pick out in advance the tragic few who do.

Rejection of the infant   Zilboorg (1933) regarded maternal rejection of the infant as the basis of puerperal psychosis and this view has been echoed by Brew and Seidenberg (1950) who inferred the presence of rejection in both schizophrenic and manic depressive mothers. In a series of patients with affective psychoses, Tetlow (1955) universally found signs of an abnormal relationship (e.g. hatred, indifference, phobia) and denial of the existence of the child was often found in schizophrenic mothers. Such feelings and abnormal relationships have been described less often by other observers (Ostwald and Regan, 1957; Seager, 1960; Jacobson, Kay and Nilsson, 1965) but were nevertheless found in a significant minority. Follow-up by Seager (1960) revealed that some mothers did develop normal relationships with their children but there were others who later developed feelings of antagonism and blame.

A study by Robson and Kumar (1980) showed that nearly 40% of a sample of first-time mothers described delays of several days before they began to feel a strong affection for their newborn. The early lack of affection was often distressing and it was clearly remembered even up to a year later; it was found to occur most often in mothers who had experienced very painful, accelerated (by amniotomy) labours. Nothing is known of the prevalence of more severe or lasting disruptions of maternal attachment, nor whether they are in any way related to brief and transient disturbances such as those described by Kumar and Robson (1984). Brockington, Winokur and Dean (1982) have described the phenomenon of 'bonding-disorder' but it is doubtful whether severe rejection and alienation from an infant can be separated from postpartum mental illness. A case study of nearly 50 women describing aversion, rejection and alienation from their newborn infants revealed the presence of significant psychiatric illness in almost every subject (Kumar, 1988).

Postnatal depression

Extent and nature of the problem
Mothers who require hospital admission after childbirth represent only a small fraction of the total sum of postnatal psychiatric illness. About 100 times as many women experience clinically significant depressive reactions. Postnatal depression is a very common sequel to childbirth, affecting at least one in every 10 women in the first two or three months after delivery (Kumar, 1982; see O'Hara and Zekoski, Chapter 2). The onset of depression is insidious and, in terms of severity, symptomatology and duration, the condition is similar to depressive neurosis occurring at other times. Clinically, such depressions may be distinguished from depressive psychotic illnesses by the absence of symptoms such as depressive or paranoid delusions, hallucinations, marked retardation or stupor. A small proportion of mothers with non-psychotic depressions are admitted to hospital possibly because they have added personal and social difficulties or because they may be experiencing severe problems in looking after their newborn (Meltzer and Kumar, 1985). Less than half of a group of depressed mothers in one survey (Kumar and Robson, 1984) made contact with their family doctors or with specialist services for help with their psychological problems; only a minority were prescribed appropriate antidepressant medication. In a few cases the depressions were severe and chronic, lasting for a year or more (Pitt, 1968; Cox, Connor and Kendell, 1982; Kumar and Robson, 1984; Watson et al., 1984). Characteristically, such depressive reactions are found more often in women with a previous predisposition to depressive disorder (Watson et al., 1984) and in subjects with significant marital difficulties. Women who had initially entertained severe doubts about the pregnancy and who had contemplated termination were also found by Kumar and Robson (1984) to be more likely to be depressed. Some investigators (e.g. Paykel et al., 1980) have found that adverse life stresses may play a part in the aetiology of postnatal depression and Kumar and Robson (1984) reported an association with premature birth.

Timing of maternal depression: search for cause and effect
The importance for the infant of depressive reactions following childbirth is highlighted by Weissman, Paykel and Klerman (1972) who described 'immobilization in their maternal role' in a few severe cases. The cardinal symptoms of depression—lowered mood, inability to cope, irritability, agitation, retardation, social isolation—may all play a part in shaping the

developing relationship between mother and child. Depressed mothers were found to describe their three-month-old infants more often in critical and negative terms (Kumar and Robson, 1984) and recent studies of the infants of such mothers followed up at three and four years of age have shown that the mothers more frequently report difficulties in their relationships with their children (Uddenberg and Englesson, 1978) and more child behavioural problems (Wrate *et al.*, 1984).

Is the timing of maternal illness important in relation to possible adverse effects on the developing child and on the mother-child relationship? The nature of the illness, the family milieu, the types of clinical and social interventions, the characteristics of the child, are all important factors which must play some part. Most of the early studies (reviewed by Rutter, 1966) sought direct links between parental mental illness and child disability, but more recently it has been argued (Billing and Moos, 1983; Rutter and Quinton, 1984) that effects on the children are mediated mainly through disturbed homes and family relationships; such disturbances may precede, or be consequent upon, parental psychiatric illness. Although the weight of evidence lies on the side of chronic adversity rather than on acute stresses at particular times leading to problems in children, 'there has been remarkably little research on the effects of acute stressors in childhood' (Rutter, 1986). A study of four-year-old first-born children, some of whose mothers experienced neurotic depressions at various times (before pregnancy, during pregnancy, in the first few months postnatally and at four years), pointed to adverse effects on children's cognitive development when maternal depression was present in the first three months of the child's life. There was also a significant and interactive influence of marital discord and of paternal psychiatric problems (Cogill *et al.*, 1986). Reported behavioural and emotional disturbances, on the other hand, were also related with concurrent maternal depression at four years (Caplan *et al.*, 1988). These observations accord with Rutter's (1986) conclusion that different sets of factors may influence a child's cognitive, behavioural and emotional development, and they underline the need for detailed and multiple measures of the development and adjustment of the child.

Studies of the mother-infant relationship

There is an extensive literature on mother-infant relationships with normal subjects. There is a small and limited literature on mother-infant relationships where the mother is psychiatrically disturbed. This literature is made up of clinical reports, small-scale case studies, and studies involving comparisons between 'disturbed' and 'normal' mothering, the 'normal' mothers being matched on sociodemographic variables or being randomly chosen. The outcomes measured in these studies are sometimes maternal variables such as degree of affection shown; sometimes infant variables such as irritability; and sometimes interaction variables such as degree of reciprocal regard. Research in this area is characterized by methodological diversity.

Methodological considerations

Methods of measuring or describing the mother-infant relationship break down into two broad classes:

(1) Maternal report techniques, i.e. questionnaires and interviews; and
(2) Direct observation techniques.

Of these two types of approach, maternal report techniques reflect the mother's perception of the mother-infant relationship and hence are likely to be influenced by her emotional and cognitive state. These influences are likely to be particularly relevant in cases of maternal psychological disturbance. Hence direct observation techniques may well have certain advantages where the mother's actual behaviour toward the infant and the infant's responses and caregiving environment are being focused on; direct observation can therefore provide objective measures which are important in themselves and which can be used to corroborate or supplement maternal self-reports.

Direct observation as a means of data collection is the most basic technique of all. The impact of ethology has led to a marked reappraisal of the potential importance of direct observation methods. Where observation techniques have progressed is firstly in terms of attempts to produce equivalent data from different observers by systematizing the vocabulary and grammar of the language of observations, and secondly by the application of new technologies of recording and analysis. Observation techniques have come to be used very heavily where young children are involved, partly because of the lack of communication options between child and researchers, and also partly because young children may not have the same need to present a 'good image' to an observer. Detailed discussion of observational techniques is provided by Hutt and Hutt (1970) and by Sackett (1978). Observational methods vary considerably and aspects of variation include:

(1) *Context of the observation*; i.e. which behaviours are to be observed in what setting. Is the situation to be structured or unstructured, are the participant's roles to be predefined, either by instruction or by the limitations of context?
(2) *Recording*; is the observation to be coded live or will it be recorded on videotape or film for later coding?
(3) *Nature of behavioural coding*; is it to be totally predefined and structured or should it be somewhat looser and less structured as when employing narrative accounts. What behaviours are to be coded? Is a comprehensive record desired or only a record of specific sorts of behaviour, e.g. verbal acts or communicative acts? Whose behaviours are to be recorded?
(4) *Length of observations*; durations can vary from a few minutes through to several hours.
(5) *Relationship between coding and time*; some methods employ continuous recording, others time sampling, and yet others event sampling. Continuous recording involves recording all behaviour of interest for the total observation period and is particularly useful if sequen'·al analysis is to be used, in that the observer can be sure of including t   h

preceding and successive behaviours to any target behaviour. Time sampling involves observations occurring at regular set time periods, and the behaviours observed are regarded as representative of the total behaviour stream. Time sampling should be restricted to observations involving frequently occurring behaviours. When certain behaviours infrequently occur event sampling is more appropriate, and observations should start upon the occurrence of a target behaviour. The time resolution of studies depends upon the detail of behaviours observed, ranging from fractions of a second up to coarse approximations of time, of the order of minutes.

(6) *Levels of description and analysis*; this is the most important aspect of differences between methodologies. The choice of the level of description and analysis which is to be used in a study will, to a large extent, determine the other characteristics of the methodology to be adopted. The level of description can be placed on a continuum of detail from the microscopic to the macroscopic. The most detailed level of description in common use is in terms of individual acts or even components of acts (as detailed as, for example, eyebrow flashes or hand movements) as the unit of analysis. In Chapter 7 of this volume, Murray describes the contribution of such studies to our understanding of normal mother-infant interaction. At less detailed levels of description it is not individual acts but behavioural categories that are the units of analysis. An example of this level of analysis is contained in the study by Persson-Blennow *et al.* (1984) of mother-neonate interaction in a group of women with a history of functional psychosis, where the description of behaviour is in terms of categories such as vocalization, physical contact and smiling. The least detailed levels of description may involve narrative and rating scales as descriptors of the interaction and they attempt to summarize the overall characteristics in terms such as 'highly involved' or 'sensitive'. The study by Davenport *et al.* (1984) of parent-infant interaction in families with a manic depressive parent and control families, uses a technique of rating by home visitors and it provides an example of the global, undetailed level of description using observation as a source of data.

At the finest levels of description, film or video recording is essential as the detail required demands close and repeated inspection of behavioural sequences. More intermediate levels of description may also use film or video recording, but as the units of observation (e.g. vocalizations, face-to-face gaze), place fewer demands on the observer's processing capacity, direct coding with pencil and paper or electronic data loggers becomes possible. At the least detailed level of description the rating scales or narrative descriptions are typically done shortly after the observation. Thus, while they are the least detailed, such methods are the least intrusive and can often be combined with other tasks, as in the study by Davenport *et al.* (1984) in which the home visit included a parental interview and ratings of the mother's caregiving were based on observations made during the whole visit. Such rating techniques, while being unintrusive, are also the most susceptible to observer bias, and the more the rating scale is anchored in readily observable, concrete behaviours the less likely is such bias to occur. As the level of description becomes less detailed so the duration of the observations increases. With the most detailed observations the detail recorded means that data are accumulated at such a rate that only brief periods of observation can be realistically analysed. As the detail of description becomes coarser, then longer periods of observation can be encompassed and the rating scale methods can be applied to almost any duration of observation but, typically, ratings cover periods of observation lasting 2–4 h.

Brief periods of detailed observation, particularly when film or video recording is necessary, demand that the situation of the observation be highly structured, with the adult participants being given set instructions, e.g. 'The mother sits down in front of him (the infant). The instructions to her are to go in and play with the baby without picking him up. No toys are provided' (Als, 1979). With less detailed techniques the situation can become progressively less structured, and more naturalistic.

For any observation there will be a set of demand characteristics and these apply particularly to the people who are being observed. In mother-infant interaction these primarily apply to the mother. The term 'demand characteristics' is here used to refer to the expectations created in participants about how they should behave. In some observation studies the demand characteristics are partially made explicit in the instructions that are given to the participants. However, the demand characteristics of the situation result not only from the explicit instructions given, but also from the observation environment and procedure and how these are perceived by the participants. One key feature is the presence of the observer, and the context of the observation is also important. The participants' behaviour is always influenced by being the focus of observation. However, the extent of such influence will vary with the demand characteristics. Some observations can be regarded as measures of interactions where the woman is interacting to the best of her ability; this is most true where the context of the observation is least naturalistic and the duration of observation is short. Writing about highly detailed observations of mother-infant interaction, Als (1979) describes the situation thus:

> 'The face-to-face laboratory situation is stressful for the interactants in that it provides no functional goals other than a situation for social interaction. In that way it forces both partners to use all skills and resources they have to engage one another in a mutually satisfying exchange.'

As the situation approximates more to the normal environment and as the woman's experience of the situation adapts her to the context, then her behaviour is increasingly likely to approximate her typical behaviour.

The susceptibility of a mentally ill mother to expectations of how she should behave (demand characteristics) is likely to be influenced by:

(1) The nature of her psychiatric disturbance.
(2) The nature of treatment received.
(3) The fact that she has been labelled 'mentally ill'.
(4) The context of observations, e.g. home, hospital or laboratory.

Such considerations should be borne in mind when interpreting the results of either psychiatric versus non-psychiatric comparisons or comparisons between psychiatric groups. It is possible to suggest hypotheses about how particular groups may be affected by such considerations. For those disorders where self-image is particularly sensitive, there is likely to be a strong motivation to present a good image and the effects of demand characteristics may well be enhanced. However, if self-esteem is low as in depression, there may be little motivation to project a good image and the distortion introduced by demand characteristics may be low. Such suggestions illustrate how different groups may respond differentially to any given observation procedure.

The existing evidence

Findings from the diverse range of studies in this area cannot be integrated without considering the methodologies that were used. This literature ranges from studies of the mother and infant at one point in time to longitudinal studies with a more complete picture, including prospective studies of high-risk families. For convenience, maternal psychiatric diagnoses will be categorized into two broad groups, the affective disorders and the schizophrenias, because most studies to date have usually been related to one or both of these major types of disorder.

Maternal affective disorder

Weissman, Paykel and Klerman (1972) did a comparative study of 40 clinically depressed women and 40 matched controls. Within this sample three of the depressed women were mothers of very young infants at the time of the study and these women were described as being 'helpless and overwhelmed . . . . they became overindulgent, overprotective or compulsive mothers'. The depressed mothers of children of whatever age showed impairments of emotional involvement, guilt, hostility, resentment and communication of affect. These difficulties emerged from a structured interview which was designed to assess social adjustment. Fraiberg (1980) reports on mother-infant pairs who had been referred because of supposed infant problems. It emerged that two mothers had recently developed reactive depressions and two mothers had endured depression for many years. The disturbances of these mother-infant relationships were discussed by Fraiberg from a psychoanalytical perspective. Such discussions may generate insights into psychological processes but generalization from such selected cases is problematic. An overview of the effects of depression on the mothering role is provided by Anthony (1983) with evidence derived from case studies. Anthony discusses the demands of mothering and how depression affects the woman's capacity to meet these demands. He argues that the normal mother can meet the demands of parenting sensitively, intuitively, flexibly and attentively. By contrast, the depressed mother is thought to exhibit a failure of mutuality in relating to the infant, with a lack of coordination with the baby's activity, and a lack of imitation and playfulness. However, such a generalization may be biased because of knowledge of the mother's depression and it overemphasizes the abilities of the 'normal mother'. The 'normal mother' is a term which hides an enormous degree of diversity in parenting techniques, and hence the comparison with the idealized 'normal mother' is not appropriate for characterizing the differences between clinically depressed and ordinary mothers.

Clinical reports of depressed mothers with infants have prompted a number of systematic observational studies. Livingood, Dean and Smith (1983) compared 25 postnatally depressed mothers with 25 matched controls. Fifteen minutes of interaction during a newborn's feed in the hospital were video taped and later analysed for the range of maternal behaviours shown. In general, the depressed mothers showed comparable behaviours to the controls, but they did tend to gaze less at the infant, show less positive emotional expression to the infant, with more shifting of position and rocking. It should be noted that the 'depressed' mothers were mildly affected and differences between the groups might have been greater if a more severely depressed group had been selected.

A rather different methodology was used by Davenport et al. (1984), who report on seven families where one of the parents was manic depressive, and 20 control families matched on sociodemographic variables. The families were seen when the infants were 12, 15 and 18 months of age. Data are reported from a questionnaire on child-bearing practices and from home visitors' ratings of the mother's caregiving. The questionnaire data revealed several differences between the index and control mothers in terms of:

(1) Less encouragement to the infant to be open to experience.
(2) Less expression of affect.
(3) More negative affect.
(4) More protective attitudes.
(5) More teaching of infants to control feelings.

The home visitor observations revealed that the mothers in the manic depressive group appeared less active, organized, happy, relaxed, consistent or effective than control mothers. As five of the seven spouses of the index subjects also showed manic depression and one spouse showed substance abuse, it is difficult from this study to differentiate effects which hold for mothers who were index cases from the mothers who were the spouses of index cases. Once again, the importance of the family context of maternal depression becomes apparent. Data for the seven index subjects and seven matched controls from the same study are presented by Gaensbauer et al. (1984). The report concerns the assessment of infant-mother attachment using the 'strange situation' described by Ainsworth et al. (1978) and the infant's emotional reactions to frustration during a developmental assessment. The 'strange situation' involves a planned sequence of stranger approach, separation from the mother and reunion, and the infant's reactions to this sequence are video taped and subsequently categorized into a measure of security of infant-mother attachment. The index infants differed from the control infants in terms of being less likely to respond more favourably to the mother than to a stranger, being less likely to be classified as securely attached to the mother and they also showed more anger during the test situation. These differences became more prominent over the period 12–18 months of age and the results were remarkably consistent for such a small sample. Where differences in child outcomes are reported and the mother is psychiatrically ill, it is possible that the result is related to the consequences of the illness rather than the illness itself. For instance, are differences in infant-mother attachment the result of maternal behaviour or are they some reflection of multiple caregivers, which themselves are a consequence for the infant of the mother's disorder?

This pattern of results is partially supported in the Rochester prospective study of schizophrenic, neurotically depressed and normal mothers and their children reported by Sameroff, Seifer and Zax (1982). This study included moderately detailed observations of mother-infant interaction in the home for two two-hour periods. They found that four months after birth the depressed mothers were observed to be less playful, happy and vocal with their infants and held them less, as compared with the normal mothers. These differences were not apparent when the infants were 12 months old and also there were no significant differences in infant-mother attachment as measured by the 'strange situation' (Ainsworth et al., 1978).

Depressed and non-depressed mothers may well behave differently but can infants differentiate between depressed and non-depressed style of interaction? Cohn and Tronick (1983) examined infants' reactions to normal mothers who were asked to act normally or to act depressed during video recording of several three-minute periods of face-to-face interaction. The depressed condition required the mothers to speak slowly in a flat monotone, with little facial expression, body movement or touch contact. The three-month-old infants reacted differently to the 'normal' and 'depressed' conditions, and the differences were maintained to some extent after the 'depressed' condition, when the mothers changed back to acting normally. The hypothesis that three-month-old infants could differentiate and were affected by simulated depression in their mothers was therefore supported. Such a study, while not of depressed mothers, has obvious relevance to understanding the impact of maternal depression on infants, and Field (1984) did a similar study comparing a group of postnatally depressed mothers and their infants with a control group. The groups were matched on sociodemographic variables. The mothers were asked to (a) act normally, (b) act depressed, and then (c) act normally in face-to-face interactions with their infants. Heart rates of infant and mother were recorded throughout. The infants in the control group were more negative in their reactions during the depressed interaction and the subsequent return to normal interaction. The infants in the depressed group showed similar behaviours across the three phases of the study. The depressed group mothers and infants showed lower heart rates throughout the interactions, so that the heart rate changes mirrored the behavioural affective changes.

A subsequent study by Field et al. (1985) involved mothers who had had pregnancy problems and subsequently were depressed and mothers who had had neither pregnancy problems nor depression. Interactions with infants showed similar characteristics to the two previous studies.

These three studies indicate the sensitivity of infants to the affective state of their mothers and suggest that depressive styles of interaction may be transmitted to infants in the early months of life. Kumar and Robson (1984) in a longitudinal study of primiparae found that depressed mothers reported more negative feelings about their three-month-old infants during interviews, revealing a similar pattern in reported feelings to that revealed by actual behaviour for depressed mothers in the observational studies of mother-infant interactions.

Both the clinical reports and more systematic studies reviewed here of depressed mothers present a unified picture of less positive expressed affect and reciprocity toward the infant. The studies involving infant and interactional measures show that the infant and the nature of interaction are affected by the mother's depression, so that as well as the mother's feelings and behaviour toward the child being influenced by depression, the child's behaviour and attachment towards the mother are similarly influenced as suggested by the study of Gaensbauer et al. (1984).

A Swedish prospective study of women with a history of functional psychosis has followed these women and their children from pregnancy through infancy and into childhood. The various stages of this study have been reported in a series of papers (McNeil, Kaij and Malmqvist-Larsson, 1984a,b; McNeil et al., 1983, 1985; Naslund et al., 1984a,b 1985; Persson-Blennow et al., 1984, 1986). In an observation of 30 minutes of feeding at three days postpartum, the manic depressed group did not differ from the control group in the quality of interaction with the infant. Subsequent observations of feeding and play interactions in naturalistic settings again revealed little difference between the manic depressed group and controls. At one year of age, the infants of this group did not differ in attachment behaviour or fear of strangers from a control group. These findings are at odds with the other studies reported so far, which have generally described a rather worse quality of interaction for mothers with manic depression. However, there are methodological differences which may account for this discrepancy. Firstly, the mothers in the Swedish study had a history of psychosis but it is not stated whether they were displaying the symptoms during the time of the study. Secondly, the differences in results may reflect differences in diagnostic practices. Thirdly, this study is one of only two studies of mothers with depression to have used a moderately detailed description of the interaction rather than a rating for an extended period of time (rather than a few minutes) in naturalistic settings. Under these conditions, the people being observed are likely to be behaving in a more typical manner than while being video taped for a few minutes when the situation is likely to lead the participants to try to produce an optimal performance. Possibly the manic depressed group and controls respond differentially to these sets of demand characteristics and hence the different methodologies produce different results.

Maternal schizophrenic disorder

Schizophrenic mothers seem to have different attitudes and beliefs concerning their infants than do 'normal' mothers. Cohler, Weiss and Grunebaum (1970) report that schizophrenic mothers tended to perceive their infants as passive, and were less likely to attribute intentionality to the infant than did mothers in a control group. This means that they interpreted cues such as smiling as 'accidental grimaces' and they played less with infants than did mothers in the control group. Mothers with a history of psychosis expressed less belief in the importance of a reciprocal relationship between themselves and their infants and in the need to differentiate their own needs from those of the infant.

A longitudinal study of 13 children born to schizophrenic mothers is reported by Fish and Alpert (1962). During infancy, the infants born to schizophrenic mothers showed greater variability in sensory responsiveness. These infants were more likely to be at the extremes of a continuum of sensory responsiveness, showing either extreme apathy or excessive irritability. Such data suggest that genetic factors may account for such a relationship. A later report by Fish and Hagin (1973) relates some aspects of these early infant data to emotional impairment in later childhood. Marcus *et al.* (1981) similarly report that the infants of schizophrenic parents show poor sensorimotor functioning as neonates and during the first year of life. Also Gamer, Gallant and Grunebaum (1976) found that one-year-old infants of schizophrenic mothers in comparison with controls, showed poorer performance on a Piagetian object permanence task indicating slower conceptual development. Irrespective of whether these differences in the infants of schizophrenic mothers derive from the parenting they receive or from biological factors, such infant characteristics are likely to influence the development of the mother-infant relationship.

Schachter *et al.* (1977) also conducted a study of mother-infant interaction in schizophrenic and non-schizophrenic women. The groups were selected on the basis of a screening questionnaire in pregnancy and a subsequent psychiatric interview. Video taping of feeding interactions took place in a laboratory furnished to resemble a living room. The feeds lasted about 15 minutes. The data from these sessions indicated that the schizophrenic mothers tended to be *more* affectionate and responsive to their infants than did the control mothers. Schacter *et al.* (1977) hypothesize that this unexpected finding may be the result of the greater anxiety experienced by the schizophrenic mothers in the video taped session. This supposition is supported by other data deriving from ratings of the adequacy of home care of these women suggesting that the video taped interactions were more positive the less adequate the home care was judged to be.

Sobel (1961) found a sample of eight families where both expectant mother and father were schizophrenic. It took two years, drawing on a population of approximately 65 000, to find these families. The aim was to observe directly the parental behaviours within the families in order to understand how these behaviours might precipitate early emotional maladjustment. The eight infants were observed in the neonatal period, after which four infants went into foster homes, and four infants returned home with their schizophrenic parents. Monthly observations of all eight infants were carried out. These observations took the form of naturalistic observations. Three of the four infants with the original schizophrenic parents developed signs of emotional disorder, whereas none of the four fostered infants did so in the first 18 months of life. The mothers of the infants who showed emotional disorder showed little play with their infants and little actively joyful interaction or positive affect toward their infants.

As part of the Rochester prospective study of children born to parents with a history of psychosis, Sameroff, Seifer and Zax (1982) compared mother-infant interactions in a group of schizophrenic mothers and a control group. The observations took place when the infants were four and 12 months of age. Schizophrenic mothers showed less spontaneous play and contact with their four-month-old infants, but for many of the mothers there was no difference when the infants were 12 months old. However, the most seriously ill mothers, whose interactive behaviour was also less happy and talkative at four months postpartum, also showed less responsive, spontaneous play with their 12-month-old infants. The infants themselves did not seem different for the schizophrenic and control groups at four months old, but by one year the infants of the most seriously ill women did appear less spontaneous in their interactions. The infants of schizophrenic mothers did not appear to be different in their attachment behaviours in the 'strange situation' (Ainsworth et al., 1978).

The Swedish prospective study revealed some differences in the characteristics of mother-infant interaction in cases where the mother was schizophrenic. These differences from the control sample were in the form of less social contact, less harmony, and greater tension, and as the infants became six months of age the differences were mostly in terms of less reciprocal social behaviours, which were most apparent during play rather than in feeding interactions. At one year of age, those infants with schizophrenic mothers were more likely to show an absence of fear of strangers and also more likely to show an anxious pattern of attachment to the mother.

There is an apparent contradiction in the studies involving schizophrenic mothers in terms of the quality of the mother-infant interactions. The findings of Schachter et al. (1977) probably reflect the ability of schizophrenic mothers to respond to the demand characteristics of the observation session and display high levels of interaction for brief periods. The more naturalistic studies with longer observation periods present a very different picture. They indicate lower levels of interaction and an impaired quality of interaction, both of which have consequences for social and attachment behaviours at one year of age.

The systematic studies of mother-infant interaction with psychotic mothers have supported the descriptions by clinical reports in several ways. However, the studies which have been conducted in this field do present some contradictions, but these can probably be accounted for by the methodological differences between studies. There is a general lack of regard for the consequences of choice of methodology for the results of studies, or indeed of consideration of which is the most appropriate methodology for the question being addressed. When the aim is to ascertain how best mothers can interact with their infants, then non-naturalistic, short duration studies can provide a wealth of finely-detailed data (indeed, the quantity of data produced is such that only small subject numbers can be realistically handled). Where the aim is to record 'typical' behaviour of mother and infant in interaction, longer duration observations where less detail is recorded and involving more naturalistic interactions are the appropriate choice.

The research into depressed mothers has been dominated by studies using short duration, recorded observations in non-naturalistic settings. Only the Rochester and Swedish prospective studies have included detailed observations of depressed mothers in naturalistic interactions and markedly different conclusions were reached. With regard to the Swedish study, because the psychiatric condition of the sample at the time of the observations was not reported, the results cannot be directly compared with the other research. The laboratory-based studies do clearly show an influence of maternal depression on the performance of mothers in interaction with their infants, particularly in terms of less overall stimulation and less expressed affect. Infants can perceive such differences in interactional style and their own behaviour is affected. There is a marked lack of information about the behaviour of depressed mothers in interaction with their infants in naturalistic settings. It should be a priority of future research in this area to fill this gap.

The conclusions that can be drawn regarding interaction between schizophrenic mothers and their infants are also tentative because of the limited data available. There is one laboratory-based study and three studies of interaction in the home. The general pattern is that of schizophrenic mothers showing less positive affect, less contact with the infants, less interaction both verbal and non-verbal, and less responsive interaction. Having a schizophrenic mother is also associated with different patterns of infant behaviour in early infancy, at one year of age, and in later childhood. The Swedish study is potentially the most useful source of data currently available in relation to both schizophrenic and affective psychosis. Should it be possible to analyse the data from this study with regard to the relationship between mother-infant interaction and *current* psychological state this would present a distinct advance. This is because a most useful source of information for understanding the impact of parental psychiatric disorder on the child is relatively detailed data on the naturalistic interactions within the family. There is a general lack of such data which is most pronounced in the case of maternal depression in contrast to the several studies with non-naturalistic interaction data.

Future research

Currently available research presents only a tentative picture of the connections between maternal psychiatric state and the development of the mother-child relationship. There is a need for further studies using systematic observational techniques which are readily applicable. Such observational studies should try to integrate observational data with data derived from self-report, the observer's report and possibly reports from significant others such as family members and/or nursing staff. Also it is necessary to have reliable assessments on current mental state as well as previous mental state; most recent studies seem to have neglected this point.

The various types of observational study have their advantages and disadvantages, and research should integrate different methodologies to answer related but separate questions. Highly detailed, short duration observations are useful in describing the interactive abilities of participants in an interaction, but may be misleading with regard to typical interactive behaviours. Less detailed, longer observations in naturalistic situations give better information about what behaviours and abilities are actually used by participants in interactions. The thoughts and feelings of participants revealed by interviews or questionnaires will aid the interpretation of data produced by observational studies. Hence integration of methodologies is an important stepping stone to progress in this field. Also the nature of the mother-child relationship will be changing as the mother's psychological state and the child's developmental status change. Hence a developmental and transactional perspective is necessary, rather than the static snapshots provided by cross-sectional research.

In addition, it should be borne in mind that as well as the mental disorder, any treatment received may well affect the course of the mother-child relationship. Hence future research should consider the impact of mental disorder and different treatments on the total caregiving environment of the child including:

(1) People at home (spouse, siblings, etc.).
(2) People in hospital (e.g. Mother and Baby Unit staff).
(3) The range of environments that both mother and baby experience.
(4) The effects of separation (e.g. when the mother is in hospital and the baby is at home).

Such research can feed into the development of methods of clinical management. Linked to such research is the question of how to assess the adequacy of the caregiving environment of the child and the 'risk' associated with different courses of clinical management. It is important to realize the impact on the caregiving environment of the child of treatment regimes as it may be dramatic. For example, the child in the Mother and Baby Unit is likely to experience an environment which is markedly different from the alternative environments associated with other forms of clinical management. The longer the child spends in an environment the greater the impact on development and such issues should be considered in decisions on clinical management. Factors to be considered include the motivation and caregiving skills of all who might be responsible for the child, including possibly other family members, as well as the stability and location of care. Where decisions are to be made about changes in caregiving environment, those involved with the different environments e.g. community-based and hospital-based staff, need to liaise closely. Such work would involve close cooperation of clinicians and researchers who will require skills to work with patients, their families and the children.

References

AINSWORTH, M.D.S., BLEHAR, M.C., WATERS, E. and WALL, S. (1978). *Patterns of Attachment: A Psychological Study of the Strange Situation*. Hillsdale, NJ: Lawrence Erlbaum Associates

ALS, H. (1979). The unfolding of behavioural organisation in the face of a biological violation. In: *Human Communication and the Joint Regulation of Behaviour*, (E. C. Tronick, ed.), Baltimore: University Park Press

ANTHONY, E.J. (1983). An overview of the effects of maternal depression on the infant and child. In: *Children of Depressed Parents: Risk, Identification and Intervention* (H. C. Morrison, ed.), Grune and Stratton

BILLING, A. G. and MOOS, R. H. (1983). Comparisons of children of depressed and non-depressed parents: a socio-environmental perspective. *Journal of Abnormal Child Psychology*, **11**, 463–486

BREW, M. F. and SEIDENBERG, R. (1950). Psychotic reactions related with pregnancy and childbirth. *Journal of Nervous and Mental Disease*, **111**, 408–423

BROCKINGTON, I. F., WINOKUR, G. and DEAN, C. (1982). Puerperal psychosis. In: *Motherhood and Mental Illness* (I. F. Brockington and R. Kumar, eds), pp. 37–69 London: Academic Press

BROCKINGTON, I.F., CERNIK, K. F., SCHOFIELD, E. M., DOWNING, A. R., FRANCIS, A. F. and KEELAN, C. (1981) Puerperal psychosis. *Archives of General Psychiatry*, **38**, 829–833

CAPLAN, H.L., COGILL, S. R., ALEXANDER, H., ROBSON, K. M. and KUMAR, R. (1988). The effect of postnatal depression on the emotional development of the child. *British Journal of Psychiatry* (in press)

CHAPMAN, A. H. (1959). Obsessions of infanticide. *Archives of General Psychiatry*, **1**, 28–31

COGILL, S., CAPLAN, H., ALEXANDRA, H., ROBSON, K. and KUMAR, R. (1986). Impact of postnatal depression on the developing child. *British Medical Journal*, **i**, 1165–1167

COHLER, B., WEISS, J. and GRUNEBAUM, H. (1970). Child-care attitudes and emotional disturbances in mothers of young children. *Genetic Psychological Monographs*, **82**, 3–47

COHN, J. F. and TRONICK, E.C. (1983). Three-month-old infants' reaction to simulated maternal depression. *Child Development*, **54**, 185–193

COX, J. L., CONNOR, Y. and KENDELL, R. E. (1982) Prospective study of the psychiatric disorders of childbirth. *British Journal of Psychiatry*, **140**, 111–117

DA SILVA, L. and JOHNSTONE, E. C. (1981). A follow-up study of severe puerperal psychiatric illness. *British Journal of Psychiatry*, **139**, 346–354

DAVENPORT, Y. B., ZAHN-WAXLER, C., ADLAND, M. L. and MAYFIELD, A. (1984). Early child rearing practices in families with a manic-depressive parent. *American Journal of Psychiatry*, **141**, 230–235

DEAN, C. and KENDELL, R. E. (1981). The symptomatology of puerperal illnesses. *British Journal of Psychiatry*, **139**, 128–133

D'ORBAN, P. T. (1979). Women who kill their children. *British Journal of Psychiatry*, **134**, 560–571

FIIELD, T. M. (1984). Early interactions between infants and their postpartum depressed mothers. *Infant Behaviour and Development*, **7**, 517–522

FIELD, T. M., SANDBERG, D., GARCIA, R., VEGA-LAHR, N., GOLDSTEIN, S. and GUY, L. (1985). Pregnancy problems, postpartum depression and early mother-infant reactions. *Developmental Psychology*, **21**, 1152–1156

FISH, B. and ALPERT, M. (1962). Abnormal states of consciousness and muscle tone in infants born to schizophrenic mothers. *American Journal of Psychiatry*, **119**, 439–445

FISH, B. and HAGIN, R. (1973). Visual-motor disorders in infants at risk for schizophrenia. *Archives of General Psychiatry*, **28**, 900–905

FRAIBERG, S. (1980). *Clinical Studies in Infant Mental Health: The First Year of Life.* London: Tavistock Publications

GAENSBAUER, T. J., HARMON, R. J., CYTRYN, L. and McKNEW, D. H. (1984). Social and affective development in infants with a manic depressive parent. *American Journal of Psychiatry*, **141**, 223–229

GAMER, E., GALLANT, D. and GRUNEBAUM, H. (1976). An evaluation of one-year-olds on a test of object permanence. *Archives of General Psychiatry*, **33**, 311–317

GIBSON, E. (1975). Homicide in England and Wales, 1967–1971. Home Office Research Study No. 31. London: HMSO

GREGGER, J. and HOFFMEYER, O. (1969). Murder of several children by schizophrenic mothers. *Psychiatrica Clinica*, **2**, 14–24

HUTT, S. J. and HUTT, C. (1970). *Direct Observation and Measurement of Behaviour.* Springfield, Illinois: Charles C. Thomas

JACOBSON, L., KAY, L. and NILSSON, A. (1965). Postpartum mental disorder in an unselected sample: frequency of symptoms and predisposing factors. *British Medical Journal*, **i**, 1640–1643

KUMAR, R. (1982). Neurotic disorders in childbearing women. In: *Motherhood and Mental Illness* (I. F. Brockington and R. Kumar, eds). London: Academic Press

KUMAR, R. (1988). Anybody's child: A study of maternal alienation from the newborn infant. In preparation

KUMAR, R. and ROBSON, K. M. (1984). A prospective study of emotional disorders in childbearing women. *British Journal of Psychiatry*, **144**, 35–47

KUMAR, R., MELTZER, E. S., HEPPELWHITE, R. and STEVENSON, A. (1986). Admitting mentally ill mothers with their babies into psychiatric hospitals. *Bulletin of the Royal College of Psychiatrists*, **10**, 169–172

LANCET (1848). Lord Denman on a case of infanticide. *Lancet*, **i**, 318–319

LIVINGOOD, A. B., DEAN, P. and SMITH, B. D. (1983). The depressed mother as a source of stimulation for her infant. *Journal of Child Psychology and Psychiatry*, **39**, 369–375

MARCUS, J., AUERBACH, J., WILKINSON, L and BURACK, C. M. (1981). Infants at risk for schizophrenia. *Archives of General Psychiatry*, **38**, 703–713

MARGISON, F. (1982). The pathology of the mother-child relationship. In: *Motherhood and Mental Illness*, (I. F. Brockington and R. Kumar, eds), pp. 191–232. London: Academic Press

MARGISON, F. and BROCKINGTON, I. F. (1982). Psychiatric mother and baby units. In: *Motherhood and Mental Illness*, (I. F. Brockington and R. Kumar, eds), pp. 233–238. London: Academic Press

McNEIL, T. F., KAIJ, L. J. and MALMQVIST-LARSSON, A. (1984a). Women with non-organic psychosis: mental disturbance during pregnancy. *Acta Psychiatrica Scandinavica*, **70**, 127–139

McNEIL, T. F., KAIJ, L. J. and MALMQVIST-LARSSON, A. (1984b). Women with non-organic psychosis: pregnancy's effect on mental health during pregnancy. *Acta Psychiatrica Scandinavica*, **70**, 140–148

McNEIL, T. F., NÄSLUND, B., PERSSON-BLENNOW, I. and KAIJ, L. J. (1983). Offspring of women with non-organic psychosis: development of a longitudinal study of children at high risk. *Acta Psychiatrica Scandinavica*, **68**, 234–250

McNEIL, T. F., NÄSLUND, B., PERSSON-BLENNOW, I. and KAIJ, L. J. (1985). Offspring of women with non-organic psychosis: mother-infant reaction at three-and-a-half and six months of age. *Acta Psychiatrica Scandinavica*, **71**, 551–558

MEARES, R., GRIMWADE, J. and WOOD, C. (1976). A possible relationship between anxiety in pregnancy and puerperal depression. *Journal of Psychosomatic Research*, **20**, 605–610

MELTZER, E. S. and KUMAR, R. (1985). Puerperal mental illness, clinical features and classification: a study of 142 mother and baby admissions. *British Journal of Psychiatry*, **147**, 647–654

NÄSLUND, B., PERSSON-BLENNOW, I., McNEIL, T. F., KAIJ, L. and MALMQVIST-LARSSON, A. (1984a). Offspring of women with non-organic psychosis: infant attachment to the mother at one year of age. *Acta Psychiatrica Scandinavica*, **69**, 231–241

NÄSLUND, B., PERSSON-BLENNOW, I., McNEIL, T. F., KAIJ, L. and MALMQVIST-LARSSON, A. (1984b). Offspring of women with non-organic psychosis: fear of strangers during the first year of life. *Acta Psychiatrica Scandinavica*, **69**, 435–444

NÄSLUND, B., PERSSON-BLENNOW, I., McNEIL, T. F. and KAIJ, L. (1985). Offspring of women with non-organic psychosis: mother-infant interaction at three and six weeks of age. *Acta Psychiatrica Scandinavica*, **71**, 441–450

OSTWALD, P.E. and REGAN, P.F. (1957). Psychiatric disorders associated with childbirth. *Journal of Nervous and Mental Disease*, **125**, 255–265

PAYKEL, E. S., EMMS, E. M., FLETCHER, J. and ROSSABY, E. S. (1980). Life events and social support in depression. *British Journal of Psychiatry*, **136**, 339–346

PERSSON-BLENNOW, I., NÄSLUND, B., McNEIL, T. F., KAIJ, L. and MALMQVIST-LARSSON, A. (1984). Offspring of women with non-organic psychosis: mother-infant interaction at three days of age. *Acta Psychiatrica Scandinavica*, **70**, 149–159

PERSSON-BLENNOW, I., NÄSLUND, B., McNEIL, T. F. and KAIJ, L. (1986). Offspring of women with non-organic psychosis: mother-infant interaction at one year of age. *Acta Psychiatrica Scandinavica*, **73**, 207–213

PITT, B. (1968). A typical depression following childbirth. *British Journal of Psychiatry*, **114**, 1325–1335

ROBSON, K. and KUMAR, R. (1980). Delayed onset of maternal affection after childbirth. *British Journal of Psychiatry*, **136**, 347–353

RUTTER, M. (1966). *Children of Sick Parents. An Environmental and Psychiatric Study.* Maudsley Monographs No. 16. London: Oxford University Press

RUTTER, M. (1986). Child psychiatry: the interface between clinical and developmental research. *Psychological Medicine*, **16**, 151–169

RUTTER, M. and QUINTON, D. (1984). Parental psychiatric disorder: effect on children. *Psychological Medicine*, **14**, 853–880

SACKETT, G. P. (1978). *Observing Behavior. Volume 2. Data Collection and Analysis Methods.* Baltimore: University Park Press

SAMEROFF, A. J., SEIFER, R. and ZAX, M. (1982). Early development of children at risk from emotional disorders. *Monographs of the Society for Research in Child Development*, **47**, No. 199

SCHACHTER, J., ELMER, E., RAGINS, N. and WIMBERLY, F. (1977). Assessment of mother-infant interaction: schizophrenic and non-schizophrenic mothers. *Merrill Palmer Quarterly*, **23**, 183–205

SEAGER, C. P. (1960). A controlled study of postpartum illness. *Journal of Mental Science*, **106**, 214–230

SOBEL, D. (1961). Children of schizophrenic parents: preliminary observations on early development. *American Journal of Psychiatry*, **118**, 512–517

STEIN, G. (1982). The maternity blues. In: *Motherhood and Mental Illness*, (I. F. Brockington and R. Kumar, eds), pp. 119–154. London: Academic Press

TETLOW, C. (1955). Psychosis of childbearing. *Journal of Mental Science*, **101**, 629–639

UDDENBERG, N. and ENGLESSON, I. (1978). Prognosis of postparatum mental disturbance. A prospective study of women and their $4^1/_2$-year-old children. *Acta Psychiatrica Scandinavica*, **58**, 201–212

WATSON, J. P., ELLIOTT, S. A., RUGG, A. J. and BROUGH, D. I. (1984). Psychiatric disorder in pregnancy and the first postnatal year. *British Journal of Psychiatry*, **144**, 453–462

WEISSMAN, M. M., PAYKEL, E. S. and KLERMAN, G. L. (1972). The depressed woman as a mother. *Social Psychiatry*, **7**, 98–108

WEST, D. J. (1965). *Murder Followed by Suicide.* London: Heinemann

WRATE, R. M., ROONEY, A. C., THOMAS, P. F. and COX, J. L. (1984). Postnatal depression and child development: a three year follow-up study. *British Journal of Psychiatry*, **146**, 622–627

ZILBOORG, G. (1933). Depressive reactions related to parenthood. *American Journal of Psychiatry*, **87**, 927–962

Chapter 9

Infant deaths: categories, causes and consequences

Kerry Bluglass

Rates of infant mortality

Infant mortality has fallen dramatically in western European countries during the past 50 years, the most striking feature in the early part of this period being the particularly steep decline in post-neonatal deaths (those occurring between one month and one year of age). In the 1960s the decline in post-neonatal mortality in the United Kingdom appeared to be slowing down while continuing at the same rate elsewhere, so that the United Kingdom lagged even further behind the Scandinavian countries, and for the first time had a rate exceeding that in France (*Figure 9.1*).

In 1984 in England and Wales, the total number of post-perinatal deaths (from one week to one year) fell to 3216, a rate of 5.1 per 1000 live births. A large part of the decline in these rates was due to the great reduction in mortality from infections, to improvements in the detection of congenital abnormalities before birth, and to the improved survival of babies with some non-lethal congenital malformations. The principal causes of death according to a 1985 DHSS survey are shown in *Table 9.1*.

The significance of 'cot deaths' in the continuum of infant mortality

As infant mortality rates have declined the phenomenon of 'cot death' or 'sudden infant death' has meanwhile come to be increasingly recognized. From 1970 'cot deaths' were recognized by OPCS and were classified as 'Sudden Death, Cause Unknown' (ICD-795). The term 'Sudden Infant Death Syndrome' was first included in the International Classification of Diseases (ICD) in the 9th revision in 1979, since when it has been an acceptable natural registrable cause of death internationally (Golding, Limerick and Macfarlane, 1985).

For the period from 1951 to 1955 the infant mortality rates in England and Wales which were ascribed to cot death and to ill-defined and unknown causes were 36 per million live births for males and 27 per million for females. They remained at this level until 1966–1970, but by 1971–1975 they had risen to 890 per million for males and 595 per million for females (OPCS, 1981). These rates have since risen further to level off at over 2000

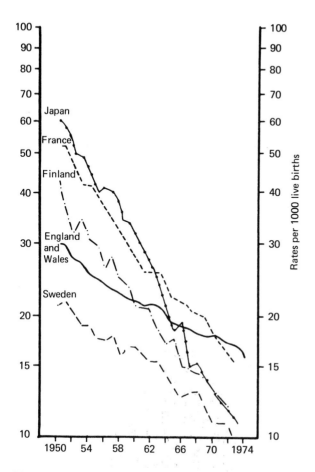

Figure 9.1 Infant mortality rates in selected countries 1950–1974. Derived from Report on the Child Health Services (1976), published by HMSO, London.

Table 9.1 Principal causes of death (DHSS, 1985)

Congenital anomalies (congenital)
Complications of prematurity (prematurity)
Violence and trauma (trauma)
Neoplasias
Cerebral meningeal symptoms (CNS)
Gastrointestinal (GI)
Upper respiratory tract (URT)
Lower respiratory tract (LRT)
Non-specific symptoms (non-specific)
Sudden unexpected death (unexpected)
Inadequate information and unclassified (not known)

per million live births (males and females), i.e. over 1500 deaths each year in the UK and, by extrapolation, about 8000 in USA. Before 1970 most of these deaths were recorded as due to respiratory disease, but with a subsequent transfer between ICD categories it was demonstrated that deaths ascribed to respiratory diseases plus cot deaths in 1971–1975 formed 19% of those from all causes, an almost identical proportion to that ascribed earlier to respiratory disease alone (*Figure 9.2*).

The increasing use of the term 'cot death' was an acknowledgement that, for many of the apparently healthy infants who were unexpectedly found dead, the cause was unknown and there was often insufficient evidence for diagnostic labels which had previously been used. The term 'cot death' ('crib death' in the USA) had originally been applied to all unexpected deaths but further information, largely from the increasingly routine post-mortem examination, explained some of them. In 1969, at the second International Conference on Causes of Sudden Death in Infants, the term 'sudden infant death syndrome' (SIDS) was proposed. These deaths were defined as 'sudden death of any infant or young child, which is unexpected by history, or in which a thorough post-mortem examination fails to demonstrate an adequate cause of death'.

Although the term 'cot death' or SIDS refers to one of the commonest causes of death in the early months of life, it is still very imprecise. The presumed mode of death and its unexpectedness, the presence or absence of an explanation and the prevailing system for classifying infant deaths are

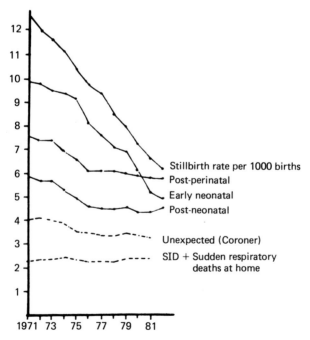

Figure 9.2 Mortality rates per 1000 live births in England and Wales 1971–1982, showing a comparison between different components of the infant mortality rates. Derived from OPCS tabulations with permission of the Controller of HMSO; Crown copyright reserved.

all important variables which can markedly influence estimates of rates of occurrence. Any definition by exclusion is dependent on the amount and quality of information that is available. In the past few years, work carried out in the various centres in the UK contributing to the DHSS study (1985), together with research by individuals and by the Foundation for the Study of Sudden Infant Deaths (UK), has increasingly demonstrated that 'diagnosis' is entirely dependent on the sophistication of the post-mortem examination. As Golding, Limerick and Macfarlane (1985) have pointed out, a major source of bias lies in the actual definition of the cases, as this relies on the techniques, experience and assiduousness with which the pathologist has carried out the post-mortem and recorded the results. The quality of post-mortem information remains variable because there is a continuing lack of trained paediatric pathologists (Bluglass, 1981, 1982). For this reason, Emery (1983) has proposed the setting up of national reference centres to help standardize autopsy reports.

The definition of a Sudden Infant Death assumes a previously *apparently* healthy baby. A detailed autopsy may, in the hands of an experienced paediatric pathologist, reveal abnormalities in some of these hitherto unexplained deaths. The demonstration of pathology helps parents to understand the loss of their child and it may help those who are supporting them to alleviate guilt and self-blame. At one time in the UK it was thought that parents would be more worried by a death certificate with the words 'sudden unexpected infant death' or 'cause unknown' rather than by 'bronchopneumonia'. The pendulum has now swung, and the proportion of sudden infant deaths which are recorded as such on death certificates has increased. There is increasing evidence that many parents are now less worried by the term 'sudden infant death' on the death certificate than by a cause such as pneumonia. However, even if the post-mortem reveals evidence of some disease process, it is often still a matter of judgement whether this can be regarded as a sufficient cause of death. Not enough is known of the significance of minor inflammation of the lungs or bronchi. Golding, Limerick and Macfarlane (1985) have stated that 'a frequent finding is of some minor inflammation of the lungs or bronchi, indicating the presence of a chest infection. The significance of this could only be validly assessed if one knew how many normal live children also showed such signs—especially during the winter months.'

Watson (1985) has highlighted the frequency with which subsequent virological or detailed histological studies have resulted in a revision of the 'unexpected, unexplained', 'cot death' label. The revised diagnosis is not always communicated to the parents who are left in uncertainty (*see* review by Valdes Dapena, 1980). The *antemortem* history is also important. Careful enquiry of parents, relatives and health professionals may provide evidence of previous illness in the child which may suggest that death was not sudden or at least not entirely unexpected.

Another problem arising from the use of the term SIDS is that it encourages a view of the syndrome as a clinical entity which may have a single cause or at least a final common pathway. Many possible aetiological hypotheses have now been discarded and the present state of knowledge suggests that the sudden infant death syndrome has a multifactorial basis. The relative importance of cot death or sudden death syndrome to overall numbers of infant mortality in the 1980s (approximately 50% in some years) explains the greater emphasis on these deaths in this chapter. The special circumstances of SIDS cases (suddenness, lack of medical explanation, accentuation of parental guilt or self-blame, lack of public education and social support for the problem) are well known vulnerability factors in bereavement, and therefore they indicate a need for particular care in therapeutic management of the patients. Because the distinction in aetiological terms between SIDS and infant deaths from other causes is to some extent arbitrary, the consequences and management of other deaths must be considered too. Because their numbers are small, not much is known about such cases.

Categories of infant deaths and their relationship to parental reactions

The upsurge of interest in SIDS at the end of the 1970s focused our attention for the first time on the potential consequences for the parents. To understand the absence of studies in this area it is necessary to look at historical trends in the UK in attitudes to deaths of children. In earlier centuries, with very high child mortality and infant wastage, social and family attitudes to the loss of infants were often less intense or, at best, philosophical as can be observed in early tombstones and memorials (Page-Phillips, 1970). Many children, as in developing countries elsewhere today, were conceived and born with the expectation that very few would survive infancy or childhood; economies were often dependent on child labour and this fact tended to keep birth rates high but survival low. The French essayist de Montaigne wrote in the 16th century, 'I have lost two or three children in their infancy, not without regret, but without great sorrow'. Even in the 17th, 18th and, to a lesser extent, the 19th century, the deaths of children were still so common as to occasion little public concern for the bereaved. Despite the resigned acceptance of infant death by society as a whole, there is no doubt that individual parents did indeed mourn.

> Parental helplessness and grief over the serious illness and impending death of a child, and joy over miraculous cures, are not uncommon themes in the saints' lives of these centuries. (Walzer, 1976)

There is no doubt, however, that greater familiarity with death and different social attitudes to mourning before the 20th century seem to have resulted in more public, less inhibited, expression of grief (Longford, 1964). Parkes (1972) whose work on the loss of a spouse has illuminated the processes of bereavement and grief, also suggests that as we have fewer children today, the tie between each child and its mother may be correspondingly greater. In other words, he suggests that the 'bonding' capacity or potential is not infinite but distributed between those children who are born, so that it might be relatively easier to accept the loss of one child from a family of 10 than to lose one child from a family of two. The expectation of loss may, however, be more important. According to Parkes (1972), 'in a society in which the death of a child is statistically rare, parents are likely to be particularly unprepared for those that do occur'. Wretmark's (1959) study of 28 bereaved psychiatric patients in Sweden found 'extremely severe and incapacitating reactions amongst mothers who had lost small infants'; in eight of these parents the illness had followed the loss of a child. Gorer, the English sociologist who studied grief and mourning in Britain in the 1960s, suggested that the loss of a child was likely to be the 'most distressing and long lasting of all griefs'. Parkes (1972) has also considered possible differences between loss of an adult spouse and that of a child, and there have since been a number of systematic attempts to describe bereavement reactions that are particular to parents following the loss of a child (Cornwell, Nurcombe and Stevens, 1977; Defrain and Ernst, 1978; Bluglass, 1978, 1979; Drotar and Irvin, 1979).

Following bereavement, the amount or lack of social support and other secondary stresses are clearly also important. Previous work with bereaved adults suggests that a proportion of parents who lose a child in early infancy will suffer damage to their physical and/or mental health (Parkes, 1972). More detailed discussion of risk factors is found in Parkes and Weiss (1983) and Osterweiss, Solomon and Green (1984). It has been suggested that mothers may be more vulnerable than fathers and that the first year of bereavement is the time when most of the difficulties may arise, but many professionals now working with bereaved parents recognize the great individual variation in reactions and in the length of time taken for adaptation to occur. One of the aims of bereavement research is the identification of those people most likely to experience greatest psychiatric, physical and social adjustment difficulties, to whom it may be appropriate to offer counselling or other forms of help after bereavement. Parents whose child dies suddenly in infancy would seem to merit special consideration but, until recently, they have been a particularly neglected group. Such studies as have been attempted will be discussed in a later section, but first it is worth asking why there has been so little research. A list of factors influencing the outcome after bereavement is given in *Table 9.2*.

The first problem is one of recognition and the second is one of resistance to accepting bereavement as an appropriate area for study. Until

Table 9.2 Factors influencing outcome after bereavement

Previous mental illness, especially depressive illness
Life crises prior to the bereavement
Closeness of relationship to the deceased
The strength and quality of attachment
The presence or absence of ambivalence in the relationship
The mode of death
The degree of preparation for bereavement
The age, sex, and personality of the bereaved
Socio-economic status
Nationality
Degree of religious faith or ritual
Culture
Previous experience of separation and loss
Other factors influencing the expression of grief

relatively recently in the UK and to a lesser degree in the USA, professional as well as general public education about bereavement was extremely limited. Beliefs were still prevalent that serious clinical studies of the bereaved might be harmful or dangerous. Cultural attitudes in the UK about the desirability of the suppression of grief and of intolerable feelings may have led to the belief that to encourage the expression of such feelings might in some way produce psychological damage. The evidence (Raphael, 1983) is in fact to the contrary. The facilitation of appropriate mourning reactions, the acknowledgement of painful feelings and support from family, friends and community as well as professional intervention have been shown to forestall later difficulties (Black and Urbanowitz, 1987). Education of professionals and the training of bereavement counsellors and of 'befrienders' by various organizations, for example CRUSE, have enormously improved the care of bereaved people and have led to greater public awareness. Much more research is, however, needed (Osterweiss, Solomon and Green, 1984).

Grief

The most comprehensive and authoritative account of the clinical theory of normal and abnormal grief is that of Raphael (1983), but a brief summary of the present understanding of normal and abnormal grief may be appropriate here.

Grief is the most prominent emotion that is experienced following a major loss such as that of a partner, parent, child or even a limb or other body part. Bereavement is the state of loss, and mourning or grieving is the state of expressing the emotion of grief, but is also used synonymously for certain rituals or activities which may vary from person to person depending on their cultural and religious or secular background.

Many of the immediate effects of loss, although to some extent culturally determined, can be helpfully understood in terms of the effects of separation. The immediate behavioural reactions can be understood in terms of the ethological survival of the human organism's response to threat and actual separation (Bowlby, 1969, 1973). Familiarity with the immediate effects such as numbness and 'denial', bewilderment, anger and hostility (which may be directed at the medical attendants, the deceased or the self), will minimize the sense of strangeness and the feeling that the bereaved is 'going mad'. Young parents who have not previously experienced bereavement may feel bewildered by their emotions and quite alienated from those around them. Their bewilderment may be heightened by a perfectly normal experience, the so-called 'pseudo-hallucination' of bereavement in which the bereaved may sense the presence or hear the voice of the deceased, not necessarily in a frightening, but often in a comforting manner. In supporting and counselling the bereaved, including parents after the death of an infant, it is most important to understand that such experiences are common and quite normal (Rees, 1971).

The sadness, weeping, disturbed sleep and apathy which succeed the first period of numbness, although similar to depressed mood, are usually a transient manifestation of loss. Most experienced clinicians who work with bereaved people now believe that whereas it is most important not to under-treat depression which may coexist with bereavement (as for example, in a patient who has a previous history of depressive episodes), so it is essential that the normal process of adaptation to loss should not be over-treated either—as by the inappropriate use of antidepressants (Oster-weiss, Solomon and Green, 1984). The prescription of antidepressants for bereaved individuals was quite common medical practice until recently and, unfortunately, as we now know, suppression of the normal experience of bereavement, for example by 'denial', may result in the later develop-ment of depression or other psychiatric problems (Parkes, 1984). Inappropriate medication may inhibit the expression of emotion and it may delay or impede normal adaptation. Most bereaved parents do not need antidepressant medication, but it is often helpful to prescribe a very limited course of short-acting hypnotics in order to promote sleep for those individuals whose daily life is being disrupted by insomnia. Most people will respond to reassurance that this stage will pass.

Most parents feel that the existence of other children in the family does provide a distraction from the immediate pangs of grief and a reason to preserve the normality of daily life. Many parents have commented to me that they would not have been able to cope had they not had their other children to care for. Parents, however, may often grieve differently and 'recover' at different rates from each other. Working fathers may be both distracted and relieved by social and occupational activities and this may promote their apparently earlier 'recovery' which may prove baffling to many mothers who may feel that their husbands are less sensitive to the loss. Men in our society are conditioned to avoid the open expression of grief or the discussion of inner feelings, particularly painful ones, and this may result in their being quite unable to talk about their loss unless given positive opportunity to do so (Mandell, MacAnulty and Reece, 1980).

The purpose of counselling, whether by a professional or a 'befriender' is to try to prevent later difficulties by facilitating the expression of emotions in an acceptable and accepting way. Excellent information for parents which complements the work of counsellors and which may help parents to understand their reactions, is available in leaflets from organizations such as the Foundation for the Study of Infant Deaths, CRUSE, the Com-passionate Friends and others (*see* Appendix 1 at the end of this chapter).

Pathological grief reactions
Pathological grief reactions are excessive in either quantity or quality and in such reactions some of the most negative but usually 'normal' ex-periences of early grief may become entrenched or chronic, such as self-blame, guilt, anger, hostility or 'denial' of the death. At times, inexperienced and young parents are so terrified by the experience that they readily believe in 'spirits' and hauntings. They are often rather suggestible people and can usually be helped by simple reassurance and explanation. However, one mother, faced with the normal toddler behav-iour of a surviving twin (after a cot death) with which she was quite unable to cope, began to identify it as the 'spirit' of the deceased twin. Her family colluded with her in scapegoating the surviving twin who eventually had to be taken into care as his physical safety was in jeopardy (Bluglass, Green and Proops, 1980).

Patients with chronic syndromes are difficult to treat, and when in doubt counsellors and professionals are best advised to seek early specialist advice (Worden, 1983). The long-term psychosocial morbidity in parents who lose small infants and children seems, from clinic populations at least, to be more responsive to preventive counselling than that of parents who lose an older or grown-up child. Apart from Gorer's (1966) observations, little is known about the community prevalence of parents' difficulties following the death of a young adult, but the referred population of parents with chronic grief syndromes following an adult child's death leaves an impression of intractable problems. Such patients need 'permission' to relinquish the deceased and behavioural techniques (Mawson *et al.*, 1981) are useful in effecting this (*see* p. 228).

Parental grief reactions following infant loss

American paediatric literature in the 1970s, often with arresting titles, usually derived from retrospective studies of small numbers of subjects, began to suggest the potential for damage to mental health of parents following the death of a small infant (Halpern, 1972; Beckwith, 1975). The early commentary by Wretmark (1959) described a 'clinic' population, which is important since we need to know the prevalence of mothers and fathers coming to psychiatric attention following such a major life event. This tells us nothing, however, of the range of consequences for the whole population of parents who may suffer such an event. Systematic study of parental bereavement has been sparse. Wretmark (1959) described eight cases (seven mothers and one father) in which the loss of a small infant was associated with psychiatric breakdown and admission to hospital. Reactions to loss were described as 'particularly severe and long-lasting'. These cases represent the extreme end of the spectrum, i.e. those parents who were so severely affected as to come to clinical attention.

We need information about the prevalence of such severe bereavement reactions compared with the whole range of response. Is the loss of an infant a more potent 'vulnerability factor' for the later development of mental illness than other major 'negative' life events? What is the normal process of adaptation to the loss of an infant and does it differ from that found in other forms of bereavement? What factors may modify such reactions and how might one try to prevent the occurrence of 'pathological' grief? Perhaps the lack of information about this subject reflects the attitudes of professionals who may not regard it as a serious or sizeable subject for study. Furthermore, in contrast with studies of reactions to deaths of older children from leukaemia, for example (Lansky *et al.*, 1979), professionals may believe that loss after the brief existence of the infant is likely to be less distressing to the parent than the loss of an older child. Yet it is during the first weeks and months of life that 'primary maternal preoccupation' (Winnicott, 1964) is most evident and this, with or without the complicating existence of postnatal depression, would suggest that mothers of young infants are also at risk of developing pathological grief reactions. Their condition may in turn affect the partnership, parenting and their existing or subsequent children.

Cain and Cain (1964) have described, from a psychoanalytical viewpoint, the consequences of 'replacing' a child following a death. Their very small and selected sample (six cases) and their unstandardized methods place limits on the validity of their conclusion, that the subsequent child is likely—due to distortions of its upbringing—to develop schizophrenia.

In the 1970s the interest shown in SIDS, together with increasing psychiatric, social work and nursing interest in bereavement, led to recognition that there might be sensitizing factors to later psychological morbidity following the deaths of children and, in particular, following the enigmatic deaths from SIDS. Some workers, such as Schodt (1976), took the likelihood of morbidity for granted and therefore suggested ways of management and intervention. Their efforts improved the recognition of parental needs as did the study of parental reactions by Defrain and Ernst (1978, 1982).

Other reports in the American literature by Mandell and Wolfe (1975) and Bergman (1979) also described emotional sequelae. Cornwell, Nurcombe and Stevens (1977) in Australia found a range of psychosocial difficulties including emotional and marital problems in a study of 11 families. They described anxiety when a new baby was born, physical deterioration in the parents and relative unconcern on the part of medical practitioners. Defrain and Ernst (1978, 1982) in Nebraska conducted surveys by postal questionnaire over a period of five years (three studies producing cumulative data in 112 families). They acknowledged sample bias; for example, the final group was recruited through national newspaper advertisements. The information thus obtained about personal reactions to the deaths of babies, although anecdotal, nevertheless pointed to the need to support distressed parents. Lewis (1981a,b) described maternal anxiety in a small study of mothers and discussed the effects of such anxiety on the emotional security of subsequent infants. Needless to say, most of the emphasis had been on the effects of the loss on the mother. Changing patterns of child care, including the increasing contact of young men with their children, emphasizes the need to study the reactions of fathers as well as of mothers.

Mandell, MacAnulty and Reece (1980) explored the extent to which fathers' responses to the loss of an infant from SIDS differed from those of their wives; they described 28 fathers (in a study of 46 families) who were present at a single interview with a community nurse. The authors identified several patterns of behaviour which were more typical of the fathers than of mothers. For example, they needed to 'keep busy' and to work more, they had feelings of diminished self-worth, and self-blame because of their lack of care and involvement with the child who had died. They had a limited ability to ask for help and a greater tendency to deny the reality of the child's death and thus to avoid the pain of mourning. They were more angry and aggressive than the mothers. Mandell, Mac-Anulty and Reece (1980) considered that these patterns of behaviour obstructed the full expression of grief and that they were often reinforced by care givers who were anxious to help fathers fulfil social expectations of 'masculine' strength. The fact that only 28 out of 46 fathers were available for interview will not surprise professionals who work clinically with bereaved parents.

Between 1977 and 1981 the causes of post-neonatal deaths in infants were studied in detail in 13 centres in the UK; the aim was to identify ways of preventing such deaths. The findings of this study which was directed by Professor Knowlden in Sheffield were published in 1985 (DHSS, 1985). During the course of this multi-centre study I was able to approach all the families at one of the centres and to interview them in depth at home in order to assess their reactions to the loss of their baby. This was, as far as I am aware, the first prospective study of parental bereavement reactions following all the consecutive infant deaths in one city in the UK (Birmingham).

In this follow-up study of 100 families all of them were interviewed at home every three months until 15 months after the death. It was unusual to find both parents available for the initial interview, despite efforts to ensure this. Amongst those fathers who could be interviewed, accounts of great emotional distress were common; they also resented the greater attention which was given by the professionals to their wives and the expectation that they would be strong and provide support. There were descriptions of similar reactions in their partners by the wives in those instances when the partners were unavailable for direct interview.

Case example 1. Two elderly parents, both of whom already had children by other associations, lost their only child together and the news of the death produced near-suicidal behaviour. The mother later told the interviewer that the father had been found wandering by the nearby canal, contemplating suicide. They were a sad couple, living in a deprived area above a shop from which they were trying to make a living. Since the business was also their home, the father probably had more daily contact with the baby than many others.

Case example 2. Another baby died, with her mother, in a household fire. This family was one of the most severely affected in the study for a variety of reasons. On learning of the deaths the young father rushed outside and began to kick the nearest object, a car, fracturing bones in his foot. He was one of the fathers who most quickly and severely developed dependence on alcohol—but it should be remembered that his wife had died, as well as the baby.

A fear for the integrity of one's own life and health is a normal reponse to a sudden death but the effects in several cases were handicapping. In a pilot study of parental reactions to SIDS (Bluglass, 1979), two fathers with no premorbid history developed severe hypochondriasis. Two other fathers featured among the small number with significant psychiatric morbidity also with well defined illness phobias. In the main study of 100 families, five fathers (out of many who turned to increased alcohol consumption in the early stages) had become established in patterns of alcohol abuse, with consequent risks to marriage and family.

It is quite clear that the response of father and mother differ for many couples. The mother tends to be more depressed, withdrawn. Her grief seems more intense, prolonged. She weeps. Her life seems more disrupted by her loss. The father's response style tends to be more like that described for perinatal deaths. He takes over protective, management functions, suppresses his feelings, deals with his distress by keeping himself busy and active. He seems to get over his grief more quickly and cannot understand his wife's continuing preoccupation with it. (Raphael, 1983)

Cornwell, Nurcombe and Stevens (1977) found the average time of return to normal function was 10.3 months for the mother and 3.6 months for the father. These observations are reinforced by the study of Mandell, MacAnulty and Reece (1980).

In Birmingham major psychiatric morbidity in most families was rare (Bluglass, 1981) and no mother required hospital admission. One mother from the earlier pilot study had taken a series of overdoses and had numerous psychiatric admissions with a diagnosis of depression. In the main study, two mothers were recommended to seek consultation with their GP for depressive symptoms. The most severely depressed mother of all was, in fact, a foster mother of a baby who died.

Anxiety, on the other hand (as evidenced by General Health Questionnaire scores), increased smoking, medicine consumption and more frequent attendance at GP surgeries, was common in 'cot death' mothers in the subsequent pregnancy and early months of a new baby's life, whereas in the families of babies dying from other causes, mild, understandable apprehension in late pregnancy was relieved by the arrival of a healthy subsequent child. The birth of a subsequent child, when this occurred, did not always bring the relief and comfort expected.

Siblings' reactions

Studies of surviving children who manifested behaviour disorders (e.g. Drotar and Irvin, 1979) have been based on 'clinic' rather than on community populations. The recent community study by Dyregrof (see Chapter 11 of this volume) has, however, also described emotional and behavioural reactions of siblings in families which lost an infant. The behaviour of surviving children was found to be disturbed in nearly 80% of the families studied by DeFrain and Ernst (1982). Problems included nightmares, bed wetting, school problems, discipline problems, increased crying, blackout spells and being over-protected by their parents. Similar findings have been reported by Cornwell, Nurcombe and Stevens (1977).

Mothers' accounts of their surviving children following infant loss during one year of the DHSS multicentre study (1985) were also studied in the prospective study of the psychosocial consequences of such deaths (Bluglass, 1981). In the cohort of 100 families in Birmingham approximately 50% suffered cot deaths and the remainder deaths from congenital or infective causes. Surviving siblings showed mainly minor and transient difficulties in the immediate mourning period. Few emotional difficulties requiring medical attention persisted in the longer term. One explanation for lower than expected morbidity is that such difficulties as may occur, may be latent and may only come to light in later years. Preoccupied, grieving parents may under-report behaviour problems and symptoms in surviving children and it is also possible that, in the majority of children, such effects are indeed minor and transient unless other adverse factors are present.

Osterweiss, Solomon and Green (1984) have drawn attention to the difficulties in drawing conclusions about long-term consequences. In the years since the study was conducted in Birmingham, and following completion of the Multicentre Study (DHSS, 1985), changing circumstances may have influenced psychiatric morbidity in surviving family members. Initially there was heightened interest and awareness on the part of health professionals, but then lack of resources stopped the regular study case conferences which had provided a forum for professionals to examine the preventable and unpreventable baby deaths in the city. In 1982, however, a parents' self-help group was formed in Birmingham as a subsidiary of the national group, and it provided support at a parent-to-parent befriending level as well as providing information for professionals in the city. It is hard to quantify the extent to which the existence of such a group changed the understanding of the need for family support for these parents. It is therefore difficult now to estimate the 'uncontaminated' rate of childhood behaviour disorder following infant deaths in Birmingham. Socio-economic factors are often implicated in family disharmony and in child behaviour problems; the Birmingham parents were predominantly drawn from social class III and below, unlike those in the survey carried out by the Foundation for the Study of Infant Deaths (*see* Golding, Limerick and Macfarlane 1985). Despite the socio-economic grouping of the Birmingham parents, the reported 'problems' in children were minor and probably little different from reactions to any major family upheaval such as moving house.

The individual consequences, including subsequent pregnancy, the 'replacement child' and other aspects of the bereavement will be discussed together as, in general, they do not greatly differ from one cause of death to another, and the management is largely the same.

Parental reactions to infant death due to congenital causes

Savage (Chapter 10) covers perinatal death while this chapter focuses on post-neonatal death. The special circumstances of parents whose baby dies in infancy of a major congenital malformation have been described by Bluglass (1984). In this chapter the effect of the delivery of a malformed or handicapped baby who survives, or who may survive, is compared with the death of such a child. The birth of a handicapped baby is a very powerful source of loss and grief for the parents; the 'loss' of the expected 'perfect' infant has to be mourned (Solnit and Stark, 1961; Olshansky, 1962).

The effect on parents and other family members of the birth of a damaged infant is often more difficult for health professionals and the general public to understand. There may be ambivalent feelings about the survival of such a baby, and medical and nursing staff may have unrealistic expectations of the parents' emotions, underestimating their complexity. The parents, moreover, may react quite differently from one another.

Case example 1. The birth of an achondroplastic baby caused major marital problems for one couple. There was no family history and the diagnosis and appearance of the baby was a considerable shock to the mother who found this 'repellent'. Her husband, on the other hand, who came from a family with a tradition and experience of working with handicapped children, 'bonded' immediately to the little boy and was perplexed by his wife's inability to accept him.

Case example 2. The situation was seen in reverse during a programme of prenatal screening for neural tube defects in an Asian family living in the Midlands of England. The father completely refused to accept the second child who was born with Down's syndrome. He asked for the baby to be institutionalized, to the great distress of the mother. For his wife, however, his refusal to allow her to bring the baby home produced an understandable bereavement reaction.

It has generally been assumed that the longer the period of gestation, or the older the baby, the more close will be the mother's attachment to the baby and, therefore, the greater the feelings of bereavement if the baby does not survive. However, not all mothers show immediate 'ideal' attachment to live healthy babies (Kennell, Slyter and Klaus, 1970; Sluckin, Herbert and Sluckin, 1983). The knowledge that the baby may not survive or that it has a progressive, fatal disease may be accompanied by a process of adaptation to impending loss. Such 'anticipatory grieving', if it occurs, may have advantages and disadvantages, but it seems likely that some opportunity to anticipate later difficulties, including death of the baby, may improve the eventual response to the bereavement (Clayton *et al.*, 1973; Parkes and Weiss, 1983; Osterweiss, Solomon and Green, 1984; Worden, 1983). For example, as has been seen in parents of leukaemic children in relapse/remission cycles, or in parents who have children suffering chronic episodic deterioration of health as in cystic fibrosis, the opportunity to grieve a possible death in advance is modified by the other demands on a parent. It is hard for a mother or father to mourn in advance the death of one child, while still attempting to live in the here and now of work, support of the other parent, and parenting of healthy siblings (Burton, 1979).

In the study of families whose infants died in the first year of life (Bluglass, 1981), bereavement outcome was considered 15–18 months later. Estimates of maternal morbidity in psychological terms in a subsequent pregnancy and during the first few months after delivery showed that those mothers who had lost their babies from congenital malformation were less anxious, and generally rated as 'recovered', (self and interviewer's rating) as compared with mothers in those families who had suffered a sudden infant death. This result, however, may be a reflection of the excellent regional genetic counselling service that was available. Genetic counselling traditionally focuses on the estimation of risk and only relatively recently have the psychological needs of parents following infant death from genetic causes been considered (Emery and Pullen, 1984).

So far we have considered the effects on parents and families of an infant loss occurring from 'natural causes'. In most bereaved people, encouragement of the normal expression of feelings results in adaptation to the loss with time—a 'good' outcome. Occasionally pathological reactions may occur, but these are in a minority. Premorbid history of emotional difficulties was not present in those parents in the study who experienced greater than average problems. For those with known vulnerability, however, bereavement by loss of a child, as with any major life event, may be implicated in the precipitation of a new episode of illness. The perception of guilt which is a common feature of these parents (as in SIDS where no clear medical explanation can be given), may be confused with the guilt and self-blame of depression. The management of these syndromes, however, will be considered generally below.

Recovery from bereavement

Allowing for the normal recurrence of sad feelings at about the time of the anniversary, many parents describe a lessening of grief continuing throughout the first year and up to and beyond the anniversary. My own clinical experience, derived from the follow-up study described above, and from work with other bereaved families suggests that for parents experiencing the death of a child the conventionally accepted period may be an underestimate, and that the older the child who dies, the longer is the bereavement process. Many parents are still suffering from quite profound feelings of loss in the second year, but their difficulties do eventually resolve and there is considerable individual variation. Much can be done to support parents through prolonged grief reactions before assuming that their experience is either abnormal or that it heralds more serious disorder.

'Adaptation' or 'adjustment' are perhaps more appropriate terms, since most parents feel that they will never 'recover' from the experience. In clinical terms, however, the absence of identifiable illness is clearly one good prognostic sign and, at a practical level, the ability to function reasonably effectively in all the dimensions of one's life (parent, spouse, worker, community member) is another.

Anxiety

Anxiety is one of the most striking psychiatric symptoms when parents have another baby after a cot death. The hypothesis that parental anxiety about the next child would be more prominent following cot death than after infant death for other reasons was confirmed by Bluglass (1981). The explanation lies in the lack of certainty that the event will not repeat itself in the next baby. Statistically, there is a slightly increased risk and most professionals feel that it is futile to conceal this fact from the parents.

> *Case example* The expression of anxiety can be severe, as in a father whose health visitor reported that he was over-protecting their nine-month-old subsequent baby and 'affecting his development'. The mother, conversely, had settled well with the birth of the new baby and was managing him totally appropriately. However, the father needed advice and reassurance in order to allow the baby to learn to play, crawl and walk.

Most commonly, anxiety expresses itself in over-protection of the subsequent baby, fears about picking the baby up at night, or frequent attendance at the general practitioner. In one practice this was managed by diminishing the number of calls on the practitioner himself by a therapeutic contract agreeing a number of home visits and attendances at the clinic to see the practice health visitor. The existence of anxiety, however, must be assessed and appropriate action taken if necessary, since it may affect subsequent fertility and the healthy progress of a subsequent pregnancy (Record and Armstrong, 1980). Behavioural regimes, rather than medication, can be very helpful because they enable the parents to gain some sense of mastery over their lives.

Unnatural and other causes of death

Non-accidental injury

In epidemiological terms, deaths from cot deaths (SIDS) have been considered by the coroner to be deaths from *'natural'* causes after full investigation and post-mortem examination. These deaths greatly outnumber deaths from *non-accidental injury*. The level of awareness of the public and of professionals to the existence of non-accidental injury, whether or not resulting in death, has led to some misunderstanding about cot death and SIDS. Great distress has been caused to parents, the majority of whose babies undoubtedly died from natural causes, by suggestions that a proportion were due to a 'missed' or covert form of child abuse. Emery (1972) has coined the term 'gently battered baby' to explain the possible existence of a very small number of deaths which may possibly occur following parental desperation, fatigue or exasperation when a baby has cried incessantly. In the UK in 1983 and 1984, great controversy was aroused when a pathologist (Wayte, 1984) suggested, on the basis of his own local experience, that non-accidental injury accounted for a large proportion of deaths labelled as SIDS. In the view of the Foundation for the Study of Infant Deaths and the DHSS Multicentre Study (1985) this view is untenable and calls into question the competence of many able and careful pathologists around the country. The lack of standardized post-mortem examinations by qualified paediatric pathologists does lead to variation but it does not necessarily imply a large overlap between 'natural' or 'unnatural' deaths. Roberts et al. (1984) have challenged Wayte's conclusions and have shown that factors predictive of non-accidental injury do not predict SIDS families.

Even in situations where the death of a child has resulted from non-accidental injury (Smith, 1979), it would be a crude oversimplification to suppose that these parents had planned or wished for the deaths of their children. The way in which parents deal with the sequelae of bereavement is likely to be influenced by the reaction of those around them. Thus the horror, repugnance and avoidance which is likely to face parents suspected of having contributed to their child's death may account for the lack of awareness of their deep distress and sense of loss. Raphael (1983) remarks, 'parental grief and mourning are often ignored alongside society's enormous anger towards parents who cause the deaths of their children'. Failure to take account of this in case work or therapy may deprive the parents of an opportunity for change and development in personal terms, and may result in the too rapid flight into a subsequent pregnancy with further difficult consequences, for example, removal of the next child at birth.

Infanticide

Margison (1982) discussed the relationship of infanticide to some cases of maternal depression or severe psychosis, citing D'Orban's (1979) series of 89 women, 56% of whom had psychiatric symptoms. Studies of the forensic aspects of infanticide do not usually consider the management of the bereavement.

> *Case example.* Following an apparently normal delivery, a 26-year-old primipara was admitted to a psychiatric hospital at two weeks postpartum, having inexplicably strangled her baby in the Maternity Unit. She had already been examined by two psychiatrists who found her to be anxious but not psychotic. In her case marital problems and immaturity appeared more likely than mental illness to have contributed to the death of the infant. Her management included careful assessment of the need for bereavement work in the early treatment plan. Staff and patients alike were appropriately sensitive to the fact that the unit contained at the time not only this mother whose baby had died by her own hand, but at various times concurrently two, and subsequently three, other mothers with relatively young babies. The father's needs were not forgotten. Very early on in the admission the loss of his baby and his angry feelings were acknowledged and discussed with him. He was able to help in the treatment of his wife by recalling photographs taken in the first few days after birth, which were also used constructively in counselling him. He agreed to the therapist keeping copies of the photographs until such time as it was considered therapeutically helpful for his wife to see them. Gradually the question of the photographs was introduced and the mother was helped to look at these, largely using a 'guided mourning' technique (Mawson *et al.*, 1981). With the mother's permission a nurse was able to sit in on this guided mourning session, not only for support for the mother, but also to introduce the nurse to the techniques of counselling. She in turn was able to report back to the other nursing staff on the progress of the session.

Infant loss and maternal mental illness

Impaired care

Do mothers who suffer from postnatal mental illness provide impaired care for their infants, both in terms of quality and amount? Do such impairments contribute to the incidence of SIDS? In the study by Bluglass (1981) there were no mothers whose mental state could be considered, from the evidence available, as having contributed to the death of the baby. There were clearly several families where less than ideal social circumstances, inadequate knowledge of the needs of infants and restricted access to medical services may have played a part; these are the circumstances of inner city deprivation. Where such deprivation exists, perceived social support is often lacking and the presence of postnatal depression may be unnoticed.

In the case of mothers suffering with major psychotic illnesses, the care of the baby is clearly uppermost in the minds of professionals. If maternal care is not adequate, then the baby is likely to be cared for by others, or the care may be supervised by others. The quality of care and attention to the baby is likely to be adversely affected by postnatal depression, but there is no evidence to suggest a link between postnatal depression and SIDS; this question has, however, not been directly investigated.

Loss of a baby and subsequent maternal illness

As indicated above, bereavement, like many negative or stressful life events, is a possible vulnerability factor in the development of later difficulties, particularly in those already at risk for depressive illness or where other vulnerability factors already exist (Brown and Harris, 1978). These include: little perceived social support, ambivalent relationship with the deceased, concurrent life crises, early loss of mother, three or more children under five years, no close confiding relationship, previously unresolved losses, and sudden or unexpected deaths. Not all mothers, of course, will succumb to these vulnerability factors, but when they are known to be present it may be possible to prevent later problems by means of careful continuing assessment and appropriate intervention.

Lewis (1976, 1979) has suggested that grief may be psychologically inhibited by pregnancy, so that the notion should be considered that delayed grief may manifest itself in the next puerperium. Our clinical experience with bereaved patients confirms that mixed feelings, lack of the anticipated relief, and delight at the next safe delivery may not only surprise obstetric staff but also the parents themselves. Often this is a 'protective phase' and will pass with support—but this kind of detachment may add to a mother's emotions of guilt, failure and lack of confidence and may reinforce 'depressed' feelings. This indicates the necessity for adequate, initial bereavement counselling so that both parents and the next baby are not followed by 'shadow grief'—a phrase coined by Peppers and Knapp (1980) to describe unresolved parental bereavement.

Maternal mental illness as an aetiological factor in SIDS

There is, as yet, no single causal explanation for SIDS and, moreover, no real agreed standards of post-mortem findings upon which to base comparisons of possible causal factors. Two large research projects in the UK, the Oxford Record Linkage Study (1966–70 and 1971–75) and the DHSS Multicentre Postneonatal Mortality Study (1985) have collected some relevant information. In the Oxford project the hospital admission records of 168 mothers of sudden infant deaths were compared with those of 510 mothers of control infants in the first ORLS study (*see* Golding, Limerick and Macfarlane, 1985).

Records of all non-obstetric hospital admissions during the period under consideration were obtained and coded according to whether maternal hospital admission had occurred (a) before pregnancy, (b) during the pregnancy, (c) after delivery but before the death occurred, and (d) after the death (*Table 9.3*). Altogether there were more admissions of mothers of sudden infant deaths than of control mothers. The difference, however, was mainly in admissions after the death had occurred, as can be seen from *Table 9.3*. After the sudden deaths, 16 mothers of cases had 21 admissions, more than would have been expected from the admission rate of mothers of controls.

Table 9.3 Comparisons of hospital admissions of mothers of sudden infant deaths with matched controls, excluding all admissions for obstetric/gynaecological reasons. (ORLS, 1966–70).

No. of hospital admissions	Mother of sudden infant deaths (n = 168)	Mother of control infants (n = 510)	Statistical significance
Prior to pregnancy	9 (8)	20 (18)	N.S.
During the pregnancy	4 (3)	3 (3)	N.S.
From delivery to death	2 (2)	4 (4)	N.S.
After death	21 (16)	32 (24)	$P < 0.05$
Total	36 (24)	59 (45)	N.S.

No. of women involved are shown in parentheses.

Four of the admissions after death were associated with overdoses and a further three with depression. Another woman had schizophrenia and one woman was a long-standing alcoholic, indeed she had had an admission during the pregnancy itself for alcoholism. Another woman was admitted in an hysterical state. Altogether, therefore, there were eight women with admissions for depression or psychosis after the death had occurred. This may be compared with only three such women among the controls.

To assess whether the mothers of sudden infant deaths are overall mentally more unstable than controls, admissions prior to the death should be analysed. Only three of the mothers of sudden infant deaths had such admissions prior to the death compared with six of the controls. It does, therefore, appear that the excess of post-mortality mental disorders among mothers who had had a sudden infant death was in response to the death rather than being a characteristic of the mothers themselves.

Any association with florid, puerperal psychosis would be identified more readily from psychiatric records and, since these mothers require regular medical follow-up, it is unlikely that a subsequent association with a 'cot death' would fail to attract attention. As far as can be ascertained no such association has been described.

At the less severe end of the spectrum of postnatal illness a study is under way in Sheffield (Emery, Sneddon and Taylor, personal communication), the aim of which is to test whether there is any link between postnatal depression and sudden infant death. One of the most difficult aspects of the problem is the fact that 'postnatal depression' is not always clearly defined, especially when non-psychiatrists use the term. For well defined cases the prevalence is 10–15% (*see* O'Hara, Chapter 2) and, therefore, many mothers will be suffering from definite and often un-diagnosed depression at the point of maximum incidence (three months) of SIDS. A prospective investigation of SIDS which occurs in about two out of every 1000 infants, and postnatal depression which is found in about 10% of mothers, is the only satisfactory way of testing for a link. The resources required would be enormous and it must be said that no study of postnatal depression has so far hinted at an association, but the numbers of subjects have been small.

Does a sudden infant death predispose vulnerable women to develop a postnatal illness after the next pregnancy? The only information which at present exists is anecdotal. The largest number of individual accounts of subsequent deliveries has been given to the Foundation for the Study of Infant Deaths but this is not a wholly representative sample. *Table 9.4* compares possible correlates of puerperal illness and SIDS. As can be seen there is no clear association.

In the bereavement period some of the concomitants of grief may summate with previous 'depression'. Unless a careful history is taken, symptoms of grief such as sadness, apathy, poor sleep, anorexia and poor concentration may be assumed to be due to a pre-existing postnatal depression.

It can, therefore, be seen that in the present state of knowledge it is not possible to define clear associations. It makes sense, however, to take

Table 9.4 Comparison of some correlates of postnatal mental illness and of SIDS

	Postnatal illness	*SIDS*
Time of occurrence	Onset of psychosis typically within 2 weeks of delivery. Onset of depression typically within 6 weeks of delivery.	Peak occurrence at 3 months
Sex difference	–	Boys more than girls
Seasonal	–	More common in winter
Social class	–	More common in working class families
Maternal age	?	Young mothers
Parity	–	High parity
Interbirth interval	–	Short interval
Illegitimacy	?	–
Multiple births	–	–
Low birth weight	?	Yes
Congenital defect	Reactive depression	No direct association
Knowledge of last menstrual period	–	No knowledge
Smoking	–	Yes
Opiate addiction	–	Occasionally reported

account of pre-existing depression and anxiety and their likely recurrence, in the individual management of all families who lose an infant from whatever cause.

Management

Advice to family, friends and grandparents

The professional, if asked, can greatly help the bereaved parents by encouraging family and friends to be available and to continue to stay with the parents, responding to their needs. Many parents, experiencing death of infants for any reason, describe their sense of isolation and avoidance by others when, for example, they first return to school to collect an older child after a death. They often learn that if they wish to hold a conversation they themselves have to initiate this. If one is asked to see a family very early on after a death it is helpful to prepare parents by explaining that such reactions in others do often occur.

Health professionals

The last five years have seen an increase in sensible and practical literature on the theory of bereavement and loss and the book by Worden (1983) is indispensable. This book is a manual of practical advice for those who work with bereaved people. Counselling courses, particularly those which allow for some experiential work, should be utilized to the full. Together with relevant organizations, a list of useful visual aids on the subject is given in Appendix 2 at the end of this chapter.

Information for parents and professionals

For SIDS parents, professionals and the community, distress can be reduced by clear information available from the Foundation for the Study of Infant Deaths. Leaflets, however useful, cannot supplant the personal support that is necessary following any loss. Furthermore, the medicolegal complications in SIDS require particular explanation and interpretation for parents and grandparents. Better community education about the nature and consequences of loss and bereavement through responsible journalism, television and even, as proposed by CRUSE, by the use of educational material for primary and secondary schools, will inevitably improve the awareness of parents' needs. Education of health professionals at student and postgraduate levels has, until recently, lacked consistent content in this area, but it is improving. In many parts of the country the immediate management of SIDS by the police is becoming more sensitive following the use of appropriate training materials (supplied by the Foundation for the Study of Infant Deaths).

Self-help groups

Apart from the help which family and health professionals (family doctors, health visitors) can provide, many parents whose babies die from SIDS, as well as from other causes, may derive benefit from sharing experiences with others as part of a mutual or self-help group. The advantages and disadvantages of such groups are discussed by Silverman (1980) and by Robinson and Henry (1977). In general, the important point seems to be one of supervision and access to professional advice (Parkes, 1980). In the study of Cornwell, Nurcombe and Stevens (1977), SIDS parents in Australia preferred a 'professionally led' group. In the United Kingdom such groups (e.g. Friends of the Foundation, SANDS, Compassionate Friends) are becoming more accessible and open to professional support, and are also playing an important part in improving professional awareness. A recent British development in Birmingham has been the innovation of a cooperative venture involving various parent groups concerned with all childrens' deaths (up to the age of 18) and the relevant professional agencies. The aim is to try to improve communications and services for parents and to try to eliminate unnecessary bureaucratic sources of distress (for example, sending a clinic follow-up appointment for a baby who has died). An innovation of this kind is not without initial difficulties but it is a logical step towards improving care for families and thus potentially reducing psychosocial morbidity.

It is important, however, that in times of reduced resources, professionals remain clear about the limitations of 'befriending' by parents and do not expect them to carry out sophisticated professional tasks which are inappropriate, may lead to failure and may tarnish the image of the befriender.

Identification of pathological or morbid grief

Professionals and befrienders alike should be able to recognize pathological developments, and psychiatric assessment and possible intervention earlier rather than later can prevent later difficulties. Facilitation of normal grief, which is appropriate for non-specialized professionals, 'grief counsellors' and befrienders has to be distinguished from 'grief therapy' which is a specialized task (see Worden, 1983) using various forms of behavioural (Mawson et al., 1981) and other psychotherapies.

Breast feeding

In the immediate crisis surrounding the death of a baby it is often easy to overlook the fact that the mother was breast feeding. If the mother is not given advice about the suppression of lactation, its continuation can be very distressing both physically and emotionally. Ideally, the general practitioner, midwife or health visitor who is most closely in touch with the mother is the appropriate person to provide this information, but hospital staff must also be ready to do so. Sometimes the immediate shock of the death may in itself diminish or spontaneously suppress lactation but it may return later and appropriate advice will be needed.

Limerick (1984) describes the comments of a few mothers who found it helpful to donate milk to a milk bank but it is very doubtful that this is a common experience or, indeed, whether it is psychologically advisable. Counselling support will explore and take account of individual mothers' wishes, and useful information for parents, written by a parent, is available in Luben (1986).

The use of medication

The place of mild night sedation and antidepressants has been thoroughly discussed by Parkes (1984). He is not opposed to the use of appropriate short-acting night sedation on a limited basis where parents are having difficulty carrying out other practical tasks because of lack of sleep. Similarly, he argues, it is appropriate to prescribe antidepressant medication when a depressive illness occurs with biological features, including retardation, anorexia, malaise. Parkes deplores the use of night sedation or antidepressants as an alternative to supportive counselling and he points out that there is a risk that antidepressant medication, where no true depressive illness exists, may inhibit the expression of appropriate emotions. Since it has been suggested (Raphael, 1983; Parkes, 1984) that the suppression of grief in the early stages of bereavement may be followed by later depressive syndromes or other forms of pathological grief (e.g. 'blocked' or denied grief), it is wise to avoid routine or indiscriminate prescription of antidepressants for bereaved parents. Osterweiss, Solomon and Green (1984), however, point out that although little systematic evidence has been collected to support this view, the consensus of opinion of clinicians favours caution—'the final resolution of loss is better accomplished by psychological help than by the use of drugs . . . . their use is adjunctive, symptomatic and limited in time'.

Case example. A 36-year-old mother lost her second child five months earlier and active, concerned support by the local SIDS befrienders failed to produce any comfort or relief. In fact it seemed as though her symptoms were worsening during that time. When a request for psychiatric consultation was made she was indeed preoccupied with the loss of the baby, but had biological features of depression and some suicidal ideation. In addition to this she had underlying problems related to over-idealization of the baby, explaining that until this baby was born she had expected it to solve all her feelings of loneliness and rejection. This mother, and another 'referred' by befrienders, worried about her lack of response to their help, was quite inaccessible to supportive counselling until her depression had been treated appropriately. For this reason it is important that lay befrienders in self-help groups are regularly helped to understand the limitations of their activities and to learn to recognize parents who need specialized help.

Appendix 1: useful addresses

United Kingdom

The Foundation for the Study of Infant Deaths (Cot Death Research and Support)

14–15 Belgrave Square
London SW1X 8PS
Tel: (01) 235 1721
Registered charity No. 262191

Leaflets:
    Information for Parents following the Sudden and Unexpected Death of
       their Baby
    Your Next Child
    When to Consult a Doctor About Your Baby
    GP Check List
    Guidelines for Accident and Emergency Departments
    (Reference list of articles)
    16mm film and/or video (VHS, U-matic and Betamax):
       After Our Baby Died
       You are Not Alone
       A Call for Help
       The Purple Line
       My Beautiful Baby is Dead
       I'm Sorry Your Baby is Dead but I Can't Tell You Why

The Compassionate Friends

(An international organization of bereaved parents offering friendship and
    understanding to other bereaved parents)
National Secretary: Mrs Gill Hodder,
6 Denmark Street,
Clifton,
Bristol BS1 5DQ
Tel: (0272) 292778
Registered charity No. 263463

Leaflets:
    No Death So Sad
    Bereaved Parents and the Professional
    When a Child in your School is Bereaved
Library of books on child bereavement

Good Grief

School Pack, Edited by Barbara Ward and Jamie Houghton,
In association with Cruse, 1987.

Price £15 + £1.50 p & p (UK) from:
Cruse,
126 Sheen Road
Richmond
Surrey
TW9 1UR

The Stillbirth and Neonatal Death Society

Argyle House,
29–31 Euston Road
London NW1 2SD
Tel: (01) 833 2851
Registered charity No: 281905

Leaflets:
   The Loss of Your Baby at Birth or Shortly After (Stillbirth or Neonatal
      Death) available from Health Education Council
   Notes on Initial Visit by a Befriending Parent
   Guidelines for Bereavement Support Groups with Regard to Stillbirths
      and Neonatal Deaths

The Miscarriage Association

18 Stoneybrook Close
West Bretton
Wakefield WF4 4TP
Tel: (0924) 85515

United States of America

SIDS Clearing House,
1555 Wilson Boulevard, Suite 600,
Rosslyn, VA 22209.
Tel: (703) 522 0870.

National Sudden Infant Death Syndrome Foundation
(NSIDSF),
8201 Greensboro Drive, Suite 600,
McLean,
Virginia 22102.
Tel: (703) 821 8955.

International Council for Infant Survival (ICIS),
c/o Nina Copp, President,
2956 Eric Lane,
Dallas, Texas 75234.

Australia

Australia Capital Territories

SID Association (ACT) Inc.
PO Box 58, Jamison,
ACT 2614.
Tel: 58 7509

New South Wales

SID Association of NSW,
PO Box 172, St. Ives,
Sydney 2075.
Tel: 534 9045

Queensland

Queensland SID Research Foundation,
The Secretary, PO Box 1987
Brisbane 4001.
Tel: 370 1311

South Australia

Sudden Infant Death Association, South Australia,
2 Wicks Avenue,
Campbell Town,
Southern Australia 5074.
Tel: 336 8727

Tasmania

c/o Mrs M. Ballen,
109 Howick Street,
Launceston, Tasmania.
Tel: 31 3806 (W); 1905 (H)

Victoria

SID Research Foundation,
2 Barkley Avenue,
Malvern 3144,
Australia.
Tel: 509 7722

Western Australia

SIDS Foundation,
c/o Mr F. Watson (Vice-President)
219 Hamilton Street,
Queens Park
Tel: 451 4607

Canada

Canadian Foundation for the
Study of Infant Deaths,
4 Lawton Boulevard,
Toronto, Ontario
M4B 124.
Tel: 416 967 1314

New Zealand

Cot Death Division,
National Children's Health Research Foundation,
c/o Mrs A. McDonald,
668 Remuera Road,
Remuera, Auckland 5

South Africa

Cot Death Society
c/o Mrs J. Marais,
PO Box 11306
Vlaeberg 8012

Other organizations

The Hon. Secretary,
The Coroner's Society of England and Wales,
77 Fulham Palace Road,
London W6.

Twins and Multiple Births Association,
54 Broad Lane,
Hampton,
Middlesex TW12 3BG.

The National Childbirth Trust,
9 Queensborough Terrace,
Bayswater,
London W2 3TB.

Appendix 2: Resource List

Information list available from: The Foundation For The Study Of Infant Deaths, 15 Belgrave Square, London SW1X 8PS. Tel. 01–235 1721

Title	Written for	Description of contents	Price per copy (Postage is extra)
Information for Parents Following the Sudden and Unexpected Death of their Baby (leaflet)	Beareaved parents	Explains what little is known and what the post-mortem may show, answers the most usual questions and describes normal grief reactions; explains coroner's role and where to seek further help.	Free for bereaved parents or 3p for educational or training purposes.
Your Next Child (leaflet)	Formerly bereaved parents	Advice to help parents with their anxieties when contemplating, expecting or caring for a subsequent baby.	As above
When to consult a Doctor about your Baby (Green Card)	New mothers, (not just formerly bereaved parents)	The green card describes urgent and sometimes serious symptoms of illness in babies; reverse side gives infant care guidance on feeding, crying, sleeping position and temperature.	5p + postage and packing up to 1000. 3p + postage and packing over 1000 cards.
Support for Parents Bereaved by an Unexpected Infant Death (leaflet)	Health professionals, enquirers, parent groups	Single sheet outlines parents' needs, the role of health professionals, and the information and support offered by the Foundation.	3p for educational or training purposes.
Cot Death Check List for GPs (leaflet)	General practitioners	Brief advice on immediate support needs of the family	3p for educational or training purposes
Guidelines for Accident and Emergency Departments (orange card)	Accident and Emergency Dept staff	Brief guidelines for the management of a sudden infant death brought to hospital casualty departments	Free for hospitals

Newsletters	Parents, supporters of the Foundation, all enquirers	Published twice a year to keep parents and others on mailing list informed of research findings and activities of the Foundation.	Free, stamped addressed envelope or donation welcome.
Reference List of Welfare and Health Education articles	Health visitors, nurses and midwives, health students, doctors	Selected list of articles published in UK since 1971 relevant to the welfare and health educational aspects of the problem.	25p
List of Foundation's Research Projects	Doctors	Researcher's name outlines objectives of each research project; gives references to published results.	£1.00
Cot Death Research and Support slip	Public	Brief objects of the Foundation; welfare and information activities; financial needs.	Free
Appeals Leaflet (picture on cover)	Public and contributors	Work of the Foundation; research for which funds are needed. Deed of Covenant form enclosed.	Free
Annual Report and Accounts of FSID	Members of Foundation and supporters	Reviews scientific, welfare and information and fundraising activities, Chairman's and Treasurer's reports.	Free on request
Sheffield Centile Weight Charts		New centile weight charts have been designed for infants in the first year of life, based upon measurements made at 2-week intervals on 259 infants studied in Sheffield in the 1970s. The charts are on sale from the Foundation (which has been granted the copyright) and are available in two sizes:-	
	For parents:	An envelope containing 2 × A1 centile weight charts (1 boy, 1 girl), weight chart instruction sheet, 6 × symptom charts, general information and green card giving advice on signs and symptoms of illness in babies.	£1 (incl P&P)

Title	Written for	Description of contents	Price per copy (Postage is extra)
	For Health Authorities:	A3 size centile weight charts for boys and girls, plus instructions.	10p per chart. Large orders of 1000 or more at 7p per chart. Postage and packing extra.
Sudden Infant Death: Patterns, Puzzles and Problems by J. Golding, S. Limerick and A. Macfarlane (1985) (Book)	Paediatricians, family doctors, social workers, parents	Contents: Part I: Setting the Scene; Part II: Epidemiological Studies; Part III: Possible Causes of Sudden Infant Death; Part IV: Reactions to Death; Part V: The Way Ahead?: Glossary; References; Index.	Paperback Edition is available from FSID £7.60 inclusive of packing. Published by Open Books, Beaumont House, New St, Wells, Somerset BA5 2LD
Videos: The US Dept of Health Education and Welfare films, *You Are Not Alone, After Our Baby Died, A Call For Help*	Bereaved parents, health professionals, police	*You Are Not Alone* (30 min) portrays the reactions of several couples to a sudden infant death, and is designed to help parents and professionals who are supporting newly bereaved families. *After Our Baby Died* (30 min) intended to arouse discussion about the counselling needs of bereaved parents and is meant to be introduced with a short talk about sudden infant deaths. *A Call For Help* (20 min) is a training film for police forces. It explains about sudden infant death syndrome and examines the immediate handling of a natural sudden infant death.	Films are available on video cassettes in 3 systems, VHS, Betamax and Sony U-Matic. The first two films are on one video cassette, the police film is separate. Each cassette may be borrowed from FSID. Please book in advance and send £3 to cover outgoing P & P. Return registered post to be paid additionally by the borrower.

TV South films *The Purple Line, My Beautiful Baby is Dead*	Public, health professionals and groups	*The Purple Line* (1 hour) H V Surveillance of 'high risk' infants. *My Beautiful Baby is Dead* (20 min) work of the Hampshire Parents Support Group.	Both films on same cassette. Available VHS, Betamax, Sony U-Matic
Leap for Life film *I'm Sorry Your Baby is Dead But I can't Tell You Why*	Health professionals, ambulance staff, police	Designed to help professionals understand the needs of bereaved parents (33 min).	VHS, Betamax, Sony U-Matic. For sale in VHS and Beta (£25 inc P & P)

References

BECKWITH, J. B. (1975). *The Sudden Infant Death Syndrome*. Washington, DC: US Department of Health, Education and Welfare

BERGMAN, A. B. (1979). The sudden infant death syndrome—what can you do? *Medical Times*, **107**, 32–36

BLACK, D. and URBANOWITZ, M. A. (1987). Family intervention with bereaved children. *Journal of Child Psychology and Psychiatry*, **28**, 467–476

BLUGLASS, K. (1978). Bereavement and sudden infant death syndrome. *Midlands Medical Review*, **13**, 30–37

BLUGLASS, K. (1979). Psychiatric morbidity after cot death. *Practitioner*, **224**, 533–539

BLUGLASS, K. (1981). Psychosocial aspects of the sudden infant death syndrome ('cot death'). *Journal of Child Psychology and Psychiatry*, **22**, 411–421

BLUGLASS, K. (1982). Problems with perinatal pathology. *British Medical Journal*, **285**, 736

BLUGLASS, K. (1984). Early infant loss and multiple congenital abnormalities. In: *Psychological Aspects of Genetic Counselling*, (A. E. H. Emery and I. M. Pullen, eds), London: Academic Press

BLUGLASS, K., GREEN, S. and PROOPS, R. (1980). The surviving twin. *British Medical Journal*, **i**, 1796

BOWLBY, J. (1969). Attachment and loss. In: *Separation: Anxiety and Anger*, Vol. 1, (M. M. R. Khan, ed.), London: Holgarth Press

BOWLBY, J. (1973). Attachment and loss. In *Separation: Anxiety and Anger*, Vol. 2, (M. M. R. Khan ed.), London: Holgarth Press

BROWN, G. W. and HARRIS, T. (1978). *Social Origins of Depression. A Study of Psychiatric Disorder in Women*. London: Tavistock Publications

BURTON, L. (1979). *The Family Life of Sick Children*. London: Routledge and Kegan Paul

CAIN, A. C. and CAIN, B. S. (1964). On replacing a child. *Journal of the American Academy of Child Psychiatry*, **3**, 433–456

CLAYTON, P. J., HALIKAS, J. A., MAURICE, W. L. and ROBINS, E. (1973). Anticipatory grief and widowhood. *British Journal of Psychiatry*, **122**, 47–51

CORNWELL, J., NURCOMBE, B. and STEVENS, L. (1977). Family response to loss of a child by sudden infant death syndrome. *Medical Journal of Australia*, **1**, 656–659

DEFRAIN, J. and ERNST, L. (1978). The psychological effects of sudden infant death on surviving family members. *Journal of Family Practice*, **6**, 895–99

DEFRAIN, J. and ERNST, L. (1982). *Coping with Sudden Infant Death*. Toronto: Lexington Books

DHSS (1985). *Post-Neonatal Mortality: A Multi-Centre Study Undertaken by the Medical Care Unit, University of Sheffield*. London: HMSO

D'ORBAN, P. T. (1979). Women who kill their children. *British Journal of Psychiatry*, **134**, 560–571

DROTAR, D. and IRVIN, N. (1979). Disturbed maternal bereavement after infant death. *Child Care, Health and Development*, **5**, 239–247

EMERY, A. E. H. and PULLEN, I. M. (1984). *Psychological Aspects of Genetic Counselling*. London: Academic Press

EMERY, J. L. (1972). Welfare of children found unexpectedly dead (cot death). *British Medical Journal*, **i**, 612–615

EMERY, J. L. (1983). The necropsy and cot death. *British Medical Journal*, **287**, 77–78

GOLDING, J., LIMERICK, S. and MACFARLANE, A. (eds) (1985). *Sudden Infant Death—Patterns, Puzzles and Problems*. Somerset: Open Books

GORER, G. (1965). *Death, Grief and Mourning in Contemporary Britain*. London: Cresset

HALPERN, W. I. (1972). Some psychiatric sequelae to crib death. *American Journal of Psychiatry*, **129**, 58–62

KENNELL, J. H., SLYTER, H. and KLAUS, M. K. (1970). The mourning response of parents to the death of a newborn infant. *New England Journal of Medicine*, **283**, 344–349

LANSKY, S. B. *et al.* (1979). Childhood cancer, non-medical costs of illness. *Cancer*, **43**, 403–408

LEWIS, E. (1976). The management of still-birth—coping with an unreality. *Lancet*, **ii**, 619–620

LEWIS, E. (1979). Inhibition of mourning by pregnancy. *British Medical Journal*, **ii**, 27–28

LEWIS, S. N. (1981a). Maternal anxiety following bereavement by cot death and emotional security of subsequent infants. *Child Psychiatry and Human Development*, **14**, 55–61

LEWIS, S. N. (1981b). Some psychological consequences of bereavement by sudden infant death syndrome. *Health Visitor*, **54**, 322–325

LIMERICK, S. R. L. (1984). In: *Sudden Infant Death—Patterns, Puzzles and Problems*, (J. Golding, S.R. L. Limerick, and A. Macfarlane, eds), p. 147. Somerset: Open Books

LONGFORD, E. (1964). *Victoria, R. I.* London: Pan Books

LUBEN, J. (1986). *Cot Death.* Northampton: Thorson Press

MANDELL, F. and WOLFE, L. (1975). Sudden infant death syndrome and subsequent pregnancy. *Pediatrics*, **56**, 774–776

MANDELL, F., MACANULTY, E. and REECE, R. (1980). Observations of paternal response to sudden unanticipated infant death. *Pediatrics*, **136**, 1152–1156

MARGISON, F. (1982). The pathology of the mother-child relationship. In: *Motherhood and Mental Illness*, (I. F. Brockington anda R. Kumar, eds), pp. 191–232. London: Academic Press

MAWSON, D., MARKS, I. M., RAMM, L. and STERN, R. S. (1981). Guided mourning for morbid grief: a controlled study. *British Journal of Psychiatry*, **138**, 185–93

DE MONTAIGNE, M. (1978). *Essais.* London: Athlone Press

OLSHANSKY, S. (1962). Chronic sorrow: a response to having a mentally defective child. *Social Casework*, **43**, 190

OPCS (1981). Mortality statistics: children. Review of the Registrar General on Deaths in England and Wales, 1981. Series DH3, No. 10. London: HMSO

OSTERWEISS, K., SOLOMON, F. and GREEN, M. (1984). *Bereavement: Reactions, Consequences and Care.* Washington: National Academy Press

PAGE-PHILLIPS, J. (1970). *Children on Brasses.* London: Allen and Unwin

PARKES, C. M. (1972). *Bereavement: Studies of Grief in Adult Life.* London: Tavistock Publications

PARKES, C. M. (1980). Bereavement counselling, does it work? *British Medical Journal*, **281**, 3–6

PARKES, C. M. (1984). Bereavement. *British Journal of Psychiatry*, **146,** 11–17

PARKES, C. M. and WEISS, R. S. (1983). *Recovery from Bereavement.* New York: Basic Books

PEPPERS, L. G. and KNAPP, R. J. (1980). *Motherhood and Mourning.* New York: Praeger

RAPHAEL, B. (1983). *The Anatomy of Bereavement.* London: Basic Books

RECORD, R. and ARMSTRONG, E. M. (1980). The influence of the birth of a malformed child on the mother's future reproduction. *British Journal of Preventative and Social Medicine*, **29**, 267–269

REES, W. D. (1971). The hallucinations of widowhood. *British Medical Journal*, **iv**, 37–41.

ROBERTS, J., GOLDING, J., KEELING, J., SUTTON, B. and LYNCH, M. A. (1984). Is there a link between cot death and child abuse? *British Medical Journal*, **289**, 789–91

ROBINSON, D. and HENRY, S. (1977). *Self-Help and Health—Mutual Aid for Modern Problems.* London: Robertson

SCHODT, C. M. (1976). *The Effect of Nursing Crisis Intervention on Maternal Response to the Loss of the Infant from Sudden Infant Death Syndrome.* Pennsylvania: School of Nursing

SILVERMAN, P. R. (1980). *Mutual Aid Groups—Organisation and Development.* London: Sage

SLUCKIN, W., HERBERT, M. and SLUCKIN, A. (1983). *Maternal Bonding.* Oxford: Blackwell

SMITH, S. M. (1979). *The Battered Child Syndrome.* London: Butterworths

SOLNIT, A. J. and STARK, M. H. (1961). Mourning and the birth of a defective child. *Psychoanalytic Study of the Child*, **6**, 523–527

VALDES DAPENA, M. (1980). Sudden infant death syndrome: a review of the medical literature 1974–79. *Pediatrics*, **66**, 597–614

WALZER, J. F. (1976). Survivors and surrogates. In: *The History of Childhood*, (L. de Mause, ed.), p. 153. London: Souvenir Press

WATSON, E. (1985). Changes in verdict of sudden infant deaths. *Lancet*, **i**, 635

WAYTE, D. (1984). Smothering, suffocation and cot death. *Lancet*, **i**, 114

WINNICOTT, D. W. (1964). *The Child, The Family, and the Outside World*. London: Penguin

WORDEN, J. W. (1983). *Grief Counselling and Grief Therapy*. London: Tavistock Publications

WRETMARK, G. (1959). A study in grief reactions. *Acta Psychiatrica Scandinavica, Suppl.*, **136**, 292–299

Chapter 10

The active management of perinatal death

Wendy Savage

Introduction

It is only comparatively recently that the medical and midwifery profes-
sions have begun to recognize how deeply parents grieve when a baby dies
soon before or after birth.

Fifty years ago one woman in 16 lost her baby in the perinatal period but
in addition one woman in 250 lost her own life in association with
pregnancy. It is therefore understandable that obstetricians have concentrated on the mother's physical, rather than on her emotional needs. Now,
one woman in 100 in England and Wales will leave hospital without a live
baby, but the risk of losing a baby is almost twice as high for working class
women as it is for middle and upper social classes (OPCS, 1987). Only one
woman in 10 000 now dies in association with pregnancy.

In England and Wales in 1986, 2789 women lost a baby in the first week
of life and 3549 gave birth to a stillborn child, whilst 661 018 women
delivered a live baby. On average, an obstetrician can therefore expect to
see between five and ten women a year who will experience a perinatal
death or, looked at another way, once every month or two he and his team
will need to comfort grieving parents. In addition, advances in prenatal
screening mean that one or two women a year in his practice will have a
pregnancy terminated because of a neural tube defect or a chromosome
anomaly. The grief that these women feel is similar to that experienced
when a baby is stillborn or dies neonatally (Lloyd and Laurence, 1985).

Women under 20 and over 35 years of age are more likely to leave
hospital without a live baby, and the loss may be experienced more keenly
by them, because young women are more likely to be unsupported mothers
or immigrants and those who are older may have had previous losses
including miscarriage, or they may have suffered from infertility.

Despite the fact that obstetricians have written extensively about
perinatal death and have used the fall in perinatal mortality rate as the
yardstick by which to measure the success of their management policies, it
is paediatricians and child psychiatrists in this country, and particularly
nurses in the USA, who have done most of the work with bereaved
parents. A child psychiatrist, Stanford Bourne, first drew attention to the
attitudes of doctors towards stillbirth. He circulated a questionnaire to the
general practitioners (GPs) of women who had had a stillborn baby and

compared the doctors' reactions to women whose babies had lived with their reactions to those who had stillbirths. Writing in 1968 Bourne stated: 'there was a strong reluctance for doctors to know, notice or remember about the woman who has had a stillbirth'. He also drew attention to the paucity of the medical literature on this common and devastating tragedy.

My own interest in the problem began in 1971 when I delivered a woman of a live baby one year after she had experienced a stillbirth due to an error of management (Savage, 1978a). The reluctance of the staff to discuss this episode and the way its significance was seemingly ignored puzzled me. I then began to notice how women who had delivered a stillborn child were given a separate room,'missed' by the ward round, not allocated a student and, if they defaulted from their postnatal appointment, were usually not given another one.

The first reference to the mixed emotions felt by women who had experienced a stillbirth and to the reactions of the nursing staff in a maternity ward, is contained in a study by a nurse in Boston (Bruce, 1962). She pointed out that nursing staff needed to recognize their own grief and guilt in order to deal sympathetically with the woman's feelings. Later that year McLenahan (1962), then Assistant Professor of Obstetric Nursing in Pittsburgh, wrote movingly about the feelings of nurses and mothers.

The growth of awareness of the importance of perinatal death

Amongst doctors, David Morris, Stanford Bourne and Emanuel Lewis have led a campaign to put perinatal bereavement on the medical agenda. In 1976, the section of paediatrics at the Royal Society of Medicine held a meeting entitled 'Family Reactions to Child Bereavement'. Morris (1976) and Jolly (1976) presented papers which were very influential in changing attitudes in maternity units in which paediatricians and obstetricians worked closely together. In the correspondence which followed, Parkes (1977) drew on his work with widows and discussed the importance of family and community involvement. Following this meeting, a study group was formed by Morris, a consultant paediatrician, who had worked with parents of stillborn babies as well as with those whose child had died after birth. He invited a number of people, including an obstetrician and midwives, a child psychiatrist from Charing Cross, Emanuel Lewis, and Hazelanne Lewis, a psychiatric social worker who had herself experienced perinatal bereavement. They wrote articles and produced a leaflet for parents which was published in the *British Medical Journal* (Beard *et al.*, 1978) and which was subsequently modified following comments. This leaflet was then published in conjunction with MIND and the Health Education Council, who circulated it to all consultant obstetricians in the country in 1979. Many copies of this leaflet have been circulated and kept by staff for educational purposes (Morris, 1983).

Hazelanne Lewis founded the Stillbirth Society in 1976 and this group has worked hard to educate the professionals involved and, in addition, has provided support for bereaved parents. In 1984 the name of the Society was changed to the Stillbirth And Neonatal Death Society (SANDS).

In 1978, the National Childbirth Trust brought professionals together with women who had experienced a perinatal loss in a series of seminars led by Kathy Sylva, a child psychologist; she was herself, like many of the participants, a bereaved mother. These multidisciplinary discussions led to the publication of a series of papers in midwifery journals (Savage 1978; Bourne, 1979; Sylva and Bryce, 1979), thus bringing the theory and practice of the management of stillbirth to the attention of the midwifery profession.

It seems obvious that helping a couple to come to terms with their grief will reduce the mourning period and will help them to rebuild their lives again after their tragedy. Negative outcomes following badly handled perinatal deaths have been reported on an individual level, and the importance of perinatal bereavement as a trigger for long lasting mental illness still represents an unanswered question. The emotions felt by bereaved parents are as deep as those following the loss of an adult member of the family, and stillbirth itself is more difficult to cope with, if the quality of 'unreality' which was described by Lewis (1976) is not recognized.

Describing the reactions of women and the family to perinatal death

Although the physical and psychological reactions of the acutely bereaved person were described by Lindemann (1944), it was not until 1963 that Williams, in Australia, reiterated the importance of the doctor's role in helping parents to understand their child's death. He stressed the need to educate students about bereavement. Bruce (1962) had made a similar point about the education of nurses when she described the confused emotions of 25 women who had delivered a stillborn child and of the 25 graduate nurses who had cared for them.

In 1970, a group from Chicago (Wolff and Nielson, 1970) reported on 40 of 50 women who had been followed for 1–3 years after delivering a stillborn child. They conducted several interviews in the postpartum period in which women were able to ventilate their feelings and they found no serious psychiatric sequelae. All subjects had experienced a typical grief reaction and, by the end of the study, half of them had become pregnant again. The women were not randomly selected and it seems possible that those who do become significantly depressed or otherwise disturbed may be less likely to enter such a study and more likely to drop out during follow-up. Kennell, Slyter and Klaus (1970) described the 'mourning response of parents to the death of a newborn infant', and in a study of 20 mothers they noted that contact with the sick baby enhanced the ability to mourn.

The first Commonwealth obstetrician to write about perinatal death was Giles (1970) from Perth in Australia. He interviewed 40 women who had lost babies in the perinatal period, 20 of whom had definite views about seeing a stillborn or very sick child at delivery. Six out of the 20 women were glad that they had done so and 14 had not wanted to, fearing that it would 'imprint the child too strongly in their minds'. Fifteen had strong opinions about seeing the child after death, eight were against it and seven felt, 'as one woman put it, "that every woman would want to, though it would break her heart"'. He also found that they had varying reactions to sedation, the use of single rooms and the sort of help they had from doctors. Giles concluded that: 'Although doctors treated the women's physical symptoms and prescribed sedatives liberally, in about half of the cases they avoided discussing the death of the baby. These women need a sympathetic listener and his reassuring explanation to remove misconceptions and guilt, and to provide confidence for the future.'

Cullberg (1972) reported that 19 of 56 mothers who had lost their babies in the perinatal period had developed severe psychiatric disorders including psychoses, anxiety attacks, phobias, obsessive thoughts and deep depressions in the 1–2-year period following the death. Four other bereaved mothers had moved away and two more could not be contacted for follow-up. It is not clear from his paper how many were still experiencing symptoms at the follow-up interview, but he noted that the 11 women who initially had 'no reaction' were more likely to take longer to recover from their grief and they took longer to return to work. He thought that only nine women had been helped by professionals to understand the emotions roused by the death and in four cases the support had been provided by a nurse.

In 1978 I wrote about the reactions of the staff as well as of the mother to perinatal loss (Savage, 1978b). Obstetricians and midwives need to understand the normal grief reaction of shock and disbelief, followed by anger, guilt and shame, sadness, and the importance of explanation and the usefulness of the post-mortem examination as well as the difficulties associated with obtaining consent. It is essential to help the doctor and midwife, as well as the parents, to realize what has happened, so that they can all come to terms with the loss.

How to help the bereaved parents

Before 1970 it was common practice for the parents not to be shown their stillborn child and for the body to be wrapped up and taken out of the delivery room. Hospitals usually offered to dispose of the child. In the USA the child was usually cremated and in the UK it shared a common grave or had no gravestone. We all thought we were helping the parents, saving them the trauma of making funeral arrangements and the expense of burying the child. Experience has taught us that we were wrong. We were preventing the parents from taking the practical steps which could help them to accept the reality of the stillborn child. Not all parents want to be involved, however, as was shown by Cooper (1980), who followed up 17 sets of parents after stillbirth; none of them wanted to see the child or to take part in a funeral. On the other hand, Lewis and Page (1978) have vividly described some of the reactions of parents if there is no funeral.

> The atmosphere was tense. The mother explained that she was too upset and incompetent to be trusted with her baby. She hated her daughter (i.e. the live newborn) . . . we asked her to tell us about her dead baby. She sobbed convulsively, and through her sobs she said that she felt that the dead woman in the common grave would not take proper care of her son.

> Procedures vary around the country . . . anything from one to two hundred babies can be buried together in the same grave. Some funeral directors for the

same money will allow the parents to attend the funeral; other hospitals will not even tell the parents where the baby is buried, although actually they do have the right to know. (Lewis, 1982)

It is important, therefore, for a senior person to discuss the wishes and needs of individual parents.

Seeing and holding the dead baby, keeping a photograph or a memento such as a lock of hair or, in the USA, footprints, naming the baby and holding a religious ceremony to mark the baby's existence, albeit *in utero* in the case of a stillbirth, can help the parents and friends to grieve and can overcome the 'conspiracy of silence'.

The reactions of the mother

Shock is usually the first reaction when a women herself detects the loss of fetal movements, or to the news that others cannot hear the fetal heart (a professional diagnosis). Shock may be followed by numbness, disbelief or denial. The woman who reported to my registrar that she had felt no movements for two days, said, when she saw me a week later 'I can feel the movements again—the doctor told me that there was a 95% chance that the baby was dead'. I listened. There was no fetal heart. Her husband also heard the silence when the handheld ultrasound failed to pick up the heart beat. They listened to my explanations about placental sounds and how perception of wind in the bowel could be interpreted as fetal movements. The mother burst into tears, 'If there was even a 5% chance why did the doctor send me home? Perhaps the baby could have been saved'. She and her husband were eventually able to accept that it was the doctor's way of trying to soften the blow and not having to say the words, 'I'm sorry but your baby has died'.

Intervention before the woman has accepted emotionally that the baby has died may lead to later difficulties, but leaving the woman for too long before induction of labour is performed may make her feel like 'a walking coffin'. One midwife described to me the need of one of her patients to wash herself obsessively during labour because she felt 'unclean'. Some women feel 'nothing'—the numbness and emptiness expressed as a calm demeanour which the staff may welcome, thinking that the woman is 'taking it well' but this reaction may be followed by delayed and long lasting grief. Personal accounts which describe very well the severity and length of the grief which follows a perinatal death have been written in recent years by Oglethorpe (1983) in this country and Elliot and Hein (1978) in the USA. After the initial acute symptoms of grief have passed, the woman may be surprised and shocked to find that she may relive the whole experience some months after the event and that the first annivers-ary of the death may also be followed by a period of renewed sadness. Few women will have recovered fully from a perinatal death until at least this time is past although some women may feel that after six months they are coping reasonably well.

Guilt is prominent in the feelings of women who have lost a baby in the perinatal period; they search for an explanation and criticize themselves for actions such as drinking, smoking or sexual activity during pregnancy or their lapses in attendance at clinics, failures to follow the doctor's instructions or not eating the right foods. They often feel that they have failed and blame themselves, in particular their bodies, which have let them down and not produced a live baby.

Anger may be displayed towards members of the obstetric team, especially if they are perceived as cold or unsympathetic (Anonymous, 1987). If there have been failures in care or communication, hostility may be expressed in formal complaints or litigation; this is especially likely if there has been negligence which has been denied by the professionals, or, if the problems have not been shared honestly with the couple. A woman whose baby suffered anoxic brain damage accepted the explanation that although the second stage of labour had lasted too long and her desire for operative help with the delivery and her feeling of exhaustion had not been understood, this was not deliberate. Duty staff had made genuine attempts to do their best, but with hindsight one could see where mistakes had been made. She sought compensation, which was justified. Months later she was able to express her anger to me about the doctors who had looked after her.

Acceptance and search for meaning follow the stage of yearning and confusion, but these 'stages' do not follow each other as neatly as set out here. Confusion may be worsened by different members of staff explaining the events using different words, and misunderstanding can add to the woman's distress.

Reconstruction of the woman's life after a period of mourning may take different forms. For example, many primigravid women soon become pregnant again, whereas multigravidae may seek sterilization, or they may find a new job. For some women involvement in, or starting a self-help organization, writing or making a film about their experience, makes a positive contribution to their recovery by helping other couples who have lost a baby.

The reaction of the family

In our society men are expected to control their emotions more than women, to support their partners after a baby has died, to cope with the registration of the birth and death, and to return to work quickly as if nothing had happened. However, a man can experience grief which may be more severe than that of his partner. He also may feel a failure especially if the child has died as a result of a congenital abnormality (Johns, 1971). It is no longer common to tell the man about an intrauterine death and to ask him to keep this knowledge from the mother until she has delivered. This added burden of responsibility not only weighed heavily on the man but by disrupting the shared experience of the parents has in my experience created difficulties—in one case leading to marital disharmony and sexual withdrawal for over two years.

Wijma and coworkers (1983) have compared mothers' and fathers' reactions in 10 couples out of 15 selected from those who had had an intrauterine death in one hospital in the Netherlands in one year. They found that men were less likely to be depressed than their partners. They tended to react more 'rationally', and to cope with the loss themselves rather than talk about it with other people. These workers considered that the men tended to suppress their emotions, felt excluded by the obstetrician or other people present at the birth, and were ambivalent about their emotions, on one hand wanting to deal with their feelings alone but on the other resenting the attention paid to their wives. In other studies in which the father is mentioned, his own voice is incompletely or rarely heard and his own emotional needs are rarely recognized by professionals (Lewis, 1976; Bourne, 1983).

Because parents may go through the stages of grief at different rates there are ample opportunities for misunderstandings. Coupled with differing patterns of sexual response (loss of libido or increased sexual desire as a means of showing closeness or reassurance), relationships can be broken if partners are not aware of each others' reactions. Kennell and Trause (1978) describe a pattern of increased activity that is displayed by some American fathers and they comment that inability to share the sadness may drive the couple apart.

The effect of a stillbirth on the children of the family has been described by Elliot and Hein (1978) from a personal viewpoint, the idealization of the replacement child by Cain and Cain (1964), Poznanski (1972), Lewis (1982), and Lewis and Page (1978), and the disturbed reactions of children harbouring destructive fantasies by Lewis (1972). Earl (1978) mentioned that 'grandparents, too, can feel bereaved. My wife and I were, I think, surprised at our own sense of loss'. Cooper (1980) found that sharing the emotions within the extended family was helpful whilst Lewis (1982) described the break-up of a close family after a disastrous stillbirth during which the mother herself was in danger.

The next pregnancy is a time of stress for the whole family and the parents may be saddened and surprised by their mixed feelings towards the new baby—especially if the child is conceived too soon after the previous child's death (Lewis and Page, 1978).

The long-term effects of perinatal death have not been systematically studied over several years. Individual case studies suggest that the effect of a perinatal death can be felt and reactivated after many years and it may even affect the children of a bereaved family when they become parents themselves. One woman who was admitted several times during her pregnancy with abdominal pain for which no cause was found, finally revealed that her mother had delivered three abnormal babies that had died in the neonatal period. Discussion about her feelings as a child coupled with genetic advice enabled her to remain out of hospital and she had a normal delivery of a healthy child at term. Another woman was always accompanied by her silent but palpably anxious mother. It was only after her successful delivery that the woman told me that her mother had experienced a stillbirth in the pregnancy before she herself had been born.

The active management of perinatal death

The fundamental principles of what I have called the 'active management of perinatal death' are set out below:

(1) Honesty with the woman and her partner.
(2) Discussion of treatment or management options with parents.

(3) Clear delineation of responsibilities of the medical/midwifery team.
(4) Consultant involvement with couple and staff.
(5) Recognition of denial and shock thus allowing time for the woman to reverse initial decisions.
(6) Continuity of care and responsibility by one medical person.

The discussion of treatment or management options includes decisions about seeing and touching the dead baby, naming and/or blessing the child, speaking to the hospital chaplain and whether or not to have a funeral. I share my experience both personal and that gained from the literature to encourage the couple to see and hold their dead baby and to commemorate the death in some way.

Case example   One young woman was deserted by her steady boyfriend of five years soon after she embarked on the pregnancy that they both had planned. She had a baby with intrauterine growth retardation (Potter's syndrome* was suspected but not proven until after birth), and was delivered under general anaesthetic because the baby developed fetal distress. Soon after she woke I asked her if she wished to see the baby who had died. She did not. I asked the midwives to keep the baby overnight in the labour ward, and the next day I spoke to her again and explained that I had never seen a woman who regretted seeing her dead baby but many others had told me how they had regretted not doing so when they had got over the initial shock. I carried the dead baby wrapped in a shawl to her in the single bay in the antenatal ward. As I uncovered his head, discoloured on the side he had been lying overnight, she said 'Isn't he beautiful', and held out her arms. She commented on his fair hair, and remembered that part of her baby whilst accepting his small shrunken chest and the lividity naturally and completely. I left her alone with him so she could say goodbye and later she was able to persuade her mother against her initial objections (her father had died the year before) that a family funeral would be the right course to take. The baby was buried in the family grave and despite her sadness at the loss of her baby, of her boyfriend and of her father all within a year, she grieved and had recovered to take up her everyday life by the time she was interviewed a year later.

Discussion with the parents

It is best to discuss the stillbirth with the parents in an informal way because they are likely to be feeling confused, sad and angry and to be going through the mourning sequence at different rates. There may be a secondary revival of mourning after they think they have overcome the initial sadness. They may find that their friends have difficulties in expressing their own sadness and sympathy, and hence may feel even more empty and lonely on returning home. They may have physical symptoms, possibly 'hallucinations' of the dead child, and feelings of jealousy when

---

*Potter's syndrome is a congenital abnormality of unknown aetiology in which the kidneys do not develop or are extremely hypoplastic. There is poor lung development associated with the reduction in liquor, and the babies have a 'pixie' like face.

seeing other women with a new baby. It is important not to overload parents with sets of instructions, but better to listen and to answer questions. The staff should discuss how best to do this so that they do not use different terminology which can further confuse the woman. Everyone who speaks to her should record the salient features of their discussion in the notes so that the next midwife or junior doctor who sees her is aware of what has been said. All questions should be answered honestly and one's lack of knowledge about the reasons for a particular death should be clearly stated. The admission of obstetric errors which may have prevented a death is a delicate matter and the parent's feelings of guilt and blame should not be reinforced by refusals of staff to accept responsibility where it is due. The situation I find most difficult is one in which the error is not my own but that of a member of the junior staff to whom I have delegated responsibility. Being honest with the parents whilst not blaming the trainee doctor or midwife can be very difficult (Savage, 1986), especially if the other person has handled the parents badly because of inexperience or personal distress at death.

The management of an intrauterine death

In the case of an intrauterine death the woman is involved in decisions about the necessity for induction and its timing and mode. Fears can be aired about the way the baby will look after being dead inside the uterus for some time. I explain that although the skin may peel the liquor helps to preserve the baby. Some women fear that the body may be putrefied; one woman was able to share her fear about maggots which she had seen on dead animals after some days in a warm climate. I used to think that nothing could be worse than going through the pain of labour without a live baby to show for it, but I have learnt that 'doing the labour well' can reassure many women that they are not complete failures. I also think that the heavy sedation we used in the past, or the well-meaning offers of an epidural nowadays, may contribute to the unreality of the experience of stillbirth. I discuss these matters beforehand, and some women have commented to me afterwards that the labour was less painful than previous labours and that they were glad not to have missed the physical sensations of birth. But one cannot generalize that one particular course is right for all women. If after my explanation a mother wants an epidural I will help her to have one. Anticipatory mourning does occur and obstetricians may find it easier to deal with intrauterine death than with intrapartum stillbirths or very early neonatal deaths, in which their own feelings of regret and guilt may intrude. These reactions may interfere with their ability to help the parents adequately. Junior medical or midwifery staff often have to deal with perinatal death (Smith, 1977) and calling the consultant as soon as possible can help trainee obstetricians and paediatricians to cope with their own feelings by allowing them to observe a more experienced person's technique. It is also beneficial for the parents who appreciate the consultant's presence and greater experience, and it helps to ensure continuity of care.

Viewing a child with a congenital abnormality

Most people's fantasies are worse than the reality, and parents usually retain some positive image of the dead baby; they may forget or not see the abnormality in the way that professionals do. Sensitivity is essential. Forcing a couple to look at a severely deformed baby can be as traumatic and wounding as careless or callous remarks by the staff. The child should be wrapped in a shawl or towel, held in one's arms like a live newborn baby and shown to the parents. One can then explain in simple words what the abnormality is, and if one or other of the parents wishes to hold the baby, pass the baby to them. Some will want to unwrap the coverings themselves, some prefer the doctor or midwife to do it. After the initial explanation it is better to let the parents ask questions than to embark on a long theoretical lecture—intellectualization being a coping mechanism often used by doctors. The way in which some mothers have already built up a picture of a baby which extends far into the future was brought home to me when talking to an 18-year-old about her baby who died soon after birth with hydranencephaly. She wanted to know how handicapped he would have been had he lived, and whether this would have affected his ability to have children. There is so much variation between individuals that one must be guided by their questions and responses and not think that 'checklists' can meaningfully structure these discussions. Checklists (Beckley et al., 1985) may nevertheless be useful aide memoires for staff to ensure that all aspects of management are dealt with.

Breaking the news

If possible it is best to have both partners present, or a friend or relative in the case of a single mother. A woman who fears for her baby's safety because of absent or diminished fetal movements often brings someone with her to the clinic. It is worth checking this before listening for the fetal heart and asking her if she wants the person to come in with her. Since the advent of ultrasound, the absence of the fetal heart sounds cannot be denied by the obstetrician or midwife, but often confirmation of this by real-time ultrasound or by the use of X-rays to show Spalding's sign* or gas in the great vessels is as useful to couples as it is to the obstetrician in establishing the reality of the baby's death.

Radiographers, according to their code of practice, cannot communicate results to patients and this can cause problems as couples can see the ultrasound pictures. The training of radiographers should include some instruction in how to deal with intrauterine death or fetal abnormality if they are to continue to deal with the majority of ultrasound scans performed on pregnant women in England and Wales. Moves are being made to allow them to talk more freely to patients. In the meantime, a sufficiently senior obstetrician or midwife who knows the woman should be called to explain the results. Sending the woman home to await the next antenatal clinic is indefensible.

---

*Spalding's sign is overlapping of the skull bones as the brain tissue begins to lessen in volume.

In the labour ward it is essential to share one's fears with the woman; relays of increasingly senior staff listening for the fetal heart, looking worried, but smiling reassuringly, have the effect of destroying any confidence that the woman has in the clinical team. Phases that soften the bald statement that one cannot hear the fetal heart are also important, 'I'm sorry but I can't hear your baby's heart' is accurate and conveys sympathy whereas 'I'm not sure if the heart beat is still there' implies that something more should be done such as calling another person who may be better at hearing it or getting a different machine. Statements such as 'the fetal heart has gone' may be interpreted as cold or uncaring by the bereaved parents who are acutely sensitive to the way messages are conveyed.

If the condition of the baby is poor at birth, one must admit one's uncertainty when the woman asks 'Is the baby alright?' Saying that the baby is being a bit slow to breathe but suction is being done or oxygen given or a tube is being passed to help breathing informs and reassures the couple, whereas saying 'yes' to this question when the paediatrician or midwife are anxiously working on the baby, does not. If the baby is obviously malformed, an appropriate response which is gently informative will be accepted whilst bland reassurance when sight of the baby is withheld is not. This is a situation which requires experience, and calling the obstetric and paediatric consultants immediately may help everybody when the baby has finally expired.

In the case of the sick neonate, especially in the neonatal intensive care unit, paediatricians usually know when a baby is no longer responding to treatment and can arrange for the person who knows the couple to come, even if the initial breaking of the news is done by one of the doctors in the unit. Decisions about holding the baby after disconnecting life support systems so that the infant can die in its parent's arms can also be discussed in some cases, and arrangements made for other family members to come to support the parents.

The post-mortem examination and arrangements for registration and burial

I always used to find it very difficult to ask the parents to consent to a post-mortem, but as I learnt more about parents' reactions to perinatal death it became clear that, handled carefully, this could be useful in helping the parents in their 'search for meaning' and eventual acceptance of the death. It is important to explain that in about half of cases no additional information can be found about the reason for the death. In such cases many parents find it comforting that the baby is internally normal, whereas obstetricians tend to feel even worse that they have lost a 'normal baby'. One must also allow the couple to express any fantasies they may have about the post-mortem itself. Arranging a visit in one or two weeks to discuss the report prevents the long wait until the traditional six-week postnatal examination, which should not be held in a routine postnatal clinic along with mothers and their healthy babies. It is important that a special appointment is made with adequate time for discussion in some other place such as in the gynaecological clinic.

Forrest, Standish and Baum (1981) wrote about the formalities of registration of a stillbirth and neonatal death. Parents have often not understood why they have to do the former and have been upset by the fact that they were not able to register the baby's name if stillborn (due to the efforts of the Stillbirth Society this has now been changed). Burial can be arranged for stillborn babies by the hospital, and a gravestone can be erected at a later date. It is possible to arrange for babies to be given a funeral at less cost than for an adult, and hospitals should be aware of local arrangements. The same holds for the burial of babies under 28 weeks and such information may be important if one twin is stillborn and another lives for a few hours. Information about such formalities should be incorporated in the labour ward protocol (Horwell, 1983).

Other practical points in management

Women should be offered the choice of a single room or a bed in the postnatal ward with other mothers and babies. If they have been in hospital for a long time antenatally, they may prefer to return to the ward where they know patients and staff—but in that case the doctor must prepare the other women in the ward, many of whom are at high risk or have already lost a baby, by breaking the news to them and explaining the grief reaction briefly. On the few occasions a woman has chosen this option I have been impressed by the support the other woman have given to the bereaved mother. The provision of a bed for the partner in a single room can be enormously helpful to both, as the woman often sleeps poorly and wakes in the night desperately lonely without her baby. If the partner does not stay, he should be allowed unlimited visiting, and the woman's preferences about other visitors should be accepted.

In busy units some method of marking the notes and the room, e.g. using a coloured sticker, will prevent the unthinking hurtfulness of staff members asking casually about the baby. 'Handover' between different staff members should ensure that all know what has happened. Having as few people as possible looking after the woman is important and one doctor should be given responsibility for her overall management.

The leaflet *The Loss of Your Baby* can be given before going to the postnatal ward and can help the woman when she wakes and does not want to disturb the midwives, but it is important that this is seen as an adjunct to talking and being with the woman—not a substitute which enables the staff to avoid her. Sedation is usually unhelpful, and it is better for the woman to have a hot milky drink over which she talks with the midwife in the middle of the night rather than an automatic nighttime hypnotic which leaves her feeling confused and detached the next day.

Lactation is often an unwelcome surprise and needs to be discussed—few women have chosen to have suppression with bromocryptine since I began to discuss this. Some women have offered to donate milk to the milk bank and should be allowed to express their maternal feelings in this way if they wish to do so.

If early discharge is chosen by the woman, as it often is, the GP and midwife should be told by the obstetrician before discharge and it is often helpful if the woman can be seen in hospital by them, with the staff who know the circumstances of the baby's death.

If the perineum is intact, intercourse may be resumed earlier than if a live baby is waking the parents, so contraception should be discussed and the possibility that sexual feelings may differ between the couple (some people wanting the closeness and warmth of sexual expression whereas the other partner loses all libido) in the postpartum period can be introduced. I advise them not to embark upon a pregnancy until at least six months after the birth and give them the evidence for that advice, and tell them both at discharge and at further follow-up to expect the mourning process to last for six months to a year.

Suggesting that a relative informs their family and friends can avoid painful encounters whilst the couple are still in a state of shock. If the woman is isolated I try and get her to stay in hospital a bit longer—in the gynaecology ward if she finds that more acceptable—and with her permission inform her social worker if she has one, her local priest or contact SANDS. The London Hospital now has a bereavement service staffed by volunteers trained by Dr C. Murray Parkes and this initiative is likely to spread to other units in time.

In the case of an abnormality, genetic counselling may be arranged and appropriate blood tests done before the postnatal visit. If a caesarean section has been done, X-rays of the pelvis should be obtained so that all possible information is available to the mother prior to her next pregnancy. The GP then continues follow-up, unless the woman seems to be developing an abnormal grief reaction in which case referral to a psychiatrist can be offered.

As well as the routine postnatal check at six weeks, another appointment at 2–3 weeks with the consultant or registrar who has cared for the couple to discuss the post-mortem findings is important. Many couples have reported distress when attending after the long wait for this information at six weeks only to find that they are met by a new doctor in a busy clinic, the result of the post-mortem is not in the notes and cannot be found. This visit may be arranged in the community where the GP and health visitor can sit in if the couple want this formal transfer of care.

Support for the medical and midwifery staff can be shared between the consultant and a senior midwife. Kirk (1984) has described the programme at Oregon Health Sciences University where in 208 cases of perinatal death, over 70% follow-up was achieved using a nurse coordinator; discussions with the staff were part of this scheme. Medical students should also be included in discussions about the case and enabled to discuss their own feelings.

How do doctors and midwives learn to cope with perinatal death?

It is by no means certain that medical students and doctors in training are adequately prepared to face a woman who has lost her baby. The support available to them to cope with their own feelings is variable, and it may well be related to the fortuitious presence of an individual who is there at the right time rather than to a supportive system based on knowledge of the reactions of doctors and patients.

Survey of medical and midwifery schools' teaching

In 1984 I undertook a questionnaire study in which I asked all the Professors of Obstetrics and Gynaecology in the UK and Eire about, firstly, the education given to medical students about the management of perinatal death, postnatal depression, psychology of pregnancy and psychosexual problems and, secondly, about the in-service education that was given to their trainee doctors about the management of perinatal death.

By August 1985, replies had been received from all of the medical schools. There were 25 undergraduate and two postgraduate schools in England, one each in Wales and Northern Ireland, four in Scotland and five in Eire, a total of 37. Only one professor considered that the topic of perinatal bereavement was outside the scope of undergraduate teaching, and 85% of them completed the questionnaires themselves, suggesting that they thought this was an important subject.

All 153 midwifery schools in England were circulated with a similar questionnaire and two-thirds of the midwifery tutors replied to a single mailing.

Results of the survey
The results showed that 60% of the schools taught about the management of perinatal death during the obstetric course, and 54% used formal lectures and 92% had seminars or discussion groups to teach about the psychology of pregnancy, perinatal death, postnatal depression and psychosexual problems. Almost all said that these topics were taught on ward rounds and 81% reported that perinatal meetings were also held for teaching purposes. The midwifery tutors who replied (66%) all said they devoted many more hours of formal teaching by lectures and in seminars to this topic, but rather fewer considered ward rounds and perinatal meetings suitable for teaching. Midwives were also much more likely than obstetricians to involve outside professionals such as psychologists, psychiatrists and social workers and also lay counsellors and self-help groups.

The greatest contrast was in the use of video tapes, films and books (*see* Appendix 1); 64% of the midwifery tutors used films and videotapes (e.g. Bel Mooney's film about stillbirth and a recent TV film *The Lost Babies*) and almost 90% recommended a number of books including *Minds, Mothers and Midwives* which could usefully be read by medical students and doctors, whereas only 35% of the medical schools used visual material and only two mentioned specific books. The responses of the 13 schools that mentioned films or videos all referred to postnatal depression or psychosexual problems. Seven schools mentioned books mostly of a general nature; two had a recommended reading list and *Sexual Problems in Medical Practice* by Judy Greenwood was mentioned by one, and *Postnatal Depression* by Vivian Welbourne and *Motherhood and Mental*

Illness (Brockington and Kumar, 1982) by another. One medical and one midwifery school mentioned taped discussions with the parents.

Practical management of perinatal death
There were some differences in practice (midwifery tutors were not asked this question as they were not responsible for hospital policy) and all the respondents replied 'yes' to the question 'are couples encouraged to see the dead child?', although one said 'allowed', and one questioned the word 'encouraged' and a third said 'if they wished'. In only half of the units was a specific doctor given responsibility for the couple—and one of those where they were not replied that specific midwives were given this responsibility. 90% of the units gave the woman a choice of a single room or a bed in the ward and almost two-thirds arranged an appointment to discuss the post-mortem result within three weeks of the birth. None of the Irish and 68% of the British schools gave the parents the leaflet *The Loss of Your Baby*. One of those who did not use it wrote that they preferred individual counselling and had links with a lay group who provided postnatal support at home.

Student involvement
Almost a fifth of the schools routinely excluded students from the care of a woman with an intrauterine death during labour and one gave as the reason 'the possibility that the student was unprepared to cope'. Fewer (10%) did not expect students to care for women who had had a stillborn baby or whose infant was sick, and another 40% said that their involvement was variable depending both on the wishes of the parents and on the views of individual consultants. The chances of a student being involved with a woman who had a perinatal death ranged from the lowest figure of one or two deaths per set of 25 students to the highest of 11 per set of 20 students, which would suggest that at best no more than one student in four is likely to gain first hand experience. In practice I have found that unless a consultant is actively involved, the duty staff often 'forget' to include the student which probably means that less than 10% of students are able to observe the poignancy of the situation directly.

Training of junior doctors in the management of perinatal death
Seventy-four per cent of the respondents said that they did not have formal training for junior staff in the management of perinatal death. Descriptions by the remainder of how this was done, suggested that only six of the ten who considered they did have 'formal' training, had a programme. The others relied on informal teaching with the trainee sitting in with the consultant or by means of perinatal mortality meetings. One of the six schools mentioned the DRCOG course and three had regular seminars, two with the paediatricians, and one mentioned specific instruction by obstetric and paediatric consultants. The last school had regular meetings once every six months for junior doctors run by a member of SANDS who lived nearby.

In response to the questions 'Do you have any meetings specifically designed so that junior staff can meet and discuss the emotional impact of perinatal death on (a) patients and (b) staff. If yes, please describe and if no, do you think such a group would be valuable?' over 60% answered 'no' to both questions. Of those who answered 'yes', most dealt with these emotions as they arose in the course of weekly clinical or less frequent perinatal meetings and not at a *specific* meeting. Three met irregularly at anywhere between monthly or six-monthly intervals. Regular meetings to deal with the staff emotions were held in only three schools, two run by psychiatrists and one by the hospital chaplain.

A similar proportion of the midwifery tutors said that specific meetings were held to deal with feelings, 38% for patients and 34% for staff, but 75% of them thought it would be a good idea to hold such a meeting and only 10% felt it would not be useful.

How did the teachers rate their training?

Only three of the professors rated their training as good, 23 (almost 60%) said their training was adequate and one said it was improving. Eleven rated it as poor, and four of these ratings were made by the six individuals who completed the questionnaire on behalf of their professors—a statistically significant difference in perception.

As far as medical student teaching was concerned, almost half thought that their teaching was adequate (although one commented that a six-week course was too short), a third thought it was not, and the remainder were unsure. By contrast, 85% of the midwifery tutors rated their teaching as good and only 2% saw the training in practical management as poor, which probably reflected the greater breadth of their programmes and their personal involvement in practical training with the small groups of students during an 18-month training period.

What do trainees think of their training?

After analysing the responses of the teachers, I circulated a questionnaire to 112 doctors for whom I could find an address of the 118 who had worked in the Obstetrics Department of the London Hospital in the seven years between 1977 and 1984. Replies were received (after three mailings) from 98 doctors (almost 90%). They were asked to rate their training as poor, adequate or good, to make suggestions for improvements, whether they now felt able to cope with parents who had experienced a perinatal death, if other parts of their training had helped and whether they felt their own feelings had been adequately dealt with at the time they were in training.

Two-thirds rated their training as poor and only seven as good; 75% of the respondents had done only six months of training in obstetrics as senior house officers. Of the remainder who had trained for longer and in higher grades (registrars or senior registrars), half rated their training as adequate or good compared with only 20% of the junior trainees (SHOs), a difference which is statistically significant ($P<0.01$). The seniors were not more likely to have attended formal teaching, films or seminars than the SHOs but they had had more practical experience of perinatal deaths. Two doctors felt that they could not cope with a perinatal death and a further 14 were uncertain about their abilities for all categories of perinatal death, i.e. intrauterine prior to labour, intrapartum stillbirth and neonatal death and another eight were unsure about an intrapartum death, i.e. those in which their own feelings of guilt or responsibility would be most likely to be present.

Thirty-four doctors thought that their own emotions had been dealt with adequately, 12 were unsure and 51 said that they were not dealt with. Two who had become obstetricians, wrote: 'It hadn't occurred to me that my own feelings were important', and 'I don't think much help can be given here'; a third wrote, 'I think I was partly at fault in that I did not want to become "involved" in these situations. Now, when one is going to see the couple in subsequent pregnancies, the importance of this management together with laying down some degree of rapport for the future becomes apparent.'

Nineteen doctors had regularly attended a weekly support group run by a child psychiatrist which had been held over a two-year period, and six had attended on one occasion. Those with regular attendance were much more likely to have rated their training as good and expressed positive feelings about the usefulness of this session in helping them to understand and deal with their own emotions. Some of the doctors had also attended seminars as students and Marks (1986) has shown that students did remember the theoretical and practical aspects of the management of perinatal death that they had been taught, and in my study several commented that this background was helpful when they came to their SHO posts in obstetrics. As one of the 118 trainees who were surveyed wrote, 'the meetings were a tremendous help to all of us, giving us permission to admit to feelings and fears and to discover we were not alone with these feelings, and opportunity to talk about one's emotional reactions, doubt, guilt in a safe place—no danger of criticisms/blame/being labelled as not tough enough to cope with the work'. Psychiatrists can offer their assistance in running such groups, which from the survey of professors would I think be accepted by some academic departments of obstetrics, and from informal discussions, I suspect, many district hospital departments.

Does the active management of perinatal death work?

Parkes (1980) reviewed the literature about bereavement counselling in relation to adult deaths and concluded that:

> The evidence presented here suggests that professional services and professionally supported voluntary and self-help groups are capable of reducing the risk of psychiatric and psychosomatic disorders resulting from bereavement. Services are most beneficial amongst bereaved people who perceive their families as unsupportive or who, for other reasons, are thought to be at special risk. We should not assume that every bereaved person will need counselling, but those who do need it seem to benefit from opportunities to express grief, reassurances about the normality of the physiological accompaniments of grief, and the chance to take stock of their life situation and to start discovering new directions.

Anecdotally doctors accept that a perinatal death is more likely than a live birth to be followed by psychiatric disturbance, and Pitt (1968) and Rees and Lutkins (1967) showed in a hospital sample and in general practice that depression was more common following a perinatal death than after a normal delivery. Clarke and Williams (1979) questioned these findings and, in their important population study, all women who had experienced a perinatal death in Leicestershire were asked to complete the Beck inventory at 48 h, six weeks and six months postpartum. As expected, women who had experienced a perinatal death were more likely to have high scores confirming depression at the two earlier points than women who had had a live birth. At six months 12.1% versus 5% of the total sample had scores of 17 or over, but when corrected for age these differences were not statistically significant. However it seems possible that those most at risk of psychiatric disorder might have been lost to follow-up as 86% of the 408 cases completed the first questionnaire compared with 93% of the controls, and by six months the proportions had fallen to 77% and 89% respectively. Those who did not respond were more likely to have an initial Beck score over 13 and to be mothers of illegitimate children, and this bias may explain their unexpected findings. Clyman et al. (1979) observed that single teenage mothers were the least likely to make use of offers of physician follow-up, and Clarke and Williams (1979) found that there was a high rate of depression in these young women even if they had had a live birth.

Although perinatal bereavement services have been described in a few places in the USA, e.g. Wolff and Nielson (1970), Kirkley-Best and Kellner (1982), and by Davies (1983) in the UK, the only study in which randomization was used to divide 50 bereaved parents into a group who received extra support and one that did not is that described by Forrest, Standish and Baum (1982) in Oxford. Active management of perinatal death was offered to the study group followed by counselling interviews for as long as the parents needed them by either a medical social worker or by a midwife. Follow-up appointments with an obstetrician and a geneticist were offered. The contrast group had the routine care provided by the consultant obstetrician which, in a few cases, meant not seeing the baby, a single room on the isolation floor, discharge within 24 h and no hospital follow-up. Semi-structured interviews at home were conducted at 6 and 14 months by a trained interviewer who did not know to which group the couples had been assigned, and the General Health Questionnaire (Goldberg et al., 1970) and Leeds self-administered questionnaires (Snaith, Bridge and Hamilton, 1976) were also completed. The authors' summary states:

> Two of sixteen mothers in the supported group showed psychiatric disorder at six months compared with 10 of 19 in the contrast group ($P<0.01$, Fisher's exact test). There was no significant difference between the two groups at 14 months when 80% of all the women studied had recovered from psychiatric symptoms. Socially isolated women and those whose marital relations lacked intimacy had a higher incidence of symptoms at six months. Early pregnancy (within six months) was associated with a higher incidence of psychiatric symptoms in the unsupported group. The duration of bereavement reaction was appreciably shortened by support and counselling.

Standish (1982), a psychiatric social worker, wrote movingly of the strong emotions still present 'under the surface' in the women who had apparently returned to normal in this study.

Bourne and Lewis (1984) pointed out the high rate of loss to follow-up (30% at six months and 40% at 14 months) and commented that:

> Outcome studies in psychotherapy and psychological treatments are notoriously riddled with pitfalls. They are far better based frankly on clinical experience, intuition, hunches, or even prejudices rather than on a supposedly "scientific" basis, wide open to criticism. A prime snag in "scientific" studies is the extraordinary difficulty in agreeing on what is a good result.

They go on to ask what is the meaning of the study and whether the results of different styles of management after months can be useful in predicting long-term results. The contrast between the studies of Clarke and Williams (1979) and Forrest, Standish and Baum (1982) and the descriptive studies of Bourne and Lewis (1984) does highlight a fundamental difference in approach between psychiatrists, i.e. between analytically trained doctors and between epidemiologists or those with a more 'scientific' bent. However, generations of guilt-ridden mothers of autistic children bear witness to the intuitive interventions of some analysts who ascribed their childrens' illness to 'defective' mothering in early childhood.

East London study of women with postnatal depression cared for by one consultant

In 1981–1982 Schwartz (M. Schwartz, 1981, unpublished dissertation) interviewed 12 out of 22 women who had lost a baby in the perinatal period under my care between 1st August 1977 and 31st July 1980. The policy had been for the women to see the baby, and all but one had done so. The one woman who was the exception did not regret her decision but she had bad dreams during the next pregnancy. One man had not wanted his wife to see the baby but I had discussed it with them both and the woman had seen the child.

The follow-up interview was done 1–4 years after the index pregnancy and therefore, as the women were at different stages, it was decided not to use a formal depression questionnaire but rather a semi-structured in-depth interview. The interviewer then judged whether or not the woman was depressed, whether she was still grieving and how she was coping.

All the women interviewed accepted the death, but one still did not understand why it had happened. One woman was clinically depressed two years after the birth. She was a multigravida who had not planned the pregnancy and had wanted a termination but her husband did not. She had gone into premature labour, and the baby had died neonatally. Her viewing of the body after death was not well handled and she had been distressed by the way the baby had been presented to her and she wished she had retained her memory of the baby in the incubator. There were many social problems and she had previously been depressed. One other woman cried 'now and again'.

The subjects in this study were too few and 'drop-outs' too many to permit any conclusions about the relationship between perinatal death and subsequent depression. Nevertheless, the comments these women made about their care were revealing.

The things that they had found helpful were:

(1) Continuity of care antenatally and once death had occurred.
(2) Being able to see and hold the baby.
(3) Being given a room away from crying babies.
(4) Having the postnatal examination away from women with babies.
(5) Health workers who had time to talk and express sympathy.

The things they had found distressing were:

(1) Poor explanation of tests and procedures.
(2) Separation from an ill baby or being denied the chance to see the dead child.
(3) Hearing babies crying on the postnatal ward.
(4) The pain and unexpectedness of lactation.
(5) Unsupportive professional staff.

After the study the following changes in management were instituted:

(1) Bromocryptine was offered for lactation suppression.
(2) A photograph of the stillborn child was taken with the parent's permission and kept until needed in some cases.
(3) A lock of hair was given to parents if possible.
(4) GPs were encouraged to visit women in hospital.

It seemed that women had found that the active management of perinatal death had helped to make the experience of stillbirth real, and that sensitive handling did make grieving a little easier. All the women expressed thanks to the interviewer and said that it had been very helpful to talk at such length to a sympathetic listener. Husbands who were at home tended to hover at the edge of the conversation, but some joined in and found it helpful.

Morris, Tew and Lawrence (1984) interviewed 60 women several years after the birth of an anencephalic stillborn baby. They found that:

> Just over half of the 60 women who were interviewed 10 and 20 years after they were delivered of a stillborn malformed baby, seem to have resolved their grief completely and have accepted the stillbirth. The remainder have become clinically depressed or have shown physical symptoms typical of anxiety states. Factors contributing to this unresolved mourning were: (1) failure on the doctor's part to explain, comprehensively, the reason for the stillbirth; (2) lack of emotional support during and after the stillbirth.

Conclusion—the future

Further research is needed into the incidence of pathological grief reactions and into how long the normal grieving process lasts after a perinatal death, as well as into the most effective way of helping bereaved parents.

The reluctance of many professionals to face the pain of the suffering parents must be overcome by increased education about grief reactions, especially following stillbirth. The groundwork for this needs to be done during the student years and reinforced during postgraduate obstetric training. Formal teaching by lectures, films and seminars should be supplemented by discussions with a psychiatrist, social worker, psychologist, or chaplain or lay person who has experience of managing perinatal death. Staff also need a safe place where they can express their own feelings so that they can understand and work through their emotions in a constructive way, in order to help the parents.

At the practical level, all labour ward protocols should include a section on the practical steps necessary for the parents when a perinatal death occurs, and should contain a guideline for staff. There is, however, a tendency among staff to hide their feelings behind a set of instructions or procedures (Menzies, 1970) or behind a leaflet, to avoid pain and to impose order when chaos occurs in the guise of an unexpected perinatal death.

It costs nothing to involve the GP and midwife before the woman leaves the hospital, and to arrange follow-up within two or three weeks with the person she knows best in the obstetric team. Personal involvement helps the couple and the single mother to cope with her feelings of isolation and grief. Lay counsellors may be of great value by providing continuing help and support at home.

Society as a whole needs to be more aware of the problems associated with perinatal death and this can probably be done through the mass media. Parents have expressed the view that the possibility of perinatal death should be raised in antenatal classes and this might well help the couples who have a live baby to take home to understand the loss of the unfortunate few who experience a stillbirth. They may be more able to talk to them about the loss rather than, as so often happens, avoiding them and thus adding to their isolation and distress.

Appendix 1: films and videos helpful in teaching about perinatal death

Stillbirth 16mm Sound/Colour, 15 min, Bel Mooney (1978). The journalist Bel Mooney speaks to Sheila Hancock about her own experience of stillbirth.

Death of a Newborn 16mm Sound/Colour, 32 min, USA (1978). Marshall Klaus interviews a couple $3^1/2$ months after their premature firstborn died aged three weeks.

The Lost Babies Videotape Sound/Colour, 55 min, BBC (1983). Esther Rantzen interviews parents who have lost babies in the perinatal period—one couple 30 years ago. (Reviewed by Morris, (1983) *British Medical Journal*, **287**, 1543).

Available from Concord Films Council, 201 Felixstowe Road, Ipswich, Suffolk IP3 9BJ, UK.

References

ANONYMOUS (1987). Personal view. *British Medical Journal*, **294**, 437

BEARD, R. W., BECKLEY, J., BLACK, D. *et al.* (1978). Help for parents after stillbirth. *British Medical Journal*, **i**, 172–173

BECKLEY, R. D., PRICE, R. A., OKERSON, M. and WALKER RILEY, K.(1985). Development of a Perinatal Grief Checklist. *Journal of Obstetrics and Gynaecology and Neonatal Nursing*, May/June, 194–196

BOURNE, S. (1968). The psychological effects of stillbirths on women and their doctors. *Journal of the Royal College of General Practitioners*, **16**, 103–112

BOURNE, S. (1979). Coping with perinatal death. Part I: After effects and theory. Part II: Management problems and strategies. *Midwife, Health Visitor and Community Nurse*, **15**, 59–62; 89–92

BOURNE, S. (1983). Psychological impact of stillbirth. *Practitioner*, **227**, 53–60

BOURNE, S. and LEWIS, E. (1984). Delayed psychological effects of perinatal deaths: the next pregnancy and the next generation *British Medical Journal*, **289**, 147–148

BRUCE, S. J. (1962). Reactions of nurses and mothers to stillbirths. *Nursing Outlook*, **10**, 88–91

CAIN, A. and CAIN, B. (1964). On replacing a child. *Journal of the American Academy of Child Psychiatry*, **3**, 443–445

CLARKE, M. and WILLIAMS, A. J. (1979). Depression in women after perinatal death. *Lancet*, **i**, 916–917

CLYMAN, R. I., GREEN, CH., MIKKELSEN, C., ROWE, J. and ATAIDE, L. (1979). Do parents utilize physician follow-up after the death of their newborn? *Pediatrics*, **64**, 665–667

COOPER, J. D. (1980). Parental reactions to stillbirths. *British Journal of Social Work*, **10**, 55–69

CULLBERG, J. (1972). Mental reaction of women to perinatal death In: *Psychosomatic Medicine in Obstetrics and Gynaecology*, 3rd International Congress, London, 1971, (N. Morris, ed.), pp. 326–329. Basel: Karger

DAVIES, D. P. (1983). Support after perinatal death: a study of support and counselling after perinatal bereavement. *British Medical Journal*, **286**, 144–145

EARL, W. J. H. (1978). Help for parents after stillbirth. *British Medical Journal*, **i**, 505 (letter)

ELLIOT, B. A. and HEIN, H. A. (1978). Neonatal death: reflections for physicians. *Pediatrics*, **62**, 96–102

FORREST, G. C., CLARIDGE, R. S. and BAUM, J. D. (1981). Practical management of perinatal death. *British Medical Journal*, **282**, 31–32

FORREST, G. C., STANDISH, E. and BAUM, J. D. (1982). Support after perinatal death: a study of support and counselling after perinatal bereavement. *British Medical Journal*, **285**, 1475–1479

GILES, P. F. H. (1970). Reactions of women to perinatal death. *Australian and New Zealand Journal of Obstetrics and Gynaecology*, **10**, 207–210

GOLDBERG, D. P., COOPER, B., EASTWOOD, M. R., KEDWARD, H. B. and SHEPHERD, M. (1970). A standardised psychiatric interview for use in community surveys. *British Journal of Preventative and Social Medicine*, **24**, 18–23

HORWELL, D. H. (1983). Stillbirth: a personal experience. *British Medical Journal*, **287**, 1467 (letter)

JOHNS, N. (1971). Family reaction to the birth of a child with congenital abnormality. *Medical Journal of Australia*, **1**, 227–282

JOLLY, H. (1976). Family reaction to stillbirth. *Proceedings of the Royal Society of Medicine*, **69**, 835–837

KENNELL, J. H. and TRAUSE, M. A. (1978). Helping parents cope with perinatal death. *Contemporary Obstetrician and Gynaecologist*, **12**, 53–68

KENNELL, J. H., SLYTER, H. and KLAUS, M. H. (1970). The mourning response of parents to death of newborn infant. *New England Journal of Medicine*, **283**, 344–349

KIRK, E. P. (1984). Psychological effect and management of perinatal loss. *American Journal of Obstetrics and Gynecology*, **149**, 46–51

KIRKLEY-BEST, E. and KELLNER, K. R. (1982). The forgotten grief: a review of the psychology of stillbirth. *American Journal of Orthopsychiatry*, **52**, 420–428

LEWIS, E. (1972). Reaction to stillbirth. In: *Psychosomatic Medicine in Obstetrics and Gynaecology*, 3rd International Congress, London, 1971, (N. Morris, ed.), pp. 323–325. Basel: Karger

LEWIS, E. (1976). The management of stillbirth: coping with an unreality. *Lancet*, **ii**, 619–620

LEWIS, E. and PAGE, A. (1978). Failure to mourn a stillbirth: an overlooked catastrophe. *British Journal of Medical Psychology*, **51**, 237–241

LEWIS, H. (1982). Stillbirth: immediate impact on family and staff and some long-term effects on the family. In: *A New Baby in the Family*, pp. 393–397. National Association for Mother and Child Welfare

LINDEMANN, E. (1944). Symptomatology and management of acute grief. *American Journal of Psychiatry*, **101**, 141–148

LLOYD, J. and LAURENCE, K. M. (1985). Sequelae and support after termination of pregnancy for fetal malformation. *British Medical Journal*, **290**, 907–909

MARKS, F. (1986). Seminars for medical students on the management of stillbirth. Proceedings of First International Symposium of Grief and Bereavement, Israel, 1986

McLENAHAN, I. G. (1962). Helping the mother who has no baby to take home. *American Journal of Nursing*, **62**, 70–71

MENZIES, I. E. P. (1970). *The Functioning of Social Systems as a Defence Against Anxiety*. London: Tavistock Institute of Human Relations

MORRIS, D. (1976). Parental reaction to perinatal death. *Proceedings of the Royal Society of Medicine*, **69**, 837–839

MORRIS, D. (1983). Stillbirth: a personal experience. *British Medical Journal*, **286**, 396 (letter)

MORRIS, J., TEW, B. and LAWRENCE, K. M. (1984). Long-term reactions following a stillbirth with a congenital abnormality: a preliminary report. *Zeitschrift fur Kinderchirurgie*, **39**, Supplement 2, 117–119

OFFICE OF POPULATION CENSUSES AND SURVEYS (OPCS) (1987). Infant and perinatal mortality 1985. Monitor DH3 87/1

OGLETHORPE, R. J. L. (1983). Stillbirth: a personal experience. *British Medical Journal*, **287**, 1197

PARKES, C. M. (1977). Family reactions to child bereavement. *Proceedings of the Royal Society of Medicine*, **70**, 54–55

PARKES, C. M. (1980). Bereavement counselling: does it work? *British Medical Journal*, **iii**, 3–6

PITT, B. (1968). Atypical depression following childbirth. *British Journal of Psychiatry*, **114**, 132–134

POZNANSKI, E. O. (1972). The replacement child: a saga of unresolved parental grief. *Journal of Pediatrics*, **81**, 1190–1193

REES, W. and LUTKINS, S. (1967). Mortality of bereavement. *British Medical Journal*, **iv**, 13–16

SAVAGE, W. (1978a). Perinatal loss and the medical team. Part 1. *Midwife, Health Visitor and Community Nurse*, **14**, 292–295

SAVAGE, W. (1978b) Perinatal loss and the medical team Part 2. *Midwife Health Visitor and Community Nurse*, **14**, 348–351

SAVAGE, W. (1986). *A Savage Enquiry*. London: Virago

SMITH, A. M. (1977). The abhorrence of stillbirth. *Lancet*, **i**, 1315 (letter)

SNAITH, R. P., BRIDGE, G. W. and HAMILTON, A. (1976). Leeds scale for the self-assessment of anxiety and depression. *British Journal of Psychiatry*, **128**, 156–165

STANDISH, L. (1982). The loss of a baby. *Lancet*, **i**, 611–612

SYLVA, K. and BRYCE, A. (1979). Coping with stillbirth. *Midwives Chronicle*, **92**, 35–36

WIJMA, K., HUISJES, H. J., WESTERHOF, R. and BOEKE, P. E. (1983). Comparison of mothers and fathers coping with late fetal death. Paper presented at 7th International Congress of Psychosomatic Obstetrics and Gynaecology

WILLIAMS, H. (1970). On a teaching hospital's responsibility to counsel parents concerning their child's death. *Medical Journal of Australia*, **2**, 643–645

WOLFF, J. R. and NIELSON, P. E. (1970). The emotional reaction to stillbirth. *American Journal of Obstetrics and Gynecology*, **108**, 73–77

Chapter 11

The loss of a child: the sibling's perspective

Atle Dyregrov

Introduction

For many years it was held that children were unable to understand death and thus were unable to experience grief. To a small degree, some still argue that this is true. However, we have gradually come to recognize and acknowledge that children do experience grief after the death of a close family member.

Through the work of Bowlby (1961, 1980) our knowledge of children's reactions to bereavement and separations has been greatly improved. Yet our knowledge is largely limited to the impact of parental loss on children. In this area, even though there still is some controversy, there seems to be increasing evidence for a relation between parental loss and psychopathology (Black, 1976a,b; Lifshitz et al., 1977; Kaffman and Elizur, 1979, 1983; Elizur and Kaffman, 1982; Raphael, 1982; Van Eerdewegh et al., 1982).

The loss of a sibling, however, is an area that has received less attention. The clinical and research literature that does exist on childrens' reactions to the loss of a sibling is primarily based on children who have later developed serious psychological problems requiring medical or clinical intervention (Rosenzweig and Bray, 1943; Pollock, 1962, 1972; Rogers, 1966; Hilgard, 1969; Lampl-De Groot, 1976). The reactions of 'normal' children to the loss of a sibling have been less frequently examined.

One area where 'normal' children's reactions to the death of a sibling have received some attention is in families which have experienced a 'sudden infant death syndrome' (SIDS, sometimes inappropriately called 'cot death') (Watson, 1981; Williams, 1981; Mandell, MacAnulty and Carlson, 1983). In these studies the behaviours most commonly displayed by children after sibling loss were found to be: anxiety (including increased clinging, insecurity, and uncertainty—with the latter being especially focused on what might happen to them or their parents); anger, guilt, and sadness; sleep disturbances; and changes in social interaction.

Rejection of parents, especially mothers, by the surviving siblings has also been reported (Cornwell, Nurcombe and Stevens, 1977). These reactions are similar to those reported in longitudinal studies of children following parental death (Kaffman and Elizur, 1979, 1983; Elizur and

Kaffman, 1982; Raphael, 1982; Van Eerdewegh *et al.*, 1982), although the reactions to sibling loss seem to be less intense and less prolonged.

The children's reactions are to some extent a mirror of how their parents cope with the event, and some relevant parental reactions will briefly be mentioned. Parents show increased protectiveness of their remaining children (Kennell, Slyter and Klaus, 1970; Cornwell, Nurcombe and Stevens, 1977; DeFrain and Ernst, 1978; Clyman *et al.*, 1980). Parents also feel the need to be physically closer to surviving children, apparently because of the comfort it provides (Mandell, MacAnulty and Carlson, 1983). The tragic event may have some positive consequences, as many parents feel that they have improved as parents for their surviving children in the year following the loss of an infant (Cornwell, Nurcombe and Stevens, 1977).

A common finding has been the suppression of discussion and of feelings related to the death due to the parents' own mourning process (Williams, 1983; Mandell, MacAnulty and Carlson, 1983). Parents struggling with the loss of a child are, at times, found to be less able to show empathy and understanding towards the surviving child or children (Halpern, 1972), and many parents also find their surviving children more active and demanding in the months immediately after an infant loss (Drotar and Irvin, 1979). Parents may feel overwhelmed by their children's need for comfort, and this sometimes leads to the parent partially rejecting the surviving child or children (Halpern, 1972; Drotar and Irvin, 1979).

A Norwegian study

In a study of some of the main problem areas in the lives of children surviving the death of a sibling in Norway, we obtained both qualitative and quantitative data. The quantitative data presented here are based on questionnaires sent to all families who experienced the death of an infant (stillbirth, neonatal death and sudden infant death) in the years 1981–1984. The majority (55%) of the parents returned the questionnaire. Empirical data on the emotional and behavioural reactions from the 44 families who had surviving children ($n = 75$) are presented here. All these families experienced an infant loss before the clinical intervention programme described below was instigated.

The qualitative data reported were gathered as part of an intervention programme established at the Department of Pediatrics of Haukeland hospital in Bergen for families who experienced the death of an infant. Emphasis was placed on early intervention. The initial contact involved the expression of sympathy, helping the family members (generally only the parents) to express their feelings and thoughts, building a therapeutic contact to support a continuing clinical relationship, and giving them information about psychological reactions to loss. The amount of follow-up clinical contact after the infant death varied as a function of the needs of the family (and the area in which the family lived, as distance and geography sometimes set limits on the amount of follow-up possible). No families refused the follow-up services. In the follow-up, we inquired particularly about sibling reactions, and considerable time was spent on counselling the parents regarding the psychological needs of surviving children.

Most of the children studied were between three and nine years of age, and many of the remaining children were younger than three years. The situation of children in or approaching adolescence is less well reflected in our data.

Less than half of the children attended the funeral. In Norwegian society children are not naturally included in matters concerning death. Participation in the funeral is often considered to be emotionally dangerous for children, because they will be exposed to their parent's emotional anguish. Should parents want to include siblings in this event, they have to disregard resistance from their relatives and friends.

Seeing their dead sister or brother after their death is also prevented by social mores in Norwegian society; almost none of the children saw their dead siblings. The few that did all came from 'SIDS' families. Although not planned by the parents, these children saw their dead sibling because the death occurred at home. The inability of parents to allow surviving children to see a dead baby brother or sister not only reflects the parents' hesitation (and our society's mores), but also the prevailing views inside the hospital and the discomfort felt by health professionals in meeting such tragic events as a child's death.

Although it may to a certain degree be from necessity, many parents (35%) did take their surviving children along for visits to the graveyard. This event is not as emotionally laden as the funeral or the viewing of the dead child, and it is not 'forbidden' by social customs. Visiting the graveyard is an important event for the siblings; for many it represents the first opportunity for ventilating their feelings and thoughts. The majority of the children (65%) were not given this opportunity.

According to their mothers, the vast majority of the children showed grief. Taking into consideration the age range of the children (a majority of small children), this means that most young children are affected by the loss of an infant brother or sister to the extent that it is noticed by their mothers.

Guilt (a more specific emotion often reported in the clinical literature) was infrequently reported by mothers in this 'normal' population of children. Anxiety, however, was more frequently reported. One-third of the children expressed anxiety regarding parental death, while 11% did so regarding their own death. The anxiety regarding parental death is probably a reflection of separation anxiety provoked by the loss in this sample of mostly younger children. Fear of their own death may either go unreported or, more probably, will be intolerable (and therefore denied).

Information was also sought on how *each* parent saw him or herself responding to the surviving children following the loss. There was a clear increase in anxiety about the surviving children after the loss of a child, for *both* mothers and fathers. Most parents indicated a rise in anxiety. However, the rise was sharper in mothers, with almost 60% indicating that their anxiety increased very much. It is not surprising that parents having lost one child will experience anxiety for surviving children. Most parents feel more vulnerable, knowing that such an event has happened once, they fear a second disaster.

Our results suggest that most children experiencing the sudden death of a sibling will have emotional reactions to the loss and will engage in a process of coping with and understanding the event. The percentage of children experiencing anxiety and guilt is undoubtedly higher than reported in the present study, because of the retrospective nature of the investigation and because parents may deny the siblings' reactions as part of their own efforts at coping with the loss.

The siblings' reactions to, and means of coping with, the death of a young brother or sister may take various forms. It is as useful to understand the nature of such reactions as it is to know that they occurred. We can identify anxiety, attempts to understand, guilt, attempts at coping via 'blaming', and expressions of anger and aggression.

Anxiety
Most of the 'symptoms' and psychological reactions to sibling loss reported in the surviving siblings can be understood as increased anxiety. Among these are increased separation anxiety, increased anxiety about the health and safety of their parents (and themselves), and difficulties in falling to sleep (and other minor sleep disturbances). Such increased anxiety, in the short-term, is a reasonable (and probably desirable) response. It implies that the child is 'activated', concerned and curious. These are all important as a stimulus for the child to understand, grieve, and 'master' the situation.

Let us consider some examples:

A 4-year-old boy would not let his parents out of sight for a single moment after his sister died. He strongly protested against others taking care of him. Even his grandparents, whom he knew very well, were not acceptable. Several times each night he checked to see if his parents were alive and, when his father took an afternoon nap, he was uncomfortable and expressed fear that he would die.

A mother reported that her daughters (aged $5\frac{1}{2}$ and $7\frac{1}{2}$ years) had asked her: 'If you die while you sleep what are we supposed to do then?' In the night the girls would get up to check that the parents were alive (and this was particularly the case with the younger child).

A boy (aged 3 years and 10 months) was afraid of illness. When he or his parents were taken ill, he was afraid that he or they might die. He hardly ever admitted to being sick himself.

In many ways the children's anxiety parallels that of the adults. Although they do not seem to fear 'a second disaster' as much as their parents, they do seem to be more vulnerable and prone to anxiety.

Meaning
Children are, from time to time, preoccupied with what has happened to the lost sibling. The children's questions come in small bursts rather than in long conversations. It is as if they integrate small parts of what has

happened at a time. They may reflect again and again on why it happened and how it happened, and they may ask the parents over and over to tell them what happened when the baby died or about the funeral, as if each time seeking some new 'piece' of information to answer a new question or further reflect upon an old one. Gradually they thereby achieve understanding and mastery.

Surviving children may include their dead siblings in their prayers, they ask to see pictures of the child, and they may select an object that was bought for the baby and keep it. They frequently ask their parents to take them to the graveyard. If the parents are asked how many children they have and they fail to count the dead child, siblings will often correct them. Long after the death the siblings talk about the dead one, and they may even remind the parents of details they have long forgotten. They have many questions about what has come to pass: Did the baby have to climb all the way to heaven? Does the baby have clothes on in the coffin? How old would she have been now if she had lived? Is it cold down in the grave? Does the dead baby get any food?

Through asking questions they expand their knowledge of what has happened and integrate their cognitive understanding and their reactions (and those of their parents). This may also be reflected in their play, where it is common for children to carry out their own burial rites after the death of a sibling. One child, who lived near the graveyard where his baby brother was buried, visited the grave alone. One day he dug a little grave beside that of his brother and buried a bee in a self-made coffin. He informed his parents and 'ordered' that it was not to be removed. After some months he dug it out to see what had happened. Needless to say, this shows that the boy was coming to grips with some aspects of what had happened. The cognitive work children undertake also shows up in drawings of graves and crosses.

Sometimes adults use metaphorical expressions when telling the children about death and thus aggravate their fears. The mother of a three-year-old boy who lost his baby brother told her surviving son that his brother was sleeping. Afterwards she commented on how afraid he was whenever one of them (the parents) were sleeping, or when he was going to sleep himself. The use of the euphemisms 'sleep' and 'journey' to designate death is the most common example of this. In our counselling, we advise parents to refrain from using such euphemisms, as they easily give rise to additional fears.

The meaning the child ascribes to the death and his/her understanding of it, is a function of many factors. The child's age and the amount of information available for him is, of course, a central factor. The 'window of the world' that the media presents may also influence the child's perception; one little boy who heard that his friend had lost his baby sister instantly asked 'Who shot her?'

Guilt

Based on this author's experience, and the questionnaire data reported here, guilt among the surviving children has been overestimated in the clinical literature on children's thoughts after the death of a newborn sibling. The reason for this is that most researchers have generalized from a clinical population, ignoring the phenomenon in more 'normal' children. Although the role of guilt may have been overplayed in the literature, this does not mean we should not warn the parents of this possibility. For siblings of SIDS children, however, guilt does seem to play a larger role, especially when the death occurs in families where the siblings had some caretaking responsibility for the dead child. For example, a five-year-old girl thought the baby died because she had kicked her mother in the stomach during the pregnancy. The mother had more than once told her to be careful about jumping on her because of the baby. In some instances the parent's own guilt feelings, to a certain degree, will be reflected in the surviving children's beliefs and reactions.

Blame

It is not uncommon for children to blame parents for what happened. For example, a seven-year-old girl said to her mother: 'You should never have gone to the hospital, then the baby would not have been taken ill'. This 'blaming' sometimes takes the form of outright rejection. Such rejection is sometimes caused by the fear that the parent will harm (or fail to protect) them too.

We have used the playroom (and family sessions with all family members present) to overcome such fear and rejection.

Case example   A three-year-old boy totally rejected his mother after his baby sister (17 months) died of meningitis within a day after hospitalization. In a session with the parents we (the author and a paediatrician) got the strong impression that the boy's rejection of his mother stemmed from his fear that she would suddenly take him to the hospital so that he would die too. We invited the family to our playroom and while playing told him how important it was that his mother brought his sister to hospital, and that although we did everything we could for her, she died. We praised the mother for her quick response, and by different means took the 'blame' away from her. To make the loss more real for him we also invited the boy to visit the room where his sister died, something he participated in with eagerness. In a week's time his three-week-old rejection of his mother subsided.

Anger and aggression

Children, like parents, have expectations about 'soon to be born children'. These are generally ambivalent feelings. But, while there may be doubt and anger, the strongest feelings are of joy and excitement during the months preceding the birth. Children inform their playmates and friends, prepare for the newcomer, and look forward to playing with and caring for the new child. My personal impression is that children, like parents, form attachments to their unborn siblings—bonds that are broken in the event of a death.

The children's disappointment over the sudden death of the sibling often takes the form of anger combined with sadness, as shown in the following examples.

An $8\frac{1}{2}$ year-old girl very much looked forward to getting a sister or brother. When her baby sister died, she took what the mother called 'a heavy beating'. She grew aggressive and angry, and she cried a lot about not getting a new sister or brother.

A mother reported: 'My four-year-old son visited me in the obstetric department. When I told him that the baby was dead, he reacted with an outburst of anger. He cried, hit me, and said we had promised him a baby. After a while he quietened down, and we could talk about it. I told him I was very sorry that the baby died, and he consoled me. In the weeks and first months after the death he talked very little about what happened, until we all visited the grave. Then he started asking why she died, and where she was now. It was hard for him to understand that children as well as adults could die'.

The impact of parental reactions on children's reactions

The parents' own grief reactions heavily influence the children. Children may be confused, afraid or sad when viewing their parents' sadness and grief. This is illustrated by one young child who said: 'I don't want to be with mama, she is crying and crying all the time'.

Some parents report that having surviving children is supportive to them in coping with their loss. We have been impressed with the way children actively try to comfort their parents. An example of the latter behaviour is illustrated by a child who said: 'Don't be sad mama, you know you have me; I will look after you mama, and it will get better later'.

Many children experience a form of 'parental deprivation' after the loss of a sibling (Bluglass, 1980, 1981). The parents may be so preoccupied with their own loss that they are less able to show empathy and understanding towards the surviving child or children. One mother described this phenomenon as she observed it in herself:

'My seven-year-old son kept asking many questions about the death of his infant sister. I tried to answer as best I could, but it was not easy. I kept thinking to myself that I had so many questions that nobody could answer for *me*. Sometimes I got mad at him for asking but mostly I just ignored him. One day he came into the kitchen and said that he pitied me for always having to do the dishes. He asked me if I wanted a hug, because he loved me. It was a good experience, but it hurt. I felt guilty. Instead of being glad for what he said, I thought about the fact that I would never hear my daughter say the same thing. Then I felt so stupid, and a little more guilty. I had let my lost daughter mean more to me than him, when I have him and he needs me. I hugged him, and I cried. But, more, he has me again, and I'm accepting the loss better.'

Many parents also find that they experience their children as more demanding and irritating immediately after an infant loss. One of the parental grief reactions is a lack of energy and one of the grief reactions of children is generalized insecurity and the wish for more time and attention from the parents. This easily leads to negative interactions between the parents and the child or children. Some children are also physically separated from one or both parents in the first weeks after the loss, as they are placed with family or friends. This separation adds to the child's fear that their parents will die and, in our intervention efforts, we try to motivate the parents to reduce additional separation between themselves and their remaining children to a minimum.

Parents often increase their protectiveness of surviving children. They restrict their daily activities, and keep them away from everything even remotely connected with danger. Parents often ruminate over the terrible things that may happen to the children, making it necessary to check their whereabouts often to know they are safe. This may hinder the children developing independence. Some parents also express a need to be physically closer to their surviving children for comfort.

Parents with young children usually feel anxious over what to tell them about the death and how to answer their questions. The way the parents provide information will have a significant influence on the children's reaction. Open communication (and time to listen and talk) makes for better adjustment in surviving siblings. Siblings ought to get a true, prompt and factual account of what has happened. It is not uncommon that children are given confusing and inadequate explanations that may aggravate their reactions.

Parents often feel uncomfortable about letting the surviving siblings attend the funeral of the lost infant. However, we recommend it. This should not be forced, especially if the parents feel very uncomfortable about having them there. But our view is supported in the clinical literature (Buhrmann, 1970; Friedman, 1974; Moriarty, 1978; Williams, 1981). Children have the same need as adults to make the loss real, and participating in the grieving rituals helps them in this process. Children's fantasies fill them with more fear than the reality. When adults 'protect' the children from learning the facts of life, it is most often to protect themselves (rather than help the children). Some children are very direct in expressing their wish to be included in what takes place after the death. For example, one 11-year-old boy gave his parents 'clear notice' that he wanted to see his stillborn sister, and he 'defined' his request by stating that he had seen his dead grandmother, so he should be allowed to see his sister. Letting the children take part in the funeral does depend on two factors:

(1) That the parents themselves feel relatively comfortable about includ-ing the children (which counselling should help them to feel), and
(2) That an adult is responsible for following the child through the ritual, answering questions, giving support and explaining what is happening (which counselling can help them to do, or help them to identify a family member who can do).

Through our counselling we let the parents know about our knowledge and experience in this area, and we try to make them more comfortable about including the children. However, we always respect and support their decision, even if it is not in line with what we hoped to achieve.

Table 11.1 gives a summary of some of the recommendations we give to parents after the death of a child. This list may be a useful checklist for the areas to be explored with the parents, and it should be pointed out that these recommendations are also valid when a child experiences a parental death.

Table 11.1 Advice for parents in the handling of surviving children's reactions to the death of a young sibling

Open, honest communication
  Give age-appropriate explanations
  Reduce confusion
  Do not use abstract explanations
  Do not talk about journeys and sleep

Time for cognitive mastery
  Questions and short conversations
  Looking at pictures
  Visiting graveyard
  Play

Make the loss real
  Show your own emotions
  Children present at burial
  Reminders of the lost sibling present

To secure emotional mastery
  Continuity in home, school, kindergarten
  Avoid separations
  Reassurance regarding personal and parental death
  Reassurance regarding guilt

Conclusions

Children grieve when they experience the death of a newborn brother or sister. There is no *one* grief syndrome in children. They experience many of the same intense feelings as adults, and they may harbour the same 'strange' thoughts.

Their reactions may reflect the influence of the following factors:

(1) The death itself and the loss or trauma it represents;
(2) The parents' reactions to the loss as well as their anxiety for the remaining children;
(3) The parents' handling of the situation regarding information, separation, and caretaking of the surviving children.

Giving open and honest information and allowing conversation and questions about the event reduces the risk of adverse long-term consequences. As health care professionals we can provide basic information on children's level of understanding and, through counselling the parents, we can indirectly prevent later childhood disturbances.

With the increasing emphasis placed on sibling relationships generally, greater attention will hopefully be placed on the area of children's reaction to the loss of a sibling. Research in this area will help us to base our intervention on knowledge rather than mere subjective beliefs (and defensive 'wishes') about how children react in the face of a sibling's death.

Acknowledgements

Both the empirical research and the clinical experience reported here are based on work completed during a Postgraduate Clinical Research Fellowship awarded to the author by the Norwegian Research Council for Science and the Humanities (NAVF). The present manuscript is based on a paper presented at the conference on 'The Newborn Child and the Family', held in Oslo, Norway on May 3–4, 1984. The author is indebted to Gary R. VandenBos, PhD of the American Psychological Association and Jane Annunziata, PsyD of the Woodburn Community Mental Health Centre for invaluable help with the manuscript.

References

BLACK, D. (1976a). Working with widowed mothers. *Social Work Today*, **6**, 684–687

BLACK, D. (1976b). What happens to bereaved children? *Proceedings of the Royal Society of Medicine*, **69**, 842–844

BLUGLASS, K. (1980). Psychiatric morbidity after cot death. *Practitioner*, **224**, 533–539

BLUGLASS, K. (1981). Psychosocial aspects of the sudden infant death syndrome ('cot death'). *Journal of Child Psychiatry*, **22**, 411–421

BOWLBY, J. (1961). The Adolf Meyer lecture. Childhood mourning and its implications for psychiatry. *American Journal of Psychiatry*, **118**, 481–498

BOWLBY, J. (1980). *Attachment and Loss: Volume III. Loss, Sadness, and Depression*. New York, Basic Books

BUHRMANN, M. V. (1970). Death—its significance in the lives of children. *South African Medical Journal*, **44**, 586–589

CLYMAN, R. I., GREEN, C., ROWE, J., MIKKELSEN, C. and ATAIDE, L. (1980). Issues concerning parents after the death of their newborn. *Critical Care Medicine*, **8**, 215–218

CORNWELL, J., NURCOMBE, B. and STEVENS, L. (1977). Family response to loss of a child by sudden infant death syndrome. *Medical Journal of Australia*, **1**, 656–659

DeFRAIN, J. D. and ERNST, L. (1978). The psychological effects of sudden infant death syndrome on surviving family members. *Journal of Family Practice*, **6**, 985–989

DROTAR, D. and IRVIN, N. (1979). Disturbed maternal bereavement following infant death. *Child Care, Health and Development*, **5**, 239–247

ELIZUR, E. and KAFFMAN, M. (1982). Children's bereavement reactions following death of the father: II. *Journal of the American Academy of Child Psychiatry*, **21**, 474–480

FRIEDMAN, S. B. (1974). Psychological aspects of sudden unexpected death in infants and children. *Pediatric Clinics of North America*, **21**, 103–111

HALPERN, W. I. (1972). Some psychiatric sequelae to crib death. *American Journal of Psychiatry*, **129**, 58–62

HILGARD, J. R. (1969). Depressive and psychotic states as anniversaries to sibling death in childhood. *International Psychiatry Clinics*, **6**, 197–211

KAFFMAN, M. and ELIZUR, E. (1979). Children's bereavement reactions following death of the father. *International Journal of Family Therapy*, **1**, 203–231

KAFFMAN, M. and ELIZUR, E. (1983). Bereavement responses of Kibbutz and non-Kibbutz children following the death of the father. *Journal of Child Psychology and Psychiatry*, **24**, 435–442

KENNELL, J. H., SLYTER, H. and KLAUS, M. H. (1970). The mourning response of parents to the death of a newborn infant. *New England Journal of Medicine*, **283**, 344–349

LAMPL-DE GROOT, J. (1976). Mourning in a 6-year-old girl. *Psychoanalytic Study of the Child*, **33**, 273–282

LIFSHITZ, M., BERMAN, D., GALILI, A. and GILAD, D. (1977). Bereaved children: the effect of mother's perceptions and social system organization on their short-range adjustment. *Journal of the American Academy of Child Psychiatry*, **16**, 272–284

MANDELL, F., MacANULTY, E. H. and CARLSON, A. (1983). Unexpected death of an infant sibling. *Pediatrics*, **72**, 652-657

MORIARTY, I. (1978). Mourning the death of an infant: the sibling's story. *Journal of Pastoral Care*, **32**, 22–33

POLLOCK, G. H. (1962). Childhood parent and sibling loss in adult patients. *Archives of General Psychiatry*, **7**, 295–305

POLLOCK, G. H. (1972). Bertha Pappenheim's pathological mourning: possible effects of childhood sibling loss. *American Psychoanalytical Association Journal*, **20**, 476–495

RAPHAEL, B. (1982). The young child and the death of a parent. In: *The Place of Attachment in Human Behaviour*, (C. M. Parkes and J. Stevenson-Hinde, eds), pp. 131–150. London: Tavistock Publications

ROGERS, R. (1966). Children's reactions to sibling death. In: *Psychosomatic Medicine*. Proceedings of the First International Congress of the Academy of Psychosomatic Medicine, Palma de Mallorca, Spain, 12–14 September, 1966, International Congress Series No. 134 (E. Dunlop and M. N. Weisman, eds), pp. 209–212. Amsterdam: Excerpta Medica Foundation

ROSENZWEIG, S. and BRAY, D. (1943). Sibling deaths in the anamneses of schizophrenic patients. *Archives of Neurology and Psychiatry*, **49**, 71–92

VAN EERDEWEGH, M. M., BIERI, M. D., PARILLA, R. H. and CLAYTON, P. J. (1982). The bereaved child. *British Journal of Psychiatry*, **140**, 23–29

WATSON, E. (1981). An epidemiological and sociological study of unexpected death in infancy in nine areas of southern England. III. Bereavement. *Medicine, Science and Law*, **21**, 99–104

WILLIAMS, M. L. (1981). Sibling reaction to cot death. *Medical Journal of Australia*, **2**, 227–231

Index